高职高专"十二五"国际商务专业规划教材

进出口贸易业务
——模拟实训与操作指南
(第二版)

童宏祥 著

上海财经大学出版社

图书在版编目(CIP)数据

进出口贸易业务:模拟实训与操作指南/童宏祥著.—2版.—上海：上海财经大学出版社,2013.7
(高职高专"十二五"国际商务专业规划教材)
ISBN 978-7-5642-1564-4/F·1564

Ⅰ.①进… Ⅱ.①童… Ⅲ.①进出口贸易-贸易实务-高等职业教育-教材 Ⅳ.①F740.4

中国版本图书馆 CIP 数据核字(2013)第 014442 号

□ 责任编辑　刘晓燕
□ 电　话　021-65903667
□ 邮　箱　exyliu@sina.com
□ 封面设计　钱宇辰
□ 责任校对　王从远

JINCHUKOU MAOYI YEWU
进出口贸易业务
——模拟实训与操作指南
(第二版)
童宏祥　著

上海财经大学出版社出版发行
(上海市武东路 321 号乙　邮编 200434)
网　　址:http://www.sufep.com
电子邮箱:webmaster@sufep.com
全国新华书店经销
启东市人民印刷有限公司印刷装订
2013 年 7 月第 2 版　2013 年 7 月第 1 次印刷

710mm×960mm　1/16　22.25 印张　375 千字
印数:12 001—17 000　定价:34.00 元
(本书有电子课件和参考答案,欢迎与责任编辑联系)

前　言

《进出口贸易业务——模拟实训与操作指南》自2008年出版后,受到广大高职院校师生的厚爱。为了更深入地探索高职技能型人才的培养,构建以学生就业为导向、以工作岗位能力为核心、以工作任务为主线的专业实训教材,著者对本书进行再版。《进出口贸易业务——模拟实训与操作指南》(第二版)是国际商务、报关与货运、国际物流等专业的一门综合实训课程,传授进出口贸易业务的理论、国际商务单证缮制和业务处理的方法,具有较强的综合性操作技能,是国际贸易业务员、国际商务单证员、国际货运代理员等职业工作岗位的基础和起点。

本书主要以我国进出口贸易业务中的信用证、电汇、托收支付方式为背景,突出工作过程的主体地位,按照实际工作情境组织实训内容,围绕进出口贸易单证流转这一主线,系统地阐述了各项主要单证的种类、作用、格式、内容和缮制方法。在教材的结构上强调理论知识为业务操作服务,边讲边做,并在每个实训项目后设置与其相应的综合业务模拟操作,系统地设计了进出口贸易业务中信用证、电汇、托收支付方式项下的单证制作,可供学生操作之用。另外,在附录中,列入国外主要港口与货币的中英文名称、填制报关单所需的各种代码和常见的外贸英语单词与词组,为学习者提供方便。

《进出口贸易业务——模拟实训与操作指南》(第二版)的体例不同于其他实训教材,是著者在职业教育改革中的一种探索,其目的是让学生在进出口贸易业务仿真情景下,通过单证的缮制和业务的处理来掌握进出口贸易业务的知识与技能,可作为高等职业技术学院、中等职业学校的国际商务、进出口货物报关、国际货运代理和国际物流等专业的实训教材。

本书参考答案由蒋学莺、童莉莉、何民乐、曾海霞、胡娜、程欣然、朱云海、陆静文、王莉锋、刘春娣、严晓丰、张歆悦、周虹等老师编写。由于笔者的水平有限，书中难免有错误或纰漏，恳请同行和专家不吝赐教。

作　者

2012 年 12 月

目 录

前言 ··· 1

体验活动一　进出口公司的设立 ································· 1
　　工作任务一　有限责任公司设立登记 ······················· 1
　　工作任务二　对外贸易经营者税务登记 ···················· 3
　　工作任务三　对外贸易经营者备案登记 ···················· 3
　　工作任务四　对外贸易经营者海关注册登记 ··············· 4
　　工作任务五　对外贸易经营者出口货物退(免)税认定 ······ 5
　　工作任务六　对外贸易经营者办理"中国电子口岸"入网手续 ··· 6
　　工作任务七　对外贸易经营者办理核销备案登记手续 ····· 8
　　工作任务八　出入境检验检疫自理报检单位备案登记 ····· 8

体验活动二　自理出口贸易业务 ································· 9
　实训一　出口交易磋商与成本核算 ···························· 10
　　工作任务一　拟写建交函 ······································ 10
　　工作任务二　核算出口报价 ··································· 12
　　工作任务三　拟写发盘函 ······································ 15
　　工作任务四　拟写接受函 ······································ 16
　　综合业务模拟操作 ··· 17
　实训二　合同签订和审核信用证 ······························· 22
　　工作任务一　拟订售货确认书 ································ 22
　　工作任务二　审核信用证 ······································ 27
　　工作任务三　拟写改证函 ······································ 29

  综合业务模拟操作 ··· 32
 实训三 出口合同的履行——备货 ·· 39
  工作任务一 拟订加工合同书 ·· 40
  工作任务二 拟订采购合同 ·· 42
  综合业务模拟操作 ··· 43
 实训四 出口合同的履行——办理出口认证 ······································ 50
  工作任务一 申请签发输欧盟纺织品许可证 ································· 50
  工作任务二 申请签发普惠制原产地证书 ···································· 58
  综合业务模拟操作 ··· 64
 实训五 出口合同的履行——订舱、报检、报关、投保 ···················· 74
  工作任务一 办理委托订舱手续 ··· 75
  工作任务二 办理委托报关报检手续 ·· 80
  工作任务三 办理出口货物保险手续 ·· 83
  工作任务四 出口商发出装船通知 ··· 87
  综合业务模拟操作 ··· 90
 实训六 出口结汇、核销与退税 ·· 111
  工作任务一 办理议付手续 ·· 112
  工作任务二 办理出口收汇核销手续 ·· 121
  工作任务三 办理出口退汇手续 ··· 125
  综合业务模拟操作 ··· 129

体验活动三 代理出口贸易业务 ·· 133
 实训一 出口贸易合同的商订 ·· 134
  工作任务一 拟写接受函 ·· 135
  工作任务二 签订委托代理协议书 ··· 136
  工作任务三 拟订销售确认书 ··· 140
  综合业务模拟操作 ··· 141
 实训二 出口合同的履行——申请签发一般原产地证书 ··············· 145
  工作任务一 申请签发一般原产地证书 ······································ 145
  工作任务二 签发一般原产地证书 ··· 151
  综合业务模拟操作 ··· 153
 实训三 出口合同的履行——办理航空运输、报检、报关手续 ······ 163
  工作任务一 办理航空货物运输手续 ··· 163

目 录

　　工作任务二　办理出境货物报检手续 …………………… 167
　　工作任务三　办理出口货物报关手续 …………………… 172
　　工作任务四　签发空运单 ………………………………… 177
　　综合业务模拟操作 ………………………………………… 182
实训四　办理出口结汇、核销及退税 ………………………… 192
　　工作任务一　办理出口结汇手续 ………………………… 193
　　工作任务二　办理出口核销手续 ………………………… 193
　　工作任务三　办理出口退税手续 ………………………… 194
　　综合业务模拟操作 ………………………………………… 196

体验活动四　自理进口贸易业务 ………………………………… 198
实训一　进口交易磋商与合同签订 …………………………… 199
　　工作任务一　拟写询盘函 ………………………………… 200
　　工作任务二　拟写接受函 ………………………………… 201
　　工作任务三　申请签发进口许可证 ……………………… 201
　　工作任务四　拟订购货合同书 …………………………… 207
　　综合业务模拟操作 ………………………………………… 209
实训二　开立与修改信用证 …………………………………… 216
　　工作任务一　办理开证手续 ……………………………… 217
　　工作任务二　办理改证手续 ……………………………… 221
　　综合业务模拟操作 ………………………………………… 222
实训三　进口合同的履行——办理订舱投保手续 …………… 229
　　工作任务一　办理订舱手续 ……………………………… 229
　　工作任务二　办理投保手续 ……………………………… 230
　　综合业务模拟操作 ………………………………………… 232
实训四　进口合同的履行——办理报检、报关、付汇核销手续 … 238
　　工作任务一　办理审单承兑手续 ………………………… 238
　　工作任务二　办理借单手续 ……………………………… 244
　　工作任务三　办理入境货物报检手续 …………………… 247
　　工作任务四　办理进口货物报关手续 …………………… 252
　　工作任务五　办理进口付汇核销手续 …………………… 257
　　综合业务模拟操作 ………………………………………… 260

体验活动五　代理进口贸易业务 ······················· 273
　实训一　进口交易磋商与合同签订 ················· 274
　　工作任务一　拟写询盘函 ························· 275
　　工作任务二　拟写接受函 ························· 275
　　工作任务三　申请签发自动进口许可证 ··············· 276
　　工作任务四　拟订购货合同书 ······················ 278
　　综合业务模拟操作 ······························ 281
　实训二　进口贸易合同履行——汇款 ················ 289
　　工作任务一　办理电汇手续 ························ 289
　　工作任务二　审核进口单证 ························ 292
　　综合业务模拟操作 ······························ 297
　实训三　进口贸易合同履行——入境货物报检、报关、
　　　　　　汇款及核销手续 ························ 302
　　工作任务一　办理入境货物报检手续 ················ 302
　　工作任务二　办理进口货物报关手续 ················ 304
　　工作任务三　办理电汇手续 ························ 308
　　工作任务四　办理进口付汇核销手续 ················ 310
　　综合业务模拟操作 ······························ 313

附录 ··· 324
　附录1　常用出口货物报关单的填制代码 ················ 324
　附录2　各国主要航运公司及标识 ····················· 330
　附录3　国际商务单证常用英语词组、语句和缩略词 ······ 332

体验活动一　进出口公司的设立

工作情景

根据我国有关法律法规的规定,设立进出口公司必须依法办理有关备案、注册和登记手续。上海永胜进出口公司是由永胜集团出资,主要经营手工工具、棉纺织品、玩具、茶叶和文化用品等的进出口业务,为此须向主管职能部门办理备案、注册和登记手续,获得许可后开展进出口业务。

业务导入

上海永胜进出口公司计划筹建,为了取得企业法人资格,能够从事进出口业务,具备报检、报关及出口退税和核销资质,上海永胜进出口公司分别办理了相应的注册、备案登记手续。

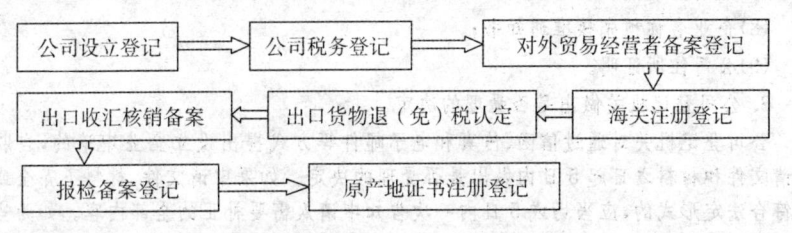

公司设立登记 → 公司税务登记 → 对外贸易经营者备案登记

出口收汇核销备案 ← 出口货物退（免）税认定 ← 海关注册登记

报检备案登记 → 原产地证书注册登记

◎ 工作任务一　　有限责任公司设立登记

上海永胜进出口公司,根据我国《公司法》和《公司登记管理条例》的有关规定,应依法到工商行政管理部门办理公司登记,依法取得法人营业执照,方可从事经营活动。

操作指南 ➡ **有限责任公司设立登记的程序**

1. 企业申请名称预先核准

企业申请名称预先核准应提交下列文件：

(1)有限责任公司的全体股东或者股份有限公司的全体发起人签署的公司名称预先核准申请书；

(2)全体股东或者发起人指定代表或者共同委托代理人的证明；

(3)国家工商行政管理总局规定要求提交的其他文件。

公司登记机关受理后做出决定。予以核准的，出具"企业名称预先核准通知书"；不予以核准的，应出具"企业名称驳回通知书"，说明不予核准的理由，并告知申请人享有依法申请行政复议或者提起行政诉讼的权利。

2. 申请企业设立登记

设立有限责任公司，应由全体股东指定的代表或者共同委托的代理人到公司登记机关，也可以通过信函、传真和电子邮件等方式提出设立登记申请，并提交有关文件。其主要有：

(1)公司法定代表人签署的设立登记申请书；

(2)全体股东指定代表或者共同委托代理人的证明；

(3)公司章程；

(4)验资机构出具的验资证明；

(5)股东的主体资格证明或者自然人身份证明；

(6)载明公司董事、监事、经理的姓名与住所的文件以及有关委派、选举或者聘用的证明；

(7)公司法定代表人任职文件和身份证明；

(8)企业名称预先核准通知书；

(9)公司住所证明。

3. 公司登记机关做出是否受理的决定

公司登记机关对通过信函、传真和电子邮件等方式提出设立企业申请的，自收到申请文件和材料之日起5日内做出是否受理的决定。如果申请文件、材料不齐全或者不符合法定形式的，应当场或5日内一次告知申请人需要补正的全部内容。如为当场告知，应将申请文件、材料退回申请人；属于5日内告知的，应当收取申请文件、材料并出具收到申请文件与材料的凭据。逾期不告知的，自收到申请文件、材料之日即为受理。

公司登记机关对受理的申请者出具"受理通知书"；对不予受理的，出具"不予受理通知书"，说明不予受理的理由，并告知申请人享有依法申请行政复议或者提起行政诉讼的权利。

续

4. 公司登记机关颁发"企业法人营业执照"

公司登记机关对申请文件等材料核准无误后,按其注册资本总额的0.8‰收取设立登记费,并颁发"企业法人营业执照"。"企业法人营业执照"签发日期为公司成立日期,设立中的公司可凭其刻制印章,开立银行账户,申请纳税登记。

工作任务二　　对外贸易经营者税务登记

上海永胜进出口公司完成工商登记之后,到上海税务局办理相应的税务登记手续,填制相应表单,提交相应文件。

操作指南

1. 网上下载税务登记表

对外贸易经营者通过上海财税网(www.csj.sh.gov.cn)下载税务登记表。

2. 现场提交税务登记资料

对外贸易经营者将填写好的税务登记表(包括房室、土地、车船情况登记表),连同办理税务登记所需的资料,向上海市国家税务局、地方税务局税务登记受理处,或上海市国家税务局、地方税务局各区县税务分局,或上海市国家税务局、地方税务局第三、第七分局申请办理税务登记。

3. 开立存款账户

对外贸易经营者应当按国家有关规定,持税务登记证件在银行或者其他金融机构开立基本存款账户和其他存款账户,并将其全部账号向税务机关报告。

银行和其他金融机构应在对外贸易经营者的账户中登录税务登记证件号码,并在税务登记证件中登录对外贸易经营者的账户。

工作任务三　　对外贸易经营者备案登记

上海永胜进出口公司作为一家专门从事进出口业务的公司,按照《对外贸易经营者备案登记办法》的规定,应当向国务院对外贸易主管部门或者其委托的机构办理备案登记。否则,海关不予办理进出口货物的报关和验放手续。

操作指南　　对外贸易经营者备案登记的程序

1. 领取"对外贸易经营者备案登记表"

对外贸易经营者可以通过商务部政府网站(http://www.mofcom.gov.cn)下载，或到所在地备案登记机关领取"对外贸易经营者备案登记表"，也可以网上填写备案登记表。

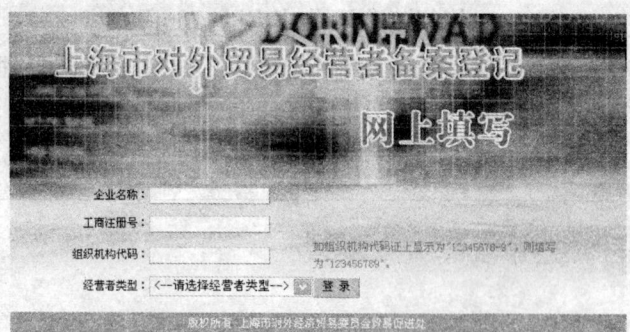

2. 填写"对外贸易经营者备案登记表"

对外贸易经营者应按"对外贸易经营者备案登记表"的要求，如实地填写各项内容，认真地阅读该表背面的条款，并由企业法人代表签字、盖章。

3. 提交备案登记材料

向备案登记机关提交的备案登记材料如下：

(1)按要求填写的"对外贸易经营者备案登记表"；

(2)营业执照复印件；

(3)组织机构代码证书复印件；

(4)如为外商投资企业，应提交外商投资企业批准证书复印件。如为个体工商户(独资经营者)，需提交合法的公证机构出具的财产公证证明。如为外国(地区)企业，需提交合法的公证机构出具的资金信用证明文件。

4. 受理备案登记

备案登记机关应自收到对外贸易经营者提交的上述材料之日起5日内办理备案登记手续，符合规定的，在"对外贸易经营者备案登记表"上加盖备案登记印章，并将其信息和材料建立备案登记档案。

工作任务四　　对外贸易经营者海关注册登记

上海永胜进出口公司为了取得报关权，还需要到海关办理相应的注册登记，这样可以在中华人民共和国关境内各个口岸地或者海关监管业务集中点办理企业的报关业务，方便业务的开展。

操作指南 ➡ **对外贸易经营者海关注册登记程序**

1. 申请注册登记
对外贸易经营者（进出口货物收发货人）应当按照规定到所在地海关办理报关单位注册登记手续，并提交有关证件材料。其主要材料如下：
(1) 企业法人营业执照副本复印件（个人独资、合伙企业或者个体工商户提交营业执照）；
(2) 对外贸易经营者登记备案表复印件（法律、行政法规或者商务部规定不需要备案登记的除外）；
(3) 企业章程复印件（非企业法人免提交）；
(4) 税务登记证书副本复印件；
(5) 银行开户证明复印件；
(6) 组织机构代码证书副本复印件；
(7) 报关单位情况登记表与报关单位管理人员情况登记表；
(8) 其他与注册登记有关的文件材料。
2. 海关审核申请人材料
注册地海关依法对申请注册登记材料是否齐全、是否符合法定形式进行核对。申请材料齐全是指申请人按照海关所公布的规定，如数提交全部材料。申请材料的法定形式是指申请人提交材料的时间必须符合法定的时限，记载事项和文书格式要符合法定的要求。
3. 海关核发注册登记证书
注册地海关接受申请后3日内办妥注册登记，并对申请材料齐全、符合法定形式的申请人核发"中华人民共和国海关进出口货物收发货人报关注册登记证书"，有效期限为3年，报关单位凭其办理报关业务。

◎ 工作任务五 对外贸易经营者出口货物退（免）税认定

上海永胜进出口公司办理好备案登记后，持对外贸易经营者备案登记表、工商营业执照、税务登记证、银行基本账户号码和海关进出口企业代码等文件，填写出口货物退（免）税认定表，到所在地主管出口退税的税务机关办理出口货物退（免）税认定手续。

操作指南 ➡ **对外贸易经营者出口货物退（免）税认定程序及随付材料**

1. 出口货物退（免）税认定程序
(1) 有关证件的送验及登记表的领取。企业在取得有关部门批准其经营出口产品业务的文件和工商行政管理部门核发的工商登记证明后，应于30日内办理出口企业退税登记。

续

(2)退税登记的申报和受理。企业领到"出口企业退税登记表"后,应按登记表及有关要求填写,加盖企业公章和有关人员印章,连同出口产品经营权批准文件、工商登记证明等证明资料一起报送税务机关,税务机关审核无误后,即受理登记。

(3)填发出口退税登记证。税务机关接到企业的正式申请,经审核无误并按规定的程序批准后,核发给企业"出口退税登记证"。

2. 出口退税随附材料

(1)报关单。报关单是指货物进口或出口时进出口企业向海关办理申报手续,以便海关凭此查验和放行货物而填具的单据。

(2)出口销售发票。这是出口企业根据与出口购货方签订的销售合同填开的单证,是外商购货的主要凭证,也是出口企业财会部门凭此记账的依据。

(3)进货发票。提供进货发票主要是为了确定出口产品的供货单位、产品名称、计量单位、数量,是否是生产企业的销售价格,以便划分和计算其进货费用等。

(4)结汇水单或收汇通知书。

(5)属于生产企业直接出口或委托出口的自制产品,凡以到岸价CIF结算的,还应附送出口货物运单和出口保险单。

(6)有进料加工复出口产品业务的企业,还应向税务机关报送进口料件的合同编号、日期、进口料件名称、数量、复出口产品名称、进料成本金额和实纳各种税的金额等。

(7)产品征税证明。

(8)出口收汇已核销证明。

(9)与出口退税有关的其他材料。

工作任务六 对外贸易经营者办理"中国电子口岸"入网手续

上海永胜进出口公司办理好出口货物退(免)税认定手续后,到海关办理"中国电子口岸"入网手续,到有关部门办理"中国电子口岸"企业法人IC卡和"中国电子口岸"企业操作员IC卡电子认证,并赴本地外汇管理局办理核销备案登记手续。

操作指南 ➡ 对外贸易经营者办理"中国电子口岸"入网手续

1. 领取有关表格

对外贸易经营者持组织机构代码证、企业法人营业执照、税务登记证、中华人民共和国进出口企业资格证书、报关单位登记注册证明等证件向海关索取中国电子口岸入网资格审核申请表、中国电子口岸企业情况登记表和中国电子口岸企业IC卡登记表。

续

2. 职能部门审核

(1)质量技术监督局审核

对外贸易经营者持中国电子口岸入网资格审核申请表和组织机构代码证到质量技术监督局,由质量技术监督局的工作人员对组织机构代码证原件与复印件的一致性进行审核。确认后,在该审核申请表内批注签章,并将资料退回企业。

(2)工商局审核

对外贸易经营者持中国电子口岸入网资格审核申请表、企业法人营业执照的原件与复印件到工商局,由工商局的工作人员对企业法人营业执照原件与复印件的真实性进行审核。确认后,在该审核申请表内批注签章,并将资料退回企业。

(3)国税局审核

对外贸易经营者持中国电子口岸入网资格审核申请表、税务登记证原件与复印件到国税局,由国税局的工作人员对税务登记证的原件与复印件进行一致性审核。审核通过的,在该审核申请表的相应栏目内批注签章,并将资料退回企业。

(4)外经贸主管部门审核

对外贸易经营者持中国电子口岸入网资格审核申请表、中华人民共和国进出口企业资格证书的原件与复印件到外经贸主管部门,由外经贸主管部门的工作人员对进出口企业资格证书的原件与复印件进行真实性审核。确认后,在该审核申请表的相应栏目内批注签章,并将资料退回企业。

(5)外汇管理局审核

对外贸易经营者持中国电子口岸入网资格审核申请表、核销员证、中国电子口岸企业情况登记表、中国电子口岸企业IC卡登记表到外汇管理局,由外汇管理局的工作人员对核销员证的原件与复印件的真实性,以及中国电子口岸企业情况登记表、中国电子口岸企业IC卡登记表进行审核。审核通过的,在该审核申请表的相应栏目内批注签章,并将资料退回企业。

(6)海关审核

对外贸易经营者持中国电子口岸入网资格审核申请表、报关单位登记注册证明、报关员证的原件与复印件、中国电子口岸企业情况登记表和中国电子口岸企业IC卡登记表到海关监管处企业备案管理科,由海关的工作人员对报关单位登记注册证明、报关员证的原件与复印件的真实性,以及中国电子口岸企业情况登记表、中国电子口岸企业IC卡登记表进行审核。审核通过的,在该审核申请表的相应栏目内批注签章,并将资料整理后装订成册,退回企业。

对外贸易经营者持中国电子口岸入网资格审核申请表到海关技术处综合科购买IC卡、读卡器、数据库软盘,交预录入费,由经办人员在该审核申请表的相应栏目内记录并盖章。然后,将资料交通关管理处业务规范科。

◎ 工作任务七　对外贸易经营者办理核销备案登记手续

上海永胜进出口公司按照相关规定,到外汇管理局办理核销备案手续,便于对所发生的外汇收支进行管理。

操作指南　➡　对外贸易经营者办理出口收汇核销备案登记

办理出口收汇核销备案登记可在办理第一笔出口业务需要领取核销单时,到外汇管理局同时办理。办理核销备案登记手续所需材料主要有:单位介绍信、申请书,外经贸部门批准经营进出口业务的批件正本及复印件,企业法人营业执照(副本)或企业营业执照(副本)及复印件,"中华人民共和国组织机构代码证"正本及复印件,海关注册登记证明书正本及复印件,外汇管理局要求提供的其他材料。

◎ 工作任务八　出入境检验检疫自理报检单位备案登记

上海永胜进出口公司为了更好地开展业务,到国家质检总局办理相应的备案登记,取得自理报检的资格。

操作指南　➡　自理报检单位备案登记程序

1. 登录中国电子检验检疫业务网

点击"自理报检单位备案登记(企业用户)"项,选择"新注册单位",登录,点击"登记备案申请"页面链接,进入自理报检单位登记备案管理。

2. 按提示输入各项基本信息

点击"申请"按钮,提交申请数据,并打印"自理报检单位登记备案申请表"。

3. 持下列有关资料到检验检疫局本部咨询窗口核查

(1)"自理报检单位备案登记申请表"正本,需法定代表人签字,单位盖公章;

(2)申请单位的"企业法人营业执照"(复印件和正本);

(3)由国家质量技术监督局颁发的申请单位组织机构代码证(复印件和正本);

(4)有进出口经营权的企业须提供上级主管部门批准企业成立的批准证书/资格证书(复印件和正本)等。

4. 检验检疫机构对申请人提供的资料等进行审核,核准后予以备案登记,并颁发"自理报检单位备案登记证明书"。

体验活动二　自理出口贸易业务

工作情景

　　近日，上海永胜进出口公司利用公司网站发布供货信息，得知英国 MANDARS IMPORTS CO. LTD. 对纯棉女裙产品感兴趣。于是，上海永胜进出口公司方达先生与 MANDARS IMPORTS CO. LTD. 的 SMITH 经理进行交易磋商，采取信用证支付方式，签订销售合同。当上海永胜进出口公司收到 MANDARS IMPORTS CO. LTD. 开立的信用证后，选择加工企业，采购原材料，委托金友国际货代公司办理托运、报检和报关手续，并向当地保险公司办理投保，确保合同的履行。

自理出口业务流程如图所示：

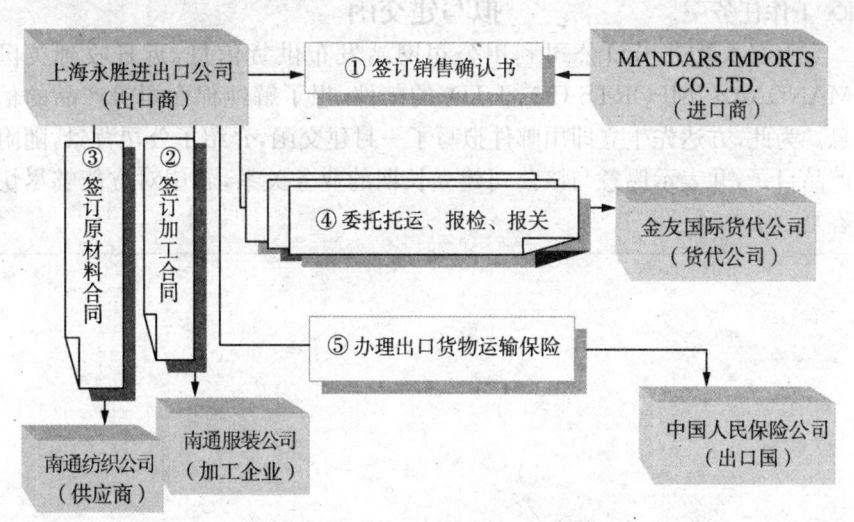

```
上海永胜进出口公司      ①签订销售确认书      MANDARS IMPORTS
   （出口商）      ─────────────▶      CO. LTD.
                                           （进口商）

  ③签订原材料合同   ②签订加工合同

              ④委托托运、报检、报关  ──▶  金友国际货代公司
                                              （货代公司）

              ⑤办理出口货物运输保险  ──▶  中国人民保险公司
                                              （出口国）

   南通纺织公司     南通服装公司
    （供应商）     （加工企业）
```

实训一　出口交易磋商与成本核算

业务导入

上海永胜进出口公司与英国 MANDARS IMPORTS CO. LTD. 就纯棉女裙的交易条件用电子邮件进行磋商。方达先生在收到 MANDARS IMPORTS CO. LTD. 客商的询盘后进行价格核算,并向客商发盘。经过一番讨价还价后,双方终于达成交易。

交易磋商的业务环节如下图所示:

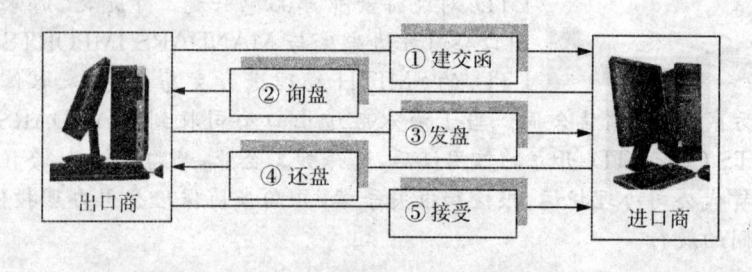

```
出口商  ←① 建交函──  进口商
        ──② 询盘 →
        ←③ 发盘──
        ──④ 还盘 →
        ←⑤ 接受──
```

◎ 工作任务一　　　拟写建交函

上海永胜进出口公司利用公司网站发布供货信息,近日收到英国 MANDARS IMPORTS CO. LTD. 的邮件,想了解纯棉女裙等产品的信息。为此,方达先生立即用邮件拟写了一封建交函,介绍了公司背景,随附产品目录,并表示愿意与该公司建立长期的业务关系,希望对方能够尽快答复。

体验活动二　自理出口贸易业务

| 答复 | 答复全部 | 转发▼ | 删除 | 永久删除 | 转到▼ |

发件人： FANGDASH@163.COM
收件人： MANDARS@HOTMAIL.COM
主　题： ESTABLISH BUSINESS RELATIONS

Dear Mr Smith,

　　We learned from the Internet that you are in the market for textiles, which falls within our business scope, so we avail ourselves of this opportunity to approach you for the establishment of the business relations with you.

　　We are a leading trading company in Shanghai, We have good connections with some reputable manufactures.

　　In order to acquaint you with our business lines, we enclose a copy of our latest catalogue and price list.

　　If any items interest you, please let me know. We shall be glad to give you our lowest quotations upon receipt of your detailed requirement.

　　We are looking forward to your favorable reply.

Your sincerely,
SHANGHAI YONGSHENG IMP. & EXP. CO.
Da Fang
MAR. 7, 2012

操作指南　➡　建交函的内容

　　建交函是贸易公司在寻求国外合作伙伴并期望与其建立和发展业务关系时，向对方介绍本公司经营特点和产品特色的函电。一份建交函通常包括以下内容：

1. 信息来源

　　We have obtained your name and address though the Commercial Counselor's Office of your Embassy in Shanghai.

　　We learned from the Internet that you are in the market for textiles, so we would like to establish business relations with you.

　　Your firm had been recommended to us by ABC Co., as large importers of furniture.

2. 致函目的

　　The purpose of this letter is to explore the possibilities of developing trade with you.

　　We are glad to send you this introductory letter, hoping that it will be the prelude to mutually beneficial relations between us.

3. 公司介绍

We are a state-operated corporation, handling both the import and export of textile.

Being specialized in export of Chinese Arts and Crafts goods, we express our desire to trade with you in this line.

With years of effort we have already been the leading manufactures of light industrial products.

4. 产品介绍

This kind of toy is of supreme quality and fine workmanship, with high popularity in America.

Since there are more than 100 items for your choice, we would like to attach the latest catalogue of our products.

5. 期盼答复

Your immediate reply would be highly appreciated.

We are looking forward to your earliest reply.

If you have any questions, please let us know.

工作任务二　　核算出口报价

2012年3月9日,上海永胜进出口公司收到英国 MANDARS IMPORTS CO. LTD. 的邮件。该电函称,上海永胜进出口公司的产品款式新颖,品质出众,对其中货号为 MA212129 的纯棉女裙感兴趣,有意向订购,要求报 CIF LONDON 价格,并愿意建立长期的业务关系。对此,上海永胜进出口公司方达先生根据成本、有关费用和预期利润计算出口价格,进行报价。

一、出口报价核算资料

供货价格	52元/件,均包含17%的增值税,出口纺织品的退税率为5%。
国内费用	运杂费1 000元、商检费500元、报关费50元。港区港杂费1 000元、业务费2 000元、其他费用1 000元。
海运运费	从上海出口棉制品到英国伦敦,一个20英尺集装箱的包箱费率为1 700美元。
货运保险	CIF 的基础上加成10%投保中国人民保险公司海运货物保险条款中的一切险和战争险。费率为0.5%和0.1%。
报价利润	报价的15%。
汇　率	8元人民币兑换1美元。

二、计算步骤

CIF 报价＝成本＋费用＋利润

实际成本＝供货价格(采购成本)/(1＋增值税率)
　　　　　×(1＋增值税率－退税率)
　　　　＝52/(1＋17%)×(1＋17%－5%)
　　　　＝49.78(元)

国内费用＝(1 000＋500＋50＋1 000＋2 000＋1 000)/18 000
　　　　＝0.31(元)

运费　　＝1 700×8/18 000
　　　　＝0.76(元)

保险费　＝CIF 价格×(1＋10%)×(0.5%＋0.1%)

利润　　＝CIF 价格×15%

CIF 报价＝(实际成本＋国内费用＋运费)/8＋保险费＋预期利润
　　　　＝(49.78＋0.31＋0.76)/8＋CIF 价格×(1＋10%)×
　　　　　(0.5%＋0.1%)＋CIF 价格×15%

三、计算结果

货号 MA212129 纯棉女裙的 CIF 报价为 7.5 美元。

操作指南 ➡ 出口报价核算

1. 出口商品价格构成
　　出口商品价格＝成本＋费用＋利润
2. 成本核算公式
　　实际成本＝采购成本－出口退税额
　　实际成本＝货价×(1＋增值税率－退税率)
　　出口退税额＝采购成本/(1＋增值税率)×出口退税率
　　采购成本＝货价＋增值税额
　　　　　　＝货价＋货价×增值税率
　　　　　　＝货价×(1＋增值税率)
　　货价＝采购成本/(1＋增值税率)
　　实际成本＝采购成本－出口退税额
　　　　　　＝货价×(1＋增值税率)－货价×退税率
　　　　　　＝货价×(1＋增值税率－退税率)
3. 海洋运费的计算
(1)班轮(散货)运费的计算

续

公式：$F = F_b \times (1 + \sum S) \times Q$

注：F 为班轮运费，F_b 为基本运费率，$\sum S$ 为附加运费率之和，Q 为总运量。

计算步骤：选择适合的运价表；根据货物名称，在货物分级表中查询货物等级(Class)和运费计算标准(Basis)；在等级费率表中，按照货物等级，根据相应的航线、装运港、目的港查出基本运价；在附加费率表中查出应付的附加运费项目和数额（或百分比）及货币种类；根据基本运价和附加运价算出实际运价；根据货物的数量算出应付运费总额。

(2) 班轮集装箱运费计算的种类

拼箱货的运费计算与传统班轮散装货运费计算方法相同。

整箱货的运费计算是按一个货柜计收运费的，即包箱费率。

常见的包箱费率有三种：FAK 包箱费率(Freight for All Kinds)，即对每个集装箱不分货物种类，也不计货量统一收取的运价。FCS 包箱费率(Freight for Class)，即按不同货物的等级制定的包箱费率。集装箱普通货物的等级与班轮散货运输一样，分为20级，可以在货物分级表中查到。FCB 包箱费率(Freight for Class or Basis)，即按不同货物的等级或货物类别以及计算标准制定的费率。

(3) 集装箱运费的计算程序

选择适合的运价表。

确定所运输的货物为拼箱货还是整箱货。

根据货物名称，在货物分级表中查询货物等级，然后按照货物的等级和航线在费率表中查出整箱货或拼箱货的基本费率。

对于拼箱货，参照班轮散货运费的计算方法。对于整箱货，根据所选取的集装箱的尺码，直接按表中给出的单箱运费计算即可。

4. 保险费的计算

公式：保险金额＝CIF（或 CIP）×（1＋投保加成率）

保险费＝保险金额×保险费率

计算步骤：根据投保加成率计算保险金额，根据所投保险别的保险费率和保险金额计算保险费。

5. 出口关税的计算

公式：出口货物应纳关税＝出口货物完税价格×出口货物关税税率

按照 FOB 价格成交，出口货物的完税价格＝FOB 价／(1＋出口关税税率)

按照 CFR 价格成交，出口货物的完税价格＝(CFR 价－运费)／
(1＋出口关税税率)

按照 CIF 价格成交，出口货物的完税价格＝(CIF 价－运费－保险费)／
(1＋出口关税税率)

6. 利润的计算

公式：销售利润＝销售价格×利润率

🔲 工作任务三　　　　　拟写发盘函

上海永胜进出口公司方达先生于 3 月 10 日向英国 MANDARS IMPORTS CO. LTD. 发盘,确定各项交易条件,并根据核算的结果进行报价,希望外商尽快订货,3 月 13 日复到有效。

📩 答复　　📩 答复全部　　➡ 转发 ▼　　🗑 删除　　✖ 永久删除　　📁 转到 ▼

发件人：FANGDASH@163.COM
收件人：MANDARS@HOTMAIL.COM
主　题：OFFER

Dear Mr. Smith,
　　We are pleased to receive your inquiry of MAR. 09, 2012 and to hear that you are interested in our products.
　　In reply, we offer firm, subject to your reply reaching us on or before MAR. 13.
　　Unit price：USD 7.50 per piece CIF LONDON
　　Packing：18 pieces /ctn
　　Shipment：not later than MAY 30, 2012
　　Insurance：For 110 percent of the invoice value covering ALL RISKS & WAR RISK
　　Payment：By L/C at 60 days sight after B/L
　　We are looking forward to your initial order.

　　　　　　　　　　　　　　　　　　　　　　　　　Yours truly,
　　　　　　　　　　　　　　　　　　SHANGHAI YONGSHENG IMP. & EXP. CO.
　　　　　　　　　　　　　　　　　　　　　　　　　　Da Fang
　　　　　　　　　　　　　　　　　　　　　　　　　MAR. 10, 2012

操作指南 ➡ 发盘函的内容

　　发盘,法律上称为要约,是买卖双方中的一方向对方提出各项交易条件,并愿意按这些条件达成交易、订立合同的一种肯定表示。
　　发盘一般采用 offer, quote 或 bid 等来表示。
　　一份发盘函通常包括以下内容：
　　1. 阐明各项主要交易条件
　　100 dozen of deerskin handbags style No. BW120 at ＄100.00 per dozen CIF London.

For the Brand AGT-4Garment sewing machine, the best price is $80.00 per set FOB Shanghai, the minimum quantity is one 20'FCL and with the purchase of two or more containers, the price is reduced by 3%.

2. 规定发盘的有效期及其他约束条件

This offer is valid for ten days.

We offer firm, subject to your reply reaching us on or before Jan. 30.

This offer is subject to our final confirmation.

3. 明确表示商品质量的完好和订单的顺利进行

We can effect shipment within one month after your order has been confirmed.

Any order you place will be processed promptly.

4. 期望对方尽早下订单

We trust the above will be acceptable to you and await with keen interest your trial order.

We are awaiting your immediate reply.

工作任务四　　　　拟写接受函

3月12日上海永胜进出口公司方达先生收到英国 MANDARS IMPORTS CO. LTD. 还盘，其称价格太高，希望由原来的每件7.50美元降为7.00美元。为此，方达先生对还价进行了利润核算，经过再三考虑，决定接受外商提出的价格，随即拟写接受函。

一、方达先生核算利润率

CIF 报价 = 7.00×8 = 56.00(元)

CIF 报价 = 成本 + 费用 + 利润

实际成本 = 供货价格(采购成本)/(1+增值税率)×(1+增值税率－退税率)

　　　　 = 50/(1+17%)×(1+17%－5%) = 47.86(元)

国内费用 = (1 000＋500＋50＋1 000＋2 000＋1 000)/18 000

　　　　 = 0.31(元)

运费 = 1 700×8/18 000

　　 = 0.76(元)

保险费＝CIF 价格×(1＋10％)×(0.5％＋0.1％)
　　　＝0.004 62×8＝0.037(元)

预期利润＝CIF 报价－实际成本－国内费用－运费－保险费
　　　＝56.00－47.68－0.31－0.76－0.037
　　　＝7.213(元)

利润率＝7.213/56＝13％

二、方达先生拟写接受函

发件人：FANGDASH@163.COM
收件人：MANDARS@HOTMAIL.COM
主　题：ACCEPTANCE

Dear Mr. Smith,

Thank you for your letter of MAR. 12, 2012.

We would like to inform you that in view of our long-standing business relationship, we accept your proposal for price, other conditions remain unchanged. We will draw up sale contract and send it to you as soon as possible.

　　　　　　　　　　　　　　　　　　　　　　Yours truly,
　　　　　　　　　　　　　　　SHANGHAI YONGSHENG IMP. & EXP. CO.
　　　　　　　　　　　　　　　　　　　　　　　Da Fang
　　　　　　　　　　　　　　　　　　　　　　MAR. 13, 2012

综合业务模拟操作

操作一

1. 操作资料

南京永发进出口公司主要经营各种手工工具、电动工具等轻工业产品，销往东南亚、欧美等国际市场，具有一定的声誉。在本年度广交会上获悉新加坡 JIM KING IMPORT & EXPORT CORPORATION 经理 YANG 先生对本公司的电动钻头感兴趣。对此，双方进行交易磋商，具体内容如下：

(1) 9 月 21 日 JIM KING 进出口贸易公司来函：
"对贵公司的电动钻头感兴趣，预计订货数量 1 800 套，请报价 CIF SINGAPORE。"

(2) 收到对方公司的询盘，我方核算出口商品的价格。核算资料如下：

供货价格	25元/套,均包含17%的增值税,出口手工工具的退税率为9%。
国内费用	运杂费1 000元、商检费100元、报关费50元。港区港杂费600元、业务费1 180元、其他费用420元。
海运运费	集装箱运输,从连云港出口手工制品到新加坡,一个20英尺集装箱的包箱费率为1 100美元。
货运保险	CIF的基础上加成10%投保中国人民保险公司海运货物保险条款中的一切险和战争险。费率为0.5%和0.15%。
报价利润	报价的10%。
汇率	8元人民币兑换1美元。

(3)9月22日南京永发进出口公司发函,报价如下:

"电动钻头:CIF SINGAPORE No. TY242 每套 USD 4.20,不可撤销即期信用证,每10套装一个纸箱,交货时间不迟于2012年10月30日。"

(4)9月23日 JIM KING 进出口贸易公司来函:

"如能将支付方式改为见票日后30天付款,愿意订购1 800套,其他条件可以接受。"

(5)9月24日南京永发进出口公司发函:

"同意贵方提出的支付方式要求,其他交易条件不变。"

买方地址:No. 206 CHANG NORTH STREET SINGAPORE

　　　　　TEL:218-76911　　FAX:218-76912

　　　　　电子信箱地址:JIM KING@666. SI

卖方地址:中国江苏省南京市中山路1321号

　　　　　TEL:025-23501111　　FAX:025-23502222

　　　　　电子信箱地址:MAOYI@168. CN

2.操作要求

(1)请你以业务员张丽的身份,根据上述资料计算每套工具CIF新加坡价。

CIF新加坡价格

(2)请你以业务员张丽的身份,根据上述资料用英语拟写一份发盘函和接受函,要求内容正确和完整。

OFFER

ACCEPTANCE

操作二

1. 操作资料

广州纺织品进出口公司(地址:广州市北京路530号　TEL:(020)64043030　FAX:(020)64043031　电子信箱地址:WANJU@168.CN)主要经营各种纺织品和服装等进出口业务,在欧美、日本等国际市场上有一定的声誉。业务员王伟在互联网上获悉法国OLAEARA TRADE CO. LTD(地址:310-224 HOLA STREET MARSEILLE FRANCE TEL:491-38241234　FAX:491-38241235　电子信箱地址:OLEARA @123. OR. JP)对男式衬衫感兴趣,于是,及时与对方取得联系并进行贸易磋商:

(1)5月11日OLAEARA公司来函:

"对你方衬衫很感兴趣,请报CIF MARSEILLE的价格。"

(2)5月12日向OLAEARA公司发报价函:

"男式衬衫,Art No. 88(BLUE)每件6.5美元,Art No. 44(BLACK)每件7.5美元,Art No. 77(RED)每件5.5美元,Art No. 66(YELLOW)每件7.8美元,Art No. 99(GREEN)每件7.9美元,CIF马赛,不可撤销即期信用证。每件装一个塑料袋,20件装一个纸箱。交货时间不迟于2012年7月31日。"

(3)5月13日OLAEARA公司来函:

"对Art No. 88(BLUE)、Art No. 44(BLACK)衬衫感兴趣,其他条件可以接受,但价格太贵。如Art No. 44(BLACK)能降0.50美元,愿意订货各3 000件。"

广州纺织品进出口公司根据OLAEARA公司提出的价格,重新核算Art No. 44(BLACK)衬衫利润率。

利润率核算资料

供货价格	48元/件,均包含17%的增值税,出口纺织品的退税率为9%。
国内费用	运杂费680元、商检费100元、报关费50元。港区港杂费600元、业务费1 200元、其他费用880元。
海运运费	集装箱运输,从广州出口棉制品到法国马赛,一个20英尺集装箱的包箱费率为2 040美元。
货运保险	CIF的基础上加成10%投保中国人民保险公司海运货物保险条款中的一切险和战争险。费率为0.5%和0.35%。
汇率	8元人民币兑换1美元。

(4)5月14日广州纺织品进出口公司发接受函:

"同意贵方的价格要求,其他交易条件不变。"

2. 实训要求

(1)请你以业务员的身份根据上述资料用英语拟写一份发盘函。

OFFER

(2)请根据 OLAEARA TRADE CO. LTD. 的还价重新核算利润率。

(3)请你以业务员的身份根据上述资料用英语拟写一份接受函。

ACCEPTANCE

实训二　合同签订和审核信用证

业务导入

上海永胜进出口公司与 MANDARS IMPORTS CO. LTD. 就弹力牛仔女裙交易条件达成一致后,拟订销售合同一式两份,双方签章后各持一份作为履行合同的依据。进口商 MANDARS IMPORTS CO. LTD. 按合同的规定开出信用证,出口商上海永胜进出口公司根据合同条款对其进行仔细审核,发现不能接受的不符点,通知进口商修改信用证。

合同签订、审证和改证业务环节如下图所示:

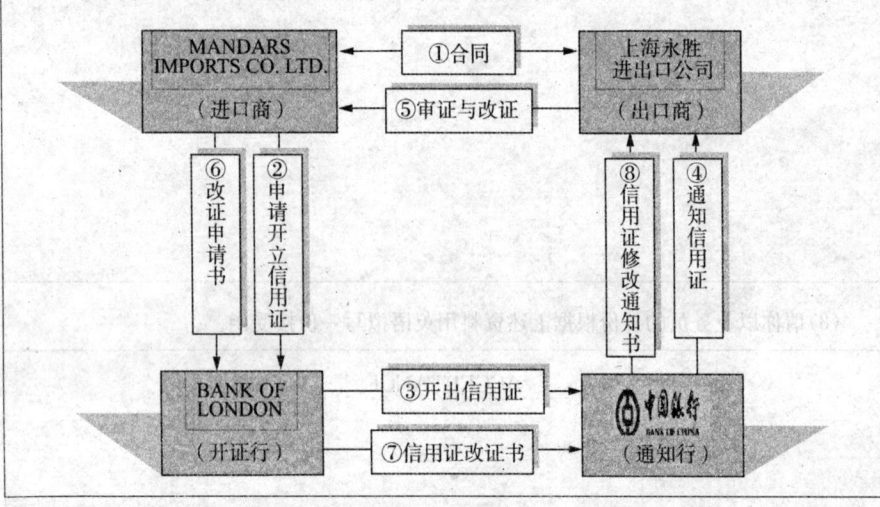

```
MANDARS                  ①合同              上海永胜
IMPORTS CO. LTD.  ←─────────────────→   进出口公司
    (进口商)         ⑤审证与改证           (出口商)
       │                                      ↑
    ⑥改证申请书  ②申请开立信用证    ⑧信用证修改通知书  ④通知信用证
       ↓                                      │
  BANK OF           ③开出信用证          中国银行
  LONDON      ─────────────────────→   BANK OF CHINA
  (开证行)          ⑦信用证改证书         (通知行)
```

◎ 工作任务一　　　　　拟订售货确认书

上海永胜进出口公司与 MANDARS IMPORTS CO. LTD. 就弹力牛仔女裙交易条件达成一致后,由方达先生拟订销售合同一式两份,并寄送进口商会签。签章后,买卖双方各持一份,作为履行合同的依据。

上海永胜进出口公司
SHANGHAI YONGSHENG IMP. & EXP. CO.
21 WEST ZHONGSHAN ROAD SHANGHAI CHINA

售货确认书

S/C No.：TXT200710

DATE：MAR. 15, 2012

POST CODE：200031
FAX：(021) 64500002
TEL：(021) 64500003
To Messrs：
 MANDARS IMPORTS CO. LTD.
 38 QUEENSWAY, 2008 UK

谨启者：兹确认售予你方下列货品，其成交条款如下：

Dear Sirs,

　　We hereby confirm having sold to you the following goods on terms and conditions as specified below：

唛 头 SHIPPING MARK	商品名称、规格及包装 NAME OF COMMODITY AND SPECIFICATIONS, PACKING	数 量 QUANTITY	单 价 UNIT PRICE	总 值 TOTAL AMOUNT
MANDARS TXT200710 LONDON C/NO.：1-UP	LADIES DENIM SKIRT FABRIC：99% COTTON 1% ELASTIC AS PER SAMPLE PACKING：FLAT PACK WITHOUT FOLDING 6 PIECES ASSORTED SIZES PER POLYBAG, 3 POLYBAGS IN A MASTER POLYBAG AND THEN INTO AN EXPORT CARTON	18 000 PCS	CIF LONDON USD 7.00	USD 126 000.00

装运港：SHANGHAI
LOADING PORT：

目的港：LONDON
DESTINATION：

装运期限：LATEST DATE OF SHIPMENT 120530
TIME OF SHIPMENT：

分批装运：ALLOWED
PARTIAL SHIPMENT：

转船：ALLOWED
TRANSSHIPMENT：

保险：FOR 110 PERCENT OF THE INVOICE VALUE COVERING ALL RISKS AND WAR RISK
INSURANCE：
付款条件：BY L/C AT 60 DAYS SIGHT AFTER B/L
TERMS OF PAYMENT：

唛头：☑由卖方指定。□由买方指定，须在信用证开出前＿＿天提出并经卖方同意，否则由卖方指定。

Shipping mark：☑To be designated by the sellers. □In case the buyers desire to designate their own shipping mark, the buyers shall advise the sellers __ days before opening L/C. And the sellers' consent must be obtained. Otherwise the shipping mark will be designated by the sellers.

买方须于 2012 年 5 月 10 日前开出本批交易的信用证（或通知卖方进口许可证号码），否则，卖方有权不经过通知取消本确认书，或向买方提出索赔。

The Buyer shall establish the covering Letter of Credit (or notify the Import License Number) before May 10, 2012, falling which the Seller reserves the right to rescind without further notice, or to accept whole or any part of this Sales Confirmation non-fulfilled by the Buyer, or to lodge claim for direct losses sustained, if any.

凡以 CIF 条件成交的业务，保额为发票价的 110%，投保险别以售货确认书中所开列的为限，买方如果要求增加保额或保险范围，应于装船前经卖方同意，因此而增加的保险费由买方负责。

For transactions conclude on CIF basis, it is understood that the insurance amount will be for 110% of the invoice value against the risks specified in Sales Confirmation. If additional insurance amount or coverage is required, the buyer must have consent of the Seller before Shipment, and the additional premium is to be borne by the Buyer.

装运单据：卖方应向议付行提供下列单据：

Shipping documents: The sellers shall present the following documents to the negotiating bank for payment：

(1) 全套清洁已装船空白抬头空白背书提单，注明运费已付。

Full set clean on board of shipped Bills of Lading made out to order and blank endorsed, mark "Freight Prepaid".

(2) 商业发票 6 份。

Commercial invoice in   6   copies.

(3) 装箱单或重量单 5 份。

The packing list or weight list in   5   copies.

(4) 可转让的保险单或保险凭证正本一份及副本 2 份。

One original and 2 duplicate copies of the transferable insurance policy or insurance certificate.

(5)买方指定的机构签发的品质、重量/数量检验证书正本一份，副本 __2__ 份。

One original and __2__ duplicate copies of inspection certificate of quality, quantity/weight issued by The Inspecting Agency Designated By The Buyer.

(6)中国商会签发的原产地证明书正本一份，副本 __1__ 份。

One original and __1__ duplicate copies of the Certificate of origin issued by The Chamber of Commerce or other authority duly entitled for this purpose.

品质/数量异议：如买方提出索赔，凡属品质异议，须于货到目的口岸之 __60__ 日内提出，凡属数量异议，须于货到目的口岸之 __30__ 日内提出，对所装货物所提的异议如属于保险公司、轮船公司等其他有关运输或邮递机构的责任范畴，卖方不负任何责任。

QUALITY /QUANTITY DISCREPANCY: In case of quality discrepancy, claim should be filed by the Buyer within __60__ days after the arrival of the goods at port of destination; while for quantity discrepancy, claim should be filed by the Buyer within __30__ days after the arrival of the goods at port of destination. It is understood that the seller shall not be liable for any discrepancy of the goods shipped due to causes for which the Insurance Company, Shipped Company and other transportation organization/or Post Office are liable.

本确认书内所述全部或部分商品，如因人力不可抗拒的原因，以致不能履约或延迟交货，卖方概不负责。

The Seller shall not be held liable for failure of delay in delivery of the entire lot or a portion of the goods under this Sales Confirmation in consequence of any Force Majeure incidents.

买方在开给卖方的信用证上请填注本确认书号码。

The Buyer is requested always to quote The Number of This Sales Confirmation in the letter of Credit to be opened in favour of the Seller.

买方收到本售货确认书后请立即签回一份，如买方对本确认书有异议，应于收到后五天内提出，否则认为买方已同意接受本确认书所规定的各项条款。

The buyer is requested to sign and return one copy of the Sales Confirmation immediately after the receipt of same. Objection, if any, should be raised by the Buyer within five days after the receipt of this Sales Confirmation, in the absence of which it is understood that the Buyer has accepted the terms and condition of the sales confirmation.

买方：MANDARS　　　　　　　　　　卖方：方达
THE BUYER：　　　　　　　　　　　　THE SELLERS：

操作指南　合同成立的有效条件

1. 当事人必须在自愿和真实的基础上达成协议

从法理上看,当事人的意思表示必须一致,分解为要约和承诺。要约人用明示的方式向受约人提出要约,要约一经承诺,合同即告成立。我国《合同法》明确规定:"合同当事人的法律地位平等,一方不得将自己的意志强加给另一方";"当事人依法享有自愿订立合同的权利,任何单位和个人不得非法干预"。

2. 当事人必须具有订立合同的行为能力

一般来说,具有法律行为能力的人是指登记注册的企业法人和自然人中的成年人。为了形成一项有效的、具有法律约束力的合同,合同双方当事人必须具有法律行为的能力。没有法律行为能力的人或限制法律行为能力的人,如未成年人和精神病患者等,都被视为没有签订合同能力的人,对其所订立的合同,视情况予以撤销或宣布无效。

3. 合同必须有对价和合法的约因

"对价"(Consideration)是指当事人为了取得合同利益所付出的代价,这是英美法的概念。例如,在买卖合同中,买方得到卖方提供的货物必须支付货款,而卖方取得买方支付的货款必须交货,买方支付和卖方交货就是买卖合同的"对价"。

"约因"(Cause)是法国法律的概念,"约因"与英美法中的"对价"相类似,是指当事人签订合同所追求的直接目的。

买卖合同在具有"对价"和"约因"的情况下,才是有效的。无"对价"或无"约因"的合同,是得不到法律保护的。

4. 合同的标的必须合法

几乎所有国家的法律都要求当事人所订立的合同标的必须合法,合法是合同的基本性质。凡是违反法律、违反公共秩序或公共政策以及违反善良风俗或道德的合同,一律无效。

5. 合同必须符合法律规定的形式

公约规定:"买卖合同无需以书面订立或证明,在形式方面不受任何其他条件的限制,买卖合同可以包括人证在内的任何方法证明。"可见,公约对国际货物买卖合同的形式不加以限制,无论采用书面还是口头方式,均不影响合同的效力。

我国《合同法》规定:"当事人订立合同,有书面形式、口头形式和其他形式",但"法律、行政法规规定采用书面形式的,应当采用书面形式。当事人约定采用书面形式的,应当采用书面形式"。

工作任务二　　　　审核信用证

上海永胜进出口公司在合同规定的开证时间内收到进口商 MANDARS IMPORTS CO. LTD. 开立的不可撤销的跟单远期信用证,方达先生依据合同条款对其进行认真的审核,如发现信用证中有不能接受的不符点,则必须要求进口商修改信用证。

信用证内容如下:

IRREVOCABLE DOCUMENTARY CREDIT

SEQUENCE OF TOTAL	*27 :	1/1
FORM OF DOC. CREDIT	*40A :	IRREVOCABLE
DOC. CREDIT NUMBER	*20 :	XT370
DATE OF ISSUE	31C :	120430
DATE AND PLACE OF EXPIRY	*31D :	DATE 120630 IN UK
APPLICANT	*50 :	MANDARS IMPORTS CO. LTD.
		38 QUEENSWAY, 2008 UK
ISSUING BANK	52A :	BANK OF LONDON
		205 QUEENSWAY, LONDON, UK
BENEFICIARY	*59 :	SHANGHAI YONGSHENG EXP. & IMP. CO.
		21 WEST ZHONGSHAN ROAD SHANGHAI CHINA
AMOUNT	*32B :	CURRENCY USD AMOUNT 126 000.00
AVAILABLE WITH/BY	*41D :	BANK OF CHINA, SHANGHAI BRANCH
DRAFTS AT ⋯	42C :	DRAFTS AT SIGHT FOR FULL INVOICE COST
DRAWEE	42A :	BANK OF LONDON
PARTIAL SHIPMENTS	43P :	ALLOWED
TRANSSHIPMENT	43T :	NOT ALLOWED
PORT OF LOADING	44E :	SHANGHAI PORT
FOR TRANSPORTATION TO ⋯	44B :	LONDON PORT
LATEST DATE OF SHIPMENT	44C :	120530
DESCRIPT OF GOODS	45A :	LADIES DENIM SKIRT AS PER S/C NO.
		TXT201210
DOCUMENTS REQUIRED	46A :	

+ SIGNED COMMERCIAL INVOICE, 2 ORIGINAL AND 4 COPIES.

+ PACKING LIST, 1 ORIGINAL AND 4 COPIES.
+ CERTIFICATE OF ORIGIN GSP CHINA FORM A AND ETC, ISSUED BY THE CHAMBER OF COMMERCE OR OTHER AUTHORITY DULY ENTITLED FOR THIS PURPOSE.
+ FULL SET OF NEGOTIABLE INSURANCE POLICY OR CERTIFICATE BLANK ENDORSED FOR 120 PERCENT OF THE INVOICE VALUE COVERING ALL RISKS & WAR RISK
+ FULL SET OF B/L CLEAN ON BOARD, MADE OUT TO ORDER OF SHIPPER AND BLANK ENDORSED AND MARKED "FREIGHT PREPAID" AND NOTIFY APPLICANT.
+ QUALITY CERTIFICATE IS TO BE EFFECTED BEFORE SHIPMENT AND IS REQUIRED FROM THE INSPECTING AGENCY DESIGNATED BY THE BUYER.

CHARGES　　　　　　　　71B：ALL BANKING CHARGES OUTSIDE UK ARE FOR ACCOUNT OF BENEFICIARY.

PERIOD FOR PRESENTATION　48：DOCUMENTS MUST BE PRESENTED WITHIN 15 DAYS AFTER THE DATE OF SHIPMENT BUT WITHIN THE VALIDITY OF THE CREDIT.

审证结果：
1. 受益人的名称错误。
2. 信用证到期的地点应为受益人国内，而非开证申请人国内。
3. 投保金额为发票金额的110％，而非120％。
4. 汇票是提单签发日60天付款，而不是即期付款。
5. 转运允许，而非不允许。
6. 删除"quality certificate is to be effected before shipment and is required from the inspecting agency designated by the buyer"，增加"quality certificate is issued by China Exit & Entry Inspection & Quarantine Bureau"。

操作指南　➡　出口商审核信用证的要点

1. 对信用证规定的品质、数量和包装的审核

信用证就商品名称、品质、数量和包装的规定须与合同一致，如发现与合同规定不符，我方又不能接受的，应要求买方改证。

续

2. 对信用证所列受益人和开证申请人的名称和地址的审核

信用证中的受益人和开证申请人的名称和地址应与合同的有关内容相一致。

3. 对信用证金额、货币的审核

信用证金额与货币应与合同一致，如合同订有溢短装条款，信用证金额亦应有相应的增减。

4. 对信用证中运输条款的审核

审核信用证规定的装运港、目的港、装运期、分批装运和转运是否与合同的规定相符。

5. 对信用证规定单据的审核

对信用证中所要求提供的单据种类、填写内容、文字说明、文件份数和填写方法等都要认真审核，凡是信用证要求的单据与我国政策相抵触或根本办不到的，应及时与对方联系修改。

6. 对信用证有效期、到期地点和装运期的审核

装运期必须与合同规定的时间相一致。如因来证太晚或发生意外情况而不能按时装运，应及时电请买方展延装运期限；如来证仅规定有效期而未规定装运期时，信用证的有效期可视为装运期，如有效期与装运期是同一个时期，需依据我方装运情况来决定是否修改，通常信用证的有效期与装运期都有一定合理时间的间隔，以便装运货物后有充足的时间办理制单、结汇工作。

对于到期地点一般要求在我国境内，如规定在国外，因不好掌握寄单时间，一般不轻易接受。

◇ **工作任务三　　　　　拟写改证函**

上海永胜进出口公司方达先生依据合同条款对信用证进行认真的审核，结果发现信用证中有几处不符点，于是拟写改证函寄至客户 MANDARS IMPORTS CO. LTD.，要求进口商及时修改信用证，以免延误装运。

发件人： FANGDASH@163.COM
收件人： MANDARS@HOTMAIL.COM
主　题： EDITING THE CREDIT

Dear Mr. Smith,

We have received your letter of credit. Thank you for your prompt issuing.

However, when we checked the L/C with the relevant contract, we found the following discrepancies:

1. the name of the beneficiary should be SHANGHAI YONGSHENG IMP. & EXP. CO.

2. the L/C expiry place should be in CHINA, not in UK.

3. the goods are insured for 110% of invoice value, not 120%.

4. the draft should be paid at 60 days after B/L date instead of at sight.

5. transshipment should be allowed, not prohibited.

6. delete the clause "quality certificate is to be effected before shipment and is required from the inspecting agency designated by the buyer", and add the wording "quality certificate is issued by CHINA EXIT & ENTRY INSPECTION & QUARANTINE BUREAU".

Please let us have your L/C amendment soon so that we may effect shipment within the contracted delivery time.

Thank you.

Yours truly,

SHANGHAI YONGSHENG IMP. & EXP. CO.

Da Fang

MAY 05, 2012

进口商 MANDARS IMPORTS CO. LTD. 针对上海永胜进出口公司提出的改证要求进行审核，确认有误后，向开证行 BANK OF LONDON 提出修改信用证的申请。开证行根据修改信用证申请书进行改证，发出信用证改证书。具体内容如下：

BANK OF LONDON
APPLICATION FOR AMENDMENT

Amendment to Credit No.: XT370
Amendment No.: XT183
To: BANK OF CHINA SHANGHAI BRANCH   Amendment Date: MAY 10, 2012

Applicant MANDARS IMPORTS CO. LTD. 38 QUEENSWAY, 2008 UK	Advising Bank BANK OF CHINA SHANGHAI BRANCH
Beneficiary (before this amendment) SHANGHAI YONGSHENG IMP. & EXP. CO. 21 WEST ZHONGSHAN ROAD SHANGHAI CHINA	Amount USD 126 000.00

The above mentioned credit is amended as follows:

1. the name of the beneficiary should be SHANGHAI YONGSHENG IMP. & EXP. CO.
2. the L/C expiry place should be in CHINA, not in UK.
3. the goods are insured for 110% of invoice value, not 120%.
4. the draft should be paid at 60 days after B/L date instead of at sight.
5. transshipment should be allowed, not prohibited.
6. delete the clause "quality certificate is to be effected before shipment and is required from the inspecting agency designated by the buyer", and add the wording "quality certificate is issued by CHINA EXIT & ENTRY INSPECTION & QUARANTINE BUREAU".

☐Banking charges:

All other terms and conditions remain unchanged.

Authorized Signature(s)
BANK OF LONDON

This Amendment is Subject to Uniform Customs and Practice for Documentary Credits (2007 Revision) International Chamber of Commerce Publication No. 600.

综合业务模拟操作

操作一

1. 操作资料

   卖　方：南京永发进出口公司
   　　　　南京中山路 1321 号
   　　　　TEL：025-23501111　　FAX：025-23502222

   买　方：JIM KING TRADING CORPORATION
   　　　　No. 206 CHANGJ NORTH STREET SINGAPORE
   　　　　TEL：218-76911　　FAX：218-76912

   货　名：电动钻头(Electric Drill) No. TY242
   数　量：1 800 套
   包　装：每 10 套装一个纸箱
   价　格：CIF SINGAPORE　No. TY242　每套 USD4.20
   支付方式：不可撤销跟单远期信用证(30 DAYS AFTER SIGHT)
   开证时间：2012 年 9 月 30 日前将不可撤销跟单远期信用证开到买方
   交货时间：不迟于 2012 年 10 月 30 日
   分批装运：不允许
   转　运：不允许
   装运港：连云港
   目的港：新加坡
   保　险：按发票金额 110％投保中国人民保险公司海洋货物运输险一切险与战争险
   合同号：wy070901　日期：2012.09.20
   唛　头：由卖方指定

2. 操作要求

   (1) 请你以南京永发进出口公司业务员张丽的身份根据上述资料拟订一份销售合同书，要求格式完整、内容正确，并要签字。

体验活动二 自理出口贸易业务

南京永发进出口公司
NANJING YONGFA IMPORT & EXPORT TRADE CORPORATION
1321 ZHONGSHAN ROAD NANJING, CHINA

SALES CONTRACT

TEL：_____   S/C NO.：_____

FAX：_____   DATE：_____

TO：

Dear Sirs,

　　We hereby confirm having sold to you the following goods on terms and conditions as specified below：

MARKS & NO.	DESCRIPTIONS OF GOODS	QUANTITY	U/ PRICE	AMOUNT

LOADING PORT：

DESTINATION：

PARTIAL SHIPMENT：

TRANSSHIPMENT：

PAYMENT：

INSURANCE：

TIME OF SHIPMENT：

THE BUYER：　　　　　　　　　　　　　　THE SELLER：

　　(2) 不久，南京永发进出口公司在合同规定的开证时间内收到客户JIM KING TRADING CORPORATION开立的信用证。请你以南京永发进出口公司业务员张丽的身份进行审证，如发现不符点，请详细记录。

IRREVOCABLE DOCUMENTARY CREDIT

SEQUENCE OF TOTAL	*27 :	1/1
FORM OF DOC. CREDIT	*40A :	IRREVOCABLE
DOC. CREDIT NUMBER	*20 :	NB4567
DATE OF ISSUE	31C :	120910
DATE AND PLACE OF EXPIRY	*31D :	DATE 121115 IN SINGAPORE
APPLICANT	*50 :	JIM KING TRADING CORPORATION
		No. 206 CHANGJ NORTH STREET SINGAPORE
ISSUING BANK	52A :	SINGAPORE BANK
		205 KAWARA, SINGAPORE
BENEFICIARY	*59 :	NANJING YONGFA IMPORT & EXPORT
		TRADE CORPORATION.
		1321 ZHONGSHAN ROAD NANJING, CHINA
AMOUNT	*32B :	CURRENCY USD AMOUNT 75 600.00
AVAILABLE WITH/BY	*41D :	BANK OF CHINA, LIANYUNGANG BRANCH
DRAFTS AT …	42C :	DRAFTS AT 30 DAYS SIGHT FOR FULL
		INVOICE COST
PARTIAL SHIPMENTS	43P :	ALLOWED
TRANSSHIPMENT	43T :	NOT ALLOWED
PORT OF LOADING	44E :	SHANGHAI PORT
FOR TRANSPORTATION TO …	44B :	SINGAPORE PORT
LATEST DATE OF SHIPMENT	44C :	121020
DESCRIPT OF GOODS	45A :	ELECTRONIC DRILL AS PER S/C NO. wy070901
DOCUMENTS REQUIRED	46A :	

+ SIGNED COMMERCIAL INVOICE, 2 ORIGINAL AND 4 COPIES.
+ PACKING LIST, 1 ORIGINAL AND 4 COPIES.
+ CERTIFICATE OF ORIGIN GSP CHINA FORM A AND ETC, ISSUED BY THE CHAMBER OF COMMERCE OR OTHER AUTHORITY DULY ENTITLED FOR THIS PURPOSE.
+ FULL SET OF NEGOTIABLE INSURANCE POLICY OR CERTIFICATE BLANK ENDORSED FOR 120 PERCENT OF THE INVOICE VALUE COVERING ALL RISKS & WAR RISK
+ FULL SET OF B/L CLEAN ON BOARD, MADE OUT TO ORDER OF SHIPPER AND BLANK ENDORSED AND MARKED " FREIGHT COLLECT "AND NOTIFY APPLICANT.
+ QUALITY CERTIFICATE IS TO BE EFFECTED BEFORE SHIPMENT AND IS REQUIRED FROM THE INSPECTING AGENCY DESIGNATED BY THE BUYER.

CHARGES 71B : ALL BANKING CHARGES OUTSIDE SINGA-
PORE ARE FOR ACCOUNT OF BENEFICIARY.

PERIOD FOR PRESENTATION 48 : DOCUMENTS MUST BE PRESENTED WITHIN 15
DAYS AFTER THE DATE OF SHIPMENT BUT
WITHIN THE VALIDITY OF THE CREDIT.

THIS DOCUMENTARY CREDIT IS SUBJECT TO THE "UNIFORM CUSTOMS AND PRACTICE FOR DOCUMENTARY CREDIT" 2007 REVISION INTERNATIONAL CHAMBER OF COMMERCE PUBLICATION NO. 600.

审证结果

操作二

1. 操作资料

THE SELLERS: GUANGZHOU TEXTILE IMPORT & EXPORT TRADE CORPORATION

  530 BEIJING ROAD GUANGZHOU, CHINA

THE BUYER: OLEARA IMPORT & EXPORT CORPORATION

  310-224 HOLA STREET MARSEILLE FRANCE

NAME OF COMMODITY:

  GENTLEMAN'S SHIRT Art No. 88(BLUE)、Art No. 44(BLACK)

QUANTITY: Art No. 88(BLUE) 3 000PCS、Art No. 44(BLACK) 3 000PCS

PACKING: PACKED IN 1 CARTON OF 20 PCS EACH

  G. W: 20.2 KGS / CTN N. W: 20 KGS / CTN MEAS: 0.2 M^3 / CYN

  PACKED IN ONE 20'CONTAINER(集装箱号: TEXU22636643)

UNIT PRICE: Art No. 88(BLUE) USD 6.50 、Art No. 44 (BLACK) USD 7.00

  CIF MARSEILLE

PAYMENT: BY L/C AT SIGHT,

  THE BUYER SHALL OPEN THROUGH A BANK ACCEPTABLE TO THE SELLERS AN IRREVOCABLE SIGHT LETTER OF CREDIT TO REACH THE SELLERS 25 DAYS BEFORE THE DAY OF SHIPMENT

SHIPMENT TIME: NOT LATER THAN JULY 31, 2012

LOADING PORT: GUANGZHOU

DESTINATION: MARSELLE

PARTIAL SHIPMENT: ALLOWED

TRANSSHIPMENT: ALLOWED

INSURANCE: FOR 110 PCT OF INVOICE VALUE COVERING ALL RISKS

S/C NO.: ST121032

DATE: JUN. 01, 2012

2. 实训要求

（1）请你以广州纺织品进出口贸易公司业务员王伟的身份根据上述资料拟订一份销售合同书，要求格式完整、内容正确，并要签字盖章。

体验活动二　自理出口贸易业务

广州纺织品进出口贸易公司
GUANGZHOU TEXTILE IMPORT & EXPORT TRADE CORPORATION
530 BEIJING ROAD GUANGZHOU, CHINA

SALES CONTRACT

TEL:＿＿＿＿＿＿　　　　　　　　　　　　　　　　INV. NO.:＿＿＿＿＿

FAX:＿＿＿＿＿＿　　　　　　　　　　　　　　　　DATE:＿＿＿＿＿＿

　　　　　　　　　　　　　　　　　　　　　　　　　S/C NO.:＿＿＿＿＿

TO:　　　　　　　　　　　　　　　　　　　　　　　L/C NO.:＿＿＿＿＿

FROM ＿＿＿＿＿＿＿＿＿＿＿　TO ＿＿＿＿＿＿＿＿＿＿＿

MARKS & NO.	DESCRIPTIONS OF GOODS	QUANTITY	U/ PRICE	AMOUNT

TOTAL AMOUNT:

WE HEREBY CERTIFY THAT THE CONTENTS OF INVOICE HEREIN ARE TRUE AND CORRECT.

　　　　　　　　　　　　　　　　　　　　　　＿＿＿＿＿＿＿＿＿＿＿＿

(2)不久，广州纺织品进出口贸易公司在合同规定的开证时间内收到客户OLEARA IMPORT & EXPORT CORPORATION开立的信用证。请你以广州纺织品进出口贸易公司业务员王伟的身份进行审证，如发现不符点，请详细记录，并拟写改证函。

CITY BANK MARSEILLE BRANCH

1025 WEST GEORGIA STREET, MARSEILLE FRANCE

DATE: 120620

PLACE: MARSEILLE

IRREVOCABLE DOCUMENTARY CREDIT	CREDIT NUMBER: 07/CB4578	ADVISING BANK'S REF. NO.
ADVISING BANK: CITY BANK SHANGHAI BRANCH 23 PUDONG ROAD, SHANGHAI CHINA		APPLICANT: OLEARA TRADING CORPORATION 310-224 HOLA STREET MARSEILLE FRANCE
BENEFICIARY: GUANGZHOU TEXTILE EXPORT & IMPORT TRADING COPORATION 530 BEIJING ROAD, GUANGZHOU CHINA		AMOUT: USD4 050.00 (US DOLLARS FOUR THOUSAND AND FIFTY ONLY)

EXPIRY DATE: AUG. 15, 2012   FOR NEGOCIATION IN APPLICANT'S COUNTRY

GENTLEMEN:

WE HEREBY OPEN OUR IRREVOCABLE LETTER OF CREDIT IN YOUR FAVOR WHICH IS AVAILABLE BY YOUR DRAFTS AT SIGHT FOR FULL INVOICE VALUE ON US ACCOMPANIED BY THE FOLLOWING DOCUMENTS:

　+SIGNED COMMERCIAL INVOICE IN 3 COPIES.

　+EEC IN COPIES.

　+PACKING LIST IN 3 COPIES.

　+CERTIFICATE OF ORIGIN GSP CHINA FORM A, ISSUED BY THE CHAMBER OF COMMERCE OR OTHER AUTHORITY DULY ENTITLED FOR THIS PURPOSE.

　+INSURANCE POLICY OR CERTIFICATE FOR 130% OF INVOICE VALUE COVERING: INSTITUTE CARGO CLAUSES (A) AS PER I.C.C DATED 1/1/1982.

　+FULL SET OF CLEAN ON BOARD OCEAN BILL OF LADING SHOWING FREIGHT PREPAID CONSIGNED TO ORDER OF THE SHIPPING INDICATING "FREIGHT PREPAID" NOTIFY APPLICANT.

　COVERING THE SHIPPMENT OF : ART NO. 88 3000 PCS   ART NO. 44 3000 PCS

　TWO ITEMS OF GENTLEMAN'S SHIRT INCLUDING:

　( )FOB/(×)CFR/( )/CIF/LONGBEACH

SHIPMENT FROM GUANGZHOU	TO MARSEILLE	LATEST 20120731	PARTIAL SHIPMENT YES	TRANSSHIPMENT NO

DRAFT TO BE PRESENTED FOR NEGOCIATION WITHIN 15 DAYS AFTER SHIPMENT, BUT WITHIN THE VALIDITY OF CREDIT.
THE CREDIT IS SUBJECT TO UCP 600.

改证函
....

实训三 出口合同的履行——备货

业务导入

上海永胜进出口公司没有自己的生产实体,在收到信用证改证书并经审核无误后,必须寻找合适的加工生产企业履行交货义务。为此,方达先生对多家服装企业的生产规模和生产能力进行调查,选择了南通服装公司作为弹力牛仔女裙的加工企业,并与其签订加工合同。与此同时,还要根据 MANDARS IMPORTS CO. LTD. 提供的样品或款式,选择合适的原材料(面料)供应商。通过对原材料市场的调查,上海永胜进出口公司选定江苏南通纺织厂为全棉弹力牛仔面料供应商,并与其签订采购合同,确保出口货物按时按质顺利完成。

备货业务环节如下图所示:

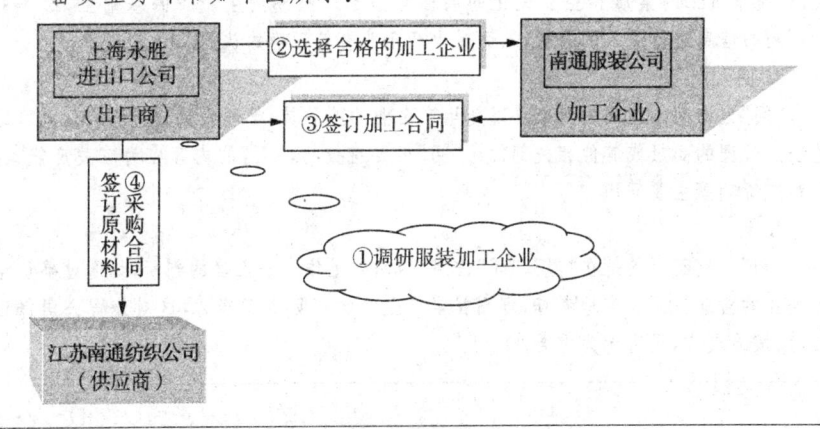

上海永胜进出口公司(出口商) —②选择合格的加工企业→ 南通服装公司(加工企业)
③签订加工合同
④签订采购原材料合同 → 江苏南通纺织公司(供应商)
①调研服装加工企业

◎ 工作任务一　　　　　拟订加工合同书

上海永胜进出口公司方达先生在收到通知行寄送的信用证改证书并经审核无误后，开始寻找合适的加工生产企业。通过对多家服装企业的生产规模、生产能力和企业管理现状进行调查，最终选择了南通服装公司作为弹力牛仔女裙的加工企业，并与其签订加工合同。

操作指南　➡　选择加工生产企业的方法

1. 望

"望"即看。一是通过"望"可掌握生产企业的基本信息。例如，核查生产企业法人登记注册事项。任何个人或组织都能到当地工商注册管理部门查询企业法人登记注册情况，包括企业法人和法定代表人姓名、经济性质、经营范围和方式、注册资本、成立时间、营业期限、经营场所等内容，这样可获得较为全面、真实的情况。在实际工作中，有些资信不良的生产企业提供的营业执照复印件有虚假现象，如不核实企业法人登记注册情况，将留下隐患。二是通过"望"确认生产企业的产能。业务员可通过实地观看生产企业的规模、生产企业的机器设备、工厂的管理、厂房的面积及安全情况等，来判断生产企业是否具备出口商品的生产能力，是否符合外国客商的评估要求。这是因为生产企业规模的大小会影响到能否按时交货，机器设备与工厂管理的好坏将直接关系到产品的质量。

2. 闻

"闻"即听。主要是从各个方面听取有关生产企业的经营管理的状况、产品信息的反馈、基本员工的素质和企业文化的层面等信息。业务员在"望"的基础上，通过对"闻"到的信息进行深入的分析，从而对生产企业有较正确的认识。

3. 问

"问"为询问。询问的对象可以是生产企业的业务员、管理人员、生产员工，也可以是企业管理的高层或其他相关部门。"问"需要有技巧，"问"的内容应为有关产能、品质和交货期等主要问题。

4. 切

"切"是判断。其是在"望"、"闻"、"问"的基础上作一个正确的判断，如通过确认生产企业的营业执照和实地考查，可测算生产企业的实际生产能力，这对外贸公司保证按时、按质交货，显得尤为重要。

上海永胜进出口公司
加工合同

编号：TXT888

甲方：上海永胜进出口公司　　　　　　　　乙方：南通服装公司
地址：中国上海市中山西路21号　　　　　　地址：南通市人民路11号
电话：(021) 64500003　　　　　　　　　　电话：0513-8836420

双方为开展来料加工业务，经友好协商，特订立本合同。

第一条　加工内容

甲方向乙方提供加工<u>蓝灰色(36、38、40、42)全棉弹力牛仔女裙 18 000</u>条所需的原材料，乙方将甲方提供的原材料加工成产品后交付甲方。

第二条　交货

甲方在<u>　2012　</u>年<u>　4　</u>月<u>　15　</u>日向乙方提供<u>22 032 米</u>原材料，并负责运至<u>南通车站</u>交付乙方；乙方在<u>　5　</u>月<u>　26　</u>日前将加工后的成品<u>18 000</u>条负责运至吴淞港口交付甲方。

第三条　来料数量与质量

甲方提供的原材料须含<u>　2　</u>％的备损率，并符合工艺单的规格标准。如甲方未能按时、按质、按量提供给乙方应交付的原材料，乙方除对无法履行本合同不负责外，还得向甲方索取停工待料的损失。

第四条　加工数量与质量

乙方如未能按时、按质、按量交付加工产品，应赔偿甲方所受的损失。

第五条　加工费与付款方式

乙方为甲方进行加工的费用，每条人民币<u>　15　</u>元。乙方收到货物后10天内向甲方支付全部加工费。

第六条　运输

甲方将成品运至乙方指定的地点，运费由甲方负责。

第七条　不可抗力

由于战争和严重的自然灾害以及双方同意的其他不可抗力引起的事故，致使一方不能履约时，该方应尽快将事故通知对方，并与对方协商延长履行合同的期限。由此而引起的损失，对方不得提出赔偿要求。

第八条　仲裁

本合同在执行期间，如发生争议，双方应本着友好方式协商解决。如未能协商解决，提请中国上海仲裁机构进行仲裁。

第九条　合同有效期

本合同自签字之日起生效。本合同正本一式两份，甲乙双方各执一份。

本合同如有未尽事宜，或遇特殊情况需要补充、变更内容，须经双方协商一致。

甲方：(盖章)　　上海永胜进出口公司　　乙方：(盖章)　　南通服装公司
　　　　　　　　　合同专用章　　　　　　　　　　　　　合同专用章

委托代理人：方达　　　　　　　　　　　　委托代理人：王达
日期：2012年3月25日　　　　　　　　　　日期：2012年3月25日

◎ 工作任务二　　　　拟订采购合同

加工合同签订后,上海永胜进出口公司方达先生通过对原材料(面料)市场进行调查,按照客户规定的原材料(面料)型号、规格等质量标准,选择合适的原材料(面料)供应商,保证加工生产的供给,确保出口产品按时按质顺利完成。上海永胜进出口公司通过对多家供应商的原材料(面料)的价格、品质等方面进行分析,决定与江苏南通纺织公司签订采购合同,由其作为全棉弹力牛仔面料的供应商。

上海永胜进出口公司
采购合同

编号：SH0731

供应商：江苏南通纺织公司　　　　　　　　　　日期：2012.3.26

请供应以下产品：

型号	品名、规格	单位	数量	单价	金额	备注
5	全棉弹力牛仔布	米	22 032	17元	374 544元	
合计	叁拾柒万肆仟伍佰肆拾肆元整					

1. 交货日期：2012年4月12日以前一次交清。
2. 交货地点：南通车站。
3. 包装条件：卷筒包装。
4. 付款方式：交货后1个月凭增值税发票付款。
5. 不合格产品处理：另议。
6. 如因交货误期、规格不符、质量不符合要求造成本公司的损失,卖方负赔偿责任。
7. 如卖方未能按期交货,必须赔偿本公司因此蒙受的一切损失。
8. 其他：

　　　　　上海永胜进出口公司　　　　　　　　江苏南通纺织公司
　　　　　　　合同专用章　　　　　　　　　　　　合同专用章

采购单位：(盖章)方达　　　　　　　　供应商：(盖章)英映

操作指南 ➡ 采购原材料的要求

1. 交货时间合理

交货时间合理是指所订购的原材料应在规定的时间内获得有效的供应。因为原材料的交货时间将直接影响到生产的进程和经营成本,如迟于生产的需求,会产生"停工待料"的现象,而过早会造成库存过多,积压订购资金,增加企业的经营成本。

2. 交货质量合理

供应商提供的原材料品质必须满足出口货物加工的要求,如原材料质量过低,将直接影响产品的品质,而质量过高,会引起采购成本的增加,缩小利润空间。

3. 交货地点合理

合理的交货地点是指可以减少企业的运输与装卸作业,其一般为港口、物流中心、企业的仓库等。否则,会增加运输、装卸和保管等方面的成本,也不利于加工企业的生产管理。

4. 交货数量合理

合理的交货数量是指每次提供的原料正好满足企业生产的需求,不产生库存,达到最佳的经济效果。这就需要业务员在原材料生产企业与加工单位之间进行有效的协调,加强沟通,及时排除不利因素。

5. 交货价格合理

合理的原材料价格应与其品质、交货时间和付款方式等条件相符。要获得合理的交货价格,可以通过询价表对多家公司进行询价,再进行"货比三家",并对选中的原材料供应商进行"杀价",挤出"水分",然后定价。

综合业务模拟操作

操作一

1. 操作资料

甲　方:南京永发进出口公司
　　　　南京中山路 1321 号
　　　　TEL:025-23501111　　FAX:025-23502222

乙　方:南京上野五金工具公司(委托代理人李廷)
　　　　南京市金陵路 19 号
　　　　TEL:025-56789877

加工合同号:NY07888

合同日期:2012 年 9 月 30 日

加工货名:电动钻头(Electric Drill)No.TY242
加工数量:1 800套
包　装:每10套装一个纸箱
加工费:每套5元,乙方结汇后45天向甲方支付全部加工费
单　耗:每套0.1米(含1‰备损率)
原料交付日期:甲方在2012年10月5日前向乙方提供原料,并负责运至南京车站交付
产品交付日期:2012年10月26日前将加工后的成品1 800套运至连云港港口指定仓库
原料货名:钢条
数　量:180米
单　价:200元/米
交货日期:2012年10月4日
交货地点:南京车站
包装条件:卷筒包装
付款方式:交货后1个月凭增值税发票付款
不合格产品处理:另议
2.操作要求
(1)请你以南京永发进出口公司业务员张丽的身份,根据上述资料、销售合同书和信用证的有关内容拟订一份加工合同书,内容正确,并要签字盖章。

南京永发进出口公司
加工合同

编号：_____

甲方：　　　　　　　　　　　　　　　乙方：
地址：　　　　　　　　　　　　　　　地址：
电话：　　　　　　　　　　　　　　　电话：

　　双方为开展来料加工业务，经友好协商，特订立本合同。
　　第一条　加工内容
　　甲方向乙方提供加工_____所需的钢条，乙方将甲方提供的钢条加工成产品后交付甲方。
　　第二条　交货
　　甲方在_____年____月____日向乙方提供_____钢条，并负责运至____车站交付乙方；乙方在_____年____月____日前将加工后的成品_____负责运至_____港口交付甲方。
　　第三条　来料数量与质量
　　甲方提供的钢条须含____%的备损率，并符合工艺单的规格标准。如甲方未能按时、按质、按量提供给乙方应交付的钢条，乙方除对无法履行本合同不负责外，还得向甲方索取停工待料的损失。
　　第四条　加工数量与质量
　　乙方如未能按时、按质、按量交付加工产品，应赔偿甲方所受的损失。
　　第五条　加工费与付款方式
　　乙方为甲方进行加工的费用，每套人民币_____元。甲方结汇后45天向乙方支付全部加工费。
　　第六条　运输
　　甲方将成品运至乙方指定的地点，运费由甲方负责。
　　第七条　不可抗力
　　由于战争和严重的自然灾害以及双方同意的其他不可抗力引起的事故，致使一方不能履约时，该方应尽快将事故通知对方，并与对方协商延长履行合同的期限。由此而引起的损失，对方不得提出赔偿要求。
　　第八条　仲裁
　　本合同在执行期间，如发生争议，双方应本着友好方式协商解决。如未能协商解决，提请中国上海仲裁机构进行仲裁。
　　第九条　合同有效期
　　本合同自签字之日起生效。本合同正本一式____份，甲乙双方各执一份。
　　本合同如有未尽事宜，或遇特殊情况需要补充、变更内容，须经双方协商一致。

甲方：（盖章）　　　　　　　　　　　乙方：（盖章）
委托代理人：　　　　　　　　　　　　委托代理人：
日期：　　　　　　　　　　　　　　　日期：

(2)南京永发进出口公司签订好加工合同后,随即与原料供应商江苏南通钢铁公司(代理人昭云)签订采购合同(编号为 NY071002、日期为 2007 年 10 月 2 日)。请你以南京永发进出口公司业务员张丽的身份,根据上述资料、销售合同书和信用证的有关内容拟订一份原材料采购合同,内容正确,并要签字盖章。

南京永发进出口公司
采购合同

编号:_____

供应商:_____ 日期:_____

请供应以下产品:

型号	品名、规格	单位	数量	单价	金额	备注
合计	万 仟 佰 拾 元 角 分						

1. 交货日期: 年   月   日以前一次交清。
2. 交货地点:_____
3. 包装条件:_____
4. 付款方式:_____
5. 不合格产品处理:_____
6. 如因交货误期、规格不符、质量不符合要求造成本公司的损失,卖方负赔偿责任。
7. 如卖方未能按期交货,必须赔偿本公司因此蒙受的一切损失。
8. 其他:_____

采购单位:(盖章)   供应商:(盖章)
日期: 日期:

操作二

1. 操作资料

甲　方：广州纺织品进出口贸易公司
　　　　广州市北京路 530 号
　　　　TEL：(020)64043030　　FAX：(020)64043031

乙　方：广州宏光服装公司(委托代理人夏力)
　　　　广州市风林路 19 号(TEL：020-56788888)

加工合同号：GH07999

合同日期：2012 年 6 月 10 日

加工货名：男式衬衫 Art No.88(蓝色)、Art No.44(黑色)

加工数量：Art No.88(蓝色)3 000 PCS，Art No.44（黑色）3 000 PCS

包　装：每 20 件装一个纸箱(G.W 为 20.2 KGS / CTN，N.W 为 20 KGS / CTN，MEAS 为 0.2 M³ / CTN)，计装入一个 20 英尺集装箱(集装箱号：TEXU22636643)

加工费：每套 20 元，乙方结汇后 45 天向甲方支付全部加工费

单　耗：每条 1.2 米，备损率为 2％

原料交付日期：甲方在 2012 年 6 月 30 日前向乙方提供原料，并负责运至广州车站交付

产品交付日期：2012 年 7 月 24 日前将加工后的成品 6 000 件运至广州港口指定仓库

原料货名：色织棉布

单　价：20 元/米

交货日期：2012 年 6 月 28 日

交货地点：广州车站

包装条件：卷筒包装

付款方式：交货后 1 个月凭增值税发票付款

不合格产品处理：另议

2. 操作要求

(1)请你以广州纺织品进出口贸易公司业务员王伟的身份，根据上述资料、销售合同书和信用证的有关内容拟订一份加工合同书，内容正确，并要签字盖章。

广州纺织品进出口贸易公司
加工合同

编号：_____

甲方：　　　　　　　　　　　　　　　　乙方：
地址：　　　　　　　　　　　　　　　　地址：
电话：　　　　　　　　　　　　　　　　电话：

　　双方为开展来料加工业务，经友好协商，特订立本合同。

　　第一条　加工内容
　　甲方向乙方提供加工_____所需的原材料，乙方将甲方提供的原材料加工成产品后交付甲方。

　　第二条　交货
　　甲方在_____年____月____日向乙方提供_____原材料，并负责运至_____车站交付乙方；乙方在_____年____月____日前将加工后的成品_____负责运至_____港口交付甲方。

　　第三条　来料数量与质量
　　甲方提供的原材料须含____%的备损率，并符合工艺单的规格标准。如甲方未能按时、按质、按量提供给乙方应交付的原材料，乙方除对无法履行本合同不负责外，还得向甲方索取停工待料的损失。

　　第四条　加工数量与质量
　　乙方如未能按时、按质、按量交付加工产品，应赔偿甲方所受的损失。

　　第五条　加工费与付款方式
　　乙方为甲方进行加工的费用，每条人民币_____元。甲方结汇后45天向乙方支付全部加工费。

　　第六条　运输
　　甲方将成品运至乙方指定的地点，运费由甲方负责。

　　第七条　不可抗力
　　由于战争和严重的自然灾害以及双方同意的其他不可抗力引起的事故，致使一方不能履约时，该方应尽快将事故通知对方，并与对方协商延长履行合同的期限。由此而引起的损失，对方不得提出赔偿要求。

　　第八条　仲裁
　　本合同在执行期间，如发生争议，双方应本着友好方式协商解决。如未能协商解决，提请中国上海仲裁机构进行仲裁。

　　第九条　合同有效期
　　本合同自签字之日起生效。本合同正本一式____份，甲乙双方各执一份。
　　本合同如有未尽事宜，或遇特殊情况需要补充、变更内容，须经双方协商一致。

甲方：(盖章)　　　　　　　　　　　　　乙方：(盖章)
委托代理人：　　　　　　　　　　　　　委托代理人：
日期：　　　　　　　　　　　　　　　　日期：

(2)广州纺织品进出口贸易公司签订好加工合同后,随即与面料供应商广州纺织公司(代理人马民)签订采购合同(编号为GZ070612、日期为2012年6月12日)。请你以广州纺织品进出口贸易公司业务员王伟的身份,根据上述资料、销售合同书和信用证的有关内容拟订一份原材料采购合同,内容正确,并要签字盖章。

广州纺织品进出口贸易公司
采购合同

编号:＿＿＿＿＿＿＿

供应商:＿＿＿＿＿＿＿＿＿＿＿＿

请供应以下产品:

型号	品名、规格	单位	数量	单价	金额	备注
合计		万 仟 佰 拾 元 角 分				

1. 交货日期:　　年　　月　　日以前一次交清。
　　　　　　分批交货,交货时间＿＿＿＿＿＿数量要求:＿＿＿＿＿＿
2. 交货地点:＿＿＿＿＿＿＿＿＿＿＿＿＿＿＿＿＿＿＿＿＿＿＿＿＿
3. 包装条件:＿＿＿＿＿＿＿＿＿＿＿＿＿＿＿＿＿＿＿＿＿＿＿＿＿
4. 付款方式:＿＿＿＿＿＿＿＿＿＿＿＿＿＿＿＿＿＿＿＿＿＿＿＿＿
5. 不合格产品处理:＿＿＿＿＿＿＿＿＿＿＿＿＿＿＿＿＿＿＿＿＿＿
6. 如因交货误期、规格不符、质量不符合要求造成本公司的损失,卖方负赔偿责任。
7. 如卖方未能按期交货,必须赔偿本公司因此蒙受的一切损失。
8. 其他:＿＿＿＿＿＿＿＿＿＿＿＿＿＿＿＿＿＿＿＿＿＿＿＿＿＿＿

采购单位:(盖章)　　　　　　　　　　　供应商:(盖章)
日期:　　　　　　　　　　　　　　　　日期:

实训四　出口合同的履行——办理出口认证

> **业务导入**
>
> 　　上海永胜进出口公司在签订加工合同与采购合同后,为了按时、按质、按量履行出口合同的交货义务,必须对生产进度、货物品质、包装等进行跟单。同时,由于纺织品出口到英国,需要办理输欧盟纺织品许可证(EEC 证书)及普惠制产地证才能出口,所以,永胜进出口公司分别到外经贸委所属许可证管理事务局及检验检疫机构办理相关证书。
>
> 　　办理输欧盟纺织品许可证与普惠制产地证书的业务环节如下图所示:
>
> ```
>         商业发票                              商业发票
>   ①纺织品临时出              普惠制产地证      ①普惠制产
>   输欧盟纺织品出   口许可证申请表   明书申请书       地证明书
>   口许可证申请表
>
>   ┌─────────┐      ┌─────────┐      ┌─────────┐
>   │许可证管理局 │      │上海永胜进出口公司│      │检验检疫局 │
>   │(出口地商委) │      │  (出口商)    │      │ (出口地)  │
>   └─────────┘      └─────────┘      └─────────┘
>      ②签发输欧盟纺织品许可证          ②签发普惠制产地证明书
> ```

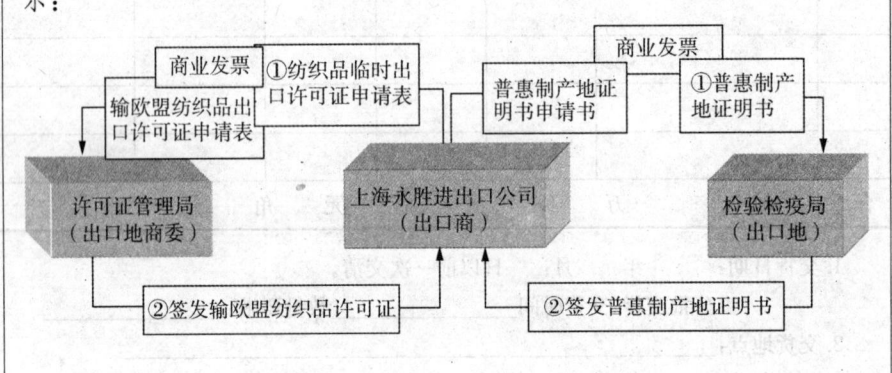

◎ 工作任务一　　申请签发输欧盟纺织品许可证

　　上海永胜进出口公司出口纺织品到英国,需要办理输欧盟纺织品许可证(EEC 证书),于是方达先生到上海市外经贸委所属许可证管理事务局办理相关手续,按照相关规定缮制输欧盟纺织品出口许可证(产地证)申请表及中华人民共和国纺织品临时出口许可证申请表并随附发票等单据。

　　方达先生缮制商业发票:

上海永胜进出口公司
SHANGHAI YONGSHENG IMP. & EXP. CO.
21 WEST ZHONGSHAN ROAD SHANGHAI, CHINA

COMMERCIAL INVOICE

TEL: 021-64500002
FAX: 021-64500003

INV. NO.: TX370
DATE: MAY 02, 2012
S/C NO.: TXT201210

TO:
MANDARS IMPORTS CO. LTD.
38 QUEENSWAY, 2008 UK

L/C NO.: XT370

FROM SHANGHAI PORT TO LONDON PORT

MARKS & NO.	DESCRIPTIONS OF GOODS	QUANTITY	U/ PRICE	AMOUNT
MANDARS TXT200710 LONDON C/NO. 1—1000	LADIES DENIM SKIRT PACKING: FLAT PACK WITHOUT FOLDING 6 PIECES ASSORTED SIZES PER POLYBAG, 3 POLYBAGS IN A MASTER POLYBAG AND THEN INTO AN EXPORT CARTON	18 000 PCS	CIF LONDON USD 7.00	USD 26 000.00

TOTAL AMOUNT: SAY US DOLLARS ONE HUNDRED AND TWENTY SIX THOUSAND ONLY.

WE HEREBY CERTIFY THAT THE CONTENTS OF INVOICE HEREIN ARE TRUE AND CORRECT.

SHANGHAI YONGSHENG IMP. & EXP. CO.
DA FANG

操作指南 ➡ 商业发票的缮制方法

1. 发票名称(Name of Document)
发票名称应用英文粗体标出"Commercial Invoice"或"Invoice"字样。如果信用证指定"Receipted Invoice"等发票名称时,应照办。

2. 发票编号(No.)
发票编号由出口公司根据本公司的实际情况自行编制,是全套结汇单据的中心编号。

3. 发票日期(Date)
发票日期应晚于合同和信用证的签发日期,在结汇单据中是最早签发的单据。

4. 信用证编号(L/C No.)
信用证项下的发票必须填入信用证号码,其他支付方式可不填。

5. 合同编号(Contract No.)
合同编号应与信用证列明的一致,其他支付方式下也必须填入。

6. 收货人(Messrs)
信用证方式下须按信用证规定的填制,一般是开证申请人。托收方式下,通常是买方。二者填写时,名称地址不应同行放置,应分行表明。

7. 航线(from…to…)
填写货物实际的起运港(地)、目的港(地),如货物需经转运,应把转运港(地)的名称表示出来。例如,From Shanghai to London W/T Rotterdam. From Guangzhou to Piraeus W/T Hongkong by steamer. 如货物运至目的港后再转运内陆城市,可在目的港下打 In transit to…to…或 In transit 字样。

8. 唛头及件号(Marks and Number)
发票唛头应按信用证或合同规定的填制,如未作具体的规定,则填写 N/M。

9. 货物描述(Description of Goods)
货物描述一般包括品名、品质、数量、包装等内容。

10. 单价及价格术语(Unit Price and Trade Terms)
完整的单价应包括计价货币、单位价格、计量单位和贸易术语四部分内容。

11. 总值(Total Amount)
发票总额不能超过信用证金额,对于佣金和折扣应按信用证规定的处理。

12. 声明文句及其他内容(Declaration and Other Contents)
根据信用证的规定或特别需要在发票上注明的内容,如参考号和证明文句等。

13. 出票人签章(Signature)
通常出票人在发票的右下角打上出口公司的名称,并由经办人签名或盖章。

方达先生填制输欧盟纺织品出口许可证(产地证)申请表：

输欧盟纺织品出口许可证(产地证)申请表

申请单位：(盖章) 上海永胜进出口公司		申请单位领导签字：黄伟		
货物运至目的地国家：UK	证书种类(由贸规处填写)：			
出口人(名称和地址)： SHANGHAI YONGSHENG IMP. & EXP. CO. 21 WEST ZHONGSHAN ROAD SHANGHAI	公司代码(13位)：3100729039727			
	类别号：27		类别标志	
	发票号码：TX370		协议年度	2012
收货人(名称和地址)： MANDARS IMPORTS CO. LTD. 38 QUEENSWAY, 2008 UK	装运地、装运期及目的地： FROM SHANGHAI TO LONDON NOT LATER THAN 120530			
	中国港口离岸价值(FOB)：			
唛头、包装件数及商品名称 　　　LADIES DENIM SKIRT MANDARS TXT200710 LONDON C/NO. 1－1000 　　　TOTAL 10 000 CARTONS	数量 18 000 PCS	单价 CIF LONDON USD 7.00		总值 USD 126 000.00
生产制造商代码：CNSHANGHAI3N				
加注内容：	货物净重(货至欧共体必须填写)： 100KGS			
	发出证书号码：			

注：以上各栏内容应以英文打字机填制

校对签字：方达

操作指南 ▶ 填制输欧盟纺织品出口许可证申请表的方法

输欧盟纺织品出口许可证(产地证)申请表要使用英文填写,一式两份。

1. 货物运至目的地国家

货物运至目的地国家应填写合同中买方所在国家的名称。

2. 证书种类

证书种类由贸规处填写,出口方不需要填写。

3. 出口人(名称和地址)

出口商业务名称、地址、国家按信用证规定的受益人名称、地址填制。

4. 收货人(名称和地址)

进口商名称、地址、国家按信用证规定的开证申请人名称、地址填写。

5. 公司代码(13位)

填写进出口企业13位代码。

6. 类别号

根据欧盟纺织品分类规则填写。

7. 发票号码

发票号码填写商业发票的号码。

8. 协议年度

填写此批货物申请使用配额的年度。

9. 装运地、装运期及目的地

装运地、装运期及目的地按照合同及信用证的规定照实填写。

10. 中国港口离岸价值(FOB)

填写FOB价格,其他贸易术语要换算成FOB价格。

11. 唛头、包装件数及商品名称

按照合同的规定填写,要求完全准确。

12. 数量、单价、总值

按照合同的成交数量、单价和总值填写。

13. 生产制造商代码

填写纺织品生产企业代码。

14. 加注内容

如有需特殊说明的内容可填写在此,如没有,可以不填写。

15. 发出证书号码

此项由发证机关即许可证管理局填写。

方达先生填制纺织品临时出口许可证申请表：

中华人民共和国纺织品临时出口许可证申请表

1. 出口商名称　　代码 3100729039727 上海永胜进出口公司 领证人姓名 　　方达　　　电话 021-64500002	3. 临时出口许可证号 输欧盟或输美许可证号 类别号 27
2. 发货人　　代码 3100729039727 上海永胜进出口公司	4. 临时出口许可证有效截止日期 　　　　　　　年　　月　　日
5. 贸易方式 一般贸易	8. 出口最终目的国（地区） 英国
6. 合同号 TXT200710	9. 付款方式 信用证
7. 报关口岸 上海	10. 运输方式 海运
11. 商品名称 全棉弹力女裙	商品编码 63025900

12. 规格、等级	13. 单位	14. 数量	15. 单价(币别)	16. 总值(币别)	17. 总值折美元
MA212129	件	18 000	USD 7.00	USD 126 000.00	USD 126 000.00
18. 总计	件	18 000		USD 126 000.00	USD 126 000.00

19. 出口商盖章 （上海永胜进出口公司 YONGSHENG IMP. & EXP. CO. SHANGHAI 印章）	20. 发证机构审核 　　　　　　年　　月　　日

中华人民共和国商务部监制

操作指南 ▶ **填制纺织品临时出口许可证申请表的方法**

1. 出口商名称、代码、领证人
填写出口商名称、进出口企业代码(13位)和实际领取许可证的人的姓名。
2. 发货人、代码
填写出口商或货运代理人名称以及进出口企业代码。
3. 临时出口许可证号、输欧盟或输美许可证号、类别号
前两项由发证方填写,类别号根据欧盟纺织品分类规则由出口商填入。
4. 临时出口许可证有效截止日期
临时出口许可证有效期一般为6个月。
5. 贸易方式
按实际贸易方式填写。
6. 出口最终目的国(地区)
按照合同及信用证规定的目的地照实填写。
7. 合同号
填写此批货物的合同号码。
8. 付款方式
填写合同规定的付款方式。
9. 报关口岸
填写货物实际离开我国关境口岸的名称。
10. 运输方式
填写合同规定的运输方式。
11. 商品名称及商品编码
填写合同规定的商品名称和《海关税则》中的10位数的商品编码。
12. 规格、等级、单位、数量、单价、总值、总值折美元
按照合同的成交商品的规格、等级、数量、单价和总值来填写。如不是按照美元计价,将价格按照外汇牌价折合成美元填入总值折美元一项。

许可证管理事务局签发输欧盟纺织品出口许可证:

输欧盟纺织品出口许可证(EEC)

1. Exporter (EID, name, full address, country) SHANGHAI YONGSHENG IMP. & EXP. CO. 21WEST ZHONGSHAN ROAD SHANGHAI	Copy	2. no CN pl
	3. Quota year 2012	4. Category number 27
5. Consignee (name, full address, country) MANDARS IMPORTS CO. LTD. 38 QUEENSWAY, 2008 UK	EXPORT LICENCE (Textile products) LICENCE D'EXPORTATION (Products textiles)	
	6. Country of origin CHINA	7. Country of destination UK
8. Place and date of shipment-Means of transport FROM SHANGHAI TO LONDON UK BY SEA LATEST DATE OF SHIPMENT 120530	9. Supplementary details CAT 2050	
10. Marks and numbers-Number and kind of packages- DESCRIPTION OF GOODS MANDARS TXT200710 LONDON C/NO. 1-1000 LADIES DENIM SKIRT M. I. D NAME: NANTONG FUSHI FACTORY ADDR: No. 11 RENMING ROAD NANTONG CHINA CITY: NANTONG CODE: NANTONG 11NT	11. Quantity 18 000 PCS	12. FOB Value USD 111 568.40
13. CERTIFICATION BY THE COMPETENT AUTHORITY-VISA DE L'AUTORITéTENTE I, the undersigned, certify that the goods described above have been charged against the quantitative limit established for the year shown in box No. 3 in respect of the category shown in box No. 4 by the provisions regulating trade textile products with the European community.		
14. competent authority (name, full address, country) SHANGHAI FOREIGN ECONOMIC RELATIONS & TRADE COMMISSION	At-A SHANGHAI on-le MAY 02,2012 方达 (Signature) (Stamp-Cachet)	

◇ 工作任务二　　申请签发普惠制原产地证书

上海永胜进出口公司申请签发普惠制原产地证书，首先要在当地出入境检验检疫局办理注册登记手续，获取普惠制原产地证明书注册登记证后，才可申请签发普惠制原产地证书。为此，方达先生根据有关规定办理注册登记，然后填写普惠制原产地证书申请书、普惠制原产地证书并随附商业发票等单据向出入境检验检疫局申请签发普惠制原产地证书。

操作指南　➡　普惠制原产地证书注册登记程序

1. 申请单位领取注册登记表

申请单位向当地出入境检验检疫机构领取"企业申请签发普惠制原产地证明书(FORM A)注册登记表"。

2. 申请单位提交材料

申请单位将填制的"企业申请签发普惠制原产地证明书(FORM A)注册登记表"呈交出入境检验检疫机构，并随附政府主管部门授予企业进出口经营权的文件、企业营业执照与组织机构代码副本、产地证手签人员授权书，如含有进口成分的商品，还需提交产品成本明细单等。

3. 出入境检验检疫机构核查

出入境检验检疫机构对申请单位提交的表格和资料进行严格审查，并派员深入调查。

4. 缴费领证

经审查合格的准予注册，给予注册编号，缴纳注册费，颁发普惠制原产地证明书注册登记证。

方达先生填制普惠制产地证书申请书：

普惠制产地证明书申请书

申请单位（加盖公章）： 　　　　　　　　　证书号：_____

申请人郑重申明： 　　　　　　　　　　　　 注册号：88559966

本人被正式授权代表本企业办理和签署本申请书。

本申请书及普惠制产地证明书格式 A 所列内容正确无误，如发现弄虚作假，冒充格式 A 所列货物，擅改证书，自愿接受签发机构的处罚并承担法律责任。现将有关情况申报如下：

生产单位	南通服装公司	生产单位联系人电话	0513-8836420
商品名称（中英文）	全棉弹力牛仔女裙 LADIES DENIM SKIRT	H.S.税目号（以六位数码计）	6302.59
商品 FOB 总值（以美元计）	111 568.40 美元	发票号	TX370
最终销售国	英国	证书种类"√"	加急证书　　普通证书√

货物拟出运日期　2012.05.30

贸易方式和企业性质（请在适用处划"√"）

正常贸易 C	来/进料加工 L	补偿贸易 B	中外合资 H	中外合作 Z	外商独资 D	零售 Y	展卖 M
√							

包装数量或毛重或其他数量　1 000 箱

原产地标准：
本项商品系在中国生产，完全符合该给惠国给惠方案规定，其原产地情况符合以下第(1)条：
　(1)"P"（完全国产，未使用任何进口原材料）；
　(2)"W"其 H.S. 税目号为_____（含进口成分）；
　(3)"F"（对加拿大出口产品，其进口成分不超过产品出厂价值的 40%）。

本批产品系：1. 直接运输从　上海　到　伦敦　；
　　　　　　2. 转口运输从_____中转国（地区）_____到_____。

申请人说明　　　　　　　　　　　领证人（签名）
　　　　　　　　　　　　　　　　电话
　　　　　　　　　　　　　　　　日期

现提交中国出口商业发票副本一份，普惠制产地证明书格式 A（FORM A）一正二副，以及其他附件一份，请予审核签证。

注：凡有进口成分的商品，必须要求提交"含进口成分受惠商品成本明细单"。

商检局联系记录

操作指南 ➡ 普惠制产地证书申请书的缮制方法

1. 申请单位(盖章)
填写申请单位全称并盖章。
2. 注册号
填写申请单位在出入境检验检疫局的注册编号,各公司注册号由当地出入境检验检疫局提供。
3. 生产单位
填写该批出口商品的生产企业单位的名称。
4. 生产单位联系人电话
填写该批出口商品的生产企业单位的电话号码。
5. 商品名称
填写中英文商品名称,并与 H.S.税目号一致。
6. H.S.税目号
填写海关《商品编码协调制度》商品8位数字的前6位。
7. 商品总值
填写以美元计的FOB价值,如是以其他贸易术语成交的,则应扣除以外汇支付的费用,如佣金、海运费、保险费等。
8. 发票号
填写对应货物的发票号码。
9. 最终销售国
填写出口商品的最终销售国家。
10. 证书种类划"√"
出入境检验检疫局可提供加急证书和普通证书,加急证书一般1天即可取得,普通证书则需3～5天,申请人可根据需要选择,并划"√"。
11. 货物拟出运日期
填写出口商品出运的日期。
12. 贸易方式和企业性质
在对应的位置划"√"。
13. 原产地标准
在(1)、(2)、(3)条中选择一条,填于空格处。符合"W"的,加列H.S.的四位税目号。
14. 本批产品的运输情况
如直接运输,填起运地(港)到目的地(港);如为转运,需增填中转国家(地区)。
15. 申请人说明
如需另作说明时,在此详述。
16. 签章
由领证人手签,加盖申请单位公章,并写明申请人的名称、电话及申请日期。

方达先生填制普惠制产地证书：

普惠制产地证书

1. Goods consigned from (Exporter's business name, address, country) SHANGHAI YONGSHENG IMP. & EXP. CO. 21WEST ZHONGSHAN ROAD SHANGHAI, CHINA	Reference No.： GENERALIZED SYSTEM OF PREFERENCES CERTIFICATE OF ORIGIN (COMBINED DECLARATION AND CERTIFICATE) FORM A ISSUED IN THE PEOPLE'S REPUBLIC OF CHINA (COUNTRY) SEE NOTES OVERLEAF
2. Goods consigned to (Consignee's name, address, country) MANDARS IMPORTS CO. LTD. 38 QUEENSWAY, 2008 UK	
3. Means of transport and route (as far as known) FROM SHANGHAI TO LONDON BY S. S	4. For official use

5. Item number	6. Marks and numbers of packages	7. Number and kind of packages; description of goods	8. Origin criterion (see notes overleaf)	9. Gross weight or other quantity G. W. 140KGS	10. Number and date of invoices
1	MANDARS TXT200710 LONDON C/NO. 1—1000	LADIES DENIM SKIRT SAY TOTAL ONE THOUSAND(1 000) CARTONS ONLY ********************	"P"		TX370 MAY 10, 2012

11. Certification is hereby certified, on the basis of control carried out, that the declaration by the exporter is correct Place and date, signature and stamp of certifying authority	12. Declaration by the exporter The undersigned hereby declares that the above details and statements are correct; that all the goods were produced in ———— CHINA ———— (country) and that they comply with the origin requirements specified for those goods in the Generalized System of Preference for goods exported to UK (importing country) SHANHGHAI MAY 10, 2012 Place and date, signature of authorized signatory

操作指南 ➡ 普惠制产地证书的填写方法

1. Goods consigned from (Exporter's business name、address、country)/发货人(出口商业务名称、地址、国家)

按信用证规定的受益人名称、地址、国别填制,如信用证未规定详细地址,可填入实际地址。

2. Goods Consigned to (Consignee's name、address、country)/收货人(出口商业务名称、地址、国家)

填给惠国的最终收货人的名称、地址和国别。信用证下一般为开证申请人,如其不是实际收货人,又不知最终收货人,可填提单被通知人或发票抬头人。

3. Means of transport and route (as far as known)/运输方式和路线(就所知而言)

按信用证规定填运输路线和运输方式,例如 By steamer（海运）、By air（空运）。如中途转运应注明转运地,例如 Via Hongkong；不知转运地则用 W/T 表示。

4. For official use/供官方使用

本栏留空,供签证机构加注说明用。

5. Item number/项目号

将同批出口不同种类的商品用阿拉伯数字进行顺序编号填入此栏,单项商品用"1"表示或不填。

6. Marks and numbers of packages/唛头及包装件数

唛头按信用证的规定填制,并与发票和提单内容相同。

7. Number & kind of packages; description of goods/包装件数、方式和品名

填出口货物最大包装件数和商品名称,如信用证规定单据要加注信用证编号或合同号码等内容,可在此显示。例如,信用证规定：All shipping documents must show the S/C No. T20031. 此栏应注明 S/C No. T20031 的合同号。

8. Origin criterion/原产地标准

根据货物原料进口成分的比例填制。"P"表示无进口成分；"W"表示含进口成分,但符合原产地标准；"F"是指出口加拿大货物中的进口成分要在40％以下。

9. Gross weight or other quantity/毛重或其他数量

按发票和提单内容填。以重量表示的商品,此栏填写毛重数量,或再加注件数。散装货填净重数量,但注明"N. W"。

10. Number and date of invoice/发票号码及日期

按发票实际内容填制。此栏填写完毕,从第5项开始用"＊"符号打成横线示意结束。

11. Certification/签证当局证明

签证当局证明已印制,此栏由签证当局盖章,由其授权人手签。出证日期和地点由申报单位填写。签证机构(出入境检验检疫局)只签发正本。

12. Declaration by the exporter/出口商申明

本栏有三个内容：A. 生产国别："China"已事先印妥；B. 出口国别：填给惠国的国名(即进口国)；C. 出口商申请日期、地点及签章。

申请单位盖章,由授权人手签并注明日期和地点,申报日期不得早于发票日期。

出入境检验检疫局签发普惠制产地证书：

1. Goods consigned from (Exporter's business name, address, country) SHANGHAI YONGSHENG IMP. & EXP. CO. 21 WEST ZHONGSHAN ROAD SHANGHAI, CHINA	Reference No. 20070590 GENERALIZED SYSTEM OF PREFERENCES CERTIFICATE OF ORIGIN (COMBINED DECLARATION AND CERTIFICATE) FORM A
2. Goods consigned to (Consignee's name, address, country) MANDARS IMPORTS CO. LTD. 38 QUEENSWAY, 2008 UK	ISSUED IN THE PEOPLE'S REPUBLIC OF CHINA (COUNTRY) SEE NOTES OVERLEAF
3. Means of transport and route (as far as known) FROM SHANGHAI TO LONDON BY S.S	4. For official use

5. Item number	6. Marks and numbers of packages	7. Number and kind of packages; description of goods	8. Origin criterion (see notes overleaf)	9. Gross weight or other quantity	10. Number and date of invoices
1	MANDARS TXT200710 LONDON C/NO. 1—1000	LADIES DENIM SKIRT SAY TOTAL ONE THOUSAND(1 000) CARTONS ONLY ********************	"P"	G.W 140KGS	TX370 MAY 02, 2012

11. Certification is hereby certified, on the basis of control carried out, that the declaration by the exporter is correct SHANGHAI MAY 22, 2012 Place and date, signature and stamp of certifying authority	12. Declaration by the exporter The undersigned hereby declares that the above details and statements are correct; that all the goods were produced in _____CHINA_____ (country) and that they comply with the origin requirements specified for those goods in the Generalized System of Preference for goods exported to _____(importing country)_____ SHANGHAI MAY 10, 2012 Place and date, signature of authorized signatory

综合业务模拟操作

操作一

1. 操作资料

卖　方：　南京永发进出口公司
　　　　　南京中山路1321号
　　　　　TEL:025-23501111　FAX:025-23502222
买　方：　JIM KING TRADING CORPORATION
　　　　　NO.206 CHANGJ NORTH STREET SINGAPORE
　　　　　TEL:218-76911　FAX:218-76912
货　名：　电动钻头(Electric Drill) No. TY242
数　量：　1 800套
包　装：　每10套装一个纸箱
价　格：　CIF SINGAPORE No. TY242 每套 USD 4.20
支付方式：不可撤销跟单远期信用证(30 DAYS AFTER SIGHT)
信用证号：NB4567
装运港：　连云港
目的港：　新加坡
合同号：　wy070901
日　期：　2012年9月20日
唛　头：　由卖方指定
发票号码：SG123
日　期：　2012年10月1号
生产单位：南京上野五金工具公司
地　址：　南京市金陵路19号
联系电话：025-56789877
商品编码：8204.1100
货物毛重：450千克　净重350千克　体积26.7立方米

2. 操作要求

(1)请你以南京永发进出口公司业务员张丽的身份,根据上述资料缮制商业发票,要求格式完整,内容正确。

体验活动二　自理出口贸易业务

南京永发进出口公司
NANJING YONGFA IMP. & EXP. CO.
21 ZHONGSHAN ROAD NANJING, CHINA

COMMERCIAL INVOICE

TEL：_____　　　　　　　　　　　INV. NO. :_____
FAX：_____　　　　　　　　　　　DATE:_____
　　　　　　　　　　　　　　　　　　　S/C NO. :_____
TO:　　　　　　　　　　　　　　　　　L/C NO. :_____

FROM _____　　　TO _____

MARKS & NO.	DESCRIPTIONS OF GOODS	QUANTITY	U/ PRICE	AMOUNT

TOTAL AMOUNT：

WE HEREBY CERTIFY THAT THE CONTENTS OF INVOICE HEREIN ARE TRUE AND CORRECT.

　　　　　　　　　　　　　　　　　　　　　　　_____

　(2)请你以南京永发进出口公司业务员张丽的身份根据上述资料填写普惠制产地证明申请书和普惠制产地证书。

普惠制产地证明书申请书

申请单位(加盖公章)：　　　　　　　　　　　　　　证书号：
申请人郑重申明：　　　　　　　　　　　　　　　　　注册号：
本人被正式授权代表本企业办理和签署本申请书。
本申请书及普惠制产地证明书格式A所列内容正确无误，如发现弄虚作假，冒充格式A所列货物，擅改证书，自愿接受签发机构的处罚并承担法律责任。现将有关情况申报如下：

生产单位				生产单位联系人电话			
商品名称 (中英文)				H.S.税目号 (以六位数码计)			
商品FOB总值(以美元计)				发票号			
最终销售国			证书种类"√"		加急证书		普通证书
货物拟出运日期							
贸易方式和企业性质(请在适用处划"√")							
正常贸易 C	来进料加工 L	补偿贸易 B	中外合资 H	中外合作 Z	外商独资 D	零售 Y	展卖 M
包装数量或毛重或其他数量							

原产地标准：
本项商品系在中国生产，完全符合该给惠国给惠方案规定，其原产地情况符合以下第　　　条；
　　(1)"P"(完全国产，未使用任何进口原材料)；
　　(2)"W"其H.S.税目号　　　　　　(含进口成分)；
　　(3)"F"(对加拿大出口产品，其进口成分不超过产品出厂价值的40%)。
本批产品系：1.直接运输从　　　　　到　　　　　；
　　　　　　2.转口运输从　　　　　中转国(地区)　　　　到　　　　。

申请人说明	领证人(签名)
	电话：
	日期：

　　现提交中国出口商业发票副本一份，普惠制产地证明书格式A(FORM A)一正二副，以及其他附件一份，请予审核签证。
　　注：凡有进口成分的商品，必须要求提交"含进口成分受惠商品成本明细单"。

商检局联系记录

1. Goods consigned from (Exporter's business name, address, country)	Reference No. GENERALIZED SYSTEM OF PREFERENCES CERTIFICATE OF ORIGIN (COMBINED DECLARATION AND CERTIFICATE) FORM A
2. Goods consigned to (Consignee's name, address, country)	ISSUED IN THE PEOPLE'S REPUBLIC OF CHINA (COUNTRY) SEE NOTES OVERLEAF
3. Means of transport and route (as far as known)	4. For official use

5. Item number	6. Marks and numbers of packages	7. Number and kind of packages; description of goods	8. Origin criterion (see notes overleaf)	9. Gross weight or other quantity	10. Number and date of invoices

11. Certification is hereby certified, on the basis of control carried out, that the declaration by the exporter is correct ··· Place and date, signature and stamp of certifying authority	12. Declaration by the exporter The undersigned hereby declares that the above details and statements are correct; that all the goods were produced in _____CHINA_____ (country) and that they comply with the origin requirements specified for those goods in the Generalized System of Preference for goods exported to _____ (importing country) ··· Place and date, signature of authorized signatory

操作二

1. 操作资料

卖　方：广州纺织品进出口公司
　　　　广州市北京路530号
　　　　TEL：(020)64043030　FAX：(020)64043031

买　方：OLEARA IMPORT & EXPORT CORPORATION
　　　　310-224 HOLA STREET MARSEILLE FRANCE

货　名：男式衬衫　Art No.88(蓝色)、Art No.44(黑色)

数　量：Art No.88(蓝色)3 000件、Art No.44(黑色)3 000件

包　装：每20件装一只纸箱，每箱毛重为20.2千克、净重为20千克、体积为0.2M³，装入一只20英尺集装箱(集装箱号：TEXU22636643)

价　格：Art No.88每件6.50美元、Art No.44每件7.00美元，CIF MARSEILLE

支付方式：不可撤销跟单即期信用证

信用证号：07/CB4578

装运港：广州

目的港：MARSELLE

合同号：ST121032

日　期：2012年6月1日

唛　头：由卖方指定

发票号码：GZT00021

日　期：2012年7月1号

生产单位：广州宏光服装公司

地　址：广州市风林路19号

联系电话：021-56788888

商品编码：6303.4500

货物毛重：6 060千克　净重6 000千克　体积60立方米

EID代码：5100729039123

MID代码：CNGUANGZHOU3

2. 操作要求

(1)请你以广州纺织品进出口贸易公司业务员王伟的身份，根据上述资料缮制商业发票，要求格式完整，内容正确。

广州纺织品进出口贸易公司
GUANGZHOU TEXTILE IMPORT & EXPORT TRADE CORPORATION
530 BEIJING ROAD GUANGZHOU, CHINA

COMMERCIAL INVOICE

TEL:_____   INV. NO.:_____

FAX:_____   DATE:_____

                                   S/C NO.:_____

TO: L/C NO.:_____

FROM _____   TO _____

MARKS & NO.	DESCRIPTIONS OF GOODS	QUANTITY	U/ PRICE	AMOUNT

TOTAL AMOUNT:

WE HEREBY CERTIFY THAT THE CONTENTS OF INVOICE HEREIN ARE TRUE AND CORRECT.

_____

(2) 请你以广州纺织品进出口贸易公司业务员王伟的身份，根据上述资料填写输欧盟纺织品出口许可证申请表和纺织品临时出口许可证申请表。

输欧盟纺织品出口许可证(产地证)申请表

申请单位:(盖章)　　　　　　　　　　　　　　　申请单位领导签字:

货物运至目的地国家:UK	证书种类(由贸规处填写):		
出口人(名称和地址):	公司代码(13位):		
	类别号:	类别标志	
	发票号码:	协议年度	
收货人(名称和地址):	装运地、装运期及目的地:		
	中国港口离岸价值(FOB):		
唛头、包装件数及商品名称	数量	单价	总值
生产制造商代码:			
加注内容:	货物净重(货至欧共体必须填写):		
	发出证书号码:		

注:以上各栏内容应以英文打字机填制

校对签字:

中华人民共和国纺织品临时出口许可证申请表

1. 出口商名称　　代码　　　　　　　　　　　　　　领证人姓名　　　　　　　　电话	3. 临时出口许可证号　　输欧盟或输美许可证号　　类别号
2. 发货人　　代码	4. 临时出口许可证有效截止日期　　　　　　　　　　　　　年　　月　　日
5. 贸易方式	8. 出口最终目的国（地区）
6. 合同号	9. 付款方式
7. 报关口岸	10. 运输方式
11. 商品名称	商品编码

12. 规格、等级	13. 单位	14. 数量	15. 单价（币别）	16. 总值（币别）	17. 总值折美元

18. 总计	
19. 出口商盖章	20. 发证机构审核　　　　　　　　　　　　　年　　月　　日

中华人民共和国商务部监制

（3）请你以广州纺织品进出口贸易公司业务员王伟的身份，根据上述资料填写普惠制产地证明申请书和普惠制产地证书。

普惠制产地证明书申请书

申请单位(加盖公章)： 证书号：

申请人郑重申明： 注册号：

本人被正式授权代表本企业办理和签署本申请书。

本申请书及普惠制产地证明书格式 A 所列内容正确无误,如发现弄虚作假,冒充格式 A 所列货物,擅改证书,自愿接受签发机构的处罚并承担法律责任。现将有关情况申报如下：

生产单位		生产单位联系人电话	
商品名称 (中英文)		H.S.税目号 (以六位数码计)	
商品 FOB 总值(以美元计)		发票号	
最终销售国		证书种类"√"	加急证书	普通证书
货物拟出运日期				

贸易方式和企业性质(请在适用处划"√")

正常贸易 C	来/进料加工 L	补偿贸易 B	中外合资 H	中外合作 Z	外商独资 D	零售 Y	展卖 M

包装数量或毛重或其他数量

原产地标准：

本项商品系在中国生产,完全符合该给惠国给惠方案规定,其原产地情况符合以下第　　条;

　　(1) "P"(完全国产,未使用任何进口原材料);

　　(2) "W"其 H.S.税目号为　　　　　(含进口成分);

　　(3) "F"(对加拿大出口产品,其进口成分不超过产品出厂价值的 40%)。

本批产品系:1. 直接运输从　　　　　到　　　　。

　　　　　　2. 转口运输从　　　　　中转国(地区)　　　　到　　　　。

申请人说明	领证人(签名)
	电话
	日期

　　现提交中国出口商业发票副本一份,普惠制产地证明书格式 A (FORM A)一正二副,以及其他附件一份,请予审核签证。

　　注:凡有进口成分的商品,必须要求提交"含进口成分受惠商品成本明细单"。

商检局联系记录

1. Goods consigned from (Exporter's business name, address, country)	Reference No. GENERALIZED SYSTEM OF PREFERENCES CERTIFICATE OF ORIGIN (COMBINED DECLARATION AND CERTIFICATE) FORM A ISSUED IN THE PEOPLE'S REPUBLIC OF CHINA (COUNTRY) SEE NOTES OVERLEAF			
2. Goods consigned to (Consignee's name, address, country)					
3. Means of transport and route (as far as known)	4. For official use			
5. Item number	6. Marks and numbers of packages	7. Number and kind of packages; description of goods	8. Origin criterion (see notes overleaf)	9. Gross weight or other quantity	10. Number and date of invoices
11. Certification is hereby certified, on the basis of control carried out, that the declaration by the exporter is correct .... Place and date, signature and stamp of certifying authority	12. Declaration by the exporter The undersigned hereby declares that the above details and statements are correct; that all the goods were produced in _____CHINA_____ (country) and that they comply with the origin requirements specified for those goods in the Generalized System of Preference for goods exported to _____ (importing country) .... Place and date, signature of authorized signatory			

实训五　出口合同的履行——订舱、报检、报关、投保

> **业务导入**

　　上海永胜进出口公司在备货的同时，为了按时履行合同的交货义务，应及时填写订舱委托书、报检委托书、报关委托书，并随附相关单据委托货运代理公司办理订舱、报检和报关手续，也可由公司自行办理。由于上海永胜进出口公司与 MANDARS IMPORTS CO. LTD. 以 CIF 价格条款成交，所以上海永胜进出口公司还需填制投保单，办理出口货物运输保险手续。货物出运后，要用传真发出装运通知，及时告知货运情况。

　　订舱、报检、报关、投保业务流程如下图所示：

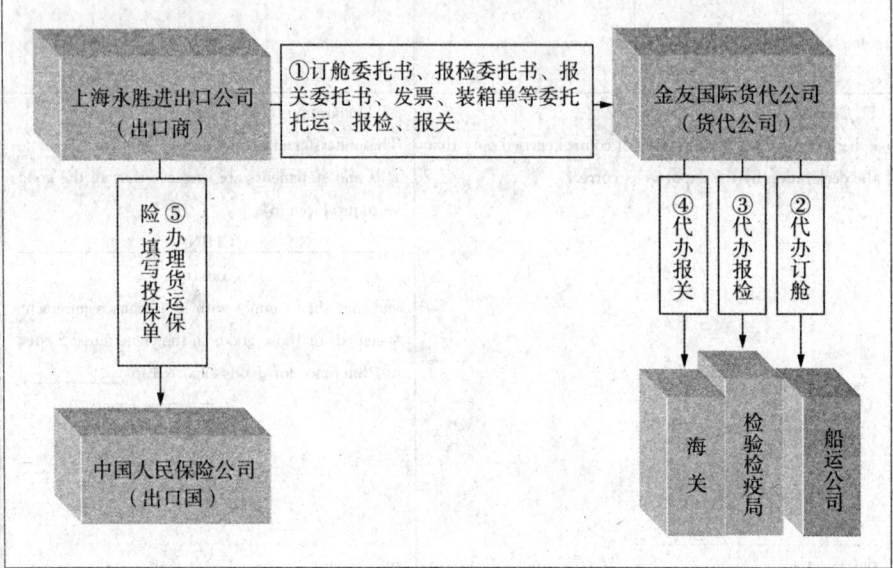

```
┌──────────────┐   ①订舱委托书、报检委托书、报   ┌──────────────┐
│ 上海永胜进出口公司 │   关委托书、发票、装箱单等委托   │ 金友国际货代公司 │
│   （出口商）    │ ─────托运、报检、报关─────→ │   （货代公司）   │
└──────┬───────┘                              └──┬───┬───┬──┘
       │⑤办理货运保险，填写投保单                    ④代办报关 ③代办报检 ②代办订舱
       ↓                                         ↓     ↓     ↓
┌──────────────┐                              ┌────┐┌──────┐┌──────┐
│ 中国人民保险公司 │                              │海关││检验检疫局││船运公司│
│   （出口国）    │                              └────┘└──────┘└──────┘
└──────────────┘
```

> ◎ **工作任务一　　办理委托订舱手续**
>
> 　　上海永胜进出口公司获取出口货物许可证后，及时向金友国际货运代理公司办理出口货物托运订舱手续，为此，方达先生缮制装箱单，填写货运委托书。金友国际货运代理公司填制集装箱货物托运单向船公司中国对外贸易运输总公司订舱，当获取船公司签发的配舱回单后，通知托运人在规定的时间内向指定的仓库发货，等候检验检疫和海关查验。

方达先生缮制装箱单：

上海永胜进出口公司
SHANGHAI YONGSHENG IMP. & EXP. CO.
21 WEST ZHONGSHAN ROAD SHANGHAI, CHINA
PACKING LIST

TEL:021-65788877	INV. NO.:TX370
FAX:021-65788876	DATE:MAY 20,2012
	S/C NO.:TXT201210
	MARKS & NOS.
TO:MANDARS IMPORTS CO. LTD.	MANDARS
38 QUEENSWAY,2008 UK	TXT201210
	LONDON
	C/NO. 1—1000

GOODS DESCRIPTION & PACKING	QTY (PCS)	CTNS	G. W (KGS)	N. W (KGS)	MEAS (M³)
LADIES DENIM SKIRT PACKING:FLAT PACK WITHOUT FOLDING 6 PIECES ASSORTED SIZES PER POLYBAG, 3 POLYBAGS IN A MASTER POLYBAG AND THEN INTO AN EXPORT CARTON	18 000	1 000	140	100	23.8
TOTAL	18 000	1 000	140	100	23.8

SAY TOTAL ONE THOUSAND CARTONS ONLY.

操作指南 ➡ 装箱单的缮制方法

1. 出口企业名称和地址（Exporter's Name and Address）
   出口企业的名称、地址应与发票同项内容一致，缮制方法相同。

2. 单据名称（Name of Document）
   单据名称通常用英文粗体标出，并与信用证的要求一致。

3. 装箱单编号（No.）
   装箱单编号一般填发票号码，也可填合同号。

4. 出单日期（Date）
   出单日期填发票签发日，不得早于发票日期，但可晚于发票日期1至2天。

5. 唛头（Shipping Mark）
   唛头制作要符合信用证的规定，并与发票的唛头相一致。

6. 品名和规格（Name of Commodity and Specifications）
   品名和规格必须与信用证的描述相符。

7. 数量（Quantity）
   数量填写实际件数，如品质规格不同应分别列出，并累计其总数。

8. 单位（Unit）
   单位填写外包装的包装单位，如箱、包、桶等。

9. 毛重（Gross Weight）
   毛重填写外包装每件重量，规格不同要分别列出，并累计其总量。

10. 净重（Net Weight）
    净重填写每件货物的实际重量并计其总量。

11. 尺码（Measurement）
    尺码填写每件包装的体积，并标明总尺码。

12. 签章（Signature）
    出单人签章应与商业发票相符，如果信用证无此项规定，此栏可不填。

方达先生填制货运委托书：

金友海运货运委托书

经营单位（托运人）	上海永胜进出口公司		金友编号	JY037001	
提单B/L项目要求	发货人：上海永胜进出口公司 Shipper： 收货人：TO ORDER OF SHIPPER Consignee： 通知人：MANDARS IMPORTS CO. LTD. Notify Party：38 QUEENSWAY, 2008 UK					
海洋运费(√) Sea freight	预付(√) 或 到付( ) Prepaid or Collect	提单份数	3	提单寄送地址	上海市中山西路21号
起运港	SHANGHAI	目的港	LONDON	可否转船	允许	可否分批	允许
集装箱预配数	20'×1 40'×		装运期限	2012.5.30	有效期限	2012.5.30
标记唛码	包装件数	中英文货号 Description of goods	毛重（公斤）	尺码（立方米）	成交条件（总价）
MANDARS TXT200710 LONDON C/NO.1-1000	1 000箱	全棉弹力牛仔女裙 LADIES DENIM SKIRT	140	23.8	USD 126 000
			特种货物 □冷藏货 □危险品	重 件：每件重量 大 件 （长×宽×高）	
内装箱(CFS)地址	上海市逸仙路2960号三号门 电话：021-6820682×215		特种集装箱：( )		
门对门装箱地址	上海市中山西路21号		物资备妥日期	2012年5月20日	
			物资进栈：自送(√) 或金友派送( )		
外币结算账号	THY6684321337		人民币结算单位账号	SZR80066686	
声明事项			托运人签章		
			电 话	64500002	
			传 真	64500003	
			联系人	方达	
			地 址	上海市中山西路21号	
			制单日期： 2012年5月20日		

77

金友货运公司填制集装箱货物托运单：

Shipper (发货人) SHANGHAI YONGSHENG IMP. & EXP. CO. 21 WEST ZHONGSHAN ROAD SHANGHAI		委托号：TX0222 Forwarding agents： B/L No.	
Consignee (收货人) TO ORDER OF SHIPPER		中国对外贸易运输总公司 集装箱货物托运单 船代留底	第二联
Notify Party (通知人) MANDARS IMPORTS CO. LTD. 38 QUEENSWAY, 2008 UK			
Pre-carriage by (前程运输)	Place of Receipt (收货地点)		
Ocean Vessel (船名)	Voy. No. (航次)	Port of Loading (装货港) SHANGHAI	Date (日期)
Port of Discharge (卸货港) LONDON	Place of Delivery (交货地点) LONDON	Final Destination for the Merchant's Reference (目的地)	

Container No. (集装箱号)	Seal No. (封志号) Marks & Nos. (标记与号码) MANDARS TXT200710 LONDON C/NO. 1-1000	No. of Containers or P'kgs (箱数与件数) 1 000 CARTONS	Kind of Packing; Description of Goods (包装种类与货名) LADIES DENIM SKIRT	Gross Weight (毛重) 140 KGS	Measurement 尺码(m³) 23.8
Total Number of Container or Package (in words) 集装箱数或件数合计(大写)			SAY TOTAL ONE THOUSAND CARTONS ONLY		
Container No. (箱号)	Seal No. (封志号)	P'kgs(件号) 1 000 CARTONS	Container No. (箱号)	Seal No. (封志号)	P'kgs(件号)
Received (实收)					By Terminal Clerk/Tally Clerk (场站员/理货员签字)

Freight & Charges	Prepaid at (预付地点)	Payable at (到付地点)	Place of Issue (签发地点)	Booking Approved by (订舱确认)
	Total Prepaid (预付总额)	No. of Original Bs/L (正本提单的份数)	货值金额	

Service Type on Receiving ☑···CY ☐···CFS ☐···DOOR	Service Type on Delivery ☑···CY ☐···CFS ☐···DOOR		Reefer Temperature Required(冷藏温度)	°F	℃
Type of Goods (种类)	☑Ordinary ☐Reefer (普通) (冷藏) ☐Liquid ☐Live Animal (液体) (活动物)	☐Dangerous ☐Auto (危险) (裸装车辆) ☐Bulk (散装)	危险品	Class: Property IMDG code Page UN No.	
发货人或代理地址：21WEST ZHONGSHAN ROAD SHANGHAI		联系人：方达	电话：64500002	
可否转船 Y	可否分批 Y	装期 MAY 30, 2012	备注	集装箱场站名称	
有效期：MAY 30, 2012		制单日期 MAY 21, 2012			
海运费由 上海永胜进出口公司 支付 如预付运费托收承付，请填银行账号 THY6684321337					

中国对外贸易运输总公司签发配舱回单：

Shipper (发货人) SHANGHAI YONGSHENG IMP. & EXP. CO. 21 WEST ZHONGSHAN ROAD SHANGHAI	D/R No. (编号) HJSHBI 1520876
Consignee (收货人) TO ORDER OF SHIPPER	中国对外贸易运输总公司 配舱回单(1) 第 八 联
Notify Party (通知人) MANDARS IMPORTS CO. LTD. 38 QUEENSWAY, 2008 UK	

Pre-carriage by (前程运输)	Place of Receipt (收货地点)	
Ocean Vessel (船名) Voy. No. (航次) DONGFANG V. 190	Port of Loading (装货港) SHANGHAI	
Port of Discharge (卸货港) LONDON	Place of Delivery (交货地点)	Final Destination for the Merchant's Reference (目的地)

Container No. (集装箱号)	Seal No. (封志号) Marks & Nos. (标记与号码)	No. of containers or p'kgs. (箱数或件数)	Kind of Package; Description of Goods (包装种类与货名)	Gross Weight 毛重(公斤)	Measurement 尺码(立方米)
GANE100067	MANDARS TXT200710 LONDON C/NO. 1–1000	1 000 CARTONS	LADIES DENIM SKIRT	140 KGS	23.8

Total Number of Containers or Packages(in words) 集装箱数或件数合计(大写)	SAY TOTAL ONE THOUSAND CARTONS ONLY

Freight & Charges (运费与附加费)	Revenue Tons (运费吨)	Rate (运费率)	Per (每)	Prepaid (运费预付) PREPAID	Collect (到付)

EX. Rate (兑换率)	Prepaid at (预付地点) SHANGHAI	Payable at (到付地点)	Place of Issue (签发地点)
	Total Prepaid (预付总额) USD1 700.00	No. of Original B(s)/L (正本提单份数) THREE	SHANGHAI

Service Type on Receiving ☑···CY □···CFS □···DOOR	Service Type on Delivery ☑···CY □···CFS □···DOOR	Reefer Temperature Required (冷藏温度) °F °C	
TYPE OF GOODS (种类)	☑ Ordinary (普通) □ Reefer (冷藏) □ Dangerous (危险) □ Auto (裸装车辆) □ Liquid (液体) □ Live Animal (活动物) □ Bulk (散装)	危险品	Class: Property: IMDG Code Page: UN No.

可否转船：Y	可否分批：Y
装 期：MAY 30, 2012	有 效 期：MAY 30, 2012
金 额：USD 1 700.00	
制单日期：MAY 22, 2012	

◇ 工作任务二　　　办理委托报关报检手续

> 上海永胜进出口公司委托上海金友国际货运代理公司代办出口货物的报检报关。为此，方达先生缮制报检委托书和报关委托书，并随附商业发票和装箱单等有关单据。由于该批货物属于法定检验的出境商品，当检验合格后获取出入境检验检疫局签发的出境货物通关单才能向海关报关。

方达先生缮制报检委托书：

报检委托书

上海市____出入境检验检疫局：

本委托人郑重声明，保证遵守出入境检验检疫法律、法规的规定。如有违法行为，自愿接受检验检疫机构的处罚并负法律责任。

本委托人委托受委托人向检验检疫机构提交"报检申请单"和各种随附单据。具体委托情况如下：

本单位将于　2012　年　5　月间出口如下货物：

品　名	全棉牛仔女裙	H.S.编码	6302.5900
数(重)量	18 000 件	合同号	TXT2007111
信用证号	XT370	审批文件	
其他特殊要求			

特委托　上海金友货运代理公司　（单位/注册登记号），代理本公司办理下列出入境检验检疫事宜：

☑1. 办理代理报检手续；
☑2. 代缴检验检疫费；
☑3. 负责与检验检疫机构联系和验货；
☑4. 领取检验检疫证书；
☐5. 其他与报检有关的事宜。

请贵局按有关法律法规规定予以办理。

委托人：上海永胜进出口公司　　　　　受委托人(公章)：上海金友国际货运代理公司

方达　　　　　　　　　　　　　　　　李明

2012 年 5 月 20 日　　　　　　　　　2012 年 5 月 20 日

本委托书有效期至 2012 年 6 月 1 日。

出入境检验检疫局签发出境货物通关单：

中华人民共和国出入境检验检疫
出境货物通关单

编号：070510

1. 收货人　　MANDARS IMPORTS CO. LTD.		5. 标记及唛码 MANDARS TXT201210 LONDON C/NO. 1－1000
2. 发货人　　上海永胜进出口公司		
3. 合同/提(运)单号 TXT200710	4. 输出国家或地区 英国	
6. 运输工具名称及号码 DONGFANG V. 190	7. 目的地 伦敦	8. 集装箱规格及数量 20'×1
9. 货物名称及规格 LADIES DENIM SKIRT	10. H. S. 编码 63025900	11. 申报总值 126 000 美元	12. 数/重量、包装数量及种类 140 千克 1 000 箱
13. 证明 　　　　上述货物业已报检/申报，请海关予以放行。 　　　　本通关单有效期至 2012 年 6 月 22 日。 签字：丁鸣　　　　　　　　　　　日期：2012 年 5 月 23 日		
14. 备注		

方达先生填写代理报关委托及委托报关协议：

代理报关委托

编号：2231458800540

上海金友国际货运代理公司：

我单位现 A（A. 逐票、B. 长期）委托贵公司代理 A、B 等通关事宜（A. 填单申报、B. 辅助查验、C. 垫缴税款、D. 办理海关证明联、E. 审批手册、F. 核销手册、G. 申办减免税手续、H. 其他）。详见《委托报关协议》。

我单位保证遵守《中华人民共和国海关法》和国家有关法规，保证所提供的情况真实、完整、单货相符。否则，愿承担相关法律责任。

本委托书有效期自签字之日起至 2012 年 6 月 1 日止。

委托方（盖章）：　[上海永胜进出口公司 印章]

法定代表人或其授权签署《代理报关委托书》的人（签字）
2012 年 5 月 20 日

委托报关协议

为明确委托报关具体事项和各自责任,双方经平等协商签订协议如下:

委托方	上海永胜进出口公司	被委托方	上海金友货运代理公司	
主要货物名称	全棉牛仔女裙	*报关单编码	No.	
H.S.编码	6302.5900	收到单证日期	2012年5月20日	
货物总价	USD 126 000.00	收到单证情况	合同☑	发票☑
进出口日期	2012年5月30日		装箱清单☑	提(运)单☐
提单号			加工贸易手册☐	许可证件☐
贸易方式	一般贸易		其他	
原产地/货源地	上海	报关收费	人民币: 元	
其他要求:		承诺说明:		
背面所列通用条款是本协议不可分割的一部分,对本协议的签署构成了对背面通用条款的同意。		背面所列通用条款是本协议不可分割的一部分,对本协议的签署构成了对背面通用条款的同意。		
委托方业务签章: （上海永胜进出口公司印章）		被委托方业务签章: 上海金友国际货运代理公司		
经办人签章:		经办报关员签章:李明		
联系电话:021-6578888 2012年5月20日		联系电话:021-56987666 2012年5月20日		

(白联:海关留存;黄联:被委托方留存;红联:委托方留存)　　中国报关协会监制

◇ 工作任务三　　办理出口货物保险手续

由于上海永胜进出口公司与 MANDARS IMPORTS CO. LTD. 以 CIF 价格条款成交,所以上海永胜进出口公司需要办理出口货物运输保险手续。为此,方达先生填制投保单,并随附商业发票向中保财产保险有限公司上海市分公司进行投保。保险公司核准投保申请后,收取保险费,签发保险单。

方达先生填写投保单：

中保财产保险有限公司上海市分公司
The People's Insurance (Property) Company of China, Ltd. Shanghai Branch
进出口货物运输保险投保单
Application From form I/E Marine Cargo Insurance

被保险人 Assured's Name	SHANGHAI YONGSHENG IMP. & EXP. CO.		
发票号码(出口用)或合同号码(进口用) Invoice No. or Contract No.	包装数量 Quantity	保险货物项目 Description of Goods	保险金额 Amount Insured
AS PER INVOICE NO. TX370	1 000 CARTONS	LADIES DENIM SKIRT	USD 138 600.00

装载运输工具 __DONGFANG__ 航次、航班或车号 __V. 190__ 开航日期 __MAY 30, 2012__
Per Conveyance　　　　　Voy. No.　　　　　　　　　Slg. Date

自 __SHANGHAI__ 至 __LONDON__ 转运地_____ 赔款地 __LONDON__
From　　　　　　To　　　　　　W/Tat　　　　　　Claim Payable at

承保险别: FOR 110% OF THE INVOICE VALUE COVERING ALL RISKS & WAR RISK AS PER Condition &/or PICC DATE 1/1/1981

Special Coverage

投保人签章及公司名称、电话、地址

Applicant's Signature and Co.'s Name, Add. And Tel. No.
SHANGHAI YONGSHENG IMP. & EXP. CO.
21 WEST ZHONGSHAN ROAD SHANGHAI
021-64500002

备注　　　　　　　　　　投保日期 2012.05.24
Remarks　　　　　　　　Date

保险公司填写:　保单号:　　　费率:　　　核保人:

操作指南 ➡ 投保单的填制要求

1. 被保险人(Assured's Name)

托收项下的保险单应填出口商名称。CIF项下的信用证应按信用证要求填制:如信用证规定"To order",此栏转om,受益人要在保险单背面作空白背书;信用证要求"To order of…或 in favor of…",此栏应填写成 To order of 加上被保险人名称,并作记名背书;信用证对此无具体规定,受益人应视为被保险人,并作空白背书。

2. 发票号码(Invoice No.)

应与本套单据发票同项内容相一致。

3. 包装数量(Quantity)

此栏填最大包装件数,并与发票、装箱单同项内容一致。散装货填"IN BULK"。如果货物价格以重量计价,除表示件数外,还应注明毛重或净重。

4. 保险货物项目(Description of Goods)

按发票品名填写,如发票品种名称繁多,可填其统称。

5. 保险金额(Amount Insured)

一般按CIF发票总值110%填写。信用证项下应按信用证规定计算填入,如无规定,应为发票总额加一成的金额。保险金额小数点后的尾数应进位取整,例如,USD 2 304.1应进位取整为 USD 2 305。

6. 装载运输工具(Per Conveyance)

海运填写船名,中途转船应在一程船名后加填二程船名,如"By S. S DONG FANG/TOKYO V. 108"。空运(By Airplane)填航班名称。

7. 航次、航班或车号(Voy. No.)

海运填航次号,空运填航班号。

8. 开航日期(Slg. Date)

一般填写本批货物运输单据的签发日期,如海运可填"As per B/L"。

9. 起讫地点(From… to…)

在From后填装运港(地)名称,To后填目的港(地)名称,转运时应在目的港(地)后加注 W/T at…(转运港/地名称)。如果海运至目的港,保险承保到内陆城市,应在目的港后注明,如"From… to Liverpool and thence to Birmingham"。

10. 赔款偿付地点(Claim Payable at)

本栏包括保险赔款的支付地点和赔付的货币名称,应按信用证规定缮制。如来证未作规定,或在托收项下,则填目的港(地)名称。

11. 承保险别(Condition)

应按合同或信用证规定的保险险别填写,并注明依据的保险条款名称及其颁布年份,如"Covering all Risks and War Risk as Per PICC 1/1/1981"。

12. 投保单位签章(Applicant's Signature and Co.'s Name, Add. And Tel. No.)

填写出口商全称、地址和电话,由经办人签名并注明日期。

保险公司签发保险单：

中保财产保险有限公司
The People's Insurance (Property) Company of China, Ltd.

发票号码
Invoice No. TX370

保险单号次
Policy No. SH053101769

海洋货物运输保险单
MARINE CARGO TRANSPORTATION INSURANCE POLICY

被保险人
Insured: SHANGHAI YONGSHENG IMP. & EXP. CO.

中保财产保险有限公司(以下简称本公司)根据被保险人的要求，及其所缴付约定的保险费，按照本保险单承担的险别和背面所载条款与下列特别条款承保下列货物运输保险，特签发本保险单。

This policy of Insurance witnesses that The People's Insurance (Property) Company of China, Ltd. (hereinafter called "The Company"), at the request of the Insured and consideration of the premium paid by the Insures, undertakes to insure the under-mentioned goods in transportation subject to the condition of this Policy as per the Clauses printed overleaf and other special clauses attached hereon.

保险货物项目 Descriptions of Goods	包装 单位 数量 Packing Unit Quantity	保险金额 Amount Insured
LADIES DENIM SKIRT	1 000 CARTONS	USD 138 600.00

承保险别: FOR 110% OF THE INVOICE VALUE COVERING　　货物标记: AS PER INVOICE NO. TX370
Condition: ALL RISKS & WAR RISK AS PER PICC DATE 1/1/1981　　Marks of Goods:

总保险金额:
Total Amount Insured: SAY US DOLLARS ONE HUNDRED AND THIRTY EIGHT THOUSAND SIX HUNDRED ONLY

保费:　　As arranged　　运输工具:　　　　　　　　开航日期:
Premium　　　　　　　　　　Per conveyance S.S DONGFANG V.190 Slg. On or abt MAY 30, 2012

起运港　SHANGHAI　　　　　　　　　　　　目的港　　LONDON
From　　　　　　　　　　　　　　　　　　　To

所保货物，如发生本保险单项下可能引起索赔的损失或损坏，应立即通知本公司下述代理人查勘。如有索赔，应向本公司提交保险单正本(本保险单共有 2 份正本)及有关文件。如一份正本已用于索赔，其余正本则自动失效。

In the event of loss or damage which may result in a claim under this Policy, immediate notice must be given to the Company's Agent as mentioned hereunder. Claims, if any, one of the Original Policy which has been issued in TWO Original (s) together with the relevant documents shall be surrendered to the Company. If one of the Original Policy has been accomplished, the others to be void.

THE PEOPLE'S INSURANCE (PROPERTY) COMPANY OF CHINA, LTD. OSAKA BRANCH
98 LSKL MACH OSAKA JAPAN
TEL: 028-543657

中保财产保险有限公司
THE PEOPLE'S INSURANCE (PROPERTY) COMPANY OF CHINA, LTD.

赔款偿付地点
Claim payable at　LONDON
日期　　　　　　　　在
Date　MAY 24, 2012　at　SHANGHAI　　General Manager: 凡培
地址:
Address:

操作指南 ➡ **保险单的缮制要求**

1. 保险单号码(Policy No.)
按保险公司指定的编号填入。

2. 货物标记(Marks of Goods)
应与发票的唛头相同,也可填"As per Invoice No. ⋯"。

3. 总保险金额(Total Amount Insured)
用英文大写表示,大小写金额须保持一致。

4. 保险费(Premium)
保险公司一般在印制保险单时已在本栏印妥"as arranged"(按约定),无需填制。如信用证要求详细列明,则应按来证要求办理,删除"as arranged"字样,填上具体保险金额。

保险费的计算公式为:保险费＝保险金额×保险费率

5. 保险勘察代理人(Insurance Survey Agent)
由保险公司指定,并注明其详细地址,以便在货物损失时,收货人可及时通知代理人进行勘察和理赔事宜。通常不接受来证中指定的理赔代理人。

6. 签发日期(Place and Date of Issue)
保险单签发日期不得晚于提单等运输单据签发日。签发地为受益人所在地,通常已事先印就在保险单上。

7. 保险公司签章(Authorized Signature)
保险单经保险公司签章后才有效,其签章一般已事先印制在保险单的右下方,然后由授权人签名即可。

工作任务四　　出口商发出装船通知

当出口货物经海关查验放行后,由船公司安排装船,货运代理公司监装。上海永胜进出口公司在货物装船后,凭装货单换取船公司签发的海运提单。此时,方达先生缮制装运通知,用传真发出,及时告知进口商有关货物的运输情况。

船公司签发海运提单：

Shipper SHANGHAI YONGSHENG IMP. & EXP. CO. 21 WEST ZHONGSHAN ROAD SHANGHAI, CHINA		B/L NO. HJSHBI 1520876 **ORIGINAL**	
Consignee or order TO ORDER OF SHIPPER		中国对外贸易运输总公司 CHINA NATIONAL FOREIGN TRADE TRANSPORT CORPORATION 直运或转船提单 BILL OF LADING DIRECT OR WITH TRANSSHIPMENT	
Notify address MANDARS IMPORTS CO., LTD. 38 QUEENSWAY, 2013 UK		SHIPPED on board in apparent good order and condition (unless otherwise indicated) the goods or packages specified herein and to be discharged or the mentioned port of discharge of as near there as the vessel may safely get and be always afloat. THE WEIGHT, measure, marks and numbers quality, contents and value, being particulars furnished by the Shipper, are not checked by the Carrier on loading. THE SHIPPER, Consignee and the Holder of this Bill of Lading hereby expressly accept and agree to all printed, written or stamped provisions, exceptions and conditions of this Bill of Loading, including those on the back hereof. IN WITNESS where of the number of original Bill of Loading stated below have been signed, one of which being accomplished, the other(s) to be void.	
Pre-carriage by	Port of loading SHANGHAI		
Vessel DONGFANG V. 190	Port of transshipment		
Port of discharge LONDON	Final destination		
Container Seal No. or Marks and Nos.	Number and kind of packages Designation of goods	Gross weight (kgs.)	Measurement (m³)
MANDARS TXT200710 LONDON C/NO. 1—1 000	LADIES DENIM SKIRT SAY ONE THOUSAND CARTONS ONLY TOTAL ONE 20' CONTAINER CFS TO CFS FREIGHT PREPAID	140 KGS	23.8CBM
REGARDING TRANSSHIPMENT INFORMATION PLEASE CONTACT			Freight and charge FREIGHT PREPAID
Ex. rate	Prepaid at	Fright payable at SHANGHAI	Place and date of issue SHANGHAI MAY 30, 2012
	Total Prepaid	Number of original Bs/L THREE	Signed for or on behalf of the Master as Agent 丁毅

体验活动二　自理出口贸易业务

方达先生缮制装船通知：

SHANGHAI YONGSHENG IMP. & EXP. CO.
21 WEST ZHONGSHAN ROAD SHANGHAI, CHINA

SHIPPING ADVICE

TEL：021-64500002　　　　　　　　　　　　　INV. NO.：TX370
FAX：021-64500003　　　　　　　　　　　　　S/C NO.：TXT201210
　　　　　　　　　　　　　　　　　　　　　　L/C NO.：XT370
TO MESSRS：　　　　　　　　　　　　　　　　DATE：MAY 20, 2012
　　MANDARS IMPORTS CO. LTD.
　　38 QUEENSWAY, 2013 UK
DEAR SIRS,
　　WE HEREBY INFORM YOU THAT THE GOODS UNDER THE ABOVE MENTIONED CREDIT HAVE BEEN SHIPPED. THE DETAILS OF THE SHIPMENT ARE STATED BELOW.

COMMODITY：	LADIES DENIM SKIRT	SHIPPING MARKS
NUMBER OF CTNS：	1 000 CARTONS	MANDARS
TOTAL GROSS WEIGHT：	140KGS	LONDON
OCEAN VESSEL：	DONGFANG V. 190	TXT201210
B/L NO.：	HJSHBI 1520876	C/NO. 1-1000
PORT OF LOADING：	SHANGHAI	
DATE OF DEPARTURE：	MAY 30, 2012	
DESTINATION：	LONDON PORT	

　　　　　　　　　　　　　　　　　　SHANGHAI YONGSHENG IMP. & EXP. CO.
　　　　　　　　　　　　　　　　　　　　　　　　　　　Da Fang

操作指南 ➡ 缮制装船通知的方法

装船通知不限格式,只要内容符合信用证的规定即可,其缮制方法如下:
1. 抬头人
  填写抬头人时应按信用证的具体要求。抬头人可以是承保该笔货物的保险公司、信用证申请人,或者是信用证规定的其他抬头人。
2. 相关单据的编号
  主要包括信用证号码和开证行名称,发票号码、日期。
3. 装船情况
  包括装运港名称、目的港名称、信用证号码和开证银行名称。
4. 货物内容
  应与发票、提单等单据的内容一致;特别注意发票金额,它是计算投保金额和保险费的基础。
5. 签署
  应由单据的出具人或负责人签字。

综合业务模拟操作

操作一

1. 操作资料

卖　方：　　南京永发进出口公司
　　　　　　南京中山路 1321 号
　　　　　　TEL:025-23501111　FAX:025-23502222
买　方：　　JIM KING TRADING CORPORATION
　　　　　　NO. 206 CHANGJ NORTH STREET SINGAPORE
　　　　　　TEL:218-76911　FAX:218-76912
合同号：　　wy070901
货　名：　　电动钻头(Electric Drill)No. TY242
数　量：　　1 800 套
包　装：　　每 10 套装一个纸箱
交货日期：　2012 年 10 月 30 日
货运代理：　南京全友货运代理公司(负责人汪铠)
船　名：　　东方号 V. 035

提单号码：　　　　　COS0215478
货运委托书编号：　　AF0387124
内装箱地址：　　　　南京金陵路 2960 号三号门
电　　话：　　　　　025-6820682×215
外币结算账号：　　　THY6684321324
人民币结算账号：　　SZR80066686
保　　险：　　　　　按发票金额 110％投保中国人民保险公司海洋货物运输险一
　　　　　　　　　　切险与战争险
保险单号：　　　　　SH061012
委托办理检验事宜：　代理报检手续，代缴检验检疫费，负责与检验检疫机构联系和
　　　　　　　　　　验货，领取检验检疫证书
报关委托书编号：　　54682455541
委托办理报关事宜：　逐票、填单申报、辅助查验、办理海关证明联
报关委托书有效期：　2012 年 11 月 10 日止
收到单证日期：　　　2012 年 10 月 20 日
收到单证名称：　　　合同、发票、装箱清单

2. 操作要求

(1)请你以南京永发进出口公司业务员张丽的身份，根据上述资料、销售合同书和信用证的有关内容缮制装箱单。

南京永发进出口公司
NANJING YONGFA IMPORT & EXPORT TRADE CORPORATION
1321 ZHONGSHAN ROAD NANJING, CHINA

PACKING LIST

TEL:＿＿＿＿＿＿＿＿

FAX:＿＿＿＿＿＿＿＿

TO:

INVOICE NO. :＿＿＿＿＿＿＿＿

DATE. :＿＿＿＿＿＿＿＿

S/C NO. :＿＿＿＿＿＿＿＿

MARKS &. NOS.

GOODS DESCRIPTION &. PACKING	QTY (PCS)	CTNS	G. W (KGS)	N. W (KGS)	MEAS (M³)
TOTAL					

SAY TOTAL

(2)请你以南京永发进出口公司业务员张丽的身份,根据上述资料、销售合同书和信用证的有关内容填写货运委托书。

南京全友货运代理公司

经营单位（托运人）				全 友 编 号	
提单 B/L 项目要求	发货人：Shipper：				
	收货人：Consignee：				
	通知人：Notify Party：				
海洋运费(√) Sea freight	预付( ) 或到付( ) Prepaid or Collect		提单份数	提单寄送地址	
起运港		目的港		可否转船	可否分批
集装箱预配数	20'× 40'×		装运期限		有效期限
标记唛码	包装件数	中英文货号 Description of goods	毛重（千克）	尺码（立方米）	成交条件（总价）
			特种货物 □冷藏货 □危险品	重 件：每件重量 大 件（长×宽×高）	
内装箱(CFS)地址					
门对门装箱地址			特种集装箱：( )		
			物资备妥日期		
外币结算账号			物资进栈：自送( ) 或全友派送( )		
声明事项			人民币结算单位账号		
			托运人签章		
			电 话		
			传 真		
			联系人		
			地 址		
			制单日期：		

(3)请你以船公司丁毅的身份,根据上述资料、销售合同书和货运委托书的有关内容填写海运提单。

Shipper			B/L NO.	**ORIGINAL**
Consignee or order			<div align="center">中 国 对 外 贸 易 运 输 总 公 司 CHINA NATIONAL FOREIGN TRADE TRANSPORT CORPORATION 直 运 或 转 船 提 单 BILL OF LADING DIRECT OR WITH TRANSSHIPMENT</div>	
Notify address			SHIPPED on board in apparent good order and condition (unless otherwise indicated) the goods or packages specified herein and to be discharged or the mentioned port of discharge of as near there as the vessel may safely get and be always afloat. THE WEIGHT, measure, marks and numbers quality, contents and value, being particulars furnished by the Shipper, are not checked by the Carrier on loading. THE SHIPPER, Consignee and the Holder of this Bill of Lading hereby expressly accept and agree to all printed, written or stamped provisions, exceptions and conditions of this Bill of Loading, including those on the back hereof. IN WITNESS where of the number of original Bill of Loading stated below have been signed, one of which being accomplished, the other(s) to be void.	
Pre-carriage by	Port of loading			
Vessel	Port of transshipment			
Port of discharge	Final destination			
Container Seal No. or Marks and Nos.	Number and kind of packages Designation of goods		Gross weight (kgs.)	Measurement (m³)
REGARDING TRANSSHIPMENT INFORMATION PLEASE CONTACT			Freight and charge	
Ex. rate	Prepaid at	Fright payable at	Place and date of issue	
	Total Prepaid	Number of original Bs/L	Signed for or on behalf of the Master as Agent	

(4)请你以南京永发进出口公司业务员张丽的身份,根据上述资料、销售合同书和信用证的有关内容填写报检委托书及报关委托书。

报检委托书

_____出入境检验检疫局：

本委托人郑重声明,保证遵守出入境检验检疫法律、法规的规定。如有违法行为,自愿接受检验检疫机构的处罚并负法律责任。

本委托人委托受委托人向检验检疫机构提交"报检申请单"和各种随附单据。具体委托情况如下：

本单位将于_____年_____月间出口如下货物：

品　名		H.S.编码	
数(重)量		合同号	
信用证号		审批文件	
其他特殊要求			

特委托_____(单位/注册登记号),代理本公司办理下列出入境检验检疫事宜：

□1.办理代理报检手续；
□2.代缴检验检疫费；
□3.负责与检验检疫机构联系和验货；
□4.领取检验检疫证书；
□5.其他与报检有关的事宜。

请贵局按有关法律法规规定予以办理。

委托人(公章)：　　　　　　　　　受委托人(公章)：

本委托书有效期至　　年　月　日

代理报关委托

编号：

_____：

  我单位现　　（A. 逐票、B. 长期）委托贵公司代理　　等通关事宜（A. 填单申报、B. 辅助查验、C. 垫缴税款、D. 办理海关证明联、E. 审批手册、F. 核销手册、G. 申办减免税手续、H. 其他）。详见《委托报关协议》。

  我单位保证遵守《中华人民共和国海关法》和国家有关法规，保证所提供的情况真实、完整、单货相符。否则，愿承担相关法律责任。

  本委托书有效期自签字之日起至　　年　月　日止。

委托方(盖章)：

法定代表人或其授权签署《代理报关委托书》的人(签字)

年　月　日

委托报关协议

为明确委托报关具体事项和各自责任,双方经平等协商签订协议如下:

委托方		被委托方		
主要货物名称		报关单编码		
H.S.编码		收到单证日期	年 月 日	
货物总价		收到单证情况	合同□	发票□
进出口日期			装箱清单□	提(运)单□
提单号			加工贸易手册□	许可证件□
贸易方式			其他	
原产地/货源地		报关收费	人民币: 元	
其他要求:		承诺说明:		
背面所列通用条款是本协议不可分割的一部分,对本协议的签署构成了对背面通用条款的同意。		背面所列通用条款是本协议不可分割的一部分,对本协议的签署构成了对背面通用条款的同意。		
委托方业务签章: 经办人签章: 联系电话:		被委托方业务签章: 经办报关员签章: 联系电话:		

(白联:海关留存;黄联:被委托方留存;红联:委托方留存)　　　　中国报关协会监制

(5)请你以南京永发进出口公司业务员张丽的身份，根据上述资料、销售合同书和信用证的有关内容填写投保单。

中保财产保险有限公司江苏省分公司

The People's Insurance (Property) Company of China, Ltd. Jiangsu Branch

进出口货物运输保险投保单

Application From form I/E Marine Cargo Insurance

被保险人 Assured's Name				
发票号码(出口用)或合同号码(进口用) Invoice No. or Contract No.		包装数量 Quantity	保险货物项目 Description of Goods	保险金额 Amount Insured

装载运输工具 _____ 航次、航班或车号 _____ 开航日期 _____
Per Conveyance　　　Voy. No.　　　　　　　Slg. Date

自 _____ 至 _____ 转运地 _____ 赔款地 _____
From　　　To　　　　W/T at　　　　Claim Payable at

承保险别：
Condition &./or
Special Coverage

投保人签章及公司名称、电话、地址：
Applicant's Signature and Co.'s Name, Add. and Tel. No.

备注：　　　　　　　　　　　投保日期：
Remarks　　　　　　　　　　Date

保险公司填写：　保单号：　　　费率：　　　核保人：

(6)请你以保险公司业务员夏丽的身份,根据上述资料、销售合同书和投保单的有关内容填写保险单。

中保财产保险有限公司
The People's Insurance (Property) Company of China, Ltd.

发票号码　　　　　　　　　　　　　　　　　　　　　　　　保险单号次
Invoice No. TX370　　　　　　　　　　　　　　　　　　　 Policy No. SH053101769

海 洋 货 物 运 输 保 险 单
MARINE CARGO TRANSPORTATION INSURANCE POLICY

被保险人
Insured:

中保财产保险有限公司(以下简称本公司)根据被保险人的要求,及其所缴付约定的保险费,按照本保险单承担的险别和背面所载条款与下列特别条款承保下列货物运输保险,特签发本保险单。

This policy of Insurance witnesses that The People's Insurance (Property) Company of China, Ltd. (hereinafter called "The Company"), at the request of the Insured and consideration of the premium paid by the Insures, undertakes to insure the under-mentioned goods in transportation subject to the condition of this Policy as per the Clauses printed overleaf and other special clauses attached hereon.

保险货物项目 Description of Goods	包装　单位　数量 Packing　Unit　Quantity	保险金额 Amount Insured

承保险别:　　　　　　　　　　　　　　　　　货物标记:
Condition:　　　　　　　　　　　　　　　　　Marks of Goods:

总 保 险 金 额:
Total Amount Insured:

保费:　　　As arranged　　运输工具:　　　　　　　　　　开航日期:
Premium　　　　　　　　　Per conveyance S.S　　　　　　Slg. On or abt

起运港　　　　　　　　　　　　　　　　　　　目的港
From　　　　　　　　　　　　　　　　　　　　To

所保货物,如发生本保险单项下可能引起索赔的损失或损坏,立即通知本公司下述代理人查勘。如有索赔,应向本公司提交保险单正本(本保险单共有____份正本)及有关文件。如一份正本已用于索赔,其余正本则自动失效。

In the event of loss or damage which may result in a claim under this Policy, immediate notice must be given to the Company's Agent as mentioned hereunder. Claims, if any, one of the Original Policy which has been issued in ____ Original(s) together with the relevant documents shall be surrendered to the Company. If one of the Original Policy has been accomplished, the others to be void.

THE PEOPLE'S INSURANCE (PROPERTY) COMPANY OF CHINA, LTD. SINGAPORE BRANCH
98 LSKL MACH SINGAPORE
TEL:026-5543657

　　　　　　　　　　　　　　　　　　　　　　中保财产保险有限公司
　　　　　　　　　　　　　　　　　　　　　　THE PEOPLE'S INSURANCE (PROPERTY) COMPANY OF CHINA, LTD.

赔款偿付地点
Claim payable at

日期　　　　　　　　　　　在
Date　　　　　　　　　　at　　　　　　　　　General Manager:

地址:
Address:

(7)请你以南京永发进出口公司业务员张丽的身份,根据上述资料、销售合同书和信用证的有关内容缮制装运通知。

NANJING YONGFA IMPORT & EXPORT TRADE CORPORATION
1321 ZHONGSHAN ROAD NANJING, CHINA

SHIPPING ADVICE

TEL:_____   INV. NO. :_____
FAX:_____   S/C NO. :_____
                     L/C NO. :_____
TO MESSRS:_____   DATE:_____

DEAR SIRS,
    WE HEREBY INFORM YOU THAT THE GOODS UNDER THE ABOVE MENTIONED CREDIT HAVE BEEN SHIPPED. THE DETAILS OF THE SHIPMENT ARE STATED BELOW.

SHIPPING MARKS:_____
TOTAL GROSS WEIGHT:_____
OCEAN VESSEL:_____
B/L NO.:_____
PORT OF LOADING:_____
DATE OF DEPARTURE:_____
DESTINATION:_____

操作二

1. 操作资料

卖　方：　　广州纺织品进出口公司
　　　　　　广州市北京路530号
　　　　　　TEL:(020)64043030　FAX:(020)64043031
买　方：　　OLEARA IMPORT & EXPORT CORPORATION
　　　　　　310—224 HOLA STREET MARSEILLE FRANCE
　　　　　　TEL:491-38241234
货　名：　　男式衬衫 Art No. 88(蓝色)、Art No. 44(黑色)
数　量：　　Art No. 88(蓝色)3 000 件、Art No. 44(黑色)3 000 件

包　　装：	每 20 件装一只纸箱，每箱毛重为 20.2 公斤、净重为 20 公斤、体积为 0.2M³，装入一只 20 英尺集装箱（集装箱号：TEXU22636643）
价　　格：	Art No.88 每件 6.50 美元、Art No.44 每件 7.00 美元 CIF MARSEILLE
支付方式：	不可撤销跟单即期信用证
信用证号：	07/CB4578
装运港：	广州
目的港：	MARSELLE
交货日期：	2012 年 7 月 31 日
合同号：	ST121032
发票号码：	GZT00021
日　　期：	2012 年 7 月 1 日
商品编码：	6303.4500
货运代理：	广州国际货运代理公司（负责人赵峡）
货运委托书编号：	JF0387124
内装箱地址：	广州市丰收路 78 号　电话：020-6820682×215
外币结算账号：	THY6684321337
人民币结算账号：	SZR80066686
提单号码：	COCS06-11861
投保单编号：	TB0562311
日　　期：	2012 年 7 月 28 日
保　　险：	按发票金额 110% 投保中国人民保险公司海洋货物运输险一切险
船　　名：	NANXING V.086
保险单号：	GZH061012
委托办理检验事宜：	代理报检手续、代缴检验检疫费、负责与检验检疫机构联系和验货、领取检验检疫证书
报关委托书编号：	12382455541
委托办理报关事宜：	逐票、填单申报、辅助查验、办理海关证明联
报关委托书有效期：	2012 年 8 月 10 日止
收到单证日期：	2012 年 7 月 2 日
收到单证名称：	合同、发票、装箱清单

2. 操作要求

(1)请你以广州纺织品进出口公司业务员王伟的身份，根据上述资料、销售合同书和信用证的有关内容缮制装箱单。

广州纺织品进出口公司
GUANGZHOU TEXTILE IMPORT & EXPORT CORPORATION
530 BEIJING ROAD GUANGZHOU, CHINA

PACKING LIST

TEL: _____
FAX: _____

TO:

INVOICE NO. : _____
DATE: _____
S/C NO. : _____

MARKS & NOS.

GOODS DESCRIPTION & PACKING	QTY (PCS)	CTNS	G. W (KGS)	N. W (KGS)	MEAS (M³)
TOTAL					

SAY TOTAL

(2) 请你以广州纺织品进出口公司业务员王伟的身份,根据上述资料、销售合同书和信用证的有关内容填写货运委托书。

广州国际货运代理公司

经营单位 (托运人)				国 际 编 号		
提单 B/L 项目 要求	发货人: Shipper:					
	收货人: Consignee:					
	通知人: Notify Party:					
海洋运费(√) Sea freight	预付( ) 或到付( ) Prepaid or Collect		提单 份数		提单寄送 地 址	
起运港		目的港		可否转船		可否分批
集装箱预配数		20'×	40'×	装运期限		有效期限
标记唛码	包装 件数	中英文货号 Description of goods		毛重 (千克)	尺码 (立方米)	成交条件 (总价)
内装箱(CFS) 地址				特种货物 □冷藏货 □危险品	重 件:每件重量 大 件 (长×宽×高)	
				特种集装箱:( )		
门对门装箱地址				物资备妥日期		
				物资进栈:自送( ) 或广州国际派送( )		
外币结算账号				人民币结算单位账号		
声明事项				托运人签章		
				电 话		
				传 真		
				联系人		
				地 址		
				制单日期:		

(3)请你以船公司业务员夏霞的身份,根据上述资料、销售合同书和货运委托书的有关内容填写海运提单。

Shipper		B/L NO. ORIGINAL		
		中 国 对 外 贸 易 运 输 总 公 司 CHINA NATIONAL FOREIGN TRADE TRANSPORT CORPORATION 直 运 或 转 船 提 单 BILL OF LADING DIRECT OR WITH TRANSSHIPMENT		
Consignee or order		SHIPPED on board in apparent good order and condition (unless otherwise indicated) the goods or packages specified herein and to be discharged or the mentioned port of discharge of as near there as the vessel may safely get and be always afloat. THE WEIGHT, measure, marks and numbers quality, contents and value, being particulars furnished by the Shipper, are not checked by the Carrier on loading. THE SHIPPER, Consignee and the Holder of this Bill of Lading hereby expressly accept and agree to all printed, written or stamped provisions, exceptions and conditions of this Bill of Loading, including those on the back hereof. IN WITNESS where of the number of original Bill of Loading stated below have been signed, one of which being accomplished, the other(s) to be void.		
Notify address		^		
Pre-carriage by	Port of loading	^		
Vessel	Port of transshipment	^		
Port of discharge	Final destination	^		
Container Seal No. or marks and Nos.	Number and kind of packages Designation of goods	Gross weight (kgs)		Measurement (m^3)
REGARDING TRANSSHIPMENT INFORMATION PLEASE CONTACT			Freight and charge	
Ex. rate	Prepaid at	Fright payable at	Place and date of issue	
	Total Prepaid	Number of original Bs/L	Signed for or on behalf of the Master as Agent	

104

(4)请你以广州纺织品进出口公司业务员王伟的身份,根据上述资料、销售合同书和信用证的有关内容填写报检委托书及报关委托书。

报检委托书

_____出入境检验检疫局:

　　本委托人郑重声明,保证遵守出入境检验检疫法律、法规的规定。如有违法行为,自愿接受检验检疫机构的处罚并负法律责任。

　　本委托人委托受委托人向检验检疫机构提交"报检申请单"和各种随附单据。具体委托情况如下:

　　本单位将于_____年_____月间出口如下货物:

品　名		H.S.编码	
数(重)量		合同号	
信用证号		审批文件	
其他特殊要求			

　　特委托_____(单位/注册登记号),代理本公司办理下列出入境检验检疫事宜:

　　□1.办理代理报检手续;
　　□2.代缴检验检疫费;
　　□3.负责与检验检疫机构联系和验货;
　　□4.领取检验检疫证书;
　　□5.其他与报检有关的事宜。
　　请贵局按有关法律法规规定予以办理。

委托人(公章):　　　　　　　　　　　受委托人(公章):

本委托书有效期至　　　年　月　日。

代理报关委托

编号：

_____：

我单位现　（A. 逐票、B. 长期）委托贵公司代理　　等通关事宜（A. 填单申报、B. 辅助查验、C. 垫缴税款、D. 办理海关证明联、E. 审批手册、F. 核销手册、G. 申办减免税手续、H. 其他）。详见《委托报关协议》。

我单位保证遵守《中华人民共和国海关法》和国家有关法规，保证所提供的情况真实、完整、单货相符。否则，愿承担相关法律责任。

本委托书有效期自签字之日起至　　年　月　日止。

委托方(盖章)：

法定代表人或其授权签署《代理报关委托书》的人（签字）

年　月　日

委托报关协议

为明确委托报关具体事项和各自责任，双方经平等协商签订协议如下：

委托方		被委托方		
主要货物名称		*报关单编码		
H.S.编码		收到单证日期	年　月　日	
货物总价		收到单证情况	合同□	发票□
进出口日期			装箱清单□	提(运)单□
提单号			加工贸易手册□	许可证件□
贸易方式			其他	
原产地/货源地		报关收费	人民币：　　　　元	
其他要求：		承诺说明：		
背面所列通用条款是本协议不可分割的一部分，对本协议的签署构成了对背面通用条款的同意。		背面所列通用条款是本协议不可分割的一部分，对本协议的签署构成了对背面通用条款的同意。		
委托方业务签章： 经办人签章： 联系电话：		被委托方业务签章： 经办报关员签章： 联系电话：		

（白联：海关留存；黄联：被委托方留存；红联：委托方留存）　　中国报关协会监制

(5)请你以广州纺织品进出口公司业务员王伟的身份,根据上述资料、销售合同书和信用证的有关内容填写投保单。

中保财产保险有限公司广东省分公司
The People's Insurance (Property) Company of China, Ltd. Guangdong Branch

进出口货物运输保险投保单
Application From form I/E Marine Cargo Insurance

被保险人 Assured's Name			
发票号码(出口用)或合同号码(进口用) Invoice No. or Contract No.	包装数量 Quantity	保险货物项目 Description of Goods	保险金额 Amount Insured

装载运输工具 _____ 航次、航班或车号 _____ 开航日期 _____
Per Conveyance   Voy. No.   Slg. Date

自 _____ 至 _____ 转运地 _____ 赔款地 _____
From   To   W/T at   Claim Payable at

承保险别:
Condition &./or
Special Coverage

投保人签章及公司名称、电话、地址:
Applicant's Signature and Co.'s Name, Add. and Tel. No.

备注: 投保日期:
Remarks   Date

保险公司填写: 保单号: 费率: 核保人:

108

体验活动二 自理出口贸易业务

(6)请你以保险公司业务员方名的身份,根据上述资料、销售合同书和投保单的有关内容填写保险单。

中保财产保险有限公司
The People's Insurance (Property) Company of China, Ltd.

发票号码
Invoice No. TX370

保险单号次
Policy No. SH053101769

海洋货物运输保险单
MARINE CARGO TRANSPORTATION INSURANCE POLICY

被保险人
Insured:

中保财产保险有限公司(以下简称本公司)根据被保险人的要求,及其所缴付约定的保险费,按照本保险单承担的险别和背面所载条款与下列特别条款承保下列货物运输保险,特签发本保险单。

This policy of Insurance witnesses that The People's Insurance (Property) Company of China, Ltd. (hereinafter called "The Company"), at the request of the Insured and consideration of the premium paid by the Insures, undertakes to insure the under-mentioned goods in transportation subject to the condition of this Policy as per the Clauses printed overleaf and other special clauses attached hereon.

保险货物项目 Description of Goods	包装 单位 数量 Packing Unit Quantity	保险金额 Amount Insured

承保险别:
Condition:

货物标记:
Marks of Goods:

总 保 险 金 额:
Total Amount Insured:

保费   As arranged
Premium

运输工具
Per conveyance S. S.

开航日期:
Slg. On or abt

起运港
From

目的港
To

所保货物,如发生本保险单项下可能引起索赔的损失或损坏,应立即通知本公司下述代理人查勘。如有索赔,应向本公司提交保险单正本(本保险单共有____份正本)及有关文件。如1份正本已用于索赔,其余正本则自动失效。

In the event of loss or damage which may result in a claim under this Policy, immediate notice must be given to the Company's Agent as mentioned hereunder. Claims, if any, one of the Original Policy which has been issued in ____ Original (s) together with the relevant documents shall be surrendered to the Company. If one of the Original Policy has been accomplished, the others to be void.

THE PEOPLE'S INSURANCE (PROPERTY) COMPANY OF CHINA, LTD. MARSEILLE BRANCH
12 LSKL MACH MARSEILLE
TEL: 22643657

中保财产保险有限公司
THE PEOPLE'S INSURANCE (PROPERTY) COMPANY OF CHINA, LTD.

赔款偿付地点
Claim payable at

日期   在
Date   at   General Manager:

地址:
Address:

(7)请你以广州纺织品进出口公司业务员王伟的身份，根据上述资料、销售合同书和信用证的有关内容缮制装运通知。

GUANGZHOU TEXTILE IMPORT & EXPORT CORPORATION
530 BEIJING ROAD GUANGZHOU, CHINA

SHIPPING ADVICE

TEL: _____
FAX: _____

TO MESSRS: _____

INV. NO.: _____
S/C NO.: _____
L/C NO.: _____
DATE: _____

DEAR SIRS,

 WE HEREBY INFORM YOU THAT THE GOODS UNDER THE ABOVE MENTIONED CREDIT HAVE BEEN SHIPPED. THE DETAILS OF THE SHIPMENT ARE STATED BELOW.

COMMODITY: _____
NUMBER OF CTNS: _____
TOTAL GROSS WEIGHT: _____
OCEAN VESSEL: _____
B/L NO.: _____
PORT OF LOADING: _____
DATE OF DEPARTURE: _____
DESTINATION: _____

SHIPPING MARKS: _____

_____

实训六　出口结汇、核销与退税

> **业务导入**

自1991年起,我国为加强出口收汇管理,实施了出口收汇核销制度,由国家职能部门对出口企业的出口货物进行"跟单"核销逐笔管理。初次办理出口收汇核销前,出口企业必须在本地外汇管理局办理核销备案登记,领取有编号的纸质核销单,并进行填制,并随附报关与议付单据进行报关议付。银行结汇后,在出口收汇核销结水单或收账通知上注明核销单号交出口企业。出口企业持经海关签章的收汇核销专用联、结水单或收账通知及报关单到外汇管理局办理核销。核销完毕后,将核销单(出口退税专用联)、报关单(退税联)、商业发票、增值税发票、出口专用缴税书等文件连同"外贸企业出口货物退税汇总申报审批表"交税务局办理退税。

出口结汇、核销与退税业务流程如下图所示:

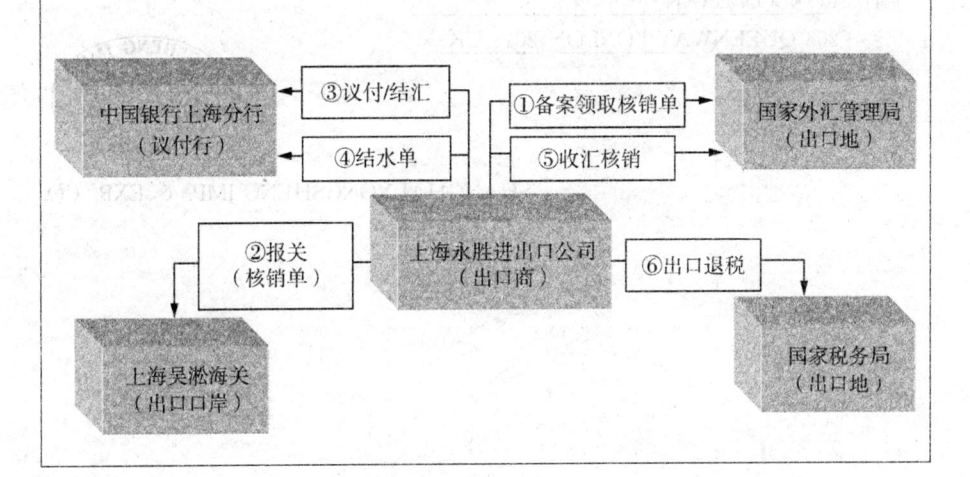

```
中国银行上海分行 ──③议付/结汇──→          ①备案领取核销单──→  国家外汇管理局
  (议付行)    ←──④结水单────           ←──⑤收汇核销────    (出口地)
                            ↑
                    上海永胜进出口公司
         ②报关        (出口商)         ⑥出口退税
        (核销单)                          ↓
                                      国家税务局
       上海吴淞海关                     (出口地)
       (出口口岸)
```

> ◎ 工作任务一　　　　办理议付手续
> 　　上海永胜进出口公司在获取海运提单和发出装运通知后，根据合同与信用证规定的交单期限进行结汇或议付。为此，方达先生制作商业汇票，并汇集有关议付单据及时向中国银行上海分行办理议付手续。

方达先生缮制商业汇票：

BILL OF EXCHANGE

No. TX370
For USD 126 000.00　　　　　　　　　　　　SHANGHAI, MAY 31, 2012
　　　　　　　　　　　　　　　　　　　　　　　　　　　Date

　　At 60 DAYS AFTER B/L DATE sight of this SECOND BILL of EXCHANGE (first of the same tenor and date unpaid) pay to the order of　BANK OF CHINA SHANGHAI BRANCH　the sum of SAY US DOLLARS ONE HUNRED AND TWENTY SIX THOUSAND ONLY.

　　Drawn under LONDON BANK
　　L/C No.　TX370　　　　　Dated　APR. 30, 2012
　　To.　LONDON BANK
　　　　205 QUEENWAY LONDON, 2013 UK

　　　　　　　　　　　　　　　　SHANGHAI YONGSHENG IMP. & EXP. CO.
　　　　　　　　　　　　　　　　　　　　Da Fang

操作指南 ➡ **汇票的缮制方法**

1. 编号(No.)

汇票编号填本套单据的发票号码。

2. 出票日期与地点(Date and Place of Issue)

信用证项下的出票日期是议付日期,出票地点是议付地,通常出口商多委托议付行在办理议付时代填。值得注意的是,汇票出票不得早于其他单据日期,也不得晚于交单期并在信用证有效期内。

3. 汇票金额(Amount)

汇票金额用数字小写和英文大写分别表明。小写金额可保留2位小数,由货币名称缩写和阿拉伯数字组成;大写金额位于 The sum of 后,习惯上句首加"SAY",意指"计",句尾由"ONLY"示意为"整",小数点用 POINT 或 SENTS 表示,大小写金额与币制必须一致。

4. 付款期限(Tenor)

必须按信用证的规定填写。即期付款在 At 与 Sight 之间填上"*"符号。远期付款主要有见票后若干天付款、出票日后若干天付款、提单日后若干天付款和定日付款。例如,信用证规定见票后90天付款(Available against your drafts drawn on us at 90 days after sight),在 at 与 sight 之间填入 90 days after,意为从承兑日后起第90天为付款期;信用证规定出票日后80天付款(Available against presentation of the documents detailed herein and of your drafts at 80 days after date of the draft),则在 at 后填入 80 days after date,将汇票上印就的"sight"划掉,其意为汇票出票日后80天付款;信用证规定提单日后70天付款(Available by beneficiary's drafts at 70 days after on board B/L date),则在 at 后填入 70 days after date of B/L,删去 sight,意为提单日后第70天付款。如果信用证汇票条款中规定远期汇票(例如,Available by your drafts at 80 days after sight on us…),在特殊条款中又规定受益人可即期收款(例如,The negotiating bank is authorized to negotiate the insurance drafts on sight bases, as acceptance commission, discount charges and interest are for account by buyer.),仍按远期(80 days after)填制,但可向议付行即期收款,其贴息由开证人负担。

5. 受款人(Payee)

汇票受款人又称抬头人或收款人,是指接受票款的当事人。汇票常见的抬头方式有:指示性抬头,即在受款人栏目中填写 Pay to the order of…,意为付给……人的指定人;限制性抬头,即在受款人栏目中填写 Pay to…only 或 Pay to…not transferable,意为仅付给……人或限付给……人,不许转让;持票人抬头,又称来人式抬头,即在受款

续

人栏目中填写 Pay to bearer,意为付给持票人。这种方式不用背书就可转让,风险较大,现极少使用。

6. 出票条款(Drawn Clause)

出票条款必须按信用证的描述填于 Drawn under 后,如信用证没有出票条款,就分别填写开证行名称、地址、信用证编号和开证日期。

信用证如有利息条款,例如,"Payable with interest at 5 per cent annum from date hereof to approximate date of arrival of cover in Tokyo,"或信用证要求汇票注明"Documents against payment"(货单付款),必须在出票条款后将其列出。

7. 付款人(Drawee)

汇票付款人即受票人,包括付款人名称和地址,在汇票中以 To…(致……)表示。付款人必须按信用证规定填制,通常为开证行。如果信用证规定"Draft drawn on applicant"或"drawn on us"或未规定付款人时,在 to 后都打上开证行名称和地址。

8. 出票人签章(Signature of the Drawer)

出票人为信用证受益人,也就是出口商。通常在右下角空白处打上出口商全称,由经办人签名,该汇票才正式生效。如果信用证规定汇票必须手签,应照办。

体验活动二　自理出口贸易业务

方达先生汇集议付单据：

上海永胜进出口公司
SHANGHAI YONGSHENG IMP. & EXP. CO.
21 WEST ZHONGSHAN ROAD SHANGHAI, CHINA
COMMERCIAL INVOICE

TEL: 021-64500002
FAX: 021-64500003

INV. NO. TX370
DATE: MAY 02, 2012
S/C NO. TXT201210
L/C NO. XT370

TO:
MANDARS IMPORTS CO. LTD.
38 QUEENSWAY, 2008 UK

FROM _____SHANGHAI PORT_____ TO _____LONDON PORT_____

MARKS & NO.	DESCRIPTION OF GOODS	QUANTITY	U/PRICE	AMOUNT
MANDARS TXT200710 LONDON C/NO. 1-1000	LADIES DENIM SKIRT PACKING: FLAT PACK WITHOUT FOLDING 6 PIECES ASSORTED SIZES PER POLYBAG, 3 POLYBAGS IN A MASTER POLYBAG AND THEN INTO AN EXPORT CARTON	18 000 PCS	CIF LONDON USD 7.00	USD 126 000.00

TOTAL AMOUNT: SAY US DOLLARS ONE HUNDRED AND TWENTY SIX THOUSAND ONLY.

WE HEREBY CERTIFY THAT THE CONTENTS OF INVOICE HEREIN ARE TRUE AND CORRECT.

SHANGHAI YONGSHENG IMP. & EXP. CO.
Da Fang

上海永胜进出口公司
SHANGHAI YONGSHENG IMP. & EXP. CO.
21 WEST ZHONGSHAN ROAD SHANGHAI, CHINA

PACKING LIST

TEL:021-65788877
FAX:021-65788876

TO: MANDARS IMPORTS CO. LTD.
38 QUEENSWAY, 2008 UK

INV. NO.: TX370
DATE: MAY 20,2012
S/C NO.: TXT201210
MARKS & NOS.
MANDARS
TXT200710
LONDON
C/NO. 1－1 000

GOODS DESCRIPTION & PACKING	QTY (PCS)	CTNS	G.W (KGS)	N.W (KGS)	MEAS (M³)
LADIES DENIM SKIRT PACKING: FLAT PACK WITHOUT FOLDING 6 PIECES ASSORTED SIZES PER POLYBAG, 3 POLYBAGS IN A MASTER POLYBAG AND THEN INTO AN EXPORT CARTON	18 000	1 000	140	100	23.8
TOTAL	18 000	1 000	140	100	23.8

SAY TOTAL ONE THOUSAND CARTONS ONLY.

SHANGHAI YONGSHENG IMP. & EXP. CO.

Da Fang

1. Goods consigned from (Exporter's business name, address, country) SHANGHAI YONGSHENG IMP. & EXP. CO. 21 WEST ZHONGSHAN ROAD SHANGHAI, CHINA	Reference No. GENERALIZED SYSTEM OF PREFERENCES CERTIFICATE OF ORIGIN (COMBINED DECLARATION AND CERTIFICATE)
2. Goods consigned to (Consignee's name, address, country) MANDARS IMPORTS CO. LTD. 38 QUEENSWAY, 2008 UK	FORM A ISSUED IN THE PEOPLE'S REPUBLIC OF CHINA (COUNTRY) SEE NOTES OVERLEAF
3. Means of transport and route (as far as known) FROM SHANGHAI TO LONDON BY S.S	4. For official use

5. Item number 1	6. Marks and numbers of packages MANDARS TXT200710 LONDON C/NO. 1—1 000	7. Number and kind of packages; description of goods LADIES DENIM SKIRT SAY TOTAL ONE THOUSAND (1 000) CARTONS ONLY ****************************	8. Origin criterion (see notes overleaf) "P"	9. Gross weight or other quantity G. W 140KGS	10. Number and date of invoices TX370 MAY 10, 2012

11. Certification is hereby certified, on the basis of control carried out, that the declaration by the exporter is correct ------------------------------------ Place and date, signature and stamp of certifying authority	12. Declaration by the exporter The undersigned hereby declares that the above details and statements are correct; that all the goods were produced in _____CHINA_____ (country) and that they comply with the origin requirements specified for those goods in the Generalized System of Preference for goods exported to ____U K____ (importing country) SHANGHAI MAY 10, 2012 方达 Place and date, signature of authorized signatory

中保财产保险有限公司
The People's Insurance (Property) Company of China, Ltd.

发票号码
Invoice No. TX370

保险单号次
Policy No. SH053101769

海洋货物运输保险单
MARINE CARGO TRANSPORTATION INSURANCE POLICY

被保险人
Insured: SHANGHAI YONGSHENG IMP. & EXP. CO.

中保财产保险有限公司(以下简称本公司)根据被保险人的要求，及其所缴付约定的保险费，按照本保险单承担的险别和背面所载条款及下列特别条款承保下列货物运输保险，特签发本保险单。

This policy of Insurance witnesses that The People's Insurance (Property) Company of China, Ltd. (hereinafter called "The Company"), at the request of the Insured and consideration of the premium paid by the Insures, undertakes to insure the under-mentioned goods in transportation subject to the condition of this Policy as per the Clauses printed overleaf and other special clauses attached hereon.

保险货物项目 Descriptions of Goods	包装 单位 数量 Packing Unit Quantity	保险金额 Amount Insured
LADIES DENIM SKIRT	1000 CARTONS	USD 138 600.00

承保险别: FOR 110% OF THE INVOICE VALUE COVERING 货物标记: AS PER INVOICE NO. TX370
Condition: ALL RISKS & WAR RISK AS PER PICC DATE 1/1/1981 Marks of Goods:

总保险金额:
Total Amount Insured: SAY US DOLLARS ONE HUNDRED AND THIRTY EIGHT THOUSAND SIX HUNDRED ONLY

保费: As arranged 运输工具: 开航日期:
Premium Per conveyance S.S DONGFANG V.190 Slg. On or abt MAY 30, 2012

起运港 目的港
From SHANGHAI To LONDON

所保货物，如发生本保险单项下可能引起索赔的损失或损坏，应立即通知本公司下述代理人查勘。如有索赔，应向本公司提交保险单正本(本保险单共有2份正本)及有关文件。如1份正本已用于索赔，其余正本则自动失效。

In the event of loss or damage which may result in a claim under this Policy, immediate notice must be given to the Company's Agent as mentioned hereunder. Claims, if any, one of the Original Policy which has been issued in TWO Original (s) together with the relevant documents shall be surrendered to the Company. If one of the Original Policy has been accomplished, the others to be void.

THE PEOPLE'S INSURANCE (PROPERTY) COMPANY OF CHINA, LTD. OSAKA BRANCH
98 LSKL MACH OSAKA JAPAN
TEL: 028-543657

中保财产保险有限公司
THE PEOPLE'S INSURANCE (PROPERTY) COMPANY OF CHINA, LTD.

赔款偿付地点
Claim payable at LONDON
日期 在
Date MAY 22, 2012 at SHANGHAI General Manager: 凡玲
地址:
Address:

Shipper SHANGHAI YONGSHENG IMP. & EXP. CO. 21 WEST ZHONGSHAN ROAD SHANGHAI CHINA		B/L NO. HJSHBI 1520876 **ORIGINAL** 中国对外贸易运输总公司 CHINA NATIONAL FOREIGN TRADE TRANSPORT CORPORATION 直运或转船提单 BILL OF LADING DIRECT OR WITH TRANSSHIPMENT
Consignee or order TO ORDER OF SHIPPER	colspan="2" rowspan="4"	SHIPPED on board in apparent good order and condition (unless otherwise indicated) the goods or packages specified herein and to be discharged or the mentioned port of discharge of as near there as the vessel may safely get and be always afloat. THE WEIGHT, measure, marks and numbers quality, contents and value, being particulars furnished by the Shipper, are not checked by the Carrier on loading. THE SHIPPER, Consignee and the Holder of this Bill of Lading hereby expressly accept and agree to all printed, written or stamped provisions, exceptions and conditions of this Bill of Lading, including those on the back hereof. IN WITNESS where of the number of original Bill of Loading stated below have been signed, one of which being accomplished, the other(s) to be void.
Notify address MANDARS IMPORTS CO. LTD. 38 QUEENSWAY, 2008 UK
Pre-carriage by	Port of loading SHANGHAI
Vessel DONGFANG V. 190	Port of transshipment
Port of discharge LONDON	Frail destination

Container Seal No. or Marks and Nos.	Number and kind of packages Designation of goods	Gross weight (kgs)	Measurement (m^3)
MANDARS TXT200710 LONDON C/NO. 1—1 000	LADIES DENIM SKIRT SAY ONE THOUSAND CARTONS ONLY TOTAL ONE 20' CONTAINER CFS TO CFS FREIGHT PREPAID	140 KGS	23.8CBM

REGARDING TRANSSHIPMENT INFORMATION PLEASE CONTACT		Freight and charge FRIGHT PREPAID
Ex. rate	Prepaid at	Fright payable at SHANGHAI	Place and date of issue SHANGHAI MAY 30, 2012
	Total Prepaid	Number of original Bs/L THREE	Signed for or on behalf of the Master as Agent 丁毅

SHANGHAI YONGSHENG IMP. & EXP. CO.
21 WEST ZHONGSHAN ROAD SHANGHAI, CHINA

SHIPPING ADVICE

TEL: 021-64500002
FAX: 021-64500003

TO MESSRS:
    MANDARS IMPORTS CO. LTD.
    38 QUEENSWAY, 2008 UK

INV. NO.: TX370
S/C NO.: TXT201210
L/C NO.: XT370
DATE: MAY 20, 2012

DEAR SIRS,
    WE HEREBY INFORM YOU THAT THE GOODS UNDER THE ABOVE MENTIONED CREDIT HAVE BEEN SHIPPED. THE DETAILS OF THE SHIPMENT ARE STATED BELOW.

COMMODITY:	LADIES DENIM SKIRT	SHIPPING MARKS
NUMBER OF CTNS:	1 000 CARTONS	MANDARS
TOTAL GROSS WEIGHT:	140 KGS	LONDON
OCEAN VESSEL:	DONGFANG V. 190	TXT201210
B/L NO.:	HJSHBI 1520876	C/NO. 1—1 000
PORT OF LOADING:	SHANGHAI	
DATE OF DEPARTURE:	MAY 30, 2012	
DESTINATION:	LONDON PORT	

SHANGHAI YONGSHENG IMP. & EXP. CO.
Da Fang

◎ 工作任务二　　办理出口收汇核销手续

初次办理出口收汇核销前，出口企业必须在本地外汇管理局办理核销备案登记，提供单位介绍信、申请书、外经贸部门批准经营进出口业务批件、企业法人营业执照、组织机构代码证和海关注册登记证明书等材料。核销备案登记后，领取有编号的纸质核销单，并进行填制，在领单90天内随附报关单据向海关报关。海关核准无误后，在核销单"海关签注栏"处加盖"验讫章"，退还出口企业。出口企业在汇票和发票上注明核销单编号，持全套结汇单据向银行办理议付。银行结汇后，在出口收汇核销结汇水单或收账通知上注明核销单号交出口企业。出口企业持经海关签章的收汇核销专用联、结汇水单或收账通知及报关单到外汇管理局办理核销。即期支付应在出口报关之日起100天内办理出口收汇核销手续，远期支付应当在合同规定收汇日起10天内办理出口收汇核销手续。外汇管理局在核销单上加盖"已核销"章后，将核销单和报关单（出口退税专用）交给出口企业。

上海永胜进出口公司方达先生填制核销单进行议付，得知本批货款已到账户上，及时到银行领取"中国银行进账单"的"收账通知"联和出口收汇核销专用"回单联"，在规定的时间内凭两票三单（外销发票、增值税发票、报关单、核销单、收汇水单）办理出口收汇核销。

中国银行开立结汇水单：
中国银行上海分行进账单(回单)

2007年8月10日　　　　　　　　　　　　　　　　第 060611 号

出票人	全称	MANDARS IMPORTS CO. LTD.	收款人	全称	上海永胜进出口贸易公司
	账号	FB44667755		账号	THY6684321337
	开户银行	LONDON BANK		开户银行	中国银行上海分行

美元：
USD 126 000.00

千	百	十	万	千	百	十	元	角	分
		1	2	6	0	0	0	0	0

票据种类	BP XT173	申报号码：
票据张数	核销单号：325623454	No.0606775588

(中国银行国际结算专用章)　　　　　　(出口收汇核销专用章)

海关返回签注的核销单：

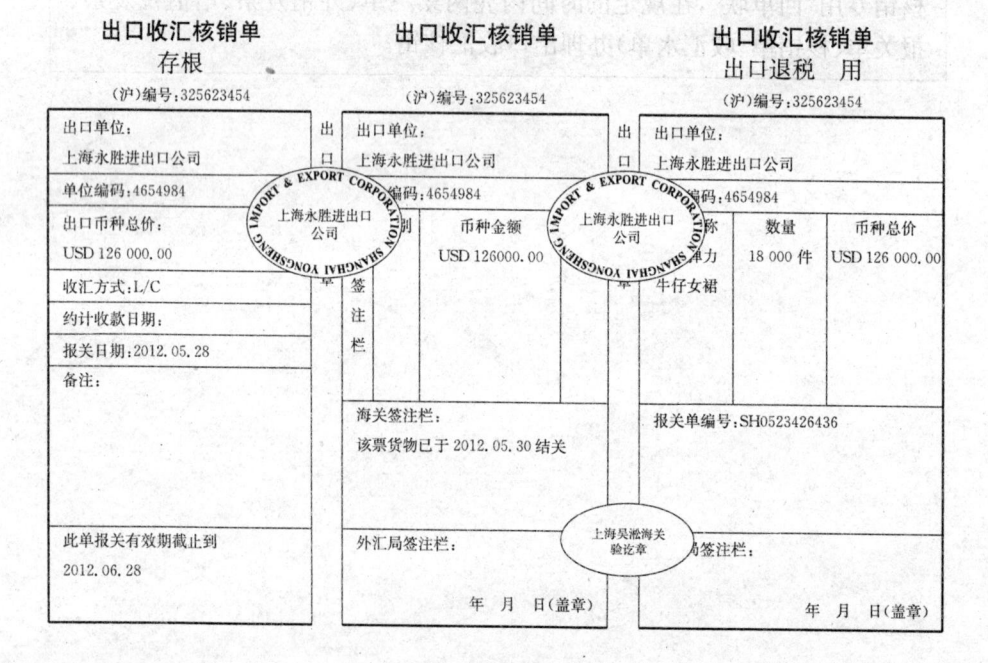

出口收汇核销单　　　**出口收汇核销单**　　　**出口收汇核销单**
　存根　　　　　　　　　　　　　　　　　　　出口退税　用

(沪)编号：325623454　　(沪)编号：325623454　　(沪)编号：325623454

出口单位：上海永胜进出口公司	出口	出口单位：上海永胜进出口公司	出口	出口单位：上海永胜进出口公司
单位编码：4654984	商品	编码：4654984	商品	编码：4654984
出口币种总价：USD 126 000.00	品名	币种金额：USD126000.00	品名规格：弹力牛仔女裙	数量：18 000 件　币种总价：USD 126 000.00
收汇方式：L/C	签注栏			
约计收款日期：				
报关日期：2012.05.28				
备注：		海关签注栏：该票货物已于2012.05.30结关		报关单编号：SH0523426436
此单报关有效期截止到 2012.06.28		外汇局签注栏： (上海吴淞海关验讫章)	签注栏：	
		年 月 日(盖章)		年 月 日(盖章)

银行返回签注的核销单：

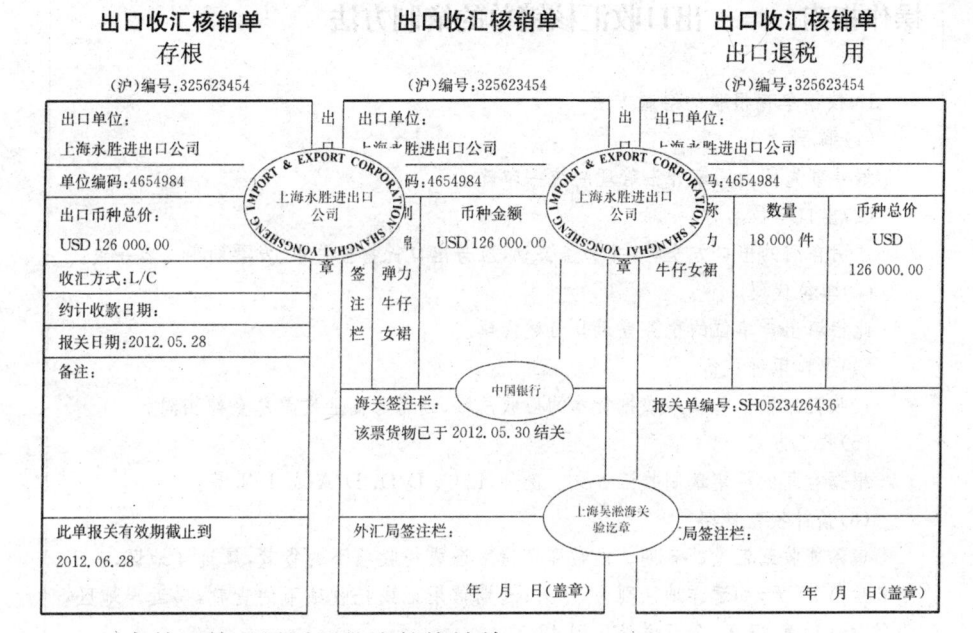

出口收汇核销单 存根	出口收汇核销单	出口收汇核销单 出口退税 用
（沪）编号：325623454	（沪）编号：325623454	（沪）编号：325623454
出口单位： 上海永胜进出口公司	出口单位： 上海永胜进出口公司	出口单位： 上海永胜进出口公司
单位编码：4654984	码：4654984	号：4654984
出口币种总价： USD 126 000.00	币种金额 USD 126 000.00	数量 18 000 件　币种总价 USD 126 000.00
收汇方式：L/C	签注栏：弹力牛仔女裙	名称：牛仔女裙
约计收款日期：		
报关日期：2012.05.28		报关单编号：SH0523426436
备注：	海关签注栏： 中国银行 该票货物已于2012.05.30结关 上海吴淞海关验讫章	
此单报关有效期截止到 2012.06.28	外汇局签注栏： 年 月 日（盖章）	局签注栏： 年 月 日（盖章）

国家外汇管理局返回签注的核销单：

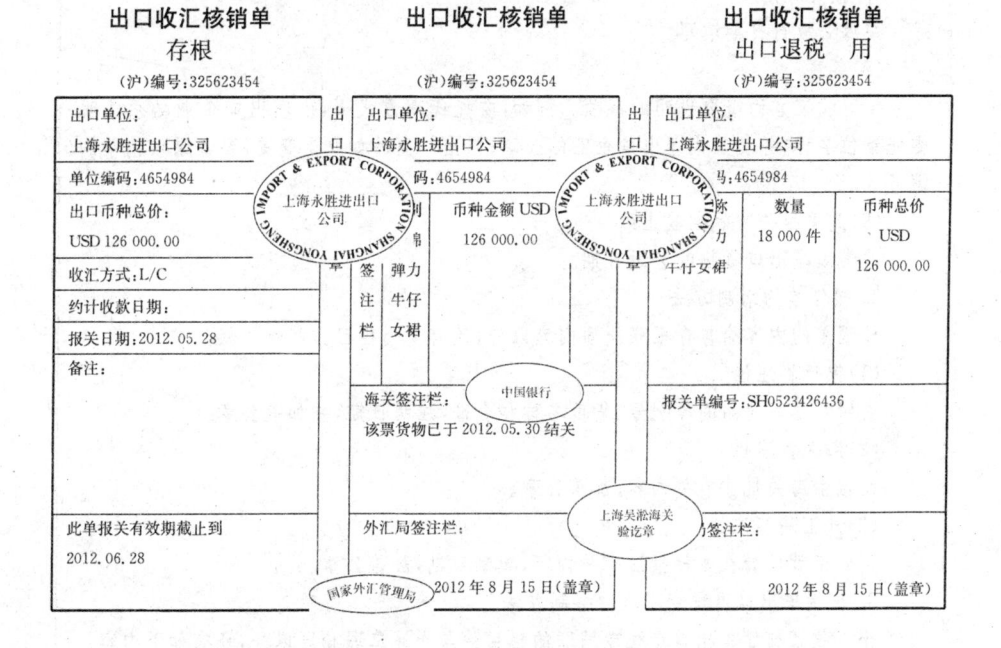

出口收汇核销单 存根	出口收汇核销单	出口收汇核销单 出口退税 用
（沪）编号：325623454	（沪）编号：325623454	（沪）编号：325623454
出口单位： 上海永胜进出口公司	出口单位： 上海永胜进出口公司	出口单位： 上海永胜进出口公司
单位编码：4654984	码：4654984	马：4654984
出口币种总价： USD 126 000.00	币种金额 USD 126 000.00	数量 18 000 件　币种总价 USD 126 000.00
收汇方式：L/C	签注栏：弹力牛仔女裙	名称：牛仔女裙
约计收款日期：		
报关日期：2012.05.28		报关单编号：SH0523426436
备注：	海关签注栏： 中国银行 该票货物已于2012.05.30结关 上海吴淞海关验讫章	
此单报关有效期截止到 2012.06.28	外汇局签注栏： 国家外汇管理局 2012年8月15日（盖章）	局签注栏： 2012年8月15日（盖章）

操作指南 ▶ 出口收汇核销单的缮制方法

1. 核销单存根联的缮制方法
(1)编号
编号事先已由国家外汇管理局统一印就。
(2)出口单位名称
注明合同的出口方全称,并加盖公章,应与出口货物报关单、发票同项内容一致。
(3)单位代码
此栏填出口单位的税务登记9位数代码。
(4)出口币种总价
按收汇的原币种填入该批货物的应收总额,通常与商业发票总金额相同。
(5)收汇方式
根据合同的规定填制收汇方式。例如,L/C、D/D、D/A 或 T/T 等。
(6)预计收款日期
填入能收到汇款的日期。通常即期信用证或托收项下的货款,属近洋地区,为寄单日后第25天,如远洋地区则为35天;远期信用证或托收项下的货款,属近洋地区,为付款日后第35天,如远洋地区则45天。
(7)报关日期
按海关放行日期填写。
(8)备注
填写收汇方面需要说明的事项。例如,委托代理方式下,代理出口企业必须注明委托单位名称,并加盖代理出口企业的公章;原出口商品如发生变更,要填原核销单的编号等。
(9)此单报关有效期截止到
通常填写出口货物的装运日期。
2. 核销单的缮制方法
核销单的内容除与存根联同项内容以外,还有下列栏目:
(1)银行签注栏
由银行填写商品的类别号、货币名称和金额,注明日期,并加盖公章。
(2)海关签注栏
此栏由海关批注有关内容,加盖公章。
(3)外汇局签注栏
由外汇管理局在本栏批注有关内容,填制日期,加盖公章。
3. 核销单出口退税专用联的缮制方法
出口收汇核销单出口退税专用联的栏目除与上述二联相同以外,还有如下内容:

续

> (1)货物名称
> 填实际出口货物名称,并与发票、出口货物报关单的品名一致。
> (2)数量
> 按包装方式的件数填写,应与报关单同项内容相符。
> (3)币种总价
> 按发票或报关单的总金额和币种填写。
> (4)报关单编号
> 按出口货报关单的实际编号填入。

工作任务三　　办理出口退汇手续

　　凡是有出口经营权并实行独立经济核算的企业单位都应向所在地主管退税业务的税务机关办理出口企业退税登记,否则不予以退税。出口企业向主管出口退税的国税机关申请退税时,须提交购进出口货物的专用发票(税款抵扣联)、经银行签章的税收(出口货物专用)缴款书、盖有海关验讫章的出口货物报关单、盖有外汇管理机关核销章的出口收汇核销单、出口销售发票和出口货物销售明细账等,并将申报出口退税的有关凭证按照顺序装订成册,以便于审核。出口企业必须在主管出口退税的国税机关规定的时间申报退税,过期退税国税机关不予受理。

　　上海永胜进出口贸易公司方达先生在办理好核销手续后,持该笔出口业务的外销发票、增值税专用发票、出口货物报关单(出口退税专用)、核销单(出口退税专用)等全套出口退税单证到国家税务局办理出口退税申报手续。

　　将核销单(出口退税专用联)、报关单(退税联)、商业发票、增值税发票、出口专用缴税书等文件连同"外贸企业出口货物退税汇总申报表"交税务局办理退税。

　　上海永胜进出口贸易公司收到增值税专用发票和税收(出口货物专用)缴款:

上海市增值税专用发票
抵扣联

开票日期：2012 年 6 月 5 日　　　　　　　　　　　　　　　　　　NO. 06053011

购货单位	名称	上海永胜进出口公司	密码区	
	纳税人识别号	3101466775532		
	地址、电话	上海市中山西路 21 号　65788877		
	开户银行及账号	中国银行上海分行　THY6684321337		

货物或应税劳务名称	规格型号	单位	数量	单价	金额	税率	税额
全棉弹力牛仔女裙		件	18 000	￥50.00	￥900 000.00	17%	￥153 000.00
合　计			18 000	￥50.00	￥900 000.00	17%	￥153 000.00

价税合计（大写）	壹拾伍万叁仟元整

销货单位	名称	南通服装公司	备注
	纳税人识别码	310457654221	
	地址、电话	南通市人民路 11 号	
	开户银行及账号	南通市工商银行人民支行 0086132733658	

注：纳税人识别号即纳税人登记号。

中华人民共和国
税收（出口货物专用）缴款

060510 号

经济类型：国有经济　　　填发日期 2012 年 6 月 30 日　　　征收机关：上海市国税局

缴款单位	税务登记号	0 3 2 0 4 8 6 5 1 2	预算科目	款	
	全称	南通服装公司		项	
	开户银行	南通市工商银行人民支行		级次	
	账号	0086132733658	收款国库	市金库	

购货企业	全称	上海永胜进出口公司	销货发票号码	06053011
	税务登记号	0 2 4 3 5 6 8 8 1 5		
	海关代码	0387124666		

税款所属时期	2012 年 6 月 30 日	税款限缴日期	2012 年 6 月 30 日

货物名称	课税数量	单位价格	计税金额	法定税率（额）	征税率	实缴税额
全棉弹力牛仔女裙	18 000 件	￥50.00	￥900 000.00	17%	17%	￥153 000.00
金额合计	（大写）壹拾伍万叁仟元整					￥153 000.00

缴款单位（盖章） （南通服装公司） 经办人：王丁	税务机关（盖章） （南通税务局） 填票人：张言	上列款项已收妥并划转缴款单位账户 （南通工商银行） 国库（银行）盖章 2012 年 6 月 30 日	备注

第二联（收据乙）国库（经收处）收款盖章后退缴款单位转交购货企业，逾期不缴按税法规定加收滞纳金

方达先生填制出口货物退税汇总申报表：

外贸企业出口货物退税汇总申报表
（适用于增值税一般纳税人）

申报年月：2012年8月 　　　　　　　　　　　　　　　　申报批次：1
纳税人识别号：0243568
海关代码：0387124666
纳税人名称(公章)：　　　　　　　日期：2012年8月31日　　　　金额单位：元至角分、美元

出口企业申报	主管退税机关审核		
出口退税出口明细申报表 1 份，记录 25 条	审单情况	机审情况	
出口发票　　1张,出口额　126 000.00 美元	本次机审通过退增值税额　　　　元		
出口报关单　　1张,	其中：上期结转疑点退增值税　　元		
代理出口货物证明　　　张,	本期申报数据退增值税　　元		
收汇核销单　1张,收汇额 126 000.00 美元			
远期收汇证明　　张,其他凭证　张	本次机审通过退消费税额　　　　元		
出口退税进货明细申报表　1份,记录 24 条	其中：上期结转疑点退消费税　　元		
增值税专用发票　1张,其中非税控专用发票　张	本期申报数据退消费税　　元		
普通发票　　1张,专用税票　　张	本次机审通过消费税额　　　　　元		
其他凭证　　张,总进货金额　　　元	结余疑点数据退增值税　　　　　元		
总进货税额　153 000.00 元,	结余疑点数据退消费税　　　　　元		
其中：增值税　153 000.00 元,消费税　　元	授权人申明		
本月申报退税额　153 000.00 元,			
其中：增值税　153 000.00 元,消费税　　元	（如果你已委托代理申报人,请填写以下资料）		
进料应抵扣税额　　元,			
申请开具单证	为代理出口货物退税申报事宜,现授权____为本纳税人的代理申报人,任何与本申报表有关的往来文件都可寄与此人。		
代理出口货物证明　　　份,记录　　条			
代理进口货物证明　　　份,记录　　条			
进料加工免税证明　　　份,记录　　条			
来料加工免税证明　　　份,记录　　条	授权人签字(盖章)		
出口货物转内销证明　　份,记录　　条			
补办报关单证明　　　　份,记录　　条			
补办收汇核销单证明　　份,记录　　条			
补办代理出口证明　　　份,记录　　条	审单人：	审核人：	
内销抵扣专用发票　1张,其他非退税专用发票　张		年　月　日	
申报人声明	签批人：(公章)		
此表各栏目填报内容是真实、合法的,与实际出口货物情况相符。此次申报的出口业务不属于"四自三不见"等违背正常出口经营程序的出口业务。否则,本企业愿承担由此产生的相关责任。			
	年　月　日		
企业填表人：方达 财务负责人：岷山 企业负责人：方达			

受理人：　　　　　　　　　　　　　　　　　　　受理日期：　年　月　日
受理税务机关(签章)：

操作指南 ➡ **外贸企业出口货物退税汇总申报表填制方法**

根据《中华人民共和国税收征收管理法实施细则》第38条及国家税务总局有关规定填制外贸企业出口退税汇总申报表。

1. 申报年月
填外贸企业出口退税申报的时间。
2. 申报批次
填外贸企业出口退税申报所属时间内第几次申报。
3. 纳税人识别号
填税务登记证号码。
4. 海关代码
填外贸企业在海关的注册编号。
5. 纳税人名称
填写纳税人单位名称全称,不得填写简称。
6. 申报日期
填外贸企业向主管退税机关申报退税的日期。
其他表内各栏的内容,根据现行退税审批政策相关的规则填写。

操作指南 ➡ **出口货物退税应注意事项**

1. 出口货物退税的范围

凡在进出口贸易中已征的产品税、增值税和特别消费税的产品,除国家明确规定不予退还以外,都予以退税。

2. 出口货物退税所具备的条件

属于增值税和消费税征税范围的货物;经出口报关离境的货物,以加盖海关验讫章的出口报关单和出口销售发票为准;出口货物必须已经结汇(部分货物除外);已在财务会计上做出口销售处理;提供退税机关规定的有关单据。

同时,国家也明确规定了少数出口产品即使具备上述条件,也不予以退税。其出口货物主要有:出口的原油,援外出口产品,国家禁止出口的产品,出口企业收购外商投资的产品,来料加工、来料装配的出口产品,军需工厂销售给军队系统的出口产品,军工系统出口的企业范围,齐鲁、扬子、大庆三大乙烯工程生产的产品等。

3. 出口货物的退税鉴定

凡经营出口产品的企业,均应填写"出口产品退税鉴定表",报经所在地主管出口

续

退税业务的税务机关审核批准后执行。

4. 出口货物的费用扣除

出口企业采购出口商品，应在库存出口商品账上将产品的出厂金额与购进等各项费用分开记账。产品出口后，出口商品销售账能反映出厂金额的，应按账上记载的出厂金额经税务机关审核后据以计算退税；出口商品销售账不能反映出厂金额的，应按库存出口商账上记载的各项费用采取核定费用扣除率的办法经税务机关审核后予以扣除。

5. 出口货物退税的单据

出口销售发票必须详细列明合同号或订单号、货物名称、规格、数量、单价、贸易总额、运输工具和起止地点，并有发货人的签名或印章。

进货发票必须有套印税务机关发票制章，并盖有供货单位的印章。工贸自营出口或委托出口的产品，非专业外贸企业出口的产品，申请退税时，必须提供银行结汇水单，并在结汇水单内注明核销单编号，税务机关查验后将其退还出口企业。专业外贸企业申请退税时提供结汇水单确有实际困难的，以及用于对外承包的成套设备和国家允许中、远期结汇的出口产品，可延期提供水单。

综合业务模拟操作

操作一

1. 操作资料

卖　方：	南京永发进出口公司
	南京中山路 1321 号
	TEL：025-23501111　FAX：025-23502222
买　方：	JIM KING TRADING CORPORATION
	No. 206 CHANGJ NORTH STREET SINGAPORE
	TEL：218-76911　FAX：218-76912
合同号：	wy070901
开证银行：	SINGAPORE BANK（地址：205 KAWARA，SINGAPORE）
信用证号：	NB4567
开证日期：	20120910
支付时间：	见票后 30 天付款
信用证金额：	7 560.00 美元
货　名：	电动钻头（Electric Drill）No. TY242
数　量：	1 800 套
发票号码：	SG123

报关单编号： NH2523426436

2.操作要求

(1)请你以南京永发进出口公司业务员张丽的身份,根据上述资料、销售合同书和信用证的有关内容填写商业汇票。

BILL OF EXCHANGE

No. _____

For _____

Date

At _____ sight of this SECOND BILL of EXCHANGE (first of the same tenor and date unpaid) pay to the order of _____ the sum of

Drawn under _____

L/C No. _____ Dated _____

To _____

(2)请你以南京永发进出口公司业务员张丽的身份,根据上述资料、销售合同书和信用证的有关内容填写出口收汇核销单。

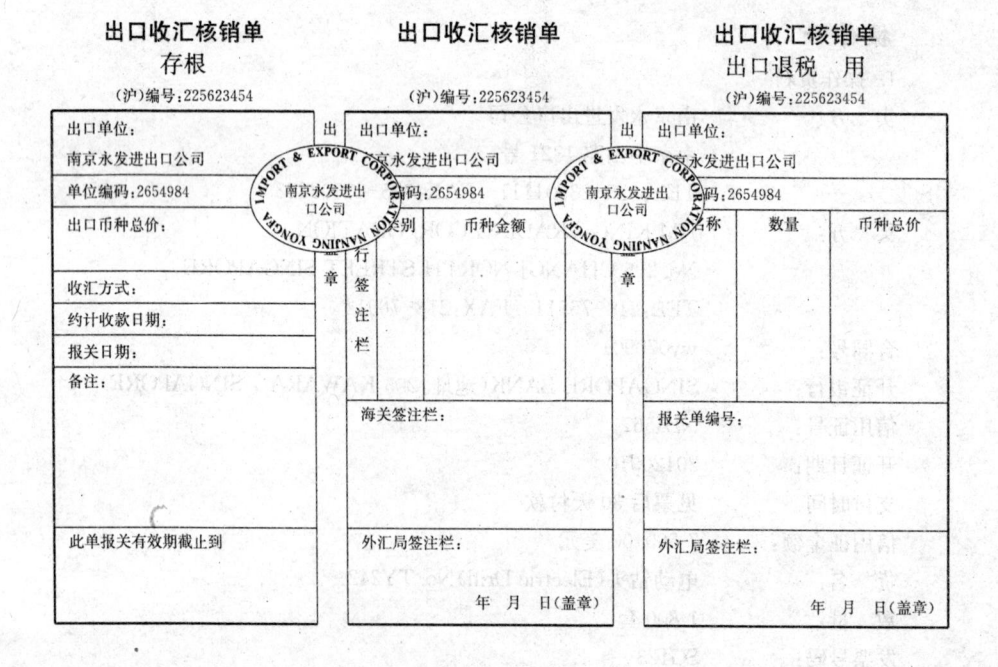

出口收汇核销单 存根	出口收汇核销单	出口收汇核销单 出口退税 用
(沪)编号:225623454	(沪)编号:225623454	(沪)编号:225623454
出口单位: 南京永发进出口公司	出口单位: 南京永发进出口公司	出口单位: 南京永发进出口公司
单位编码:2654984	编码:2654984	编码:2654984
出口币种总价:	类别 / 币种金额	名称 / 数量 / 币种总价
收汇方式:	行签注栏	
约计收款日期:		
报关日期:		
备注:	海关签注栏:	报关单编号:
此单报关有效期截止到	外汇局签注栏: 年 月 日(盖章)	外汇局签注栏: 年 月 日(盖章)

操作二

1. 操作资料

卖　方：广州纺织品进出口公司
　　　　广州市北京路 530 号
　　　　TEL:(020)64043030　FAX:(020)64043031

买　方：OLEARA IMPORT & EXPORT CORPORATION
　　　　310-224 HOLA STREET MARSEILLE FRANCE
　　　　TEL:491-38241234

合同号：　ST071032
开证银行：CITY BANK MARSEILLE BRANCH(地址:1025 WEST GEORGIA STREET MARSEILLE, FRANCE)
信用证号：07/CB4578
开证日期：2012 年 6 月 20 日
支付方式：不可撤销跟单即期信用证
信用证金额：40 500.00 美元
货　名：男式衬衫 Art No. 88(蓝色)、Art No. 44(黑色)
数　量：Art No. 88(蓝色)3 000 件、Art No. 44(黑色)3 000 件
发票号码：GZT00021
报关单编号：GZ1343426436

2. 操作要求

(1)请你以广州纺织品进出口公司业务员王伟的身份，根据上述资料、销售合同书和信用证的有关内容填写商业汇票。

BILL OF EXCHANGE

凭_____　不可撤销信用证
Drawn under　　　　　　　　　Irrevocable L/C No._____

Date _____支取 Payable With interest @ _____ %　按 _____ 息 _____ 付款

号码　　　　　　　　　　　汇票金额　　　　　　　　　上海
No. _____　　Exchange for _____　Shanghai _____

见票 _____ 日后(本汇票之副本未付)付交　　　　　　　　　金额
AT　＊　＊　＊　＊. _____ sight of this FIRST of Exchange (Second of Exchange being unpaid) Pay to the order of _____ the sum of

款已收讫
Value received _____
此致：
To _____
　　_____

_____

131

(2) 请你以广州纺织品进出口公司业务员王伟的身份，根据上述资料、销售合同书和信用证的有关内容填写出口收汇核销单。

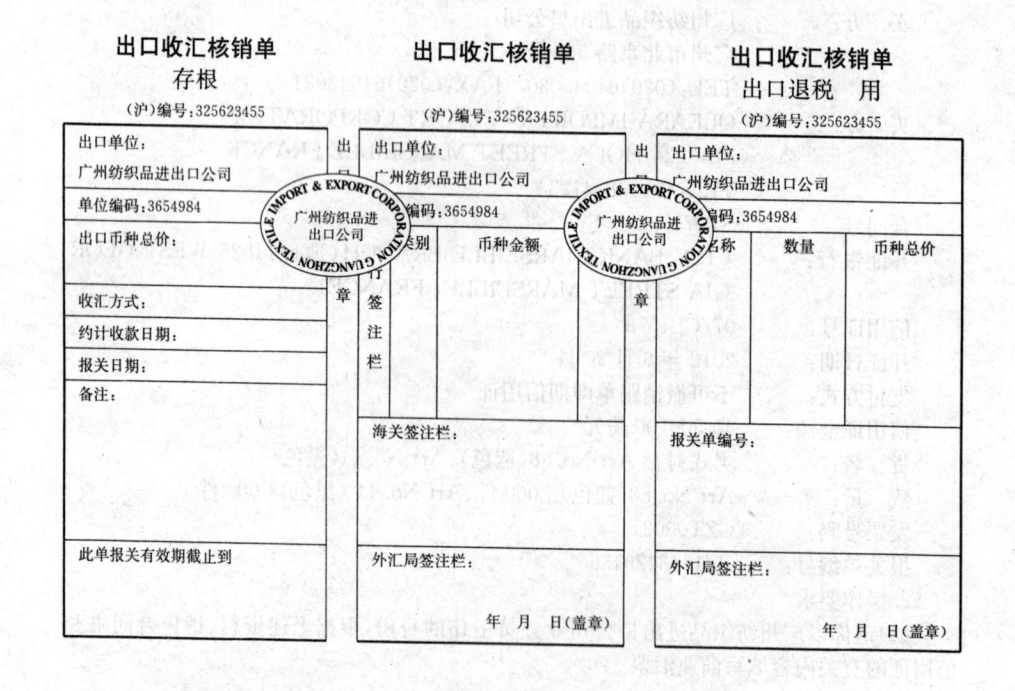

出口收汇核销单
存根

（沪）编号：325623455

出口单位：	
广州纺织品进出口公司	
单位编码：3654984	
出口币种总价：	
收汇方式：	
约计收款日期：	
报关日期：	
备注：	
此单报关有效期截止到	

出口收汇核销单

（沪）编号：325623455

出口单位：		
广州纺织品进出口公司		
编码：3654984		
类别	币种金额	
签注栏		
海关签注栏：		
外汇局签注栏：		
	年 月 日（盖章）	

出口收汇核销单
出口退税 用

（沪）编号：325623455

出口单位：		
广州纺织品进出口公司		
编码：3654984		
名称	数量	币种总价
报关单编号：		
外汇局签注栏：		
	年 月 日（盖章）	

132

体验活动三　代理出口贸易业务

工作情景

上海进出口贸易公司是一家专业进出口贸易公司，主要代理手工工具、棉纺织品、玩具、茶叶和文化用品等进出口业务，深受欧洲、北美、东南亚国家和地区的客户欢迎。在今年春季华交会上，日本客商 FUJIYAMA TRADING CORPORATION 的山本先生，对该公司展览的手工工具活络扳手样品很感兴趣，上海进出口贸易公司业务员卢珍小姐对山本先生进行了热情详细的介绍，并呈送了大量的资料和样品。山本先生回国后，将资料与活络扳手样品送至其用户进行研究和确认。数日后，山本先生获知用户对样品的质量、用材和规格予以认可，立即通过邮件与卢珍小姐联系，于是双方进行了贸易洽谈，采用CPT价格条件、航空运输和电汇支付方式。达成交易后，双方签订了销售确认书。

合同签订后，上海进出口贸易公司业务员卢珍小姐委托上海国际货代公司办理货物运输手续，与此同时，向上海出入境检验检疫局和海关办理报检和报关手续，确保按合同规定的时间履行交货义务。出口结汇后，还要办理出口收汇核销和出口退税。

代理出口业务流程如下图所示。

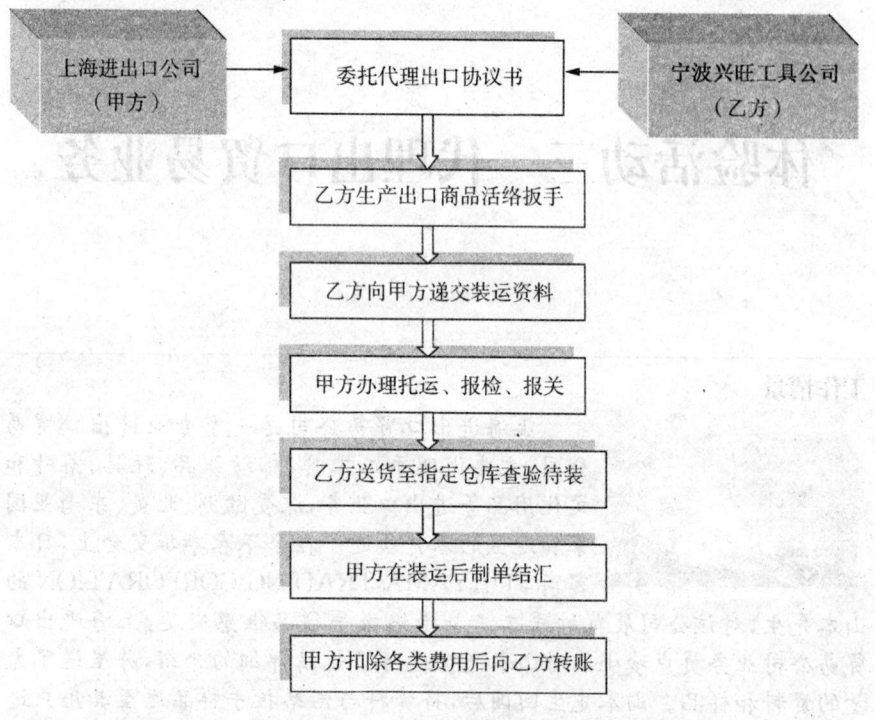

```
上海进出口公司  →  委托代理出口协议书  ←  宁波兴旺工具公司
   （甲方）                                    （乙方）
                        ↓
              乙方生产出口商品活络扳手
                        ↓
              乙方向甲方递交装运资料
                        ↓
              甲方办理托运、报检、报关
                        ↓
              乙方送货至指定仓库查验待装
                        ↓
              甲方在装运后制单结汇
                        ↓
              甲方扣除各类费用后向乙方转账
```

实训一　出口贸易合同的商订

业务导入

日本客商 FUJIYAMA TRADING CORPORATION 从春季华交会上带回的手工工具活络扳手样品经其用户确认后，山本先生用电子邮件向上海进出口贸易公司发盘。业务员卢珍小姐收到发盘后向业务经理请示，在确认同意发盘的交易条件后，写接受函发送给山本先生。数日后，卢珍小姐拟订了销售确认书，经业务经理和宁波兴旺工具厂主管确认后签章，交由 FUJIYAMA TRADING CORPORATION 客商会签。

出口贸易合同商订的业务环节如下图所示。

体验活动三 代理出口贸易业务

续

① 发盘
② 接受
③ 签订合同

出口商　　　　　　　　　　　　　　进口商

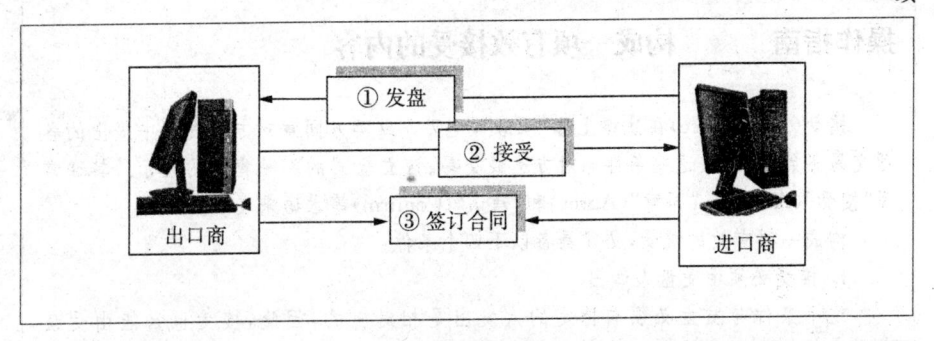

工作任务一　　　　拟写接受函

卢珍小姐收到了日本客商 FUJIYAMA TRADING CORPORATION 山本先生的发盘,随即向业务经理请示。为此,上海进出口贸易公司与宁波兴旺工具公司共同商议,决定同意发盘的全部交易条件,并请卢珍小姐写接受函发送给山本先生。

发件人：SHMYGS@HOTMAIL.COM
收件人：fujiyama@hotmail.com
主　题：ACCEPTANCE

Dear Mr. TKAMR,

Thank you for your letter of SEP. 01, 2012.

We would like to inform you that we accept your proposal as follows:

GOODS OF DESCRIPTIONS	QUANTITY	UNIT PRICE	AMOUNT
DOUBLE OPEN END SPANNER		CPT OSAKA	
8×10MM(MTM)	60 000 PCS	USD 0.50	USD 30 000.00
10×12MM(MTM)	80 000 PCS	USD 0.60	USD 48 000.00

Shipment: not later than DEC. 20, 2012 by air
Payment: by 30% T/T in advance, the others 70% T/T after shipment
Packing: Packed in 1 400 cartons of 100 pcs each
Insurance: For 110 percent of the invoice value covering all risks & war risk
We are looking forward to your initial order.

　　　　　　　　　Yours truly,
　　　　　　　　　SHANGHAI IMPORT & EXPORT CORPORATION
　　　　　　　　　ZHEN LU
　　　　　　　　　SEP. 04, 2012

操作指南 ➡ **构成一项有效接受的内容**

接受(Acceptance)在法律上称"承诺",是买方或卖方同意对方在发盘中提出的各项交易条件,并愿按这些条件与对方达成交易、订立合同的一种肯定的表示。其通常用"接受"(Accept)、"同意"(Agree)和"确认"(Confirm)等术语来表示。

构成一项有效的接受,必须具备以下四个条件:

1. 接受必须由受盘人做出

这一条件与发盘必须向特定的人发出是相对应的,因此,接受也只能由受盘人做出,才具有效力。其他任何人对发盘表示同意,不能构成接受,合同也就不会成立。

2. 接受必须表示出来

受盘人必须以口头或书面的形式向发盘人明确表示,还可用行为表示接受。例如,某进口商向出口商发盘,由于发盘内容明确,所列条件又符合出口商的要求,出口商接到发盘后,马上将货物装运出去;或买方同意卖方在发盘中提出的交易条件,并随即支付货款或开出信用证。

3. 接受必须在发盘的有效期内传达到发盘人

发盘中规定有效期是约束发盘人承担义务,在有效期内不能任意撤销或修改发盘的内容。同时,受盘人只有在有效期内作出的接受,才具备法律效力。如果发盘没有规定接受的时限,则受盘人应在合理时间内表示接受。

4. 接受必须与发盘相符

接受必须是无条件地同意发盘的全部条件,这样才能达成交易,订立合同。在实际业务中,常有这种情况,受盘人在答复中使用了"接受"、"同意"等的字眼,但又对发盘的商品价格、付款、质量、数量、交货地点和时间等实质性的内容做了增加、限制或修改,这在法律上不能构成有效的接受,其实质仍属于还盘。

▶ **工作任务二** 　　**签订委托代理协议书**

卢珍小姐向日本客商 FUJIYAMA TRADING CORPORATION 山本先生发出接受函后,由于成交的手工工具活络扳手是受宁波兴旺工具公司委托出口的,为此上海进出口贸易公司要与该公司签订该笔业务的委托代理出口协议书,作为双方各自履行合同义务的依据。

委托代理出口协议书

编号：20075612

甲方(受托方)：上海进出口贸易公司
　　　　　　上海市中山路 1321 号
　　　　　　TEL：(021) 65788877　Fax：(021) 65788876
乙方(委托方)：宁波兴旺工具公司
　　　　　　宁波市木行路 302 号
　　　　　　TEL：(0574) 65788877　Fax：(0574) 65788876

经双方友好协商，就乙方委托甲方代理出口的有关事项达成如下协议：
一、乙方委托甲方向___甲___方选定的客户 FUJIYAMA TRADING CORPORATION 代理出口，具体内容如下：
1.1　品名规格：手工工具活络扳手 8×10 MM（MTM）、10×12 MM（MTM）
1.2　品质标准：参照样品 NG07-321
1.3　数量：8×10 MM（MTM）60 000 件、10×12 MM（MTM）80 000 件
1.4　单价：8×10 MM（MTM）每件 0.50 美元、10×12 MM（MTM）每件 0.60 美元 CPT OSAKA
1.5　总金额：78 000.00 美元
1.6　支付方式：T/T
1.7　包装：每 100 件装入一个出口纸箱
1.8　装运地：上海
1.9　目的地：大阪
1.10　装运期限：2012 年 12 月 20 日
1.11　装运方式：航空运输
以上条款如有变动，以售货确认书及经双方认可的修改文件为准。
二、甲方接受乙方委托，以自己的名义代理以下事项：
2.1　对外签约
2.2　托运订舱
2.3　办理出口商检、报关
2.4　制单、结汇
2.5　涉外索赔、理赔
三、交货要求：
3.1　乙方交货期限：2012 年 12 月 10 日（或凭甲方书面通知）
3.2　交货地点：甲方指定地点
3.3　交货方式：乙方送货并承担货物到达上述地点前的各项费用

四、费用及结算：
  4.1 甲方向乙方收取出口发票金额的 3 ‰作为代理手续费。
  4.2 甲方在出口过程中垫付的费用（如报关费、商检费、运费、办证费等）均由乙方承担，在收汇后从结汇人民币金额中扣除。

五、甲方权利和义务：
  5.1 甲方根据本协议书的约定，与外商签订售货确认书。
  5.2 甲方在签订售货确认书前应将售货确认书副本送交乙方，经乙方签字认可。乙方如有异议，应于收到售货确认书副本后次日起3个工作日内以书面形式向甲方提出，逾期视为无异议。
  凡经乙方认可的售货确认书条款，乙方不得由于条款本身的缺陷引起的损失向甲方要求补偿。
  5.3 甲方如对售货确认书作重大的实质性修改或变更，事先需经乙方书面确认。
  5.4 甲方根据乙方提供的资料，按照合同规定编制托运单据，办理托运手续。事先商定凭甲方通知交货的，甲方应及时将交货时间、地点通知乙方。
  5.5 甲方应按双方商定的方式及期限与乙方结算货款、代理手续费及代垫费用。部分代垫费用一时无法结算的，甲方可先按估计金额向乙方收取，事后按实际金额结算，多退少补。
  5.6 甲方收汇后应根据乙方提供的增值税发票、税收专用缴款书等有关单据办理出口退税手续，退税所得金额由甲方划交乙方。
  5.7 外商无故不履行部分或全部合同，或拖欠货款长期不付清，甲方应负责向外商催促履约付款，或与乙方商讨采取必要措施，为此发生的一切费用及后果由乙方承担；如客户由乙方指定，甲方已与客户商定解决办法，则依乙方与客户商定的办法处理。
  5.8 本协议书签订后，由于非甲方的原因而未能签订售货确认书，甲方免除责任。售货确认书签订后，甲方应认真履行本协议书规定由其承担的义务，否则须赔偿乙方因此而造成的损失。
  5.9 因外商违约导致本协议书不能部分或全部履行，甲方免除责任，但须及时代乙方对外索赔，并将索赔所得转给乙方。索赔所发生的费用由甲方承担。若因甲方过错未及时对外索赔，损失由甲方承担，若因乙方过错未及时对外索赔，损失由乙方自负。

六、乙方权利和义务：
  6.1 乙方必须在本协议书规定的交货期前备妥委托甲方代理出口的商品，以书面形式通知甲方，并按甲方的要求将商品运到指定地点，送入指定仓库，承担相关的费用。
  6.2 乙方提供的商品必须符合本协议书规定出口商品的品质标准，同时必须符合我国知识产权法有关规定，相应承担法律责任。如果由于乙方逾期交货或所交货物产生质量问题，或因知识产权纠纷而引起外商索赔，则由乙方负全部责任，乙方必须无条件接受索赔结果并支付赔偿金。
  6.3 乙方在交货的同时必须提供完整、准确的交货单、装箱单、厂检证或换证凭单、出口包装证明等必备单据，并给予甲方合理的时间制作出口单证，安排托运。乙方需承担由于资料错误引起的后果。

6.4 乙方同意以 T/T 方式由甲方向外商收汇，在售货确认书中订明，如非甲方的过错，甲方不承担收汇的风险。

6.5 乙方应在交货后 10 天内向甲方提供增值税发票、税收专用缴款书等必备单据，供甲方办理退税手续，退税所得金额由甲方划交乙方。

6.6 当外商提出索赔时，甲方应及时向乙方转交外商提出的索赔函电复印件及有关证件，乙方收到后应及时弄清情况，通过甲方对外理赔，甲方应及时向乙方通报对外理赔情况。由于乙方的责任，未能及时对外理赔，乙方除承担对外商的一切经济、法律责任外，还应负责赔偿甲方所受到的一切损失。

6.7 发生对外理赔或索赔时，乙方应及时书面委托甲方处理，向甲方提供有效证据及预支有关费用（包括出国费用、律师费、仲裁或诉讼费等），并承担理赔、索赔后果及因乙方不作为（包括不委托、不付款等）导致的一切后果。

6.8 乙方违反本协议书时，应偿付甲方代垫的费用及利息，支付代理手续费及售货确认书总价 10 %的违约金，并承担甲方因此对外承担的责任。

七、因不可抗力事件导致本协议书不能部分或全部履行，当事方必须在事发一周内通知对方，并在30天内向对方送交有关机构的书面证明，及时协商处理未尽事宜，逾期视作违约。

八、双方在执行本协议书过程中如遇争议，应协商解决，如协商无效，任何一方都可向中国国际经济贸易仲裁委员会上海分会仲裁，或甲方所在地人民法院起诉。

九、本协议书正本一式两份，经双方签字盖章后生效。

上海进出口贸易公司　　　　　　宁波兴旺工具公司
　　合同专用章　　　　　　　　　　合同专用章

甲方(盖章)：卢珍　　　　　　　乙方(盖章)：李江
日期：2012年9月8日　　　　　日期：2012年9月8日
地点：上海　　　　　　　　　　　地点：上海

> ### ◎ 工作任务三　　　　拟订销售确认书
>
> 　　上海进出口贸易公司与宁波兴旺工具公司签订该笔业务的委托代理出口协议后，卢珍小姐根据接受函和协议的规定拟订销售确认书一式两份，经业务经理和宁波兴旺工具公司主管确认后签章，并交由 FUJIYAMA TRADING CORPORATION 客商会签。合同经进出口双方签章后生效，双方各持一份，作为合同履行的依据。

上海进出口贸易公司
SHANGHAI IMPORT & EXPORT TRADE CORPORATION
1321 ZHONGSHAN ROAD SHANGHAI CHINA
SALES CONFIRMATION

Post code: 200032　　　　　　　　　　　　　S/C No.: TXT06081
Fax: (021) 65788876
TEL: (021) 65788877　　　　　　　　　　　　DATE: SEP. 10, 2012
TO MESSRS:
　　FUJIYAMA TRADING CORPORATION
　　121, KAWARA MACH OSAKA JAPAN

Dear Sirs,
　　We hereby confirm having sold to you the following goods on terms and conditions as specified below:

GOODS OF DESCRIPTIONS	QUANTITY	UNIT PRICE	AMOUNT
DOUBLE OPEN END SPANNER		CPT OSAKA	
8×10MM (MTM)	60 000 PCS	USD 0.50	USD 30 000.00
10×12MM (MTM)	80 000 PCS	USD 0.60	USD 48 000.00

　1) TERMS OF PAYMENT: 30% T/T IN ADVANCE, THE OTHERS 70% T/T AFTER SHIPMENT.
　2) AIRPORT OF DEPARTURE: PUDONG AIRPORT SHANGHAI, CHINA
　3) AIRPORT OF DESTINATION: OSAKA AIRPORT JAPAN
　4) LATEST DATE OF SHIPMENT: DEC. 20, 2012
　5) PACKED IN 1 400 CARTONS OF 100 PCS EACH.
OUR BANK INFORMATION IS AS BELOW:
BANK NAME: BANK OF CHINA SHANGHAI BRANCH
ACCOUNT NO.: RMB80456861

THE BUYER: FUJIYAMA TRADING CORPORATION　　　　THE SELLER 上海进出口贸易公司 合同专用章
　　　　　　山本　　　　　　　　　　　　　　　　　　　　　　　卢珍

综合业务模拟操作

操作一

1. 操作资料

在本年度华交会上,日本 YAMADA TRADE CO.,LTD(地址:310 SKURAMAJI OSAKA JAPAN TEL:028-38241234 FAX:028-38241235)的山田社长对苏州玩具进出口贸易公司(苏州市虎丘路130号;TEL:0512-64043030;FAX:0512-64043030)的展品汽车模型玩具很感兴趣。展销会结束后,苏州玩具进出口贸易公司业务员李霞小姐向日本客户发送邮件。报价如下:"货号:Art No.101(BLUE)每只4.2美元,Art No.102(BLACK)每只4.2美元,Art No.103(RED)每只4美元,Art No.104(YELLOW)每只3美元,CPT大阪;支付方式:30%前 T/T,70%后 T//T;包装:每只玩具装一个泡沫塑料袋,再装入一个小纸箱中,20只小纸箱装一个出口纸箱,由卖方制定唛头;交货时间:不迟于2012年5月31日;运输方式:航空运输。"YAMADA TRADE CO.,LTD 收到发盘后,经研究决定同意苏州玩具进出口贸易公司提出的交易条件,进口数量为每种型号各30 000只。

补充资料:

(1)分批装运:不允许

(2)转　　运:不允许

(3)装运地:苏州

(4)目的地:大阪

(5)合同号:SZHTY070315

(6)合同日期:2012.03.15

2. 实训要求

(1)请你以苏州玩具进出口公司业务员李霞的身份,根据上述资料用英语拟写一份发盘函,要求内容正确,格式完整。

```
                          OFFER
_____




```

(2)请你以苏州玩具进出口公司业务员李霞的身份，根据上述资料拟订一份销售确认书，要求格式完整、内容正确，并要签字盖章。

苏州玩具进出口公司
SUZHOU TOY IMPORT & EXPORT CORPORATION
130 HUQIU ROAD SUZHOU, CHINA
SALES CONFIRMATION

TEL:_____   S/C NO.:_____
FAX:_____   DATE:_____
TO:_____

Dear Sirs,
　　We hereby confirm having sold to you the following goods on terms and conditions as specified below:

MARKS & NO.	DESCRIPTIONS OF GOODS	QUANTITY	U/ PRICE	AMOUNT

LOADING PORT:_____
DESTINATION:_____
PARTIAL SHIPMENT:_____
TRANSSHIPMENT:_____
PAYMENT:_____
TIME OF SHIPMENT:_____

THE BUYER: THE SELLER:

体验活动三　代理出口贸易业务

操作二

1. 操作资料

宁波进出口贸易公司(地址：宁波市百丈路 678 号；电话：0574-87551112 传真：0574-87551113)主要经营各种手工工具、电动工具和汽车喇叭等轻工业产品。近日，该公司收到老客户美商 YAMOO IMPORT & EXPORT TRADING CORPORATION(地址：No. 206 CHANGJ NORTH STREET NEWYORK USA；TEL：212-7691134；FAX：212-76911135)的询盘，要求对汽车喇叭报价。对此，宁波进出口贸易公司业务员张力先生向美商发盘。具体内容如下："单价：CPT NEWYORK No. XY122 每套 USD1.50、No. HY132 每套 USD 2.10、No. TY242 每套 USD 4.40；支付方式：即期信用证；包装：每50 套装一个纸箱，由卖方制定唛头；运输方式：航空运输；交货时间：不迟于 2012 年 11 月31 日。"

YAMOO IMPORT & EXPORT CORPORATION 收到发盘后，经研究决定同意宁波进出口贸易公司提出的交易条件，进口数量为每种型号各 1 800 套。

补充资料：

(1)分批装运：不允许

(2)转　运：不允许

(3)装运地：宁波

(4)目的地：纽约

(5)合同号：NBIE071001

(6)合同日期：2012.10.1

2. 实训要求

(1)请你以宁波进出口贸易公司业务员张力的身份，根据上述资料用英语拟写一份发盘函。

OFFER

(2)请你以宁波进出口贸易公司业务员张力的身份,根据上述资料拟订一份销售确认书,要求格式完整、内容正确,并要签字盖章。

宁波进出口贸易公司
NINGBO IMPORT & EXPORT TRADING CORPORATION
678 BAIZHANG ROAD NINGBO , CHINA
SALES CONFIRMATION

TEL:_____ S/C NO. :_____
FAX:_____ DATE:_____
TO:

Dear Sirs,
　　We hereby confirm having sold to you the following goods on terms and conditions as specified below:

MARKS & NO.	DESCRIPTIONS OF GOODS	QUANTITY	U/ PRICE	AMOUNT

LOADING PORT:_____
DESTINATION:_____
PARTIAL SHIPMENT:_____
TRANSSHIPMENT:_____
PAYMENT:_____
TIME OF SHIPMENT:_____

THE BUYER:　　　　　　　　　　　　　　　　THE SELLER:

实训二　出口合同的履行——申请签发一般原产地证书

业务导入

上海进出口贸易公司卢珍小姐通过中外运—欧西爱斯国际快递公司用文件专递将销售确认书一式两份（卖方已签章）向日商 FUJIYAMA TRADING CORPORATION 发出，经其会签后合同即告成立。由于日商要求我方提供一般原产地证书，因此上海进出口贸易公司收到 FUJIYAMA TRADING CORPORATION 30%电汇货款的银行到账通知后，向中国国际贸易促进委员会上海分会主管部门申请签发。为此，卢珍小姐要缮制商业发票一份、一般原产地证明书申请书一份、一般原产地证书一套。

申请签发一般原产地证书业务环节如下图所示。

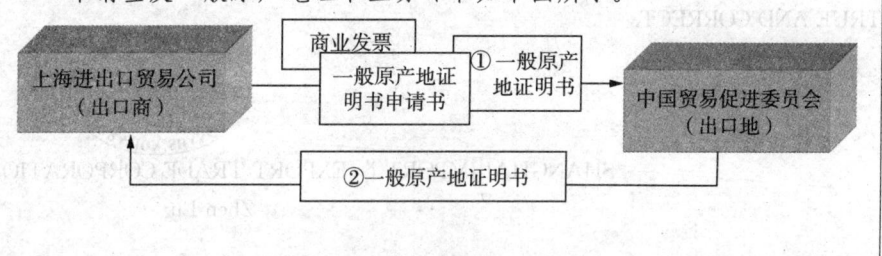

```
┌──────────────┐   商业发票        ┌──────────────┐
│ 上海进出口贸易公司 │ ─一般原产地── ①一般原产地 →│  中国贸易促进委员会 │
│   （出口商）   │   证明书申请书    证明书       │   （出口地）    │
└──────────────┘ ←────②一般原产地证明书────── └──────────────┘
```

▣ 工作任务一　　　　申请签发一般原产地证书

上海进出口贸易公司收到日商 30%电汇货款后，通知宁波兴旺工具公司着手备货，并根据 FUJIYAMA 公司的要求向中国国际贸易促进委员会上海分会主管部门申请签发一般原产地证书。对此，卢珍小姐按照申请签发一般原产地证书的规定缮制一般原产地证明书申请书、一般原产地证书和商业发票一份。

卢珍小姐缮制商业发票：

上海进出口贸易公司
SHANGHAI IMPORT& EXPORT TRADING CORPORATION
1321 ZHONGSHAN ROAD SHANGHAI, CHINA
COMMERCIAL INVOICE

TEL：021-65788876
FAX：021-65788877

INV. NO.：XH05111
DATE：DEC. 02, 2012
S/C NO.：TXT12081

TO: FUJIYAMA TRADING CORPORATION
121, KAWARA MACH OSAKA JAPAN

FROM　PUDONG AIRPORT SHANGHAI　　　TO　OSAKA AIRPORT

MARKS & NO.	DESCRIPTIONS OF GOODS	QUANTITY	U/PRICE	AMOUNT
N/M	DOUBLE OPEN END SPANNER		CPT OSAKA	
	8×10MM(MTM)	60 000PCS	USD 0.50	USD 30 000.00
	10×12MM(MTM)	80 000PCS	USD 0.60	USD 48 000.00
TOTAL:		140 000PCS		USD 78 000.00

TOTAL AMOUNT：SAY US DOLLARS SEVENTY EIGHT THOUSAND ONLY.

WE HEREBY CERTIFY THAT THE CONTENTS OF INVOICE HEREIN ARE TRUE AND CORRECT.

SHANGHAI IMPORT & EXPORT TRADE CORPORATION

Zhen Lu

卢珍小姐填制一般原产地证明书申请书：

中国贸促会上海分会
中国国际商会分会
一般原产地证明书/加工装配证明书

申 请 书

申请单位注册号：<u>866742Q</u>　　证书号：_____

申请人郑重申明：　　　　　发票号：<u>XH051111</u>

全部国产填上 P	P
含进口成分填上 W	

本人被正式授权代表本企业办理和签署本申请书。

　　本申请书及一般原产地证明书/加工装配证明书所列内容正确无误，如发现弄虚作假，冒充证书所列货物，擅改证书，愿按《中华人民共和国出口货物原产地规则》有关规定接受惩处并承担法律责任。现将有关情况申报如下：

商品名称	活络扳手	H.S. 编码（八位数）	8204.1100
商品生产、制造、加工单位、地点	宁波兴旺工具公司 宁波市木行路302号		
含进口成分产品主要制造加工工序			
商品FOB总值（以美元计）	75 500美元	最终目的地国家/地区	加拿大
拟出运日期	2012年11月20日	转口国（地区）	
包装数量或毛重或其他数量	1 400箱		
贸易方式和企业性质			
贸易方式		企业性质	
一般贸易		民营企业	

　　现提交中国出口货物商业发票副本一份，报关单一份或合同/信用证影印件，一般原产地证明书/加工装配证明书一正三副，以及其他附件　份，请予审核签证。

（上海进出口贸易公司 印章）

申领人（签名）：卢珍
电话：65788888

申请单位盖章：　　　　　　　日期：2012年12月2日

操作指南 ➡ 一般原产地证明书申请书的缮制方法

一般原产地证明书申请书共有10项内容,其各栏目缮制要点如下:
1. 商品名称
填入出口货物名称,并与发票同项内容一致。
2. H.S. 编码
H.S.是海关合作理事会《商品名称及编码协调制度》的英文缩写。商务部和海关总署根据H.S.分类编制了《中华人民共和国进出口商品的目录对照表》,规定了商品名称和编码。本栏应填入该商品的H.S.编码前八位数。
3. 商品生产、制造、加工单位、地点
填入出口货物的生产或加工单位的名称和地点。
4. 含进口成分产品主要制造加工工序
出口货物如含有进口成分,此栏注明主要制造或加工工序。
5. 商品FOB总值
填入出口货物FOB总额,如为CFR条件成交,要减去运费额。
6. 最终目的地国家/地区
填入出口货物到达的最终目的地国家或地区。
7. 拟出运日期
填入出口货物拟出运日期,必须在合同或信用证规定的装运期内。
8. 转口国(地区)
出口货物如有转口,则填入该国或地区的名称。
9. 包装数量或毛重或其他数量
填入出口货物总包装件数,或总毛重数量。
10. 贸易方式和企业性质
根据实际情况填入相应的贸易方式和企业性质。

卢珍小姐填制一般原产地证明书：

1. Exporter (full name and address) SHANGHAI IMPORT & EXPORT TRADE CORPORATION 1321 ZHONGSHAN ROAD SHANGHAI CHINA			CERTIFICATE No. : 500511266 CERTIFICATE OF ORIGIN OF THE PEOPLE'S REPUBLIC OF CHINA		
2. Consignee (full name, address, country) FUJIYAMA TRADING CORPORATION 121, KAWARA MACH OSAKA JAPAN					
3. Means of transport and route FROM SHANGHAI TO OSAKA BY AIR			5. For certifying authority use only		
4. Country/Region of Destination JAPAN					
6. Marks and numbers of packages N/M	7. Description of goods, number and kind of packages DOUBLE OPEN END SPANNER ONE THOUSAND FOUR HUNDRED (1 400) CARTONS **************		8. H. S. Code 8204.1100	9. Quantity or weight 140 000 PCS	10. Number and date of invoice XH051111 SEP. 20, 2012
11. Declaration by the exporter 　The undersigned hereby declares that the above details and statements are correct; that all the goods were produced in China and that they comply with the Rules of Origin of the People's Republic of China. SHANGHAI DEC. 02, 2012　　Zhen Lu Place and date, signature and stamp of authorized signatory			12. Certification 　It is hereby certified that the declaration by the exporter is correct. Place and date, signature and stamp of certifying authority		

操作指南 ➡ 一般原产地证书的缮制方法

一般原产地证明书共有12项内容,除按检验检疫局指定的号码填入证书编号(Certificate No.)以外,就其各栏目内容和缮制要点逐项介绍如下:

1. Exporter/出口商

此栏包括出口商的全称和地址。信用证项下的证书,一般为信用证受益人,托收项下的是卖方。

2. Consignee/收货人

填本批货物最终目的地的收货人全称和地址。信用证项下的证书一般为开证申请人,如信用证有具体规定,应按要求填写。

3. Means of transport and route/运输方式和路线

应填装运港和卸货港的名称,并说明运输方式。例如,From Shanghai to London by sea。如要转运,须注明转运地。例如,By s. s. from Shanghai to London W/T Hongkong。

4. Country/Region of Destination Port/目的国家或地区

按信用证或合同规定的目的国家或地区名称填制。

5. For certifying authority use only/供签证机构使用

本栏供检验检疫局根据需要加注说明,如补发、后发证书等事项。

6. Marks and numbers of packages/唛头及包装件数

按信用证中规定的内容进行缮制,且与发票和提单的同项一致,不得留空。

7. Description of Goods, number and kind of Packages/商品名称、包装件数及种类

填写具体的商品名称、包装件数和种类,如散装货物用"In bulk"表示。

8. H. S. code/H. S. 编码

H. S. 是海关合作理事会《商品名称及编码协调制度》的英文缩写。商务部和海关总署根据 H. S. 分类编制了《中华人民共和国进出口商品的目录对照表》,规定了商品名称和编码。本栏应按该规定填入,不同商品应分别标明不同的 H. S. 编码。

9. Quantity or weight/数量及重量

依据发票和提单有关内容填写。重量应注明毛重和净重。例如,G. W. 40 000 kgs, N. W 38 000 kgs。

10. Number and date of invoice/发票号码及日期

按发票实际号码和日期填写,月份应用英文缩写表示。例如,OCT. 3,2012。

本栏内容填写完毕,从第6项开始用"*"符号打成横线表示结束。

11. Declaration by the exporter/出口商声明

出口商声明已事先印就。内容为:"下列签署人声明,以上各项及其陈述是正确的,全部货物均在中国生产,完全符合中华人民共和国原产地规则。"在本栏仅填入申报地点和日期,加盖申请单位章,并由经办人签字。签字与图章不能重叠。

12. Certification/签证机构证明

签证机构证明事先已印制,内容为:"兹证明出口商声明是正确的。"签证机构在此注明签证日期和地点,并由授权人签名,加盖签证机构印章。两者不能重叠。

工作任务二　　　　签发一般原产地证书

中国国际贸易促进委员会上海分会的主管部门在接受上海进出口贸易公司签发一般原产地证书的申请时,要查看单证资料是否齐全,填写是否完整,文字是否清晰,印章、签字有无错漏。核准无误后予以签发,如发现不符合规定,则不接受申请。

中国贸易促进委员会签发一般原产地证明书：

1. Exporter (full name and address) SHANGHAI IMPORT & EXPORT TRADE CORPORATION 1321 ZHONGSHAN ROAD SHANGHAI CHINA	CERTIFICATE No.：500511266 CERTIFICATE OF ORIGIN OF THE PEOPLE'S REPUBLIC OF CHINA
2. Consignee (full name, address, country) FUJIYAMA TRADING CORPORATION 121, KAWARA MACH OSAKA JAPAN	
3. Means of transport and route FROM SHANGHAI TO OSAKA BY AIR	5. For certifying authority use only
4. Country/Region of Destination JAPAN	

6. Marks and numbers of packages N/M	7. Description of goods, number and kind of packages DOUBLE OPEN END SPANNER ONE THOUSAND FOUR HUNDRED (1 400) CARTONS ***************	8. H. S. Code 8204. 1100	9. Quantity or weight 140 000 PCS	10. Number and date of invoice XH051111 DEC. 02, 2012

11. Declaration by the exporter 　　The undersigned hereby declares that the above details and statements are correct, that all the goods were produced in China and that they comply with the Rules of Origin of the People's Republic of China. SHANGHAI DEC. 21, 2012　　　卢珍 Place and date, signature and stamp of authorized signatory	12. Certification 　　It is hereby certified that the declaration by the exporter is correct. SHANGHAI DEC. 22, 2012　　　丁毅 Place and date, signature and stamp of certifying authority

综合业务模拟操作

操作一

1. 操作资料

卖　方：	苏州玩具进出口公司
	苏州市虎丘路 130 号　　TEL：0512-64043030
	FAX：0512-64043030
企业性质：	民营企业
买　方：	日本 YAMADA TRADE CO．，LTD
	310 SKURAMAJI OSAKA JAPAN　　TEL：028-38241234
	FAX：028-38241235
货物名称：	汽车模型玩具（AUTO MODEL）
货物单价：	Art No. 101（BLUE）每只 4.2 美元，Art No. 102（BLACK）每只 4.2 美元，Art No. 103（RED）每只 4 美元，Art No. 104（YELLOW）每只 3 美元，CPT 大阪
货物数量：	每种型号各 30 000 只
货物包装：	每只玩具装一个泡沫塑料袋，再装入一个小纸箱中，20 只小纸箱装入一个出口纸箱，由卖方制定唛头
支付方式：	30％前 T/T，70％后 T//T
起运地：	苏州
目的地：	大阪
运输方式：	航空运输（运费 2 500 美元）

装运时间：　不迟于 2012 年 5 月 31 日
合同号：　　SZHTY120315
合同日期：　2012.03.15
H.S. 编码：　9503.9000
发票号码：　SZTY01221
发票日期：　2012 年 4 月 20 日
生产商名称：苏州红星玩具公司
　　　　　　苏州市干将路 210 号　电话：0512-35123333
　　　　　　传真：0512-35124444
申请单位注册号：Q123456

2. 实训要求

(1)请你以苏州玩具进出口公司业务员李霞的身份，根据上述资料缮制商业发票。

苏州玩具进出口公司
SUZHOU TOY IMPORT & EXPORT CORPORATION
130 HUQIU ROAD, SUZHOU
COMMERCIAL INVOICE

TEL:_____ INV. NO.:_____

FAX:_____ DATE:_____

S/C NO.:_____

TO:

FROM _____ TO _____

MARKS & NO.	DESCRIPTIONS OF GOODS	QUANTITY	U/ PRICE	AMOUNT
TOTAL:				

TOTAL AMOUNT：

    WE HEREBY CERTIFY THAT THE CONTENTS OF INVOICE HEREIN ARE TRUE AND CORRECT.

(2)请你以苏州玩具进出口公司业务员李霞的身份,根据上述资料填写一般原产地证明书申请书。

中国贸促会江苏分会
中国国际商会江苏分会
一般原产地证明书/加工装配证明书

申 请 书

申请单位注册号：_____　　证书号：_____
申请人郑重申明：　　　　　　　发票号：_____

| 全部国产填上 P |
| 含进口成分填上 W |

本人被正式授权代表本企业办理和签署本申请书。

本申请书及一般原产地证明书/加工装配证明书所列内容正确无误,如发现弄虚作假,冒充证书所列货物,擅改证书,愿按《中华人民共和国出口货物原产地规则》有关规定接受惩处并承担法律责任。现将有关情况申报如下：

商品名称		H.S. 编码（八位数）	
商品生产、制造、加工单位、地点			
含进口成分产品主要制造加工工序			
商品 FOB 总值（以美元计）		最终目的地国家/地区	
拟出运日期		转口国（地区）	
包装数量或毛重或其他数量			
贸易方式和企业性质			
贸易方式		企业性质	

现提交中国出口货物商业发票副本一份,报关单一份或合同/信用证影印件,一般原产地证明书/加工装配证明书一正三副,以及其他附件　份,请予审核签证。

　　　　　　　　　　　　　　　　　　　　申领人（签名）：
　　　　　　　　　　　　　　　　　　　　电话：
申请单位盖章：　　　　　　　　　　　　　日期：

(3)请你以苏州玩具进出口公司业务员李霞的身份,根据上述资料填写一般原产地证明书。

1. Exporter (full name and address)	CERTIFICATE No.： CERTIFICATE OF ORIGIN OF THE PEOPLE'S REPUBLIC OF CHINA			
2. Consignee (full name, address, country)	:::			
3. Means of transport and route	:::			
:::	5. For certifying authority use only			
4. Country/Region of Destination	:::			
6. Marks and numbers of packages	7. Description of goods, number and kind of packages	8. H. S. Code	9. Quantity or weight	10. Number and date of invoice
11. Declaration by the exporter 　　The undersigned hereby declares that the above details and statements are correct, that all the goods were produced in China and that they comply with the Rules of Origin of the People's Republic of China. .... Place and date, signature and stamp of authorized signatory	12. Certification 　　It is hereby certified that the declaration by the exporter is correct. .... Place and date, signature and stamp of certifying authority			

操作二

1. 操作资料

合同：

宁波进出口贸易公司
NINGBO IMPORT & EXPORT TRADING CORPORATION
678 BAIZHANG ROAD NINGBO, CHINA

SALES CONFIRMATION

TEL：(0574)87551112　　　　　　　　　　　　　　　INV. NO.：NBIE121001

FAX：(0574)87551113　　　　　　　　　　　　　　　DATE：OCT. 01, 2012

TO：YAMOO IMPORT & EXPORT CORPORATION
No. 206 CHANGJ NORTH STREET NEWYORK USA

Dear Sirs,

We hereby confirm having sold to you the following goods on terms and conditions as specified below：

MARKS & NO.	DESCRIPTIONS OF GOODS	QUANTITY	U/ PRICE	AMOUNT
YAMOO NBIE071001 NEWYORK C/NO. 1-108	CAR SPEAKER No. XY122 No. HY132 No. TY242	 1 800 SETS 1 800 SETS 1 800 SETS	CPT NEWYORK USD 1.50 USD 2.10 USD 4.40	 USD 2 700.00 USD 3 780.00 USD 7 920.00

LOADING PORT：SUZHOU AIRPORT

DESTINATION：NEWYORK AIRPORT USA

PARTIAL SHIPMENT：NOT ALLOWED

TRANSSHIPMENT：NOT ALLOWED

PAYMENT：BY L/C AT SIGHT

TIME OF SHIPMENT：NOT LATER THAN NOV. 31, 2012

THE BUYER：YAMOO IMPORT & EXPORT CORPORATION　　　THE SELLER：宁波进出口贸易公司　合同专用章

　　　　　　JOHNSON　　　　　　　　　　　　　　　　　　　　　张力

信用证：

IRREVOCABLE DOCUMENTARY CREDIT

SEQUENCE OF TOTAL	*27 :	1/1
FORM OF DOC. CREDIT	*40A :	IRREVOCABLE
DOC. CREDIT NUMBER	*20 :	NY1234
DATE OF ISSUE	31C :	121010
DATE AND PLACE OF EXPIRY	*31D :	DATE 121215 IN USA
APPLICANT	*50 :	YAMOO IMPORT & EXPORT CORPORATION
		No. 206 CHANGJ NORTH STREET NEWYORK
		USA
ISSUING BANK	52A :	CITYBANK
		205 THE NO. 5 ROAD, NEWYORK, USA
BENEFICIARY	*59 :	NINGBO IMPORT & EXPORT TRADING
		CORPORATION
		678 BAIZHANG ROAD NINGBO, CHINA
AMOUNT	*32B :	CURRENCY USD AMOUNT 8 640.00
AVAILABLE WITH/BY	*41D :	BANK OF CHINA, SHANGHAI BRANCH
DRAFTS AT…	42C :	DRAFTS AT 15 DAYS AFTER SIGHT
		FOR FULL INVOICE COST
PARTIAL SHIPMENTS	43P :	ALLOWED
TRANSSHIPMENT	43T :	NOT ALLOWED
LOADING ON BOARD	44E :	SHANGHAI
FOR TRANSPORTATION TO…	44B :	NEWYORK
LATEST DATE OF SHIPMENT	44C :	121131
DESCRIPT OF GOODS	45A :	CAR SPEAKER AS PER S/C NO. NBIE071001
DOCUMENTS REQUIRED	46A:	

+ SIGNED COMMERCIAL INVOICE, IN 4 COPIES.
+ PACKING LIST IN 4 COPIES.
+ CERTIFICATE OF ORIGIN GSP CHINA FORM A AND EEC, ISSUED BY THE CHAMBER OF COMMERCE OR OTHER AUTHORITY DULY ENTITLED FOR THIS PURPOSE.
+ QUALITY CERTIFICATE IS TO BE EFFECTED BEFORE SHIPMENT AND IS REQUIRED FROM THE INSPECTING AGENCY DESIGNATED BY THE BUYER.

CHARGES	71B :	ALL BANKING CHARGES OUTSIDE USA
		ARE FOR ACCOUNT OF BENEFICIARY.
PERIOD FOR PRESENTATION	48 :	DOCUMENTS MUST BE PRESENTED WITHIN
		15 DAYS AFTER THE DATE OF SHIPMENT
		BUT WITHIN THE VALIDITY OF THE CREDIT.

体验活动三　代理出口贸易业务

补充资料：
申请单位注册号：Q34568
企业性质：　民营企业
运输方式：　航空运输（运费600美元）
H.S.编码：　9503.9100
发票号码：　NBIE01211
发票日期：　2012年10月10日
生产商名称：　宁波玩具公司
　　　　　　宁波市人民路1210号　电话：0574-35123321　传真：0574-35123321

2.实训要求
(1)请你以宁波进出口贸易公司业务员张力的身份，根据上述资料审核信用证，填写审证结果。

审证结果

159

(2)请你以宁波进出口贸易公司业务员张力的身份，根据上述资料缮制商业发票。

宁波进出口贸易公司
NINGBO IMPORT & EXPORT TRADING CORPORATION
678 BAIZHANG ROAD NINGBO, CHINA

COMMERCIAL INVOICE

TEL: _____ INV. NO.: _____
FAX: _____ DATE: _____
　　　　　　　　　　　　　　　　　　　　S/C NO.: _____
TO:

FROM _____ TO _____

MARKS & NO.	DESCRIPTIONS OF GOODS	QUANTITY	U/PRICE	AMOUNT
TOTAL:				

TOTAL AMOUNT:

　　WE HEREBY CERTIFY THAT THE CONTENTS OF INVOICE HEREIN ARE TRUE AND CORRECT.

　　　　　　　　　　　　　　　　　　　　　_____

(3)请你以宁波进出口贸易公司业务员张力的身份,根据上述资料填写一般原产地证明书申请书。

中国贸促会浙江分会
中国国际商会浙江分会
一般原产地证明书/加工装配证明书
申　请　书

申请单位注册号:_____　证书号:_____　　全部国产填上 P

申请人郑重申明:_____　发票号:_____　　含进口成分填上 W

　　本人被正式授权代表本企业办理和签署本申请书。

　　本申请书及一般原产地证明书/加工装配证明书所列内容正确无误,如发现弄虚作假,冒充证书所列货物,擅改证书,愿按《中华人民共和国出口货物原产地规则》有关规定接受惩处并承担法律责任。现将有关情况申报如下:

商品名称	H.S. 编码(八位数)
商品生产、制造、加工单位、地点	
含进口成分产品主要制造加工工序	
商品FOB总值(以美元计)	最终目的地国家/地区
拟出运日期	转口国(地区)
包装数量或毛重或其他数量	
贸易方式和企业性质	
贸易方式	企业性质

现提交中国出口货物商业发票副本一份,报关单一份或合同/信用证影印件,一般原产地证明书/加工装配证明书一正三副,以及其他附件　份,请予审核签证。

申领人(签名):

电话:

申请单位盖章:　　　　　　　　　　　　　　　　日期:

(4)请你以宁波进出口贸易公司业务员张力的身份,根据上述资料填写一般原产地证明书。

1. Exporter (full name and address)	CERTIFICATE No.:
2. Consignee (full name, address, country)	CERTIFICATE OF ORIGIN OF THE PEOPLE'S REPUBLIC OF CHINA
3. Means of transport and route	5. For certifying authority use only
4. Country/Region of Destination	

6. Marks and numbers of packages	7. Description of goods, number and kind of packages	8. H.S. Code	9. Quantity or weight	10. Number and date of invoice

11. Declaration by the exporter	12. Certification
The undersigned hereby declares that the above details and statements are correct, that all the goods were produced in China and that they comply with the Rules of Origin of the People's Republic of China.	It is hereby certified that the declaration by the exporter is correct.
.... Place and date, signature and stamp of authorized signatory	.... Place and date, signature and stamp of certifying authority

实训三　出口合同的履行——办理航空运输、报检、报关手续

业务导入

上海进出口贸易公司向中国国际贸易促进委员会上海分会主管部门申请签发好一般原产地证书后，按照合同的约定委托上海客货运输服务公司办理航空货物运输。由于活络扳手属于法定检验检疫商品，必须经检验检疫合格并获取出境货物通关单方可报关。卢珍小姐具有报检与报关的资格，为此准备好商业发票、合同书，并缮制装箱单、报检单、出口货物报关单办理报检、报关手续。

办理航空运输、报检、报关手续业务环节如下图所示：

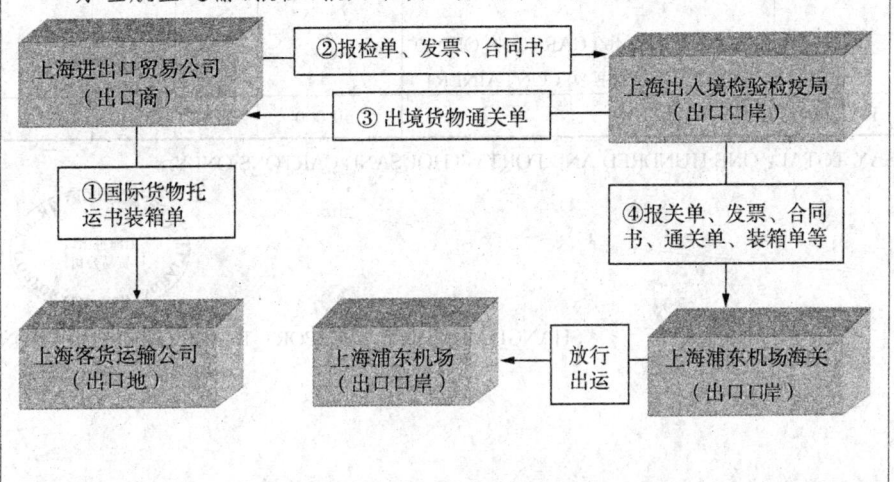

```
上海进出口贸易公司  ──②报检单、发票、合同书──→  上海出入境检验检疫局
   （出口商）       ←───③出境货物通关单───        （出口口岸）
        │                                              │
        │①国际货物托运书装箱单                          │④报关单、发票、合同
        │                                              │ 书、通关单、装箱单等
        ↓                                              ↓
  上海客货运输公司        上海浦东机场    ←─放行─  上海浦东机场海关
     （出口地）           （出口口岸）     出运      （出口口岸）
```

◇ 工作任务一　　办理航空货物运输手续

上海进出口贸易公司向中国国际贸易促进委员会上海分会主管部门申请签发好一般原产地证书后，按照合同的规定委托上海客货运输服务公司办理航空货物运输手续，以便能在合同规定的装运期内进行交货。为此，卢珍小姐缮制装箱单，填写国际货物托运书。

卢珍小姐缮制装箱单：

上海进出口贸易公司
SHANGHAI IMPORT & EXPORT TRADE CORPORATION
1321 ZHONGSHAN ROAD SHANGHAI CHINA

PACKING LIST

TEL:0512-6578876
FAX:0512-6578877
E-mail:LUZHENSH@163.COM
TO:FUJIYAMA TRADING CORPORATION
121,KAWARA MACH OSAKA JAPAN

INV. NO. : XH051111
DATE: DEC. 02,2012
S/C NO. : TXT12081
SHIPPING MARK
N/M

CASE NO.	GOODS DESCRIPTION & PACKING	QUANTITY (PCS)	G.W. (KGS)	N.W. (KGS)	MEAS (M^3)
1-600	DOUBLE OPEN END SPANNER 8×10MM(MTM)	60 000	1 200	1 080	12
601-1400	10×12MM(MTM)	80 000	2 000	1 760	8
	PACKED IN 1 400 CARTONS OF 100 PCS EACH(ONE 20'CONTAINER)				
TOTAL:		140 000	3 200	2 840	20

SAY TOTAL: ONE HUNDRED AND FORTY THOUSAND CARTONS ONLY.

SHANGHAI IMPORT & EXPORT TRADING CORPORATION
Zhen Lu

卢珍小姐填制国际货物托运书：

上海客货运输服务有限公司
SHANGHAI EXPRESS SERVICE CO., LTD.   IATA

国际货物托运书
SHIPPER'S LETTER OF INSTRUCTION   REF. NO.: XY050401

始发站 AIRPORT DEPARTURE SHANGHAI		到达站 AIRPORT OF DESTINATION OSAKA				供承运人用 FOR CARRIER ONLY	
路线及到达站 ROUTING AND DESTINATION						航班/日 FLIGHT/DAY	航班/日 FLIHT/DAY
至 TO	第一承运人 BY FIRST CARRIER	至 TO	承运人 BY	至 TO	承运人 BY	至 TO	承运人 BY	已预留吨位 BOOKED	
收货人姓名及地址 CONSIGNEE'S NAME AND ADDRESS		FUJIYAMA TRADING COR. 121, KAWARA MACH OSAKA JAPAN				运费 CHARGES: FREIGHT: PREPAID	
另行通知 ALSO NOTIFY		SAME AS CONSIGNEE					
托运人账号 SHIPPER'S ACCOUNT NUMBER		045686		托运人姓名及地址 SHIPPER'S NAME & ADDRESS		SHANGHAI IMPORT & EXPORT TRADE CORPORATION 1321 ZHONGSHAN ROAD SHANGHAI	
托运人声明的价值 SHIPPER'S DECLARED VALUE NVD		保险金额 AMOUNT OF INSURANCE		所附文件 DOCUMENTS TO ACCOMPANY AIR WAYBILL			
供运输 FOR CARRIAGE	供海关 FOR CUSTOMS						
件数 NO. OF PACKAGES	实际毛重 ACTUAL GROSS WEIGHT(KG)	运价类别 RATE CLASS		收费重量 CHARGEABLE WEIGHT	离岸 RATE CHARGE	货物名称及重量(包括体积或尺寸) NATURE AND QUANTITY OF GOODS(INCL. DIMENSIONS OF VOLUME)	
1 400 CTNS	3 200	Q		3 200		DOUBLE OPEN END SPANNER 20 CBM	

在货物不能交于收货人时,托运人指示的处理方法
SHIPPER'S INSTRUCTIONS IN CASE OF INABILITY TO DELIVER SHIPMENT AS CONSIGNED

处理情况(包括包装方式、货物标志及号码等)
HANDLING INFORMATION (INCL. METHOD OF PACKING IDENTIFYING MARKS AND NUMBERS, ETC.)

托运人证实以上所填全部属实并愿遵守托运人的一切载运章程
THE SHIPPER CERTIFIES THAT THE PARTICULARS ON THE FACE HEREOF ARE CORRECT AND AGREES TO THE CONDITIONS OF CARRIAGE OF THE CARRIER.

托运人签字：卢珍　　　日期：2012.12.05　　经办人：华民彰　　日期：2012.12.05
SIGNATURE OF SHIPPER　　DATE　　　　　　AGENT　　　　　　DATE

操作指南 ➡ 国际货物托运书的缮制方法

办理出口货物航空运输手续须填写国际货物托运书,并随附商业发票与装箱单。国际货物托运书内容和主要缮制方法如下:

1. AIRPORT DEPARTURE/始发站机场

填写货物始发站的机场的英文名称,不得简写或使用代码。

2. AIRPORT OF DESTINATION/目的地机场

填写货物目的地站的机场的英文名称,不得简写或使用代码。如有必要,填写机场所属国家、州的名称或城市的全称。

3. FOR CARRIAGER ONLY/供承运人用

此栏留空,由承运人根据需要填写。

4. ROUTING AND DESTINATION/路线及到达站

此栏留空。

5. FLIGHT/DAY/航班/日期

填写托运人事先预订的航班/日期。

6. CONSIGNEE'S NAME AND ADDRESS/收货人姓名及地址

填写收货人的全称、地址,包括邮政编码和电话号码。此栏内不可填写"TO ORDER"字样。

7. ALSO NOTIFY/另行通知

填写SAME AS CONSIGNEE。

8. SHIPPER'S ACCOUNT NUMBER/托运人账号

如果承运人需要,可填写托运人账号。

9. SHIPPER'S NAME & ADDRESS/托运人姓名及地址

填写托运人的全称、地址,包括邮政编码和电话号码。

10. SHIPPER'S DECLARED VALUE/托运人声明的价值

填写托运人向承运人办理货物声明价值的金额。托运人未办理货物声明价值,必须填写"NVD"字样。

11. CHARGES/运费

填写托运人支付货物运费的方式等项内容。

12. AMOUNT OF INSURANCE/保险金额

此栏不填,由中国民航部代理国际货物的保险业务机构填写。

13. DOCUMENTS TO ACCOMPANY AIR WAYBILL/所附文件

填写随交承运人有关文件的名称。

14. FOR CARRIAGE/供运用

此栏留空。

续

15. FOR CUSTOMS/供海关用

16. NO. OF PACKAGES/件数

填写货物的包装件数,如果使用不同的货物运价种类,应分别填写,并将总件数填入此栏。

17. ACTUAL GROSS WEIGHT(KG)/实际毛重

填写货物的总毛重。

18. RATE CLASS/运价类别

填写所使用的货物运价种类代号,如"M"代表起码运费,"N"代表45千克以下普通货物运价,"Q"代表45千克以上普通货物运价。

19. CHARGEABLE WEIGHT/收费重量

此栏留空。

20. RATE CHARGE/费率

此栏留空。

21. NATURE AND QUANTITY OF GOODS (INCL. DIMENSIONS OF VOLUME)/货物名称及重量(包括体积或尺寸)

填写具体货名与数量。货名不得用统称,危险物品应填写其标准学术名称;外包装要注明尺寸或体积,按长×宽×高×件数的顺序填写。

22. SHIPPER'S INSTRUCTIONS IN CASE OF INABILITY TO DELIVER SHIPMENT AS CONSIGNED/在货物不能交于收货人时,托运人指示的处理方法

托运人根据需要作出指示。

23. HANDLING INFORMATION (INCL. METHOD OF PACKING, IDENTIFYING MARKS AND NUMBERS ETC.)/处理情况(包括包装方式、货物标志及号码等)

填写货物在运输、中转、装卸和仓储时需要注意的事项,如货物的包装形式、标志、名称和货物外包装所用的材料,以及写明数量和包装种类。

24. SIGNATURE OF SHIPPER, DATE/托运人签字、日期

由托运人或其代理人签字或盖章,并填写托运货物的日期。

25. AGENT, DATE/经办人、日期

由承运人或其代理人的经办人签字,并填写收运货物的日期。

◆ 工作任务二　　办理出境货物报检手续

上海进出口贸易公司在委托上海客货运输服务公司办理航空货物运输后,应根据我国有关检验检疫法律法规的规定申请报检。为此,卢珍小姐在货物装运前一周,缮制报检单,并随附商业发票、装箱单、合同等有关单据向上海出入境检验检疫机构报检。出入境检验检疫机构经对货物扳手检验合格后,签发出境货物通关单。

卢珍小姐填写出境货物报检单

中华人民共和国出入境检验检疫
出境货物报检单

报检单位(加盖 [上海进出口贸易公司印章])　　　　　　　　　　　＊编号：_____

报检单位登记号：_____　联系人：卢珍　电话：65788876　报检日期：2012年12月8日

发货人	(中文)上海进出口贸易公司						
	(外文)SHANGHAI IMPORT & EXPORT TRADE CORPORATION						
收货人	(中文)						
	(外文)FUJIYAMA TRADING CORPORATION						
货物名称(中/外文)	H.S.编码	产地		数/重量	货物总值	包装种类及数量	
活络扳手 DOUBLE OPEN END SPANNER	8204.1100	中国 上海		毛重 3 200 千克 净重 2 840 千克	78 000 美元	1 400 箱	
运输工具的名称与号码	MU0752SY		贸易方式	一般贸易	货物存放地点		逸仙路9号
合同号	TXT07081		信用证号		用途		外销
发货日期	2012.12.20		输往国家(地区)	日本	许可证/审批证		
起运地	上海		到达口岸	大阪	生产单位注册号		
集装箱规格、数量及号码	1×20' 整箱 TUR060911						
合同、信用证订立的检验检疫条款或特殊要求	标记及号码 || 随附单据(划"√"或补填)					
按合同条款	N/M		☑ 合同 ☑ 信用证 ☑ 发票 ☐ 换证凭单 ☑ 装箱单 ☐ 厂检单		☐ 包装性能结果单 ☑ 许可/审批文件 ☐ ☐ ☐			
需要证单名称(划"√"或补填)			＊检验检疫费				
☑ 品质证书　　1 正 2 副 ☐ 重量证书　　__正__副 ☐ 数量证书　　__正__副 ☐ 兽医卫生证书　__正__副 ☐ 健康证书　　__正__副 ☐ 卫生证书　　__正__副 ☐ 动物卫生证书　__正__副			☐ 植物检疫证书　__正__副 ☐ 熏蒸/消毒证书　__正__副 ☐ 出境货物换证凭单　__正__副	总金额 (人民币元)			
			计费人			
			收费人			
报检人郑重声明： 　1. 本人被授权报检。 　2. 上列填写内容正确属实，货物无伪造或冒用他人的厂名、标志、认证标志的情形。					领 取 证 单		
				日期	2012.6.10		
签名：_卢 珍_				签名			

注：有"＊"号栏由出入境检验检疫机关填写。　　◆国家出入境检验检疫局制

操作指南　　出境货物报检单的填制要求

1. 编号

由检验检疫机构报检受理人员填写,前6位为检验检疫机构代码,第7位为报检类代目,第8、9位为年代码,第10至15位为流水号。实行电子报检后,该编号可在受理电子报检的回执中自动生成。

2. 报检单位

填写报检单位的全称,并盖报检单位的印章。

3. 报检单位登记号

填写报检单位在检验检疫机构备案或注册登记的代码。

4. 联系人

填写报检人员的姓名。

5. 电话

填写报检人员的联系电话。

6. 报检日期

检验检疫机构实际受理报检的日期,由检验检疫机构受理报检人员填写。

7. 发货人

预检报检的,可填写生产单位;出口报检的,应填写外贸合同中的卖方。

8. 收货人

填写外贸合同中的买方名称。

9. 货物名称

填写出口贸易合同上的货物名称及规格。

10. H.S.编码

填写本批货物的商品编码(8位数或10位数编码),以当年海关公布的商品税则编码分类为准。

11. 产地

填写本货物的生产或加工地的省、市和县名称。

12. 数/重量

填写本货物实际申请检验检疫数/重量,重量还应注明毛重或净重。

13. 货物总值

填写本批货物的总值及币种,应和出口贸易合同与发票上的货物总值一致。

14. 包装种类及数量

填写本批货物实际运输包装的种类及数量,应注明包装的材质。

续

15. 运输工具的名称与号码
填写装运本批货物的运输工具的名称和号码。
16. 合同号
填写出口贸易合同、订单或形式发票的号码。
17. 信用证号
填写本批货物的信用证编号。
18. 贸易方式
根据实际情况选择填写一般贸易、来料加工、进料加工、易货贸易和补偿贸易等。
19. 货物存放地点
填写本批货物存放的具体地点。
20. 发货日期
填写出口装运日期,预检报检可不填。
21. 输往国家(地区)
填写出口贸易合同中买方所在国家和地区,或合同注明的最终输往国家和地区。
22. 许可证/审批号
如为实施许可/审批制度管理的货物,必须填写其编号,不得留空。
23. 生产单位注册号
填写本批货物生产、加工的单位在检验检疫机构的注册登记编号,如卫生注册登记号、质量许可证号等。
24. 起运地
填写装运本批货物离境的交通工具的起运口岸/城市地区名称。
25. 到达口岸
填写本批货物最终抵达目的地停靠口岸的名称。
26. 集装箱规格、数量及号码
货物若以集装箱运输,应填写集装箱的规格、数量及号码。
27. 合同订立的特殊条款以及其他要求
填写在出口贸易合同中特别订立的有关质量、卫生等条款,或报检单位对本批货物检验检疫的特别要求。
28. 标记及号码
填写本批货物的标记及号码,如没有标记及号码,则填"N/M"。
29. 用途
根据实际情况,选填食用、观赏或演艺、伴侣动物、试验、药用、其他等。

续

30. 随附单据

根据向检验检疫机构提供的实际单据，在同名的"□"上打"√"，或在"□"后补填其名称。

31. 需要证单名称

根据需要由检验检疫机构出具的证单，在对应的"□"上打"√"或补填，并注明所需证单的正副本数量。

32. 报检人郑重声明

报检人员必须亲笔签名。

33. 检验检疫费

由检验检疫机构计费人员填写。

34. 领取证单

报检人在领取证单时填写领证日期并签名。

出入境检验检疫机构签发通关单：

中华人民共和国出入境检验检疫
出境货物通关单

编号：070688

1. 收货人　FUJIYAMA TRADING CORPORATION			5. 标记及唛码 N/M
2. 发货人　上海进出口贸易公司			
3. 合同/提(运)单号 TXT07081		4. 输出国家或地区 日本	
6. 运输工具名称及号码 MU0752SY		7. 目的地 大阪	8. 集装箱规格及数量 1×20'
9. 货物名称及规格 DOUBLE OPEN END SPANNER 8×10MM(MTM) 10×12MM(MTM)	10. H.S. 编码 8204.1100	11. 申报总值 78 000.00 美元	12. 数/重量、包装数量及种类 2 840 千克 1 400 箱

13. 证明

上述货物业已报检/申报，请海关予以放行。
本通关单有效期至 2012 年 12 月 30 日。

（中华人民共和国上海出入境检验检疫局 印章）

签字：丁鸣　　　　　　　　　　　　　日期：2012 年 12 月 12 日

14. 备注

◎ 工作任务三　　办理出口货物报关手续

上海进出口贸易公司在取得出境通关单后，应根据我国有关海关法律法规的规定，填写出口货物报关单，并随附出境货物通关单、商业发票、装箱单和合同等有关单据及时向上海浦东机场海关办理出口货物报关手续。海关经查验合格后，在报关单与装货单上加盖放行章，货物方能装运。

卢珍小姐填写出口货物报关单：

中华人民共和国海关出口货物报关单

预录入编号： 　　　　　　　　　　　　　海关编号：

出口口岸 浦东机场 2233	备案号	出口日期 2012.12.20	申报日期 2012.12.18
经营单位(3122668874) 上海进出口贸易公司	运输方式 航空运输	运输工具名称 MU0752SY	提运单号
发货单位 上海进出口贸易公司	贸易方式 一般贸易	征免性质 一般征税	结汇方式 电汇
许可证号	运抵国(地区) 日本	指运港 大阪	境内货源地 宁波
批准文号	成交方式 CPT	运费 502/2500/3	保费	杂费
合同协议号 TXT07081	件数 1 400	包装种类 纸箱	毛重(千克) 3 200	净重(千克) 2 840
集装箱号 TUR060911/20/2280	随附单据 B:070688		生产厂家 宁波兴旺工具公司
标记唛码及备注 N/M			

项号	商品编号	商品名称、规格型号	数量及单位	最终目的国(地区)	单价	总价	币制	征免
	8204.1100	活络扳手		日本		502	照章
01		8×10MM(MTM)	60 000 件		0.50	30 000.00		
02		10×12MM(MTM)	80 000 件		0.60	48 000.00		

税费征收情况

录入员	录入单位 310478965432 卢珍	兹声明以上申报无讹并承担法律责任	海关审单批注及放行日期 (签章)
报关员		申报单位 上海进出口贸易公司 报关专用章	审单　　　　审价
单位地址	上海市中山路 1321号		征税　　　　统计
邮编	电话 65756786	填制日期 2012 年 12 月 18 日	查验　　　　放行

操作指南　　出口报关单的填制规范

报关单根据业务性质的不同,分为一般贸易出口货物报关单、进料加工专用报关单、出口退税专用报关单与来料加工和补偿贸易专用报关单。其主要内容大致相同,填制方法略有差异。简介如下:

1. 预录入编号

填写申报单位或预录入单位对报关单的编号。报关单录入凭单的编号规则由申报单位自行决定。预录入报关单及 EDI 报关单的预录入编号由接受申报的海关决定。

2. 海关编号

海关接受申报时给予报关单的编号,一般为 9 位数码。此栏由海关填写。

3. 出口口岸

注明货物实际出境口岸的海关名称和代码,按《海关名称及代码表》规定填制。如"上海海关 2200"。倘若是在我国不同出口加工区之间转让的货物,则填报对方出口加工区海关名称及代码。倘若是其他无实际进出境的货物,填报接受申报的海关名称及代码。

4. 备案号

如为一般贸易,此栏留空。如为加工贸易,填报进料加工登记手册、出口货物免税证明或其他有关备案审批文件的编号。

5. 出口日期

填入申报货物的运输工具出境的日期,顺序为年、月、日,如 2012 年 8 月 10 日填为 2012.08.10。预录入报关单及 EDI 报关单均免于填报,无实际进出境货物的报关单填报办理申报手续的日期。

6. 申报日期

发货人办理货物出口报关手续的日期,年为 4 位,月、日各 2 位。

7. 经营单位

应填报出口企业中文名称及单位编码(10 位数字)。

8. 运输方式

根据实际运输方式并按海关规定的"运输方式代码表"填报,如"江海 2"。

9. 运输工具名称

将载运货物出境的运输工具的名称或运输工具编号填入此栏,一份报关单只允许填报一个运输工具名称。

10. 提运单号

填报出口货物提单或运单编号，一票货物如有多个提运单时，应分单填写。

11. 发货单位

应填报出口货物在境内的生产或销售单位的中文名称或海关注册编码。

12. 贸易方式

根据实际情况并按海关规定的"贸易方式代码表"填制相应的贸易方式简称及其代码，如"一般贸易0110"。

13. 征免性质

按海关核发的征免税证明中批注的征免性质或海关规定的征免性质代码表填报相应的征免性质简称或其代码，如"一般征税101"。

14. 结汇方式

依据合同和信用证的规定并按海关规定的"结汇方式代码表"填制，如"电汇2"。

15. 许可证号

属申领出口许可证的货物，必须填出口货物许可证的编号，不得为空。

16. 运抵国(地区)

根据出口货物直接运抵的国家(地区)，并按海关规定的"国别/地区代码表"填写，如"日本116"。

17. 指运港

填写出口货物运抵的最终目的港及海关规定的港口航线代码，如"香港0110"。

18. 境内货源地

注明出口货物在国内的产地或始发地及其国内地区代码，如"上海浦东新区31222"。

19. 批准文号

此栏应填报出口收汇核销单的编号。

20. 成交方式

根据合同的成交条件，并按成交方式代码填写，如"FOB 3"。

21. 运费

按成交价格中含有的国际运输费用的金额和货币代码填写。如"502/1100/3"，其意为总运费美元1 100("1"表示运费率，"2"表示运费单价，"3"表示运费总价)。

22. 保费

填报该批出口货物运输的保险费用和货币代码。如10 000港元保险费总价应填为"110/10000/3"("1"表示保险费率，"3"表示保险费总价)。

23. 杂费

指成交价以外应计入完税价格或应从完税价格中扣除的费用，诸如手续费、佣金和回扣等，可按杂费总价或杂费率填报。如应计入完税价格的500英镑杂费总价为"303/500/3"("1"表示杂费率，"3"表示杂费总价)。

24. 同协议号
   注明出口货物合同(协议)的全部字头和号码。
25. 件数
   按外包装的出口货物(如集装箱、托盘等)的实际件数填报,裸装货物填"1"。
26. 包装种类
   根据出口货物的实际外包装种类填制,如木箱、纸箱等。
27. 毛重(千克)
   按出口货物实际毛重(千克)填,不足1千克应填"1"。
28. 净重(千克)
   填出口货物实际重量(千克),不足1千克的填"1"。
29. 集装箱号
   填报集装箱编号,如集装箱号为 TEXU5678021 的 20 英尺集装箱,应填为 TEXU5678021/20/2280(2280 是集装箱的自重量)。
30. 随附单据
   应填写与出口货物报关单一并向海关递交的单证的名称与代码。合同、发票、装箱单和许可证等必备的随附单证可不填。
31. 生产厂家
   填出口货物的境内生产企业的名称。
32. 标记唛码及备注
   按照发票中的唛头,用除图形以外的文字和数字填制。
33. 项号
   第一行打印报关单中的商品排列序号,第二行专用于加工贸易等已备案的货物在"登记手册"中的项号。
34. 商品编号
   按海关规定的商品分类编码规则填写该出口货物的商品编号。
35. 商品名称、规格型号
   通常第一行写出口货物的中文名称,第二行表示规格型号。
36. 数量及单位
   注明出口商品的实际数量及计量单位。
37. 最终目的国(地区)
   填制出口货物的最终消费或进一步加工制造国家(地区)及其国别/地区的代码。
38. 单价
   填报同一项号下出口货物实际成交的商品单位价格。
39. 总价
   填报同一项号下出口货物实际成交的商品总价。

40. 币制
按实际成交价格的币种货币的代码填入。

41. 征免方式
按海关核发的"征免税证明"和征减免税方式的代码填写,如"全免 3"。

42. 税费征收情况
此栏留空,供海关对出口货物的税费征收、减免情况进行批注。

43. 录入员
用于预录入和 EDI 报关单,打印录入人员的姓名。

44. 录入单位
用于预录入和 EDI 报关单,打印录入单位的名称。

45. 申报单位
注明向海关申报单位的全称和代码,如为委托代理报关,应填报代理报关企业的名称及代码,由报关员填报。

46. 填制日期
指报关单的填制日期。

47. 海关审单批注栏
由海关人员填写。

◎ 工作任务四　　签发空运单

出口货物经海关查验放行后方能装运,航空公司装机后,签发空运单。空运单应由出口商填写,但在实际业务中都由航空公司填制并签发。按国际惯例,空运单正本为 3 份,分别由航空公司和发货人留存,以及随机转给收货人。

航空公司签发空运单：

Shipper'S Name and Address SHANGHAI IMPORT & EXPORT TRADE CORPORATION 132 1 ZHONGSHAN ROAD SHANGHAI CHINA	Shipper's Account Number 045686	Not negotiable **Air Waybill** 中国东方航空公司 Issued by CHINA EASTERN AIRLINES 2250 HONGQIAO ROAD SHANGHAI CHINA
Consignee's Name and Address FUJIYAMA TRADING CORPORATION 121,KAWARA MACH OSAKA JAPAN	Consignee's Account Number SO099	Copies 1,2 and 3 this Air Waybill are originals and have the same validity It is agreed that goods described herein are accepted in apparent good order and condition (except as noted) for carriage SUBJECT TO THE CONDITIONS OF CONTRACT ON THE REVERSE HEREOF. ALL GOODS MAY BE CARRIED BY ANY OTHER MEANS INCLUDING ROAD OR ANY OTHER CARRIER UNLESS SPECIFIC CONTRARY INSTRUCTIONS ARE GIVEN HEREON BY THE SHIPPER, AND SHIPPER AGREES THAT THE SHIPPMENT MAY BE CARRIED VIA INTERMEDIATE STOPPING PLACES WHICH THE CARRIER DEEMS APPROPRIATE. THE SHIPPER'S ATTENTION IS DRAWN TO THE NOTICE CONCERNING CARRIER'S LIMITATION OF LIABILITY. Shipper may increase such limitation of liability by declaring a higher value for carriage and paying a supplemental charge if required.
Issuing Carrier's Agent Name and City FUKANGWA EX3 (030-424) SEMARANG EXPRESS CO., LTD.		Accounting Information FREIGHT: PREPAID
Agents IATA Code 08321550	Account No.	D = 34 (20 C BM)

Airport of Departure (Addr. Of First Carrier) and Requested Routing
PUDONG AIRPORT

To	By First Carrier	Routing and Destination	To	By	To	By	Currency USD	Chgs Code	WT/VAL PPD COLL X X	Other PPD COLL X X	Declared Value for Carrier	Declared Value for Customs N.V.D

Airport of Destination	Requested Flight/Date MU0514/02	Amount of Insurance	If shipper requests insurance in accordance with the conditions thereof indicate amount to be insures in figures in box marked "Amount of Insurance".

Handing Information
AS PER REF. NO.: XY050401

No. of pieces	Gross Weight	kg/lb	Rate Class Commodity Item No.	Chargeable Weight	Rate / Charge	Total	Nature and Quantity of Goods (Incl. Dimensions or Volume)
1 400	3 200	K	Q	3 200	0.70	2 240.00	DOUBLE OPEN END SPANN ER 20 CBM

Prepaid Weight Charge 2 240.00	Collect	Other Charges AWB FEE : 260.00
Valuation Charge		
Tax		
Total other Charges Due Agent 260.00		Shipper certifies that particular's on the face hereof are correct and agrees THE CONDITIONS ON REVERSE HEREOF: PUDONG / AIR EXPORT 早民郭
Total other Charges Due Carrier		Signature Shipper or his Agent
Total Prepaid 2 500.00	Total Collect	Carrier certifies that the goods described hereon are accepted for carriage subject to THE CONDITION OF CONTRACT ON THE REVERSE HEREOF. The goods then being in apparent good order and condition except as noted hereon. DEC. 20,2012 SHANGHAI,CHINA CHINA EASTERN AIRLINES
Currency Conversion Rate	CC Charges in Dest. Currency	Executed on (date) at (place) Signature of Issuing Carrier
For Carriers Use only at Destination	Charges at Destination	Total Collect Charges 789-3905 0933

操作指南 ➡ 空运单的填制要求

空运单(Air Waybill)是承运人签发给托运人表示已收妥货物接受托运的货运单据,是承运人和托运人之间的运输合同和货物收据。空运单不是物权凭证,不能凭以提货或转让,其仅供收货人作为运费账单和核收货物的依据,也是承运人的计账凭证。

空运单有3份正本,其内容和主要缮制方法如下:

1. No. /编号

由航空公司编写,前3位数为国际航空公司代号。(例如,999为中国国际航空公司,131为日航代号。)

2. Air Waybill/空运单

空运单上注明"Not negotiable"(不可转让),说明其是不可转让的运输单据。

3. Shipper's Name and Address /收货人名称及地址

按信用证或合同规定填写,信用证项下一般为受益人,托收方式下通常为出口商。

4. Shipper's Account Number /发货人账号

此栏通常留空不填。

5. Consignee's Name and Address/收货人名称及地址

按信用证要求填收货人名称和地址。一般为开证行或开证人。托收方式下以代收行为收货人,可避免风险,但须征得代收行的同意。在实际业务中,通常仍是进口商。

6. Consignee's Account Number /收货人账号

除信用证特别要求外,通常不填。

7. Issuing Carrier's Agent Name and City/签单承运人的代理人名称及城市

如由货运代理公司签发,此栏填实际名称和城市名。如承运人直接签发,此栏可不填。

8. Agent's IATA Code /代理人的IATA代号

IATA为国际航空运输协会的英文缩写,填代理人在该协会的代号。

9. Agent's Account No. /代理人账号

供承运人结算使用,由代理人填写,此栏留空。

10. Airport of Departure and Requested Routing/起航机场和指定航线

填起航机场名和实际航线。

11. Accounting Information/会计结算情况

按信用证要求或实际情况填,如运费预付、运费到付等。

12. Airport of Transshipment/转运机场

按信用证规定填,如无转运,此栏留空。

13. Airport of Destination/目的地机场

按信用证或合同规定的目的地机场名称填。

14. Flight/Date <For Carrier Use Only>/航班/日期<供承运人用>

填航次与实际起飞日期。但装运期应以空运单签发日为准。

15. Currency and Charges Code/费用币制及费用代号

按货币国际标准电码表示，如 CNY(人民币)，费用代号通常不填。

16. WT/VAL and Other /运费/声明价值费和其他费用

如果运费和声明价值费或其他费用预付，在 PPD 栏(Prepaid 缩写)打"×"；如为到付，则在 COLL 栏(Collect 缩写)打"×"。

17. Declared Value for Carriage/供运输使用声明价值

按国际公约规定，托运人在交付托运货物时声明货物价值，如发生货损，承运人按其声明价值赔偿。如没有声明价值，按每千克统一规定的金额赔偿，但不超过该货到达后的价值。

声明价值必须注明币制，如不填声明价值，此栏用"N.V.D."(No Value Declared)示意无声明价值。

18. Declared Value for Customs /供海关使用声明价值

此栏所填入价值为海关征税的依据。如果以商业发票或出口报关单申报价值为征税依据，可留空不填。如作为样品等，可填 N.C.V (No Commercial Value)，示意无商业价值。

19. Handing Information/处理情况

根据信用证要求注明被通知人，或随机的单证名称，或包装情况，或托运人对货物在途中的特别要求等，一般此栏不填。

20. No. of Pieces/件数

填包装件数。

21. Gross Weight/毛重

填实际货物毛重量。

22. Kg. lb/千克或磅

按实际计量单位选择。

23. Rate class/运价分类代号

运价分类代号如下：

"M"(Minimum Charge)：起码运价

"N"(Normal Under 45 kg Rate)45 千克以下运价。

"Q"(Quantity Over 45 kg Rate)45 千克以上运价，其中又分 100 千克、250 千克多个档次。

"C"(Special Commodity Rate)特种商品运价。

续

"R"(Reduced Class Rate, Less than Normal Rate)折扣运价,低于45千克普通货物运价的等价运价。

"S"(Surcharged Class Rate, More than Normal Rate)加价运价,高于45千克普通货物运价的等价运价。

24. Commodity Item No. /商品编号

本栏留空,由航空公司按品名类别编号填写。

25. Chargeable Weight/计费重量

以重量计费,此栏填毛重,其他可不填。

26. Rate/Charge /费率

按实际计费的费率填入。

27. Total/运费总额

按(计费重量×费率=运费总额)公式计算的结果填入。

28. Nature and Quantity of Goods (incl. Dimensions or Volume)/货物的品名和数量(包括体积或容积)

按信用证或合同规定填写。

29. Weight Charge/以重量计算的运费额

将运费额按照实际情况,填入"预付"或"待付"栏中。

30. Other Charges /其他费用

其他费用主要包括运单费、仓储费和危险货物费等,按实际情况填写。

31. Total Other Charges Due Carrier/因承运人需要而产生其他费用总额

如运单费、仓储费等,按实际诸项费用相加填入。

32. Total Prepaid/预付费用总额

由运费预付额与其他费用金额构成。

33. Signature of Shipper or His Agent /发货人或代理人签名

由发货人或代理人在本栏签名,保证该货并非危险物。

34. Executed on (date)at (place), Signature of Issuing Carrier or its Agent /承运人或其代理人签字及签运单日期、地点

正本空运单必须由承运人或其代理人签字盖章才生效。本栏签发日期不得晚于合同或信用证规定的最迟装运日期。

35. Original/正本

通常为3份。

综合业务模拟操作

操作一

1. 操作资料

卖　　方：　苏州玩具进出口公司
　　　　　　苏州市虎丘路 130 号　　TEL：0512-64043030
　　　　　　FAX：0512-64043030

企业性质：　民营企业

买　　方：　日本 YAMADA TRADE CO.，LTD.
　　　　　　310 SKURAMAJI OSAKA JAPAN　　TEL：028-38241234
　　　　　　FAX：028-38241235

货物名称：　汽车模型玩具（AUTO MODEL）

货物单价：　Art No. 101(BLUE)每只 4.2 美元，Art No. 102(BLACK)每只 4.2 美元，Art No. 103(RED)每只 4 美元，Art No. 104(YELLOW)每只 3 美元，CPT 大阪

货物数量：　每种型号各 30 000 只

货物包装：　每只玩具装入一个泡沫塑料袋，再装入一个小纸箱中，20 只小纸箱装入一个出口纸箱，共计装入一个 20 英尺集装箱（集装箱号：TEXU2263999）

毛　　重：　Art No. 101 10.2KGS/CTN, Art No. 102 11.2KGS/CTN, Art No. 103 10.2KGS/CTN, Art No. 104 11.2KGS/CTN

净　　重：　Art No. 101 10KGS/CTN, Art No. 102 11KGS/CTN, Art No. 103 10KGS/CTN, Art No. 104 11KGS/CTN

体　　积：　Art No. 101 0.2CBM/CTN, Art No. 102 0.2CBM/CTN, Art No. 103 0.2CBM/CTN, Art No. 104 0.2CBM/CTN

支付方式：　30% 前 T/T, 70% 后 T//T

起运地：　　苏州

目的地：　　大阪

运输方式：　航空运输（运费 2 500 美元）

装运时间：　不迟于 2012 年 5 月 31 日

合同号：　　SZHTY070315

合同日期：　2012 年 3 月 15 日

H.S. 编码：　9503.9000

发票号码：　SZTY01221

发票日期：　2012 年 4 月 20 日

生产商名称：苏州红星玩具公司

体验活动三　代理出口贸易业务

国际货物托运书编号：JF0387124
航班号码：　　　　US00214M
报检单位登记号：　1254789479
生产单位注册号：　12345Q
海关注册号：　　　3018712462
货物存放地点：苏州市虎丘路11号
2.实训要求
(1)请你以苏州玩具进出口公司业务员李霞的身份，根据上述资料缮制装箱单。

苏 州 玩 具 进 出 口 公 司
SUZHOU TOY IMPORT & EXPORT CORPORATION
130 HUQIU ROAD, SUZHOU

PACKING LIST

TEL:_____　　　　　　　　　　　　　　　INV. NO. :_____
FAX:_____　　　　　　　　　　　　　　　DATE:_____
TO:

FROM _____ TO _____

GOODS DESCRIPTION & PACKING	QTY	CTNS	G.W.	N.W.	MEAS
TOTAL					

SAY TOTAL:

(2) 请你以苏州玩具进出口贸易公司业务员李霞的身份，根据上述资料填写国际货物托运书。

苏州客货运输服务有限公司
SUZHOU EXPRESS SERVICE CO., LTD.   IATA

国际货物托运书
SHIPPER'S LETTER OF INSTRUCTION   REF. NO.：

始发站 AIRPORT DEPARTURE		到达站 AIRPORT OF DESTINATION				供承运人用 FOR CARRIER ONLY	
路线及到达站 ROUTING AND DESTINATION						航班/日期 FLIGHT/DAY	航班/日期 FLIGHT/DAY
至 TO	第一承运人 BY FIRST CARRIER	至 TO	承运人 BY	至 TO	承运人 BY	至 TO	承运人 BY	已预留吨位 BOOKED	
收货人姓名及地址 CONSIGNEE'S NAME AND ADDRESS						运费： CHARGES：	
另行通知 ALSO NOTIFY						FREIGHT:PREPAID	
托运人账号 SHIPPER'S ACCOUNT NUMBER				托运人姓名及地址 SHIPPER'S NAME & ADDRESS			
托运人声明的价值 SHIPPER'S DECLARED VALUE		保险金额 AMOUNT OF INSURANCE		所附文件 DOCUMENTS TO ACCOMPANY AIR WAYBILL			
供运输用 FOR CARRIAGE	供海关用 FOR CUSTOMS						
件数 NO. OF PACKAGES	实际毛重 ACTUAL GROSS WEIGHT(KG)	运价类别 RATE CLASS	收费重量 CHARGEABLE WEIGHT	离岸 RATE CHARGE	货物名称及重量（包括体积或尺寸） NATURE AND QUANTITY OF GOODS(INCL. DIMENSIONS OF VOLUME)		

在货物不能交于收货人时，托运人指示的处理方法
SHIPPER'S INSTRUCTIONS IN CASE OF INABILITY TO DELIVER SHIPMENT AS CONSIGNED

处理情况（包括包装方式、货物标志及号码等）
HANDLING INFORMATION (INCL. METHOD OF PACKING DENTIFYING MARKS AND NUMBERS, ETC.)

托运人证实以上所填全部属实并愿遵守托运人的一切载运章程
THE SHIPPER CERTIFIES THAT THE PARTICULARS ON THE FACE HEREOF ARE CORRECT AND AGREES TO THE CONDITIONS OF CARRIAGE OF THE CARRIER

托运人签字： SIGNATURE OF SHIPPER	日期： DATE	经办人： AGENT	日期： DATE

(3)请你以苏州玩具进出口公司业务员李霞的身份，根据上述资料填写出境货物报检单。

中华人民共和国出入境检验检疫
出境货物报检单

报检单位(加盖公章)：   *编号：_____

报检单位登记号：_____ 联系人：_____ 电话：_____ 报检日期： 年 月 日

发货人	(中文)					
	(外文)					
收货人	(中文)					
	(外文)					

货物名称(中/外文)	H.S.编码	产地	数/重量	货物总值	包装种类及数量

运输工具的名称与号码		贸易方式		货物存放地点	
合同号		信用证号		用途	
发货日期		输往国家(地区)		许可证/审批证	
起运地		到达口岸		生产单位注册号	
集装箱规格、数量及号码					

合同、信用证订立的检验检疫条款或特殊要求	标记及号码	随附单据(划"√"或补填)	
		☐ 合同	☐ 包装性能结果单
		☐ 信用证	☐ 许可/审批文件
		☐ 发票	☐
		☐ 换证凭单	☐
		☐ 装箱单	☐
		☐ 厂检单	☐

需要证单名称(划"√"或补填)	*检验检疫费
☐ 品质证书 __正__副　☐ 植物检疫证书 __正__副	总金额
☐ 重量证书 __正__副　☐ 熏蒸/消毒证书 __正__副	(人民币元)
☐ 数量证书 __正__副　☐ 出境货物换证凭单 __正__副	
☐ 兽医卫生证书 __正__副	计费人
☐ 健康证书 __正__副	
☐ 卫生证书 __正__副	收费人
☐ 动物卫生证书 __正__副	

报检人郑重声明：	
1. 本人被授权报检。	领 取 证 单
2. 上列填写内容正确属实，货物无伪造或冒用他人的厂名、标志、认证标志的情形。	
签名：	

185

(4)请你以苏州玩具进出口公司业务员李霞的身份,根据上述资料填写出口货物报关单。

中华人民共和国海关出口货物报关单

预录入编号: 海关编号:

出口口岸	备案号		出口日期		申报日期	
经营单位	运输方式		运输工具名称		提运单号	
发货单位	贸易方式		征免性质		结汇方式	
许可证号	运抵国(地区)		指运港		境内货源地	
批准文号	成交方式	运费		保费		杂费
合同协议号	件数	包装种类		毛重(千克)		净重(千克)
集装箱号	随附单据			生产厂家		
标记唛码及备注						

项号 商品编号 商品名称、规格型号 数量及单位 最终目的国(地区) 单价   总价 币制 征免

税费征收情况			
录入员 录入单位	兹声明以上申报无讹并承担法律责任	海关审单批注及放行日期(签章)	
报关员	申报单位(签章)	审单	审价
单位地址		征税	统计
邮编 电话	填制日期	查验	放行

操作二

1. 操作资料

卖　方：　宁波进出口贸易公司
　　　　　宁波市百丈路678号　　电话:0574-87551112
　　　　　传真:0574-87551113
企业性质：民营企业
买　方：　YAMOO IMPORT & EXPORT CORPORATION
　　　　　No.206 CHANGJ NORTH STREET NEWYORK USA
　　　　　TEL:212-7691134　FAX:212-76911135
货物名称：汽车喇叭
货物单价：No. XY122 每套 USD 1.50,No. HY132 每套 USD 2.10,No. TY242 每套 USD 4.40,CPT NEWYORK
货物数量：每种型号各1 800套
货物包装：每50套装一个纸箱,计装入一个20英尺集装箱(集装箱号：TEXU2263999)
毛　重：　No. XY122 15 KGS/CTN,No. HY132 14 KGS/CTN,No. TY242 19 KGS/CTN
净　重：　No. XY122 13KGS/CTN,No. HY132 11 KGS/CTN,No. TY242 15 KGS/CTN
体　积：　No. XY122 0.2CBM/CTN, No. HY132 0.2CBM/CTN, No. TY242 0.2 CBM/CTN
支付方式：即期信用证
起运地：　苏州
目的地：　纽约
运输方式：航空运输(运费1 023美元)
装运时间：不迟于2012年11月30日
合同号：　NBIE071001
合同日期：2012年10月1日
H.S.编码：9503.9100
发票号码：NBIE01211
发票日期：2012年11月10日
国际货物托运书编号：TU0124785
航班号码：　MU00345N
报检单位登记号：1254794512
生产单位注册号：12345Q
海关注册号：3018712444
货物存放地点：宁波市百丈路11号
生产厂家：　宁波电讯公司

2. 实训要求

(1)请你以宁波进出口贸易公司业务员张力的身份,根据上述资料填写装箱单。

宁波进出口公司
NINGBO IMPORT & EXPORT TRADING CORPORATION
678 BAIZHANG ROAD NINGBO, CHINA
PACKING LIST

TEL: _____ 　　　　　　　　　　　　　INV. NO.: _____

FAX: _____ 　　　　　　　　　　　　　DATE: _____

TO:　　　　　　　　　　　　　　　　　SHIPPING MARK

GOODS DESCRIPTION & PACKING	QTY	CTNS	G.W.	N.W.	MEAS
TOTAL					

SAY TOTAL:

(2)请你以宁波进出口贸易公司业务员张力的身份,根据上述资料填写国际货物托运书。

宁波客货运输服务有限公司
NINGBO EXPRESS SERVICE CO., LTD.   IATA

国际货物托运书
SHIPPER'S LETTER OF INSTRUCTION   REF. NO.:

始发站 AIRPORT DEPARTURE		到达站 AIRPORT OF DESTINATION				供承运人用 FOR CARRIER ONLY	
路线及到达站 ROUTING AND DESTINATION						航班/日期 FLIGHT/DAY	航班/日期 FLIGHT/DAY
至 TO	第一承运人 BY FIRST CARRIER	至 TO	承运人 BY	至 TO	承运人 BY	至 TO	承运人 BY	已预留吨位 BOOKED	
收货人姓名及地址 CONSIGNEE'S NAME AND ADDRESS						运费: CHARGES:	
另行通知 ALSO NOTIFY							
托运人账号 SHIPPER'S ACCOUNT NUMBER				托运人姓名及地址 SHIPPER'S NAME & ADDRESS			
托运人声明的价值 SHIPPER'S DECLARED VALUE		保险金额 AMOUNT OF INSURANCE		所附文件 DOCUMENTS TO ACCOMPANY AIR WAYBILL			
供运输用 FOR CARRIAGE	供海关用 FOR CUSTOMS						
件数 NO. OF PACKAGES	实际毛重 ACTUAL GROSS WEIGHT(KG)	运价类别 RATE CLASS	收费重量 CHARGEABLE WEIGHT	离岸 RATE CHARGE	货物名称及重量(包括体积或尺寸) NATURE AND QUANTITY OF GOODS(INCL. DIMENSIONS OF VOLUME)		
在货物不能交于收货人时,托运人指示的处理方法 SHIPPER'S INSTRUCTIONS IN CASE OF INABILITY TO DELIVER SHIPMENT AS CONSIGNED							
处理情况(包括包装方式、货物标志及号码等) HANDLING INFORMATION (INCL. METHOD OF PACKING DENTIFYING MARKS AND NUMBERS, ETC.)							

托运人证实以上所填全部属实并愿遵守托运人的一切载运章程
THE SHIPPER CERTIFIES THAT THE PARTICULARS ON THE FACE HEREOF ARE CORRECT AND AGREES TO THE CONDITIONS OF CARRIAGE OF THE CARRIER

托运人签字: 日期: 经办人: 日期:
SIGNATURE OF SHIPPER   DATE   AGENT   DATE

(3) 请你以宁波进出口贸易公司业务员张力的身份,根据上述资料填写出境货物报检单。

中华人民共和国出入境检验检疫
出境货物报检单

报检单位(加盖公章):　　　　　　　　　　　　　　*编号:＿＿＿＿

报检单位登记号:　　　联系人:　　电话:　　　报检日期:　年　月　日

发货人	(中文)						
	(外文)						
收货人	(中文)						
	(外文)						
货物名称(中/外文)		H.S.编码	产地	数/重量	货物总值	包装种类及数量	

运输工具的名称与号码		贸易方式		货物存放地点	
合同号		信用证号		用途	
发货日期		输往国家(地区)		许可证/审批证	
起运地		到达口岸		生产单位注册号	
集装箱规格、数量及号码					

合同、信用证订立的检验检疫条款或特殊要求	标记及号码	随附单据(划"√"或补填)	
		□ 合同	□ 包装性能结果单
		□ 信用证	□ 许可/审批文件
		□ 发票	□
		□ 换证凭单	□
		□ 装箱单	□
		□ 厂检单	□

需要证单名称(划"√"或补填)		*检验检疫费
□ 品质证书　＿正＿副	□ 植物检疫证书　＿正＿副	总金额 (人民币元)
□ 重量证书　＿正＿副	□ 熏蒸/消毒证书　＿正＿副	
□ 数量证书　＿正＿副	□ 出境货物换证凭单　＿正＿副	
□ 兽医卫生证书　＿正＿副		计费人
□ 健康证书　＿正＿副		
□ 卫生证书　＿正＿副		收费人
□ 动物卫生证书　＿正＿副		

报检人郑重声明:
1. 本人被授权报检。
2. 上列填写内容正确属实,货物无伪造或冒用他人的厂名、标志、认证标志的情形。

　　　　　　　　　　签名:　　　　　　　　　　领　取　证　单

(4)请你以宁波进出口贸易公司业务员张力的身份,根据上述资料填写出口货物报关单。

中华人民共和国海关出口货物报关单

预录入编号:　　　　　　　　　　　　海关编号:

出口口岸		备案号		出口日期		申报日期	
经营单位		运输方式		运输工具名称		提运单号	
发货单位		贸易方式		征免性质		结汇方式	
许可证号		运抵国(地区)		指运港		境内货源地	
批准文号		成交方式	运费		保费		杂货
合同协议号		件数	包装种类		毛重(千克)		净重(千克)
集装箱号		随附单据			生产厂家		
标记唛码及备注							

项号 商品编号 商品名称、规格型号 数量及单位 最终目的国(地区) 单价　　总价　币制　征免

税费征收情况		
录入员　　录入单位	兹声明以上申报无讹并承担法律责任	海关审单批注及放行日期(签章)
报关员	申报单位(签章)	审单　　　　审价
单位地址		征税　　　　统计
		查验　　　　放行
邮编　　电话	填制日期	

实训四　办理出口结汇、核销及退税

业务导入

　　上海进出口贸易公司获取空运单后,卢珍小姐根据有关的规定,制作非木质包装证明,并汇集发票、装箱单和空运单等有关单据及时向中国银行上海分行办理结汇手续。当货款到账,按照合同、发票的有关内容填制出口收汇核销单,持该笔业务的有关单据向国家外汇管理局办理核销手续。核销后,持该笔出口业务的外销发票、增值税专用发票、出口货物报关单(出口退税专用)、核销单(出口退税专用)等全套出口退税单证及时到国家税务局主管退税机关办理出口退税申报手续,及时获取出口退税金额。

　　办理出口结汇、核销与退税手续业务环节如下图所示:

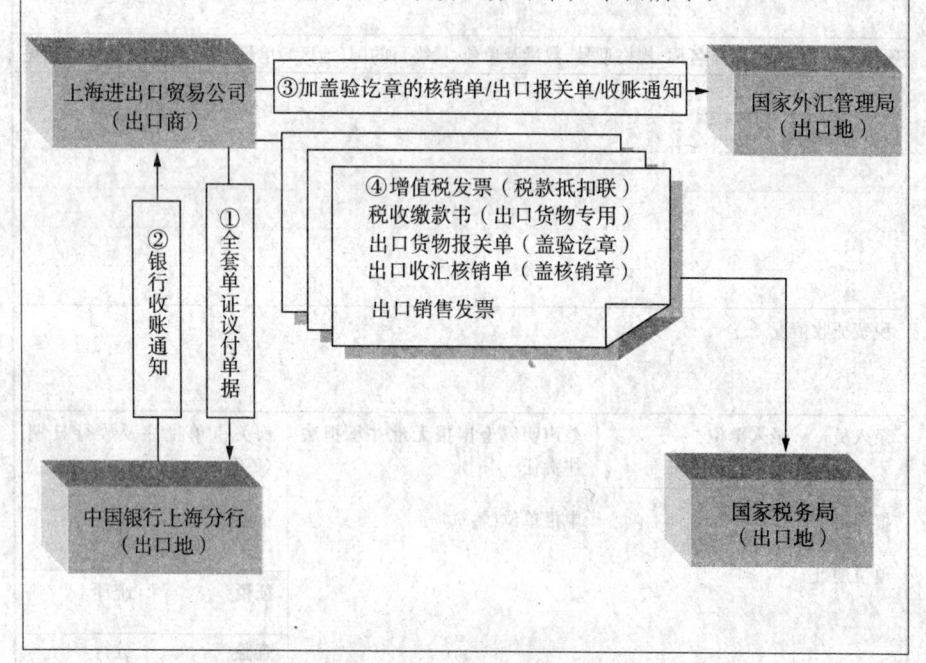

```
┌─────────────┐  ③加盖验讫章的核销单/出口报关单/收账通知  ┌─────────────┐
│上海进出口贸易│ ──────────────────────────────────────→ │国家外汇管理局│
│公司(出口商) │                                          │  (出口地)   │
└─────────────┘                                          └─────────────┘
   ↑      ↓                ④增值税发票(税款抵扣联)
   ②      ①                税收缴款书(出口货物专用)
  银行    全套             出口货物报关单(盖验讫章)
  收账    单证             出口收汇核销单(盖核销章)
  通知    议付             出口销售发票
          单据                        │
                                      ↓
┌─────────────┐                                          ┌─────────────┐
│中国银行上海 │                                          │ 国家税务局  │
│分行(出口地)│                                          │  (出口地)   │
└─────────────┘                                          └─────────────┘
```

体验活动三　代理出口贸易业务

◎ 工作任务一　　　办理出口结汇手续

上海进出口贸易公司在货物装机并获取空运单后，根据有关的规定由卢珍小姐制作非木质包装证明，汇集发票、装箱单和空运单等有关单据及时向中国银行上海分行办理结汇手续。

卢珍小姐缮制非木质包装证明：

Declaration of no-wooden Packing material

TO:
THE SERVICE OF JAPAN ENTRY & EXIT INSPECTION AND QUARANTINE
IT IS DECLARED THAT THIS SHIPMENT
COMMODITY: ___DOUBLE OPEN END SPANNER___
QUANTITY/WEIGHT: ___1 400 CARTONS___
INV. NO. : XH05111

DOES NOT CONTAIN WOOD PACKING MATERIALS.

SHANGHAI IMPORT & EXPORT CORPORATION
Zhen Lu
2012. 12. 20

◎ 工作任务二　　　办理出口核销手续

上海进出口贸易公司在货款到账后，按照合同、发票的有关内容填制出口收汇核销单，持该笔业务的有关单据向国家外汇管理局办理核销手续。

出口收汇核销单 存根	出口收汇核销单	出口收汇核销单 出口退税 用
（沪）编号：325623454	（沪）编号：325623454	（沪）编号：325623454

出口收汇核销单 存根

（沪）编号：325623454

出口单位：上海进出口贸易公司

单位编码：4654984

出口币种总价：USD 78 000.00

收汇方式：T/T

约计收款日期：

报关日期：2012.12.18

备注：

此单报关有效期截止到 2012.12.30

（盖章：上海进出口贸易公司 IMPORT & EXPORT TRADE CORPORATION SHANGHAI）

（盖章：国家外汇管理局）

出口收汇核销单

（沪）编号：325623454

出口单位：上海进出口贸易公司

单位编码：4654984

类别	币种金额	盖章
活络扳手	USD 78 000.00	

银行盖章注栏

海关签注栏：该票货物已于 2012.12.20 结关

（盖章：中国银行）

（盖章：上海吴淞海关验讫章）

外汇局签注栏：

2012 年 12 月 31 日（盖章）

出口收汇核销单 出口退税 用

（沪）编号：325623454

出口单位：上海进出口贸易公司

单位编码：4654984

货物名称	数量	币种总价
活络扳手	1 400 箱	USD 78 000.00

（盖章：上海进出口贸易公司 IMPORT & EXPORT TRADE CORPORATION SHANGHAI）

报关单编号：SH0310254665

签注栏：

2012 年 12 月 31 日（盖章）

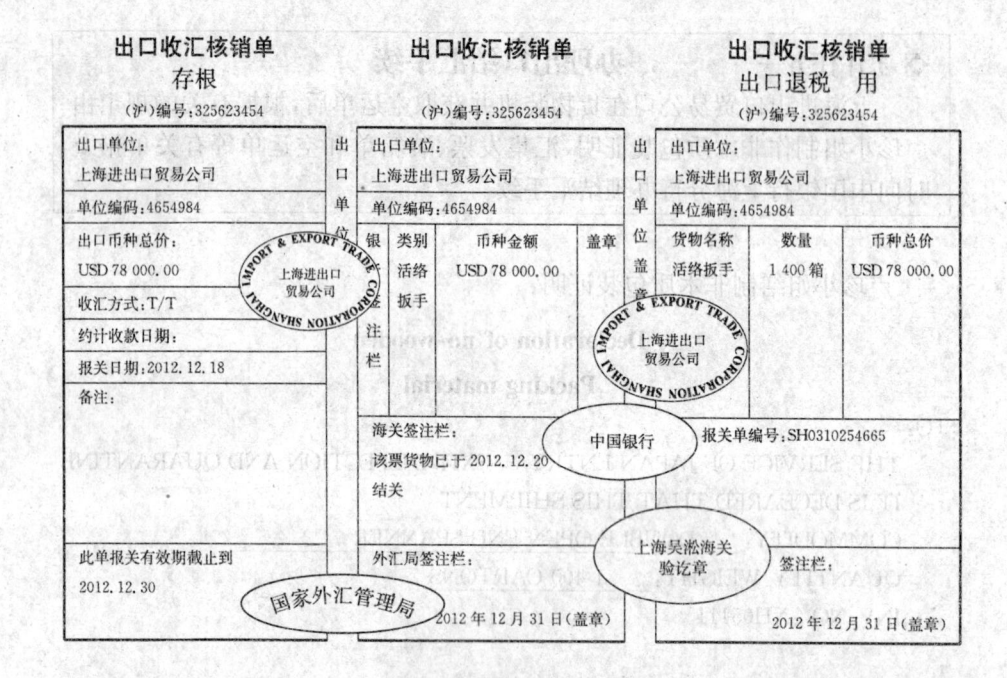

◇ 工作任务三　　办理出口退税手续

　　上海进出口贸易公司在货款到账后，按照合同、发票的有关内容填制出口收汇核销单，持该笔业务的有关单据向国家外汇管理局办理核销手续。

　　上海进出口贸易公司在货物出运后，按规定凭相关退税单据到税务局办理退税，退税办理好后，上海进出口贸易公司接到银行通知，对方货款已经进账，按照相关规定到外汇管理局办理核销手续。

体验活动三 代理出口贸易业务

上海市增值税专用发票
抵扣联

开票日期：2012 年 11 月 20 日　　　　　　　　　　　　　NO.06053011

购货单位	名称	上海进出口贸易公司	密码区	
	纳税人识别号	3101466775532		
	地址、电话	上海市中山路 1321 号 65788877		
	开户银行及账号	中国银行上海分行 SZR80066686		

货物或应税劳务名称	规格型号	单位	数量	单价	金额	税率	税额
活络扳手	8×10MM(MTM)	件	60 000	￥3.00	￥180 000	17%	￥85 000
	10×12MM(MTM)	件	80 000	￥4.00	￥320 000		
合计			140 000		￥500 000	17%	￥85 000

价税合计（大写）　捌万伍仟圆整

销货单位	名称	宁波兴旺工具公司	备注
	纳税人识别码	310457651564	
	地址、电话	宁波市木行路 302 号	
	开户银行及账号	宁波市工商银行木行支行 0086132732315	

注：纳税人识别号即纳税人登记号。

中华人民共和国
税收（出口货物专用）缴款　　060510 号

经济类型：国有经济　　填发日期：2012 年 11 月 30 日　　征收机关：上海市国税局

缴款单位	税务登记号	0 3 1 0 4 8 6 4 8 1	预算科目	款	
	全称	宁波兴旺工具公司		项	
	开户银行	宁波市工商银行木行支行		级	
	账号	0086132732315	收款国库		市金库
购货企业	全称	上海进出口贸易公司	销货发票号码		06053011
	税务登记号	0 2 4 3 5 6 8 8 1 5			
	海关代码	0387124666			

税款所属时期　2012 年 12 月 31 日　　　税款限缴日期　2012 年 12 月 31 日

货物名称	课税数量	单位价格	计税金额	法定税率（额）	征税率	实缴税额
活络扳手 8×10MM(MTM)	60 000 件	￥3.00	￥180 000.00	17%	17%	￥85 000.00
10×12MM(MTM)	80 000 件	￥4.00	￥320 000.00			
金额合计			（大写）捌万伍仟圆整			￥85 000.00

缴款单位（盖章）　宁波兴旺工具公司　　　税务机关（盖章）　上海税务　　上列款项已收妥并划转收款单位账号　　中国银行　　备注
经办人：土丁　　填票人：张言　　国库（银行）盖章 2012 年 11 月 30 日

第二联（收据乙）国库（经办处）收款盖章后退缴款单位转交购货企业，逾期不缴，按税法规定加收滞纳金

综合业务模拟操作

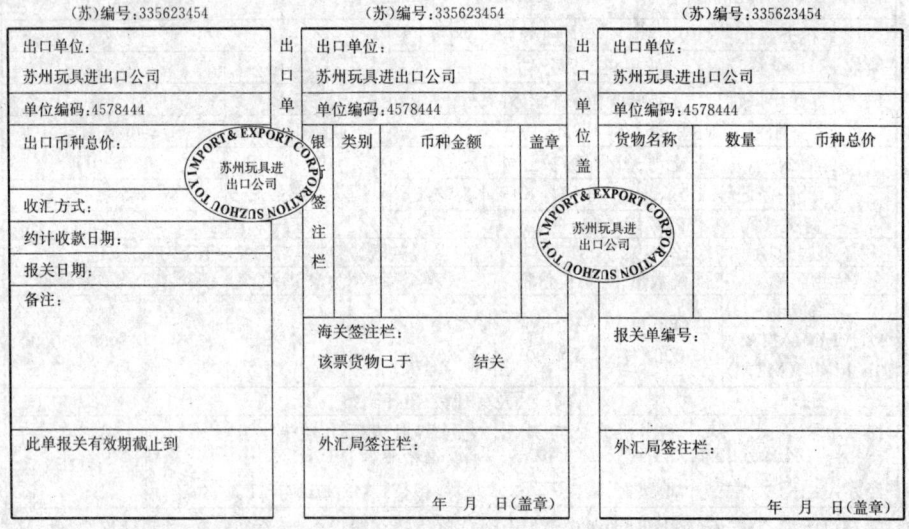

操作一

1. 操作资料

卖　方：　苏州玩具进出口公司
　　　　　苏州市虎丘路130号　　TEL:0512-64043030
　　　　　FAX:0512-64043030

企业性质：　民营企业

货物名称：　汽车模型玩具（AUTO MODEL）

货物单价：　Art No.101(BLUE)每只4.2美元，Art No.102(BLACK)每只4.2美元，Art No.103(RED)每只4美元，Art No.104(YELLOW)每只3美元，CPT大阪

货物数量：　每种型号各30 000只

支付方式：　30%前T/T，70%后T//T

报关单编号：SZ0310233548

2. 实训要求

请你以苏州玩具进出口公司业务员李霞的身份，根据上述资料填写出口收汇核销单。

出口收汇核销单 存根 (苏)编号:335623454	出口收汇核销单 (苏)编号:335623454	出口收汇核销单 出口退税 用 (苏)编号:335623454
出口单位: 苏州玩具进出口公司 单位编码:4578444 出口币种总价: 收汇方式: 约计收款日期: 报关日期: 备注: 此单报关有效期截止到	出口单位: 苏州玩具进出口公司 单位编码:4578444 银行签注栏 类别 / 币种金额 / 盖章 海关签注栏: 该票货物已于　　结关 外汇局签注栏: 　　　年　月　日(盖章)	出口单位: 苏州玩具进出口公司 单位编码:4578444 货物名称 / 数量 / 币种总价 报关单编号: 外汇局签注栏: 　　　年　月　日(盖章)

体验活动三 代理出口贸易业务

操作二

1. 操作资料

卖　方：	宁波进出口贸易公司
	宁波市百丈路 678 号　　电话:0574-87551112
	传真:0574-87551113
货物名称：	汽车喇叭
货物单价：	No.XY122 每套 USD 1.50，No.HY132 每套 USD 2.10，No.TY242 每套 USD 4.40，CPT NEWYORK
货物数量：	每种型号各 1 800 套
货物包装：	每 50 套装一个纸箱，计装入一个 20 英尺集装箱（集装箱号：TEXU2263999）
支付方式：	即期信用证
报关单编号：	SZ0310248953

2. 实训要求

请你以宁波进出口贸易公司业务员张力的身份，根据上述资料填写出口收汇核销单。

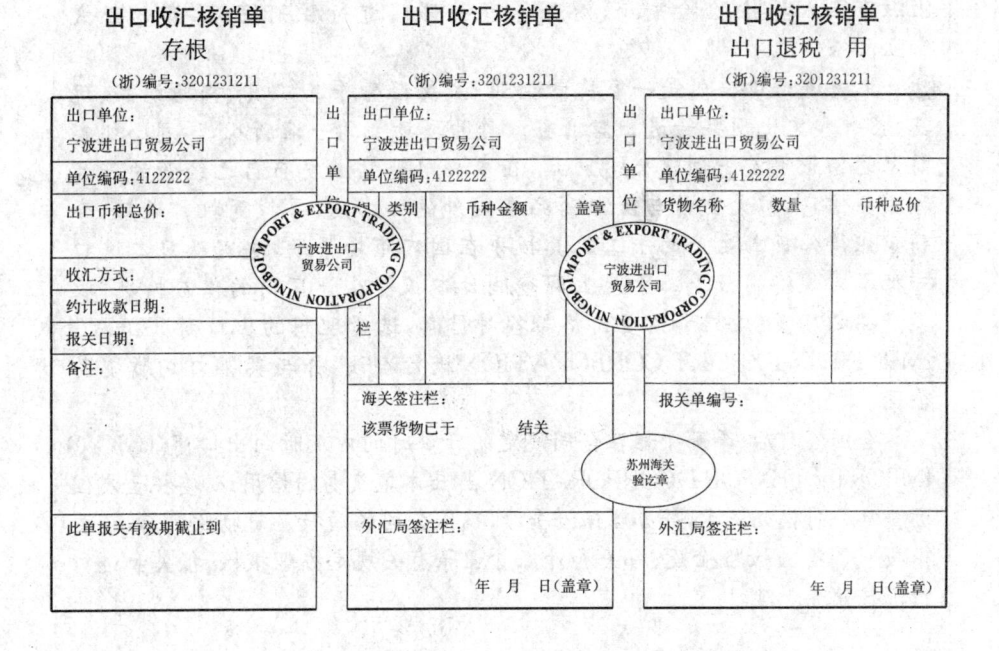

出口收汇核销单 存根
（浙）编号：3201231211

出口单位：
宁波进出口贸易公司
单位编码：4122222
出口币种总价：
收汇方式：
约计收款日期：
报关日期：
备注：
此单报关有效期截止到

出口收汇核销单
（浙）编号：3201231211

出　口　单　栏	出口单位：宁波进出口贸易公司
	单位编码：4122222
	类别　币种金额　盖章
海关签注栏：该票货物已于　　　结关
外汇局签注栏：　　　　　年　月　日（盖章）

出口收汇核销单
出口退税　用

（浙）编号：3201231211

出口单位：宁波进出口贸易公司
单位编码：4122222
货物名称　数量　币种总价
报关单编号：
（苏州海关验讫章）
外汇局签注栏：　　　　　年　月　日（盖章）

体验活动四 自理进口贸易业务

工作背景

　　李莉小姐今年毕业于上海贸易大学，面对就业市场的激烈竞争，决定放弃各种应聘机会进行创业。在父母、老师和朋友等各方面的支持下，成立了上海进出口公司。该公司在工商局、税务局和上海市对外经济贸易委员会登记核准后，并在上海市出入境检验检疫局、海关等有关部门进行注册登记，开始正式营业。

　　上海进出口公司是一家民营企业，主要经营手工工具、棉纺织品、玩具、茶叶和文化用品等进出口业务。作为商场上的一名新人，李莉小姐在前辈的指点下首先创建公司网站，在本公司网站上发布自己经营的产品和服务信息，扩大公司与出口商品在国外的知名度，寻找商机。近日，李莉小姐得知日本生产的手工工具扳手在国内市场紧缺，决定从日本进口一批不同规格的扳手。于是上网查阅日本扳手生产厂商的供应情况，收集产品的质量、规格和购货价格等各种信息，选择理想的出口商 TOKYO IMPORT & EXPORT CORPORATION 进行洽谈，并与其签订购货贸易合同。

　　合同签订后，李莉小姐在合同规定的开证时间内及时向出口商 TOKYO IMPORT & EXPORT CORPORATION 开出本笔交易的信用证，委托金友国际货代公司代办托运，并办理保险手续，确保合同的履行。货物收到后，还要根据我国有关检验检疫、海关和外汇管理等有关规定办理报检、报关和进口付汇核销等手续。

体验活动四　自理进口贸易业务

自理进口业务流程如下图所示：

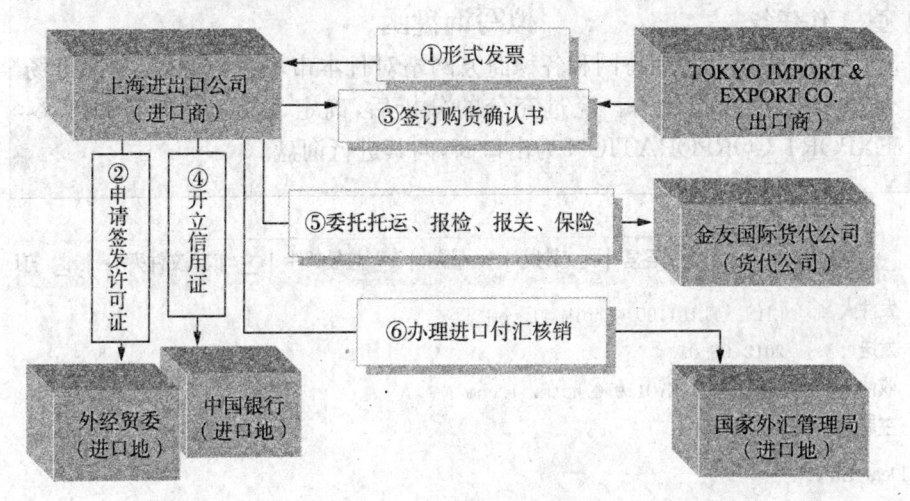

```
上海进出口公司 ←——①形式发票——— TOKYO IMPORT &
（进口商）  ——③签订购货确认书——  EXPORT CO.
                                （出口商）

②申请签发许可证   ④开立信用证
         ⑤委托托运、报检、报关、保险 → 金友国际货代公司
                                    （货代公司）

         ⑥办理进口付汇核销 → 国家外汇管理局
                              （进口地）

外经贸委   中国银行
（进口地） （进口地）
```

实训一　进口交易磋商与合同签订

业务导入

李莉小姐创建上海进出口公司后,建立了公司网站,在网站上发布自己经营的产品和服务信息。近日,李莉小姐得知日本生产的手工工具扳手在国内市场紧缺,决定从日本进口一批扳手。于是上网查阅日本扳手生产厂商的供应情况,收集产品的质量、规格和购货价格等各种信息,选择了 TOKYO IMPORT & EXPORT CORPORATION 进行洽谈。当双方达成一致意见后,TOKYO IMPORT & EXPORT CORPORATION 向上海进出口公司开出形式发票,作为办理进口许可证的材料,然后与其签订购货确认书。

合同商订的业务环节如下图所示：

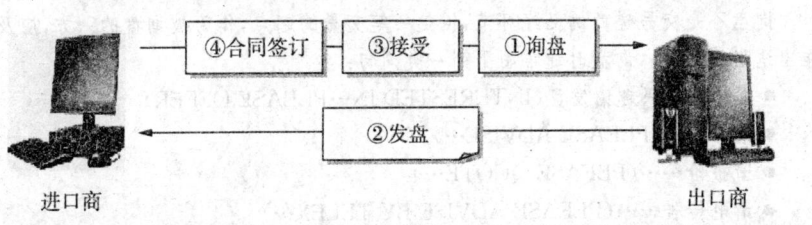

```
进口商  ④合同签订  ③接受  ①询盘  出口商
              ②发盘
```

工作任务一　　　　　　拟写询盘函

李莉小姐利用因特网和各种商务网站对日本市场进行调研,掌握市场的供求信息、价格动态。经过充分的分析后,确定 TOKYO IMPORT & EXPORT CORPORATION 为出口商,向其进行询盘。

| 答复发件人 | 全部答复 | 转发 | 删除 | 垃圾邮件 | 放入文件夹 | 打印 |

发件人： LILI < LILI100 @ hotmail.com >
发送： 2012-08-01
收件人： TOKYO < TOKYO119 @ hotmail.com >
主题： ENQUIRY

Dear Sir,

　　We are interested in your WRENCH, especially HEX DEYS WRENCH, DOUBLE RING OFFSET WRENCH, CONBINATION WRENCH and ADJUSTABLE WRENCH. We would be appreciated if you could quote us your best prices.

　　Looking forward to hearing from you.

　　　　　　　　　　　　　　　　Yours truly,
　　　　　　　　　　　　　　　　SHANGHAI IMPORT & EXPORT CORPORATION
　　　　　　　　　　　　　　　　LILI
　　　　　　　　　　　　　　　　AUG. 01, 2012

操作指南 ➡ 询盘的主要内容

　　询盘(Enquiry)是指交易的一方有意购买或出售某一种商品,向对方询问买卖该商品的有关交易条件,其内容可以是询问价格,也可询问其他一项或几项交易条件。
　　询盘不是交易磋商的必经环节,但是一笔交易的起点,作为被询盘的一方,应及时作出适当的处理。询盘时通常用下列一类词句:
- 对……有兴趣请发盘(INTERESTED IN…PLEASE OFFER)
- 请告……(PLEASE ADVISE…)
- 请报价……(PLEASE QUOTE…)
- 请电传告……(PLEASE ADVISE BY TELEX…)

工作任务二　　　　　拟写接受函

不久,上海进出口公司接到了对方的发盘,发盘中详细列明了各项交易条件,我方经慎重考虑,决定接受对方的发盘,并由李莉拟写接受函。

发送 | 保存草稿 | 附加 | 工具 | 取消

收件人:　　TOKYO < TOKYO119 @ hotmail.com >

抄送:

密件抄送:

主题:　　　ACCEPTANCE

Dear Sir,

　　Thank you for your letter of AUG. 01, 2012.

　　We would like to inform you that we accept your proposal as follows:

	PACKING	FOB TOKYO
HEX DEYS WRENCH	100 PCS/CTN	USD 10.00/SET
DOUBLE RING OFFSET WRENCH	100 PCS/CTN	USD 10.00/SET
CONBINATION WRENCH	100 PCS/CTN	USD 20.00/SET
ADJUSTABLE WRENCH	100 PCS/CTN	USD 20.00/SET

Shipment: not later than SEP. 20, 2012

Payment: by at 60 days after sight irrevocable L/C

We are glad that through our mutual effort finally we have reached the agreement.

　　　　　　　　　　　　　Yours truly,
　　　　　　　　　　　　　SHANGHAI IMPORT & EXPORT CORPORATION
　　　　　　　　　　　　　LILI
　　　　　　　　　　　　　AUG. 10, 2012

工作任务三　　　　　申请签发进口许可证

上海进出口贸易公司与日本东京进出口贸易公司就扳手交易条件达成一致意见,并要求其出具形式发票。当收到形式发票后,李莉小姐持主管部门有关批准进口文件等资料向上海市外经贸主管部门申请签发进口许可证。

日本东京进出口贸易公司出具形式发票：

TOKYO IMPORT & EXPORT CORPORATION
82-324, OTOLI MACHI TOKYO, JAPAN

PROFORMA INVOICE
(WITHOUT ENGAGEMENT)

TEL: 028-548742
FAX: 028-548743

P/I NO.: IN05791
DATE: AUG. 11, 2012
P/C NO.: TX200523

CONSIGNEE:
SHANGHAI IMPORT & EXPORT CORPORATION

FROM TOKYO, JAPAN   TO   SHANGHAI, CHINA
DELIVERY: LATEST DATE OF SHIPMENT 120920
PARTIAL SHIPMENTS ALLOWED TRANSSHIPMENT NOT ALLOWED

MARKS & NO.	DESCRIPTIONS OF GOODS	QUANTITY	UNIT PRICE	AMOUNT
TITC	HAND TOOLS		FOB TOKYO	
TX200523	HEX DEYS WRENCH	1 000 SETs	USD 10.00	USD 10 000.00
SHANGHAI	DOUBLE RING OFFSET WRENCH	1 500 SETs	USD 10.00	USD 15 000.00
C/NO. 1-60	CONBINATION WRENCH	2 000 SETs	USD 20.00	USD 40 000.00
	ADJUSTABLE WRENCH	1 500 SETs	USD 20.00	USD 30 000.00
				USD 95 000.00

SAY U.S. DOLLARS NINETY FIVE THOUSAND ONLY

TERMS: 100% PAYMENT BY IRREVOCABLE DOCUMENTARY CREDIT AT 30 DAYS AFTER SIGHT

This invoice is supplied to enable you
to apply For the necessary import licence to be valid up to

TOKYO IMPORT & EXPORT CORPORATION

山 田

上海进出口贸易公司填写进口许可证申请表：

中华人民共和国进口许可证申请表

1. 进口商：代码 1368029168 上海进出口公司					3. 进口许可证号：			
2. 收货人： 上海进出口公司 1368029168					4. 进口许可证有效截止日期： 　　　　年　　月　　日			
5. 贸易方式： 一般贸易					8. 出口国(地区)： 日本			
6. 外汇来源： 购汇					9. 原产地国(地区)： 日本			
7. 报关口岸： 吴淞海关					10. 商品用途： 自营内销			
11. 商品名称： 扳手					商品编码： 8204.1100			
12. 规格、型号	13. 单位	14. 数量	15. 单价(USD)			16. 总值(USD)		17. 总值折美元
HEX DEYS WRENCH	套	1 000	10.00			10 000.00		10 000.00
DOUBLE RING OFFSET WRENCH	套	1 500	10.00			15 000.00		15 000.00
CONBINATION WRENCH	套	2 000	20.00			40 000.00		40 000.00
ADJUSTABLE WRENCH	套	1 500	20.00			30 000.00		30 000.00
18. 总计	套	6 000				95 000.00		95 000.00
19. 领证人姓名： 李　莉 联系电话：021-56082266 申请日期：2012 年 8 月 12 日 下次联系日期：					20. 签证机构审批(初审)： 终审：			

中华人民共和国商务部监制　　　　　　　　　第一联(正本)签证机构存档

中华人民共和国进口许可证申请表

1. 进口商：代码 1368029168 上海进出口公司			3. 进口许可证号：		
2. 收货人： 上海进出口公司			4. 进口许可证有效截止日期： 年　月　日		
5. 贸易方式： 一般贸易			8. 出口国（地区）： 日本		
6. 外汇来源： 购汇			9. 原产地国（地区）： 日本		
7. 报关口岸： 吴淞海关			10. 商品用途： 自营内销		
11. 商品名称： 扳手			商品编码： 8204.1100		
12. 规格、型号	13. 单位	14. 数量	15. 单价(USD)	16. 总值(USD)	17. 总值折美元
HEX DEYS WRENCH	套	1 000	10.00	10 000.00	10 000.00
DOUBLE RING OFFSET WRENCH	套	1 500	10.00	15 000.00	15 000.00
CONBINATION WRENCH	套	2 000	20.00	40 000.00	40 000.00
ADJUSTABLE WRENCH	套	1 500	20.00	30 000.00	30 000.00
18. 总计	套	6 000		95 000.00	95 000.00
19. 领证人姓名： （上海进出口公司印章） 李莉 联系电话：021-56082266 申请日期：2012年8月12日 下次联系日期：			不能获准原因： 1. 公司无权经营； 2. 公司编码有误； 3. 到港不妥善； 4. 品名与编码不符； 5. 单价(高)低； 6. 币别有误； 7. 漏填第（　）项 8. 第（　）项须补充说明函； 9. 第（　）项与批件不符； 10. 其他。		

中华人民共和国商务部监制　　　　　　　　　　第二联（副本）取证凭证

操作指南　　进口许可证申请表缮制方法

进口货物许可证申请表一式两联,由进口商填制,其主要内容与缮制方法如下:
1. 进口商及编码
填进口商全称,注明在海关注册的企业代码。
2. 收货人
按信用证或合同规定填写。
3. 进口许可证号
此栏留空,由签证机关填制。
4. 进口许可证有效截止日期
通常为一年,由签证机关填写。
5. 贸易方式
根据实际情况填写,如一般贸易、进料加工和来料加工等贸易方式。
6. 外汇来源
根据实际情况填写,通常为银行购汇。
7. 报关口岸
即实际目的地口岸,注明全称。
8. 出口国(地区)
应填写装运港(地)国家的全称。
9. 原产地国(地区)
应填写进口货物生产国家或地区的全称。
10. 商品用途
根据实际情况填写,通常有自用、生产用、内销和外销等。
11. 商品名称及商品编码
根据《中华人民共和国海关统计商品目录》规定的商品标准名称和统一编码填写。
12. 规格、型号
填写实际规格,不同规格应分行表示,计量单位按 H.S. 编码规则填写。
13. 单位
填写与合同规定一致的计量单位名称。
14. 数量
必须填写实际出运的数量,并与发票的相关内容一致。
15. 单价
按合同成交的单价填制,并与发票的相关内容一致。
16. 总值
按合同成交的总额填写,并与发票总金额相同。
17. 总值折美元
按外汇牌价折算为美元记入。
18. 总计
各栏的合计数分别填入本栏内。
19. 领证人姓名
根据实际情况填写。
20. 签证机构审批(初审)
发证机关审核无误后盖章,由授权人签名,并注明签证日期。

上海市外经贸主管部门签发进口许可证：

中华人民共和国进口货物许可证
IMPORT LICENCE THE PEOPLE'S REPUBLIC OF CHINA

1. 我国货物成交单位 Importer 上海进出口公司	编码 1368029168	3. 进口许可证编号 Licence No.	06-JZ5661168
2. 收货单位 Consignee	上海进出口公司	4. 许可证有效期 Validity	2013年8月15日
5. 贸易方式 Terms of trade	一般贸易	8. 进口国家（地区） Country of destination	日本
6. 外汇来源 Terms of foreign exchange	购汇	9. 商品原产地 Country of origin	日本
7. 到货口岸 Port of destination	上海	10. 商品用途 Use of commodity	外贸自营内销
唛头—包装件数 Marks & numbers-number of packages		SHIE SHANGHAI C/NO. 1-60	
商品名称 Description of commodity	WRENCH	商品编码 Commodity	No. 8204.1100

13. 商品规格、型号 Specification	单位 Unit	14. 数量 Quantity	15. 单价(USD) Unit price	16 总值(USD) Amount	17. 总值折美元 Amount in USD
HEX DEYS WRENCH	套	1 000	10.00	10 000.00	10 000.00
DOUBLE RING OFFSET WRENCH	套	1 500	10.00	15 000.00	15 000.00
CONBINATION WRENCH	套	2 000	20.00	40 000.00	40 000.00
ADJUSTABLE WRENCH	套	1 500	20.00	30 000.00	30 000.00
18. 总计 Total	套	6 000		95 000.00	95 000.00

19. 备注 Supplementary details	20. 发证机关盖章 Issuing authority's stamp & signature
	发证日期 Date　2012年8月15日　（进口许可证专用章 上海）

商务部监制　　　　　　　　　　　　　　　本证不得涂改，不得转让

操作指南 ➡ 申请签发进口许可证注意事项

进口许可证自签发之日起1年内有效。如1年内尚未对外签订贸易合同,不予以展期,该证作废;如1年内已对外签订了贸易合同,但货物还未进口,可持进口合同到原发证机关申请展期。

进口许可证是国家主管机关签发的批准进口商品的证明文件,也是进口通关证据之一。我国凡列入《实施进口许可证商品目录》中的进口货物,必须申领许可证。否则海关不予以放行。

外经贸主管部门签发进口许可证。

☒ 工作任务四　　拟订购货合同书

上海进出口公司办理好进口许可证后,由李莉小姐拟订购货贸易合同一式两份,双方签章后,各留下一份作为履行合同的依据。

上海进出口公司
SHANGHAI IMPORT & EXPORT CORPORATION
1321 ZHONGSHAN ROAD SHANGHAI, CHINA
PURCHASE CONTRACT

TEL:021-56082266　　　　　　　　　　　　　P/C NO. :TX200523
FAX:021-56082265　　　　　　　　　　　　　DATE:AUG. 20,2012

买 方:
The Buyer: SHANGHAI IMPORT & EXPORT CORPORATION
　　　　　1321 ZHONGSHAN ROAD SHANGHAI, CHINA
　　　　　TEL:021-56082266　FAX:021-56082265

卖 方:
The Seller: TOKYO IMPORT & EXPORT CORPORATION
　　　　　82-324 OTOLI MACHI TOKYO, JAPAN
　　　　　TEL:028-548-742　FAX:028-548-743

The Seller and the Buyer have confirmed this Contract with the terms and conditions stipulated below.

DESCRIPTIONS OF GOODS	QUANTITY	UNIT PRICE	AMOUNT
WRENCH		FOB TOKYO	
HEX DEYS WRENCH	1 000 SETS	USD 10.00	USD 10 000.00
DOUBLE RING OFFSET WRENCH	1 500 SETS	USD 10.00	USD 15 000.00
CONBINATION WRENCH	2 000 SETS	USD 20.00	USD 40 000.00
ADJUSTABLE WRENCH	1 500 SETS	USD 20.00	USD 30 000.00

1. COUNTRY OF ORIGIN AND MANUFACTURER: TOKYO IMPORT & EXPORT CORPORATION
2. PACKING: PACKED IN 1 CARTON OF 100 SETS EACH.
3. LATEST DATE OF SHIPMENT: 120920
4. PORT OF LOADING: TOKYO, JAPAN
5. PORT OF DESTINATION: SHANGHAI, CHINA
6. PAYMENT: IRREVOCABLE DOCUMENTARY CREDIT AT 60 DAYS AFTER SIGHT.
7. PARTIAL SHIPMENTS: ALLOWED
8. TRANSSHIPMENT: NOT ALLOWED
9. INSURANCE: FOR 110 PERCENT OF THE INVOICE VALUE COVERING ALL RISKS AND WAR RISK BY THE BUYER
10. DOCUMENTS: THE SELLER SHALL PRESENT THE FOLLOWING DOCUMENTS TO THE PAYING BANK FOR NEGOTIATION:
(1) THREE COPIES OF SIGNED COMMERCIAL INVOICE INDICATING CONTRACT NUMBER.
(2) THREE COPIES OF PACKING LIST.
(3) TWO COPIES OF CERTIFICATE OF QUALITY /QUANTITY ISSUED BY MANUFACTURE.
(4) WITHIN 12 HOURS AFTER THE GOODS ARE COMPLETELY LOADED, THE SELLER SHALL FAX TO NOTIFY THE BUYER OF THE CONTRACT NUMBER, NAME OF COMMODITY, QUANTITY, GROSS WEIGHT, B/L NO. AND THE DATE OF DELIVERY.
11. INSPECTION AND CLAIMS: IF THE QUALITY/WEIGHT AND/OR THE SPECIFICATIONS OF THE GOODS SHOULD BE FOUND NOT IN LINE WITH THE CONTRACTED STIPULATIONS, OR SHOULD THE GOODS PROVE DEFECTIVE FOR ANY REASONS, INCLUDING LATENT DEFECT OR THE USE OF UNSUITABLE MATERIALS, THE BUYER WOULD ARRANGE AN INSPECTION TO BE CARRIED OUT BY THE INSPECTION BUREAU AND HAVE THE RIGHT TO CLAIM AGAINST THE SELLERS ON THE STRENGTH OF THE INSPECTION CERTIFICATE ISSUED BY THE BUREAU. ALL CLAIMS SHALL BE REGARDED AS ACCEPTED IF THE SELLERS FAIL TO REPLY WITHIN 30 DAYS AFTER RECEIPT OF THE BUYER'S CLAIM.

Buyer:
SHANGHAI IMPORT & EXPORT CORPORATION
李 莉

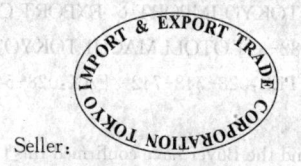

Seller:
TOKYO IMPORT & EXPORT CORPORATION
山 田

综合业务模拟操作

操作一

1. 操作资料

近日,上海玩具进出口公司要从日本进口一批电子手掌玩具(ELECTRON PALM BAUBLE),请你以公司业务员的身份上网查阅日本电子手掌玩具供应商有关产品的质量、规格和购货价格等各种信息,并选择其中一家理想的出口商(TOKYO IMPORT & EXPORT CORPORATION)进行洽谈。双方具体磋商内容如下:

(1)8月10日上海玩具进出口公司询盘:
"对贵公司的电子手掌玩具感兴趣,请报价FOB TOKYO。"

(2)8月12日上海玩具进出口公司对TOKYO IMPORT & EXPORT CORPORATION的发盘进行核定,表示接受全部发盘的条件。具体内容如下:

买　　方：　上海玩具进出口公司(SHANGHAI TOY IMPORT & EXPORT CORPORATION)
　　　　　　地址：13 FENXIANG ROAD SHANGHAI, CHINA
　　　　　　TEL：021-56082212　FAX：021-56082211

卖　　方：　TOKYO IMPORT & EXPORT CORPORATION
　　　　　　地址：82-324 OTOLI MACHI TOKYO, JAPAN
　　　　　　TEL：028-548-742　FAX：028-548-743

货名规格：　电子手掌玩具(ELECTRON PALM BAUBLE)(货号为R222S、R333H、R666W、R888A)

单　　价：　FOB TOKYO
　　　　　　R222S USD 50.00/ SET, R333H USD 45.00/ SET
　　　　　　R666W USD 35.00/ SET, R888A USD 20.00/ SET

支付方式：　不可撤销跟单即期信用证(IRREVOCABLE DOCUMENTARY CREDIT AT SIGHT)

数　　量：　R222S 1 000套(1 000 SETS)、R333H 1 000套(1 000 SETS)
　　　　　　R666W 1 000套(1 000 SETS)、R888A 1 000套(1000 SETS)

包　　装：　每50套装一个出口纸箱(PACKED IN 1 CARTON OF 50 SETS EACH)

装运期：　　不迟于2012年10月31日前装运(LATEST DATE OF SHIPMENT：20121031)

装运港：　　日本东京(TOKYO, JAPAN)

目的地港：　中国上海(SHANGHAI, CHINA)

分批装运：　允许(ALLOWED)

转运： 不允许（NOT ALLOWED）
唛头： 由卖方制定（BY THE SELLER）
合同号： TX06238
提交单据： (1) 已签字的商业发票一式三份,并显示合同号（THREE COPIES OF SIGNED COMMERCIAL INVOICE INDICATING CONTRACT NUMBER OF TX06238）；

(2) 装箱单一式三份（THREE COPIES OF PACKING LIST）；

(3) 品质证书一式二份,由厂商签发（TWO COPIES OF CERTIFICATE OF QUALITY/QUANTITY ISSUED BY MANUFACTURE）；

(4) 在装船后 12 小时内用传真向买方发出装运通知,其包含合同号、货名、数量毛重、提单号和装运日期等（WITHIN 12 HOURS AFTER THE GOODS ARE COMPLETELY LOADED, THE SELLER SHALL FAX TO NOTIFY THE BUYER OF THE CONTRACT NUMBER, NAME OF COMMODITY, QUANTITY, GROSS WEIGHT, B/L NO. AND THE DATE OF DELIVERY）。

2. 操作要求

(1)请你以上海玩具进出口公司业务员张成的身份,向日本 TOKYO IMPORT & EXPORT CORPORATION 询盘,写一封询盘函。

询盘函：

(2)请你以上海玩具进出口公司业务员张成的身份,向日本 TOKYO IMPORT & EXPORT CORPORATION 写一封接受函。

接受函：

(3) 请你以上海玩具进出口公司业务员张成的身份，与日本 TOKYO IMPORT & EXPORT CORPORATION 签订购货贸易合同书。

上海玩具进出口公司
SHANGHAI TOY IMPORT & EXPORT CORPORATION
13 FENXIANG ROAD SHANGHAI, CHINA

PURCHASE CONTRACT

TEL: _____   P/C NO.: _____
FAX: _____   DATE: _____

The Buyer:

The Seller:

The Seller and the Buyer have confirmed this Contract with the terms and conditions stipulated below.

DESCRIPTIONS OF GOODS	QUANTITY	UNIT PRICE	AMOUNT

1. COUNTRY OF ORIGIN AND MANUFACTURER:
2. PACKING:
3. LATEST DATE OF SHIPMENT:
4. PORT OF LOADING:
5. PORT OF DESTINATION:
6. PAYMENT:
7. PARTIAL SHIPMENTS:
8. TRANSSHIPMENT:
9. DOCUMENTS: THE SELLER SHALL PRESENT THE FOLLOWING DOCUMENTS TO THE PAYING BANK FOR NEGOTIATION:

(1) _____ COPIES OF SIGNED COMMERCIAL INVOICE INDICATING CONTRACT NUMBER OF _____.

(2) _____ COPIES OF PACKING LIST.

(3) TWO COPIES OF CERTIFICATE OF QUALITY/QUANTITY ISSUED BY MANUFACTURE.

(4) WITHIN _____ HOURS AFTER THE GOODS ARE COMPLETELY LOADED, THE SELLER SHALL FAX TO NOTIFY THE BUYER OF THE CONTRACT NUMBER, NAME OF COMMODITY, QUANTITY, GROSS WEIGHT, B/L NO. AND THE DATE OF DELIVERY.

10. INSPECTION AND CLAIMS: IF THE QUALITY/WEIGHT AND/OR THE SPECIFICATIONS OF THE GOODS SHOULD BE FOUND NOT IN LINE WITH THE CONTRACTED STIPULATIONS, OR SHOULD THE GOODS PROVE DEFECTIVE FOR ANY REASONS, INCLUDING LATENT DEFECT OR THE USE OF UNSUITABLE MATERIALS, THE BUYER WOULD ARRANGE AN INSPECTION TO BE CARRIED OUT BY THE INSPECTION BUREAU AND HAVE THE RIGHT TO CLAIM AGAINST THE SELLERS ON THE STRENGTH OF THE INSPECTION CERTIFICATE ISSUED BY THE BUREAU. ALL CLAIMS SHALL BE REGARDED AS ACCEPTED IF THE SELLERS FAIL TO REPLY WITHIN 30 DAYS AFTER RECEIPT OF THE BUYER'S CLAIM.

Buyer: Seller:

操作二

1. 操作资料

近日,上海进出口贸易公司要从德国进口一批彩色喷墨打印机(COLOR INKJET PRINTERS),请你以公司业务员的身份上网查阅德国有关彩色喷墨打印机供应商有关产品的质量、规格和购货价格等各种信息,并选择其中一家理想的出口商(PITER IMPORT & EXPORT CORPORATION)进行洽谈。双方具体磋商内容如下:

(1)8月21日上海进出口贸易公司询盘:

"对贵公司的彩色喷墨打印机感兴趣,请报价 FOB HAMBURG。"

(2)8月23日上海进出口贸易公司对 PITER IMPORT & EXPORT CORPORATION 的发盘进行核定,表示接受全部发盘的条件。具体内容如下:

买 方: 上海进出口贸易公司(SHANGHAI IMPORT & EXPORT TRADE CORPORATION)
21 ZHONGSHAN ROAD SHANGHAI, CHINA
TEL:021-56082266 FAX:021-56082265

卖 方: PITER IMPORT & EXPORT CORPORATION
地址: NO. 324 TOLI MACH HAMBURG, GERMANY
TEL: 128-54842 FAX:128-54843

体验活动四　自理进口贸易业务

货名规格：　彩色喷墨打印机(COLOR INKJET PRINTERS)

单　　价：　FOB HAMBURG RO123 USD 110.00/ SET，RO122 USD 125.00/ SET，RO145 USD 120.00/ SET，RO168 USD 115.00/ SET

支付方式：　见票后30天付款不可撤销跟单信用证(IRREVOCABLE DOCUMENTARY CREDIT AT 30 DAYS AFTER SIGHT)

数　　量：　RO123 1 000套(1 000 SETS)、RO122 1 000套(1 000 SETS)、RO145 1 000套(1 000 SETS)、RO168 1 000套(1 000 SETS)

包　　装：　每50套装一个出口纸箱(PACKED IN 1 CARTON OF 50 SETS EACH)

装运期：　不迟于2012年11月8日前装运(LATEST DATE OF SHIPMENT：20121108)

装运港：　德国汉堡(HAMBURG GERMANY)

目的地港：　中国上海(SHANGHAI CHINA)

分批装运：　允许(ALLOWED)

转　运：　允许(ALLOWED)

唛　头：　由卖方制定(BY THE SELLER)

合同号：　TX07238

提交单据：
(1) 已签字的商业发票一式三份，并显示合同号(THREE COPIES OF SIGNED COMMERCIAL INVOICE INDICATING CONTRACT NUMBER OF TX07238)；

(2) 装箱单一式三份(THREE COPIES OF PACKING LIST)；

(3) 品质证书一式二份，由厂商签发(TWO COPIES OF CERTIFICATE OF QUALITY/QUANTITY ISSUED BY MANUFACTURE)；

(4) 在装船后12小时内用传真向买方发出装运通知，其中包含合同号、货名、数量毛重、提单号和装运日期等(WITHIN 12 HOURS AFTER THE GOODS ARE COMPLETELY LOADED, THE SELLER SHALL FAX TO NOTIFY THE BUYER OF THE CONTRACT NUMBER, NAME OF COMMODITY, QUANTITY, GROSS WEIGHT, B/L NO. AND THE DATE OF DELIVERY).

2. 操作要求

(1) 请你以上海进出口贸易公司业务员方为的身份，向德国PITER IMPORT & EXPORT CORPORATION询盘，写一封询盘函。

询盘函：

(2)请你以上海进出口贸易公司业务员方为的身份,向德国 PITER IMPORT & EXPORT CORPORATION 写一封接受函。

接受函：

(3)请你以上海进出口贸易公司业务员方为的身份,与德国 PITER IMPORT & EXPORT CORPORATION 签订购货贸易合同书。

体验活动四　自理进口贸易业务

上海进出口贸易公司
SHANGHAI IMPORT & EXPORT TRADE CORPORATION
21 ZHONGSHAN ROAD SHANGHAI, CHINA

PURCHASE CONTRACT

TEL: _____   P/C NO.: _____
FAX: _____   DATE: _____

The Buyer:

The Seller:

The Seller and the Buyer have confirmed this Contract with the terms and conditions stipulated below.

DESCRIPTIONS OF GOODS	QUANTITY	UNIT PRICE	AMOUNT

1. COUNTRY OF ORIGIN AND MANUFACTURER:
2. PACKING:
3. LATEST DATE OF SHIPMENT:
4. PORT OF LOADING:
5. PORT OF DESTINATION:
6. PAYMENT:
7. PARTIAL SHIPMENTS:
8. TRANSSHIPMENT:
9. DOCUMENTS: THE SELLER SHALL PRESENT THE FOLLOWING DOCUMENTS TO THE PAYING BANK FOR NEGOTIATION:
    (1) _____ COPIES OF SIGNED COMMERCIAL INVOICE INDICATING CONTRACT NUMBER OF _____.
    (2) _____ COPIES OF PACKING LIST.
    (3) _____ COPIES OF CERTIFICATE OF QUALITY/QUANTITY ISSUED BY MANUFACTURE.
10. INSPECTION AND CLAIMS: IF THE QUALITY/WEIGHT AND/OR THE SPECIFICATIONS OF THE GOODS SHOULD BE FOUND NOT IN LINE WITH THE CONTRACTED STIPULATIONS, OR SHOULD THE GOODS PROVE DEFECTIVE FOR ANY REASONS, INCLUDING LATENT DEFECT OR THE USE OF UNSUITABLE MATERIALS, THE BUYER WOULD ARRANGE AN INSPECTION TO BE CARRIED OUT BY THE INSPECTION BUREAU AND HAVE THE RIGHT TO CLAIM AGAINST THE SELLERS ON THE STRENGTH OF THE INSPECTION CERTIFICATE ISSUED BY THE BUREAU. ALL CLAIMS SHALL BE REGARDED AS ACCEPTED IF THE SELLERS FAIL TO REPLY WITHIN 30 DAYS AFTER RECEIPT OF THE BUYER'S CLAIM.

Buyer: Seller:

实训二　开立与修改信用证

业务导入

　　合同签订后,李莉小姐在合同规定的开证时间内及时向中国银行上海分行申请开立信用证,为此要填写开证申请书并缴纳开证费和保证金。开证行中国银行上海分行依据开证申请书向 TOKYO IMPORT & EXPORT CORPORATION 开出本笔交易的信用证。通知行收到信用证后,进行审证,审核无误后寄送至 TOKYO IMPORT & EXPORT CORPORATION。出口商依据贸易合同再次审证,发现有多处不符点或改证要求,可书写改证函向上海进出口公司提出改证要求。李莉小姐对改证函的内容予以确认,于是向开证行提出改证要求,缴纳改证费,由中国银行上海分行开出信用证改证书,并通过 FUJI BANK 交至 TOKYO IMPORT & EXPORT CORPORATION。

　　开证与改证业务流程如下图所示:

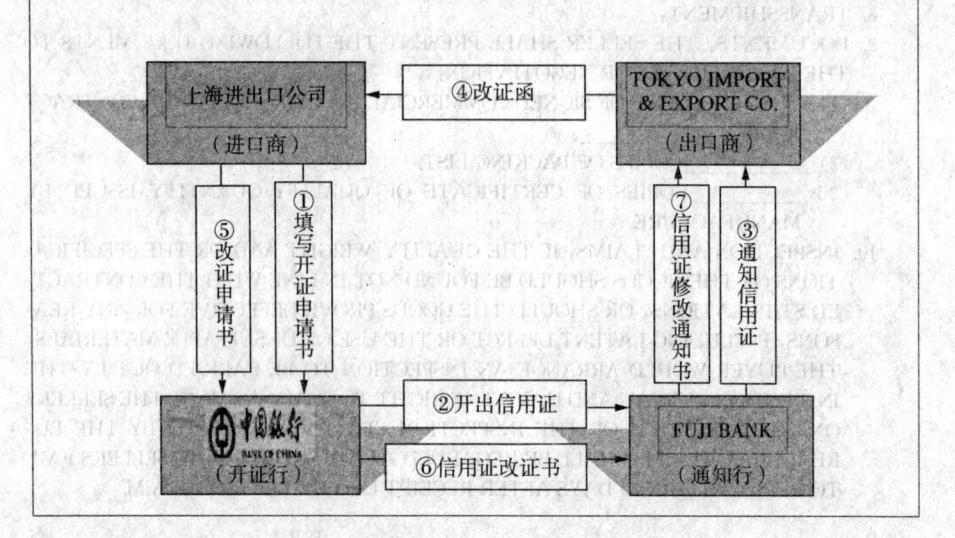

```
┌─────────────┐   ④改证函    ┌─────────────┐
│ 上海进出口公司│ ◄─────────── │TOKYO IMPORT │
│             │              │& EXPORT CO. │
│  （进口商）  │              │  （出口商）  │
└──┬───┬──────┘              └──┬───┬──────┘
   │   │                        │   │
   ⑤   ①                        ⑦   ③
  改证 填写                      信用 通知
  申请 开证                      证修 信用
   书  申请                      改通 证
       书                        知书
   │   │                        │   │
┌──▼───▼──────┐  ②开出信用证  ┌──▼───▼──────┐
│  中国银行   │ ───────────► │  FUJI BANK  │
│  （开证行）  │ ◄─────────── │  （通知行）  │
└─────────────┘  ⑥信用证改证书 └─────────────┘
```

工作任务一　　　　　　办理开证手续

上海进出口公司的外汇结算银行是中国银行上海分行，于是李莉小姐根据贸易合同的有关规定向该行办理开证手续，为此填写好开证申请书，并通知本公司财务部将保证金转账到公司的保证金账户。然后，开证行根据开证申请书的要求开出本笔交易的不可撤销信用证，正本寄送通知行，副本交给开证人备案。

IRREVOCABLE DOCUMENTARY CREDIT APPLICATION

To: BANK OF CHINA　　　　　　　　　　　Date: AUG. 22, 2012

Beneficiary (full name and address) TOKYO IMPORT & EXPORT CORPORATION 82-324 OTOLI MACHI TOKYO, JAPAN		L/C No. Ex Card No. Contract No.　　TX200523
rows		Date and place of expiry of the credit OCT. 20, 2012　　JAPAN
Partial shipments ☒allowed ☐not allowed	Transshipment ☐allowed ☒not allowed	☐ Issue by airmail　　☐ With brief advice by teletransmission ☐ Issue by express delivery ☒ Issue by teletransmission (which shall be the operative instrument)
Loading on board/dispatch taking in change at/ from TOKYO not later than SEP. 20, 2012 for transportation to SHANGHAI		Amount (both in figures and words) USD 95 000.00 SAY U. S. DOLLARS NINETY FIVE THOUSAND ONLY
Description of goods WRENCH HEX DEYS WRENCH DOUBLE RING OFFSET WRENCH CONBINATION WRENCH ADJUSTABLE WRENCH Packing: PACKED IN ONE CARTON OF 100 SETS EACH		Credit available with ☐ by sight payment ☒by acceptance ☒by negotiation ☐ by deferred payment at ☒ against the documents detailed herein and beneficiary's draft for 100% of the invoice value at USD 95 000.00 on 60 DAYS AFTER SIGHT
		☒FOB　☐CFR　☐CIF or other terms

续

Documents required: (marks with ×)
1. (×) Signed Commercial Invoice in 5 copies indicating L/C No. and Contract No.
2. ( ) Full set of clean on board ocean Bills of Landing made out to   and blank endorsed, marked "freight [ ] to collect/ [ ] prepaid [ ] showing freight amount" notifying
3. ( ) Air Way bills showing "freight [ ] to collect/ [ ] prepaid [ ] including freight amount" and consigned to
4. ( ) Memorandum issued by   consigned to
5. ( ) Insurance Policy/Certificate in copies for   % of the invoice value showing claims payable in China in currency of the draft, blank endorsed, covering ([ ] Ocean Marine Transportation / [ ] Air Transportation /[ ] Over Land Transportation) All Risks, War Risks.
6. (×) Packing List / Weight Memo in 5 copies issued by the quantity / gross and the weights of each packing and packing condition as called by the L/C.
7. ( ) Certificate of Quantity / Weight in copies issued by an independent surveyor at loading port, indicating the actual surveyed quantity / weight of shipped goods as well as the packing condition.
8. (×) Certificate of Quantity in 2 copies issued by [ ] manufacturer / [×] public recognized surveyor.
9. (×) Beneficiary's certified copy of cable dispatched to the accountees within 12 hours after shipment advising [×] name of vessel / [ ] flight No. / [ ] wagon No., date quantity, weight and value of shipment.
10. ( ) Beneficiary's Certifying that extra copies of the documents have been dispatched according to the contract terms.
11. ( ) Shipping Co's Certificate attesting that the carrying vessel is chartered or booked by accountee or their shipping agents.
12. ( ) Other documents, if any.

Additional instructions:
1. (×) All banking charges outside the opening bank are for beneficiary's account.
2. (×) Documents must be presented with 15 days after the date of issuance of the transport documents but with the validity of this credit.
3. (×) Third party as shipper is not acceptable. Short Form / Blank Back B/L is not acceptable.
4. ( ) Both quantity and amount   % more or less are allowed.
5. ( ) prepaid freight drawn in excess of L/C amount is acceptable against presentation of original charges voucher issued by shipping Co. / Air Line / or it's agent.
6. ( ) All documents to be forwarded in one cover, unless otherwise started above.
7. ( ) Other terms, if any:

Account No.: 67548211   with   BANK OF CHINA   (name of bank)
Transacted by: SHANGHAI IMPORT & EXPORT TRADE CORPORATION   (Applicant: name, signature of authorized person)
Telephone No.: 56082266   李 莉   (with seal)

操作指南 ➡ 开证申请书的缮制方法

1. Beneficiary
填写出口商的全称和详址。

2. Contract No.
填写合同号码。

3. Date and place of expiry of the credit
填写信用证的有效日期与地点。

4. Partial shipments
根据合同对分批装运的规定,用"×"选择允许或不允许。

5. Transshipment
根据合同对转运的规定,用"×"选择允许或不允许。

6. Issue by
根据合同的规定,用"×"选择开证方式。

7. Loading on board/dispatch taking in change at/from
根据合同的规定填写运输路线和装运日期。

8. Amount(both in figures and words)
按照合同总金额用大小写表示。

9. Description of goods
根据合同的规定,填写货物名称、规格和包装方式。

10. Credit available with
填写信用证的种类和汇票金额。

11. Trade terms
根据合同的规定用"×"选择贸易术语,也可补充在"other terms"后面。

12. Documents required
根据合同的规定或进口商的要求,用"×"选择单据的类别及要求。

13. Additional instructions
根据合同的规定或进口商的要求,用"×"选择相关内容。

14. Account No.
填写进口商的开户银行账号。

15. Name of bank
填写开证银行名称。

16. Transacted by
填写开证申请人及经办人名称。

17. Telephone No.
填写开证申请人的电话号码。

IRREVOCABLE DOCUMENTARY CREDIT

SEQUENCE OF TOTAL	*27 :	1/1
FORM OF DOC. CREDIT	*40A :	IRREVOCABLE
DOC. CREDIT NUMBER	*20 :	XUT17345
DATE OF ISSUE	31C :	120822
DATE AND PLACE OF EXPIRY	*31D :	DATE 121020 PLACE BENEFICIARY' COUNTRY
APPLICANT	*50 :	SHANGHAI IMPORT & EXPORT CORPORATION 1321 ZHONGSHAN ROAD SHANGHAI CHINA
ISSUING BANK	52A :	BANK OF CHINA SHANGHAI BRANCH 100 ZHONGSHAN 1 ROAD SHANGHAI CHINA
BENEFICIARY	*59 :	TOKYO IMPORT & EXPORT CORPORATION 82-324 OTOLI MACHI TOKYO JAPAN
AMOUNT	*32B :	CURRENCY USD AMOUNT 95 000.00
AVAILABLE WITH / BY	*41D :	ANY BANK IN JAPAN BY NEGOTIATION
DRAFTS AT…	42C :	DRAFTS 60 DAYS AFTER SIGHT FOR FULL INVOICE COST
DRAWEE	42A :	BANK OF CHINA SHANGHAI BRANCH
PARTIAL SHIPMENTS	43P :	ALLOWED
TRANSSHIPMENT	43T :	NOT ALLOWED
LOADING ON BOARD	44A :	TOKYO PORT
FOR TRANSPORTATION TO…	44B :	SHANGHAI PORT
LATEST DATE OF SHIPMENT	44C :	120920
DESCRIPTION OF GOODS	45A :	WRENCH AS PER S/C NO. TX200523 FOB TOKYO
DOCUMENTS REQUIRED	46A :	+SIGNED COMMERCIAL INVOICE IN 3 COPIES +PACKING LIST IN 3 COPIES +CERTIFICATE OF QUANTITY IN 2 COPIES +WITHIN 12 HOURS AFTER THE GOODS ARE COMPLETELY LOADED, THE SELLER SHALL FAX TO NOTIFY THE BUYER OF THE CONTRACT NUMBER, NAME OF COMMODITY, QUANTITY, GROSS WEIGHT, B/L NO. AND THE DATE OF DELIVERY.
CHARGES	71B :	ALL BANKING CHARGES OUTSIDE CHINA ARE FOR ACCOUNT OF BENEFICIARY.
PERIOD FOR PRESENTATION	48 :	DOCUMENTS MUST BE PRESENTED WITHIN 15 DAYS AFTER THE DATE OF SHIPMENT BUT WITHIN THE VALIDITY OF THE CREDIT.

☑ 工作任务二　　　　　办理改证手续

TOKYO IMPORT & EXPORT CORPORATION 收到信用证后，由于该公司备货有一定的困难，便向上海进出口公司提出装运期改为 2012 年 10 月 20 日，并将信用证有效期延长。为此，李莉小姐根据出口商的要求向中国银行上海分行提出修改信用证的要求。

中 国 银 行
BANK OF CHINA
信用证修改申请书
APPLICATION FOR AMENDMENT

Date of Amendment: SEP. 1, 2012　　　　　　　　No. of Amendment: SD070901
Amendment to Our Documentary Credit No. XUT17345

To: BANK OF CHINA SHANGHAI BRANCH

Applicant SHANGHAI IMPORT & EXPORT CORPORATION	Advising Bank FUJI BANK TOKYO BRANCH
Beneficiary (before this amendment) TOKYO IMPORT & EXPORT CORPORATION	Amount USD 95 000.00

The above mentioned credit is amended as follows:
☑　Shipment date extended to 　OCT. 20, 2012
☑　Expiry date extended to 　NOV. 31, 2012
☐　Amount increased/decreased by 　　　　　to 　　　　　
☐　Other terms:

☐　Banking charges:

All other terms and conditions remain unchanged.

　　　　　　　　　　　　　　　　　　　　　　　Authorized Signature(s)
　　　　　　　　　　　　　　　　　　SHANGHAI IMPORT & EXPORT CORPORATION

This Amendment is Subject to Uniform Customs and Practice for Documentary Credits (2007 Revision) International Chamber of Commerce Publication No. 600.

综合业务模拟操作

操作一

1. 操作资料

合同规定买方必须于 2012 年 9 月 30 日前,通过一家卖方可接受的银行开出不可撤销跟单即期信用证。为此,上海玩具进出口公司在规定的开证时间内向中国银行上海分行申请开证。TOKYO IMPORT & EXPORT CORPORATION 收到信用证后,由于该公司备货有一定的困难,便向上海玩具进出口贸易公司提出装运期改为 2012 年 11 月 30 日,并将信用证有效期延长。为此,张成先生根据出口商的要求向业务主管请示,获准后即向开证行申请修改信用证。

填写开证申请书的有关资料如下:

买　　方：上海玩具进出口公司(SHANGHAI TOY IMPORT & EXPORT CORPORATION)
　　　　　地址：13 FENXIANG ROAD SHANGHAI, CHINA
　　　　　TEL：021-56082212　FAX：021-56082211

银行账号：WT056742

卖　　方：TOKYO IMPORT & EXPORT CORPORATION
　　　　　地址：82-324 OTOLI MACHI TOKYO, JAPAN
　　　　　TEL：028-548-742　FAX：028-548-743

货名规格：电子手掌玩具(ELECTRON PALM BAUBLE)(货号为 R222S、R333H、R666W、R888A)

单　　价：FOB TOKYO R222S USD 50.00/ SET, R333H USD 45.00/ SET, R666W USD 35.00/ SET, R888A USD 20.00/ SET

支付方式：不可撤销跟单即期信用证(IRREVOCABLE DOCUMENTARY CREIDT AT SIGHT)

数　　量：R222S 1 000 套(1 000 SETS)、R333H 1 000 套(1 000 SETS) R666W 1 000 套(1 000 SETS)、R888A 1 000 套(1 000 SETS)

包　　装：每 50 套装一个出口纸箱(PACKED IN 1 CARTON OF 50 SETS EACH)

装 运 期：不迟于 2012 年 10 月 31 日前装运(LATEST DATE OF SHIPMENT: 20121031)

装 运 港：日本东京(TOKYO, JAPAN)

目的地港：中国上海(SHANGHAI, CHINA)

分批装运：允许(ALLOWED)

转　　运：不允许(NOT ALLOWED)

合 同 号：TX06238

信用证号：XUT17123

信用证有效期：2012 年 11 月 20 日

提交单据：(1) 已签字的商业发票一式三份，并显示合同号(THREE COPIES OF SIGNED COMMERCIAL INVOICE INDICATING CONTRACT NUMBER OF TX06238)；

(2) 装箱单一式三份(THREE COPIES OF PACKING LIST)；

(3) 品质证书一式二份，由厂商签发(TWO COPIES OF CERTIFICATE OF QUALITY/QUANTITY ISSUED BY MANUFACTURE)

(4) 在装船后12小时内用传真向买方发出装运通知，其包含合同号、货名、数量毛重、提单号和装运日期等(WITHIN 12 HOURS AFTER THE GOODS ARE COMPLETELY LOADED, THE SELLER SHALL FAX TO NOTIFY THE BUYER OF THE CONTRACT NUMBER, NAME OF COMMODITY, QUANTITY, GROSS WEIGHT, B/L NO. AND THE DATE OF DELIVERY)

通知银行：FUJI BANK TOKYO BRANCH

2. 操作要求

(1)请你以上海玩具进出口公司业务员张成的身份，根据上述资料填写开证申请书。

To：BANK OF CHINA　　　　　　　　　　　　　　Date：

Beneficiary (full name and address)	L/C No. Ex Card No. Contract No.
	Date and place of expiry of the credit
Partial shipments ☐allowed ☐not allowed	Transshipment ☐allowed ☐not allowed	☐ Issue by airmail　☐ With brief advice by teletransmission ☐ Issue by express delivery ☐ Issue by teletransmission (which shall be the operative instrument)
Loading on board/dispatch taking in change at/from not later than or transportation to	Amount (both in figures and words)
Description of goods Packing：	Credit available with ☐ by sight payment　☐ by acceptance ☐ by negotiation ☐ by deferred payment at against the documents detailed herein ☐ and beneficiary's draft for 100% of the invoice value at on
	☐FOB　☐CFR　☐CIF or other terms

223

Documents required: (marks with ×)
1. (　) Signed Commercial Invoice in _____ copies indicating L/C No. and Contract No.
2. (　) Full set of clean on board ocean Bills of Landing made out to order of shipper and blank endorsed, marked "freight [　] to collect/ [　] prepaid [　] showing freight amount" notifying applicant.
3. (　) Air Waybills showing "freight [　] to collect/ [　] prepaid [　] including freight amount" and consigned to .
4. (　) Memorandum issued by   consigned to
5. (　) Insurance Policy/Certificate in copies for   % of the invoice value showing claims payable in China in currency of the draft, blank endorsed, covering ([　] Ocean Marine Transportation / [　] Air Transportation /[　] Over Land Transportation) All Risks.
6. (　) Packing List / Weight Memo in _____ copies issued by the quantity / gross and the weights of each packing and packing condition as called by the L/C.
7. (　) Certificate of Quantity / Weight in copies issued by an independent surveyor at loading port, indicating the actual surveyed quantity / weight of shipped goods as well as the packing condition.
8. (　) Certificate of Quantity in 2 copies issued by [　] manufacturer / [　] public recognized surveyor / [　]
9. (　) Beneficiary's certified copy of cable dispatched to the accountees within _____ hours after shipment advising [　] name of vessel / [　] flight No. / [　] wagon No., date quantity, weight and value of shipment.
10. (　) Beneficiary's Certifying that extra copies of the documents have been dispatched according to the contract terms.
11. (　) Shipping Co's Certificate attesting that the carrying vessel is chartered or booked by accountee or their shipping agents.
12. (　) Other documents, if any.

Additional instructions:
1. (　) All banking charges outside the opening bank are for beneficiary's account.
2. (　) Documents must be presented with 15 days after the date of issuance of the transport documents but with the validity of this credit.
3. (　) Third party as shipper is not acceptable. Short Form / Blank Back B/L is not acceptable.
4. (　) Both quantity and amount   % more or less are allowed.
5. (　) prepaid freight drawn in excess of L/C amount is acceptable against presentation of original charges voucher issued by shipping Co. / Air Line / or it's agent.
6. (　) All documents to be forwarded in one cover, unless otherwise started above.
7. (　) Other terms, if any.

Account No.:   with _____ (name of bank)
Transacted by: (Applicant: name, signature of authorized person)
Telephone No.:   (with seal)

(2)请你以上海玩具进出口公司业务员张成的身份,根据上述资料填写信用证修改申请书。

中 国 银 行
BANK OF CHINA
信用证修改申请书
APPLICATION FOR AMENDMENT

Date of Amendment: No. of Amendment: SD070930
Amendment to Our Documentary Credit No.

To: BANK OF CHINA SHANGHAI BRANCH

Applicant	Advising Bank
Beneficiary (before this amendment)	Amount

The above mentioned credit is amended as follows:
☐ Shipment date extended to _____
☐ Expiry date extended to _____
☐ Amount increased/decreased by _____ to _____
☐ Other terms:

☐ Banking charges:

All other terms and conditions remain unchanged.

Authorized Signature(s)
SHANGHAI TOY IMPORT & EXPORT CORPORATION

This Amendment is Subject to Uniform Customs and Practice for Documentary Credits (2007 Revision) International Chamber of Commerce Publication No. 600.

操作二

1. 操作资料

合同规定买方必须于 2012 年 9 月 10 日前,通过一家卖方可接受的银行开出不可撤销跟单即期信用证。为此,上海进出口贸易公司在规定的开证时间内填写开证申请书,向中国银行上海分行申请开证。

填写开证申请书的有关资料如下:

银行账号:WT012342

买　　方:上海进出口贸易公司(SHANGHAI IMPORT & EXPORT TRADE COR-
　　　　　PORATION)
　　　　　21 ZHONGSHAN ROAD SHANGHAI, CHINA
　　　　　TEL:021-56082266　FAX:021-56082265

卖　　方:PITER IMPORT & EXPORT CORPORATION
　　　　　地址:NO. 324 TOLI MACH HAMBURG, GERMANY
　　　　　TEL:128-54842　FAX:128-54843

货名规格:彩色喷墨打印机(COLOR INKJET PRINTERS)

单　　价:FOB HAMBURG RO123 USD 110.00/ SET,RO122 USD 125.00/ SET,
　　　　　RO145 USD 120.00/ SET,RO168 USD 115.00/ SET

支付方式:见票后 30 天付款不可撤销跟单信用证(IRREVOCABLE DOCUMENTA-
　　　　　RY CREDIT AT 30 DAYS AFTER SIGHT)

数　　量:RO123 1 000 套(1 000 SETS)、RO122 1 000 套(1 000 SETS)
　　　　　RO145 1 000 套(1 000 SETS)、RO168 1 000 套(1000 SETS)

包　　装:每 50 套装一个出口纸箱(PACKED IN 1 CARTON OF 50 SETS EACH)

装 运 期:不迟于 2012 年 11 月 8 日前装运(LATEST DATE OF SHIPMENT:
　　　　　20121108)

装 运 港:德国汉堡(HAMBURG, GERMANY)

目的地港:中国上海(SHANGHAI, CHINA)

分批装运:允许(ALLOWED)

转　　运:允许(ALLOWED)

唛　　头:由卖方制定(BY THE SELLER)

合 同 号:TX07238

信用证有效期:2012 年 12 月 8 日

提交单据:(1) 已签字的商业发票一式三份,并显示合同号(THREE COPIES OF
　　　　　　　SIGNED COMMERCIAL INVOICE INDICATING CONTRACT
　　　　　　　NUMBER OF TX07238);
　　　　　(2) 装箱单一式三份(THREE COPIES OF PACKING LIST);
　　　　　(3) 品质证书一式二份,由厂商签发(TWO COPIES OF CERTIFICATE

OF QUALITY/QUANTITY ISSUED BY MANUFACTURE);

(4) 在装船后 12 小时内用传真向买方发出装运通知,其中包含合同号、货名、数量毛重、提单号和装运日期等(WITHIN 12 HOURS AFTER THE GOODS ARE COMPLETELY LOADED, THE SELLER SHALL FAX TO NOTIFY THE BUYER OF THE CONTRACT NUMBER, NAME OF COMMODITY, QUANTITY, GROSS WEIGHT, B/L NO. AND THE DATE OF DELIVERY).

2.操作要求

请你以上海进出口贸易公司业务员方为的身份,根据上述资料填写开证申请书,向中国银行上海分行申请开立信用证。

To: BANK OF CHINA   Date:

Beneficiary (full name and address)	L/C No. Ex Card No. Contract No.	
	Date and place of expiry of the credit	
Partial shipments ☐allowed ☐not allowed	Transshipment ☐allowed ☐not allowed	☐ Issue by airmail ☐With brief advice by teletransmission ☐ Issue by express delivery ☐ Issue by teletransmission (which shall be the operative instrument)
Loading on board/dispatch taking in change at/from not later than or transportation to	Amount (both in figures and words)	
Description of goods	Credit available with ☐ by sight payment ☐ by acceptance ☐ by negotiation ☐ by deferred payment at against the documents detailed herein ☐ and beneficiary's draft for 100% of the invoice value at on	
Packing:	☐FOB ☐CFR ☐CIF or other terms	

Documents required: (marks with ×)
1. ( ) Signed Commercial Invoice in _____ copies indicating L/C No. and Contract No.
2. ( ) Full set of clean on board ocean Bills of Landing made out to order of shipper and blank endorsed, marked "freight [ ] to collect/ [ ] prepaid [ ] showing freight amount" notifying applicant.
3. ( ) Air Waybills showing "freight [ ] to collect/ [ ] prepaid [ ] including freight amount" and consigned to
4. ( ) Memorandum issued by   consigned to
5. ( ) Insurance Policy/Certificate in copies for   % of the invoice value showing claims payable in China in currency of the draft, blank endorsed, covering ([ ] Ocean Marine Transportation/[ ] Air Transportation /[ ] Over Land Transportation) All Risks.
6. ( ) Packing List / Weight Memo in _____ copies issued by the quantity / gross and the weights of each packing and packing condition as called by the L/C.
7. ( ) Certificate of Quantity / Weight in copies issued by an independent surveyor at loading port, indicating the actual surveyed quantity / weight of shipped goods as well as the packing condition.
8. ( ) Certificate of Quantity in 2 copies issued by [ ] manufacturer / [ ] public recognized surveyor / [ ]
9. ( ) Beneficiary's certified copy of cable dispatched to the accountees within _____ hours after shipment advising [ ] name of vessel / [ ] flight No. / [ ] wagon No., date quantity, weight and value of shipment.
10. ( ) Beneficiary's Certifying that extra copies of the documents have been dispatched according to the contract terms.
11. ( ) Shipping Co's Certificate attesting that the carrying vessel is chartered or booked by accountee or their shipping agents.
12. ( ) Other documents, if any:

Additional instructions:
1. ( ) All banking charges outside the opening bank are for beneficiary's account.
2. ( ) Documents must be presented with 15 days after the date of issuance of the transport documents but with the validity of this credit.
3. ( ) Third party as shipper is not acceptable. Short Form / Blank Back B/L is not acceptable.
4. ( ) Both quantity and amount   % more or less are allowed.
5. ( ) prepaid freight drawn in excess of L/C amount is acceptable against presentation of original charges voucher issued by shipping Co. / Air Line / or it's agent.
6. ( ) All documents to be forwarded in one cover, unless otherwise started above.
7. ( ) Other terms, if any:

Account No.:   with _____ (name of bank)
Transacted by: (Applicant: name, signature of authorized person)
Telephone No.:   (with seal)

实训三　进口合同的履行——
办理订舱投保手续

业务导入

上海进出口公司在合同规定的开证时间内,及时向 TOKYO IMPORT & EXPORT CORPORATION 开出本笔交易的信用证后,李莉小姐填写订舱委托书并随附相关单据委托金友国际货代公司代办托运手续。订舱确认后,向出口商发出装船通知,让其做好装运货物的准备。

订舱与投保业务流程如下图所示:

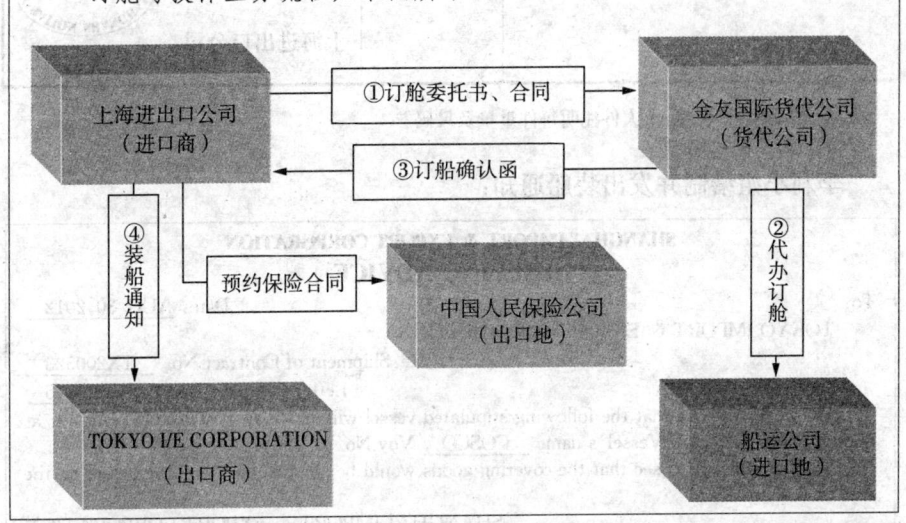

```
上海进出口公司 ──①订舱委托书、合同──→ 金友国际货代公司
（进口商）   ←───③订船确认函───       （货代公司）
   │                                        │
   ④装船通知    预约保险合同                 ②代办订舱
   │              ↓                         │
   ↓        中国人民保险公司                  ↓
TOKYO I/E CORPORATION   （出口地）          船运公司
（出口商）                                  （进口地）
```

🔾 工作任务一　　　　办理订舱手续

上海进出口公司在办理好改证手续后,及时向上海金友货运代理公司办理订舱委托,根据合同有关内容填写进口订舱委托书。当进口货物运输手续办妥之后,李莉小姐向 TOKYO IMPORT & EXPORT CORPORATION 发出装船通知,告知其船名、航次和到达装运港的时间,以便出口商做好装运货物的准备。

李莉小姐填写进口订舱委托书：

进口订舱委托书

编号：XT051147　　　　　　　　　　　　　　　日期：2012年8月29日

货　名（英文）	扳手 WRENCH		
重　量	175KGS	尺　码	7M³
合同号	TX200523	包　装	60箱
装运港	东京港	交货期	2012年9月20日
装货条款	(1)2012年9月19日到达东京港装运 (2)不允许转船 (3)允许分批装运		
发货人名称、地址	TOKYO IMPORT & EXPORT CORPORATION 82-324 OTOLI MACHI TOKYO, JAPAN		
发货人电挂	028-548-743		
订妥船名	COSCO V. 861	预抵港口	上海港
备　注		委托单位 上海进出口公司 李莉	

1. 危险品须注明性能，重大件注明每件重量及尺码。
2. 装货条款须详细注明。

李莉小姐缮制并发出装船通知：

SHANGHAI IMPORT & EXPORT CORPORATION
SHIPPING ADVICE

To:　　　　　　　　　　　　　　　　　　　　Date：AUG. 30, 2012
TOKYO IMPORT & EXPORT CORPORATION
　　　　　　　　　　　　　Re：Shipment of Contract No.　TX200523
　　　　　　　　　　　　　　　Letter of Credit No.　XUT17345

We wish to advise that the following stipulated vessel will arrive at　TOKYO　port, on/about　SEP. 19, 2012　Vessel's name　COSCO　Voy No.　V. 861.
We'll appreciate to see that the covering goods would be shipped on the above vessel on the date of L/C called.

　　　　　　　　　SHANGHAI IMPORT & EXPORT CORPORATION
　　　　　　　　　　　　　　　　　　　　　　　　LILI

◎ 工作任务二　　　办理投保手续

李莉小姐发出装船通知后，及时向中国人民保险公司上海分公司办理进口货物运输保险，根据购货合同保险条款有关内容的规定签订进口货物运输预约保险合同。出口商在装船后向保险公司发出装运通知，该批进口货物便自动被承保。

中国人民保险公司
进口货物运输预约保险合同

合同号：TX200523　　　　　　　　　　　　　　　日期：2012年9月15日
甲方：上海进出口公司
乙方：中国人民保险公司上海分公司

双方就进口货物的运输预约保险拟订以下条款，以资共同遵守：

一、保险范围

甲方从国外进口的全部货物，不论运输方式，凡贸易条款规定由买方办理保险的，都属于本合同范围之内。甲方应根据本合同规定，向乙方办理投保手续并支付保险费。

乙方对上述保险范围内的货物，负有自动承保的责任，在发生本合同规定范围内的损失时，均按本合同的规定，负责赔偿。

二、保险金额

保险金额以货物的到岸价（CIF）即货价加运费加保险费为准（运费可用实际运费，亦可由双方协定一个平均运费率计算）。

三、保险险别和费率

各种货物需要投保的险别由甲方选定并在投保单中填明。乙方根据不同的险别规定不同的费率。现暂定如下：

货物种类	运输方式	保险险别	保险费率
扳手	江海运输	一切险、战争险	按约定

四、保险责任

各种险别的责任范围，按照所属乙方制定的"海洋货物运输保险条款"、"海洋运输货物战争险条款"、"海运进口货物国内转动期间保险责任扩展条款"、"航空运输一切险条款"和其他有关条款的规定为准。

五、投保手续

甲方一经掌握货物发运情况，即应向乙方寄送起运通知书，办理投保手续。通知书一式五份，由保险公司签认后，退回一份。如不办理投保，货物发生损失，乙方不予赔偿。

六、保险费

乙方按甲方寄送的起运通知书照前列相应的费率逐笔计收保费，甲方应及时付费。

七、索赔手续和期限

本合同所保货物发生保险责任范围内的损失时，乙方应按制定的"关于海运进口保险货物残损检验的赔款给付办法"和"进口货物施救整理费用支付办法"迅速处理。甲方应尽力采取防止货物扩大受损的措施，对已遭受损失的货物必须积极抢救，尽量减少货物的损失。向乙方办理索赔的有效期限，以保险货物卸离海港之日起满一年终止。如有特殊需要，可向乙方提出延长索赔期。

八、合同期限

本合同自2012年9月15日起开始生效。

甲方：李莉　　　　　　　　　　　　　　　　　　乙方：丁君

综合业务模拟操作

操作一

1. 操作资料

上海玩具进出口公司向中国银行上海分行申请改证后,及时向上海国际货运代理公司办理订舱委托手续,根据合同有关内容填写进口订舱委托书。当进口货物运输手续办妥之后,向出口商 TOKYO IMPORT & EXPORT CORPORATION 发出装船通知,告知其船名、航次和到达装运港的时间,以便做好装运货物的准备。

填写进口订舱委托书的有关资料如下:

订舱委托书号:JF1899W
合 同 号:TX06238
信 用 证 号:XUT17123
卖　　　方:TOKYO IMPORT & EXPORT CORPORATION
　　　　　TEL:028-548-742　FAX:028-548-743
买　　　方:上海玩具进出口公司
货名规格:电子手掌玩具(ELECTRON PALM BAUBLE)
数　　　量:R222S 1 000 套,R333H 1 000 套,R666W 1 000 套,R888A 1 000 套
包　　　装:每 50 套装一个出口纸箱
毛　　　重:每箱 2.5 KGS
净　　　重:每箱 2.0 KGS
体　　　积:每箱 0.2 CBM
装 运 期:不迟于 2012 年 10 月 31 日前装运
装 运 港:日本东京
目的地港:中国上海
分批装运:允许
转　　　运:不允许
船　　　名:HONDA V.026
保险险别:投保一切险
预约保险合同号:HY098765

2. 操作要求

(1)请你以上海玩具进出口公司业务员张成的身份,根据上述资料填写进口订舱委托书。

体验活动四　自理进口贸易业务

进口订舱委托书

编号：　　　　　　　　　　　　　　　　　　　　日期：

货　名 （英文）			
重　量		尺　码	
合同号		包　装	
装运港		交货期	
装货条款			
发货人 名称、地址			
发货人电挂			
订妥船名		预抵港口	
备　注		委托单位	

1. 危险品须注明性能，重大件注明每件重量及尺码。
2. 装货条款须详细注明。

(2) 请你以上海玩具进出口公司业务员张成的身份，根据上述资料填写装船通知。

SHANGHAI IMPORT & EXPORT CORPORATION
SHIPPING ADVICE

To:　　　　　　　　　　　　　　　　　　　　　　Date:＿＿＿＿＿

　　　　　　　　　　　　　　　Re:Shipment of Contract No. ＿＿＿＿＿
　　　　　　　　　　　　　　　Letter of Credit No. ＿＿＿＿＿

　We wish to advise that the following stipulated vessel will arrive at ＿＿＿＿ port,on/about ＿＿＿＿＿ Vessel's name ＿＿＿＿＿ Voy No. ＿＿＿＿

　We'll appreciate to see that the covering goods would be shipped on the above vessel on the date of L/C called.

（3）请你以上海玩具进出口公司业务员张成的身份，根据上述资料与中国人民保险公司签订进口货物运输预约保险合同。

中国人民保险公司
进口货物运输预约保险合同

合同号：　　　　　　　　　　　　　　　　　　　　　日期：

甲方：

乙方：

双方就进口货物的运输预约保险拟订以下条款，以资共同遵守：

一、保险范围

甲方从国外进口的全部货物，不论运输方式，凡贸易条款规定由买方办理保险的，都属于本合同范围之内。甲方应根据本合同规定，向乙方办理投保手续并支付保险费。

乙方对上述保险范围内的货物，负有自动承保的责任，在发生本合同规定范围内的损失时，均按本合同的规定，负责赔偿。

二、保险金额

保险金额以货物的到岸价(CIF)即货价加运费加保险费为准（运费可用实际运费，亦可由双方协定一个平均运费率计算）。

三、保险险别和费率

各种货物需要投保的险别由甲方选定并在投保单中填明。乙方根据不同的险别规定不同的费率。现暂定如下：

货物种类	运输方式	保险险别	保险费率

四、保险责任

各种险别的责任范围，按照所属乙方制定的"海洋货物运输保险条款"、"海洋运输货物战争险条款"、"海运进口货物国内转动期间保险责任扩展条款"、"航空运输一切险条款"和其他有关条款的规定为准。

五、投保手续

甲方一经掌握货物发运情况，即应向乙方寄送起运通知书，办理投保手续。通知书一式五份，由保险公司签认后，退回一份。如不办理投保，货物发生损失，乙方不予赔偿。

六、保险费

乙方按甲方寄送的起运通知书照前列相应的费率逐笔计收保费，甲方应及时付费。

七、索赔手续和期限

本合同所保货物发生保险责任范围内的损失时，乙方应按制定的"关于海运进口保险货物残损检验的赔款给付办法"和"进口货物施救整理费用支付办法"迅速处理。甲方应尽力采取防止货物扩大受损的措施，对已遭受损失的货物必须积极抢救，尽量减少货物的损失。向乙方办理索赔的有效期限，以保险货物卸离海港之日起满一年终止。如有特殊需要，可向乙方提出延长索赔期。

八、合同期限

本合同自　　年　月　日起开始生效。

甲方：　　　　　　　　　　　　　　　　　　　　　乙方：

操作二

1. 操作资料

上海进出口贸易公司向中国银行上海分行申请开证后,及时向金发国际货运代理公司办理订舱委托手续,根据合同有关内容填写进口订舱委托书。当进口货物运输手续办妥之后,向出口商 PITER IMPORT & EXPORT CORPORATION 发出装船通知,告知其船名、航次和到达装运港的时间,以便做好装运货物的准备。

填写进口订舱委托书的有关资料如下:

订舱委托书号:0699W

合　同　号:TX07238

买　　方:上海进出口贸易公司(SHANGHAI IMPORT & EXPORT TRADE COR-
　　　　　PORATION)21 ZHONGSHAN ROAD SHANGHAI, CHINA
　　　　　TEL:021-56082266　　FAX:021-56082265

卖　　方:PITER IMPORT & EXPORT CORPORATION
　　　　　地址:NO. 324 TOLI MACH HAMBURG, GERMANY
　　　　　TEL:128-54842　　FAX:128-54843

货名规格:彩色喷墨打印机(COLOR INKJET PRINTERS)

数　　量:RO123 1 000 套(1 000 SETS)、RO122 1 000 套(1 000 SETS)
　　　　　RO145 1 000 套(1 000 SETS)、RO168 1 000 套(1 000 SETS)

包　　装:每50套装一个出口纸箱(PACKED IN 1 CARTON OF 50 SETS EACH)

毛　　重:每箱10KGS

净　　重:每箱8KGS

体　　积:每箱0.8CBM

装 运 期:不迟于2012年11月8日前装运(LATEST DATE OF SHIPMENT:
　　　　　20121108)

装 运 港:德国汉堡(HAMBURG, GERMANY)

目的地港:中国上海(SHANGHAI, CHINA)

分批装运:允许(ALLOWED)

转　　运:允许(ALLOWED)

船　　名:HOGA. V. 086

信用证号:XUT17456

保险险别:投保一切险与战争险

预约保险合同号:RY0787653

2. 操作要求

(1)请你以上海进出口贸易公司业务员方为的身份,根据上述资料填写进口订舱委托书。

进口订舱委托书

编号：　　　　　　　　　　　　　　　　　　日期：

货　名 (英文)			
重　量		尺　码	
合同号		包　装	
装运港		交货期	
装货条款			
发货人 名称、地址			
发货人电挂			
订妥船名		预抵港口	
备　注		委托单位	

1. 危险品须注明性能，重大件注明每件重量及尺码。
2. 装货条款须详细注明。

(2) 请你以上海进出口贸易公司业务员方为的身份，根据上述资料填写装船通知。

SHANGHAI IMPORT & EXPORT TRADE CORPORATION
SHIPPING ADVICE

To：　　　　　　　　　　　　　　　　　　Date：_____

　　　　　　　　　　　Re：Shipment of Contract No. _____
　　　　　　　　　　　Letter of Credit No. _____

We wish to advise that the following stipulated vessel will arrive at _____ port, on/about _____ Vessel's name _____ Voy No. _____

We'll appreciate to see that the covering goods would be shipped on the above vessel on the date of L/C called.

(3)请你以上海进出口贸易公司业务员方为的身份,根据上述资料与中国人民保险公司签订进口货物运输预约保险合同。

中国人民保险公司
进口货物运输预约保险合同

合同号:　　　　　　　　　　　　　　　　　　　　　　日期:

甲方:

乙方:

双方就进口货物的运输预约保险拟订以下条款,以资共同遵守:

一、保险范围

甲方从国外进口的全部货物,不论运输方式,凡贸易条款规定由买方办理保险的,都属于本合同范围之内。甲方应根据本合同规定,向乙方办理投保手续并支付保险费。

乙方对上述保险范围内的货物,负有自动承保的责任,在发生本合同规定范围内的损失时,均按本合同的规定,负责赔偿。

二、保险金额

保险金额以货物的到岸价(CIF)即货价加运费加保险费为准(运费可用实际运费,亦可由双方协定一个平均运费率计算)。

三、保险险别和费率

各种货物需要投保的险别由甲方选定并在投保单中填明。乙方根据不同的险别规定不同的费率。现暂定如下:

货物种类	运输方式	保险险别	保险费率

四、保险责任

各种险别的责任范围,按照所属乙方制定的"海洋货物运输保险条款"、"海洋运输货物战争险条款"、"海运进口货物国内转动期间保险责任扩展条款"、"航空运输一切险条款"和其他有关条款的规定为准。

五、投保手续

甲方一经掌握货物发运情况,即应向乙方寄送起运通知书,办理投保手续。通知书一式五份,由保险公司签认后,退回一份。如不办理投保,货物发生损失,乙方不予赔偿。

六、保险费

乙方按甲方寄送的起运通知书照前列相应的费率逐笔计收保费,甲方应及时付费。

七、索赔手续和期限

本合同所保货物发生保险责任范围内的损失时,乙方应按制定的"关于海运进口保险货物残损检验的赔款给付办法"和"进口货物施救整理费用支付办法"迅速处理。甲方应尽力采取防止货物扩大受损的措施,对已遭受损失的货物必须积极抢救,尽量减少货物的损失。向乙方办理索赔的有效期限,以保险货物卸离海港之日起满一年终止。如有特殊需要,可向乙方提出延长索赔期。

八、合同期限

本合同自　　年　月　日起开始生效。

甲方:　　　　　　　　　　　　　　　　　　　　　　乙方:

实训四　进口合同的履行——办理报检、报关、付汇核销手续

业务导入

当出口商 TOKYO IMPORT & EXPORT CORPORATION 按合同规定的装运时间发货后，持全套单据向 FUJI BANK 进行议付。中国银行上海分行收到该笔业务的全套单据后交付上海进出口公司，由其审单，核准无误后进行承兑。由于付款时间未到，但货物已到达上海吴淞港，为了能及时出售，上海进出口公司向中国银行上海分行借单提货。与此同时，办理进口货物的报检、报关和进口付汇核销手续。

报检、报关、付汇核销业务流程如下所示：

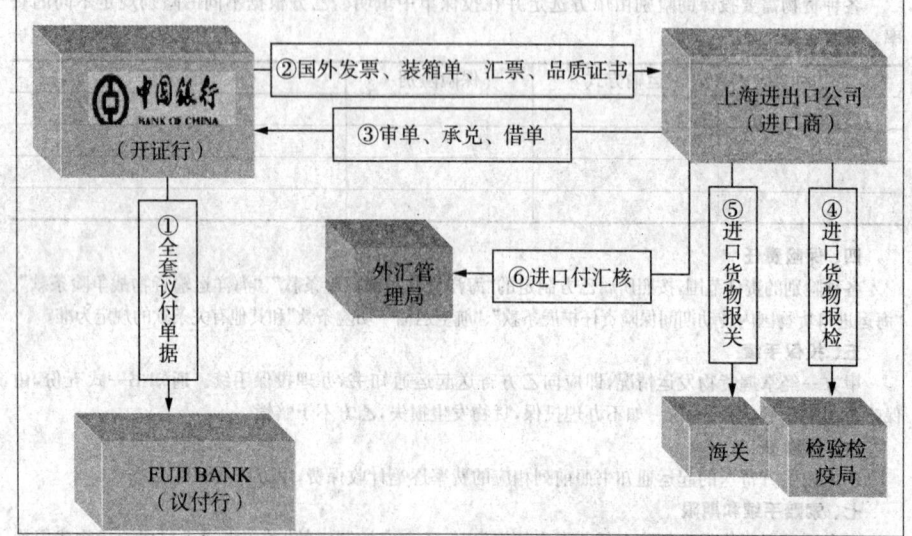

```
中国银行              ②国外发票、装箱单、汇票、品质证书         上海进出口公司
（开证行）    ←————————————————————————————→    （进口商）
              ③审单、承兑、借单
  │                                                    │  │
  │①全套议付单据                          ⑤进口货物报关 │  │ ④进口货物报检
  ↓                                                    ↓  ↓
FUJI BANK      外汇管理局  ←—⑥进口付汇核—              海关  检验检疫局
（议付行）
```

◎ 工作任务一　　办理审单承兑手续

中国银行上海分行收到议付行 FUJI BANK 该笔业务的全套议付单据后，交由上海进出口公司审单。李莉小姐根据合同与信用证的内容进行审单，核准无误后进行承兑，承兑后将全套单据交还给中国银行上海分行。

体验活动四 自理进口贸易业务

李莉小姐审单承兑：

TOKYO IMPORT & EXPORT CORPORATION

82-324 OTOLI MACHI TOKYO, JAPAN

TEL:028-548-742 FAX:028-548-743

SHANGHAI IMPORT & EXPORT CORPORATION

1321 ZHONGSHAN ROAD SHANGHAI, CHINA

TEL:021-56082266 FAX:021-56082265

COMMERCIAL INVOICE

INVOICE NO. TIEX060930

DATE: SEP. 10, 2012

PAYMENT TERMS:

60 DAYS AFTER SIGHT L/C

MARKS: TITC
TX200523
SHANGHAI
C/NO. 1-60

SHIPPED FROM	SHIPPED TO	VESSEL/VOYAGE NO.	
TOKYO	SHANGHAI	COSCO V. 861	
DESCRIPTION	QUANTITY (SET)	PRICE PER SET (USD)	TOTAL AMOUNT (USD)
WRENCH HEX DEYS WRENCH DOUBLE RING OFFSET WRENCH 　CONBINATION WRENCH 　ADJUSTABLE WRENCH L/C NO: XUT17345 P/C NO: TX200523 PACKING: PACKED IN ONE CARTON OF 100 SETS EACH	1 000 1 500 2 000 1 500	FOB TOKYO USD 10.00 USD 10.00 USD 20.00 USD 20.00	USD 10 000.00 USD 15 000.00 USD 40 000.00 USD 30 000.00 USD 95 000.00

SAY U.S. DOLLARS NINETY FIVE THOUSAND ONLY.

山 田

TOKYO IMPORT & EXPORT CORPORATION

TOKYO IMPORT & EXPORT CORPORATION

82-324 OTOLI MACHI TOKYO, JAPAN

TEL:028-548-742 FAX:028-548-743

PACKING LIST

SHANGHAI IMPORT & EXPORT CORPORATION 1321 ZHONGSHAN ROAD SHANGHAI CHINA TEL:021-56082266 FAX:021-56082265

INVOICE NO. TIEX060930
DATE: SEP. 10, 2012
PAYMENT TERMS:
60 DAYS AFTER SIGHT L/C

MARKS: TITC
TX200523
SHANGHAI
C/NO. 1-60

PACKAGES	DESCRIPTION	QUANTITY (SET)	GROSS WEIGHT (KGS)	NET WEIGHT (KGS)
60	WRENCH HEX DEYS WRENCH DOUBLE RING OFFSET WRENCH CONBINATION WRENCH ADJUSTABLE WRENCH	1 000 1 500 2 000 1 500	35 35 50 55	30 30 40 45
	L/C NO: XUT17345 PACKED IN ONE CARTON OF 100 SETS EACH	6 000	175	145

SHIPPED FROM: TOKYO
SHIPPED TO: SHANGHAI
VESSEL/VOYAGE NO.: COSCO V. 861

SAY TOTAL SIXTY(60)CARTONS ONLY.

山田

TOKYO IMPORT & EXPORT CORPORATION

体验活动四　自理进口贸易业务

Declaration of no-wooden
Packing material

To the Service of China Entry & Exit Inspection and Quarantine:

It is declared that this shipment

_____WRENCH_____ (Commodity)

__60CARTONS /175KGS__ (Quantity/Weight)

does not contain wood packing materials.

Name of Export Company:

(Stamp or Signature of Director)

TOKYO IMPORT & EXPORT CORPORATION

_____山田__ SEP. 10, 2012_____

Manager

No. TIEX060930

For USD 95 000.00　　**BILL OF EXCHANGE**　　TOKYO, SEP. 21, 2012

Date

At __60 DAYS AFTER__ sight of this SECOND BILL of EXCHANGE (first of the same tenor and date unpaid) pay to the order of __FUJI BANK TOKYO BRANCH__ the sum of SAY U.S. DOLLARS NINETY FIVE THOUSAND ONLY

Drawn under __BANK OF CHINA SHANGHAI BRANCH__

L/C No. __XUT17345__ Dated __AUG. 22, 2012__

To. __BANK OF CHINA SHANGHAI BRANCH__
　　　__100 ZHONGSHAN NO.1 ROAD SHANGHAI, CHINA__

TOKYO IMPORT &
EXPORT CORPORATION

TOKYO IMPORT & EXPORT CORPORATION

山田

中国银行
BANK OF CHINA

进口信用证付款/承兑通知书

申请人： 上海进出口公司	信用证号：XUT17345
	汇票金额：USD 95 000.00
	汇票期限：60 DAYS AFTER SIGHT
	汇票到期日：2012.11.20

寄单行：FUJI BANK TOKYO BRANCH

受益人：TOKYO IMPORT & EXPORT CORPORATION

单据	汇票	发票	海运提单	空运提单	货物收据	保险单	装箱单	重量单	产地证	装船通知
	1	2	2				2		2	1

货物：WRENCH

不符点：

上述单据已到，现将影印单据提交贵公司：

  请审核并备妥票款于2012年10月10日前来我行，如不在上述期限来我行承兑，即作为你公司同意授权我行在公司存款账户内支出票款对寄单行承兑。

  对于上述不符点，你公司如不同意接受，请于2012年10月10日前书面通知我行，如不在上述期限来我行办理拒付，又不将单据退回我行，即作为你公司接受不符点并授权我行在你公司存款账户内支出票款对寄单行承兑。

                  中国银行
                 2012年10月4日

同意付款
李莉

2012年10月6日

体验活动四　自理进口贸易业务

No. TIEX060930

For USD 95 000.00　　　　**BILL OF EXCHANGE**　　　TOKYO, SEP. 21, 2012
　　　　　　　　　　　　　　　　　　　　　　　　　　　　　　　Date

At ___60 DAYS AFTER___ sight of this SECOND BILL of EXCHANGE (first of the same tenor and date unpaid) pay to the order of ___FUJI BANK TOKYO BRANCH___ the sum of SAY U. S. DOLLARS NINETY FIVE THOUSAND ONLY

Drawn under ___BANK OF CHINA SHANGHAI BRANCH___ 2012.10.06　　┌──────┐
L/C No. ___XUT17345___　　　　　　　　　Dated ___AUG. 22, 2012___　│ 承兑 │
To. BANK OF CHINA SHANGHAI BRANCH　　　　　　　　　　　　　　　　　└──────┘
　　100 ZHONGSHAN NO. 1 ROAD SHANGHAI, CHINA

　　　　　　　　　　　　　　　　　　┌────────────────────┐
　　　　　　　　　　　　　　　　　　│ TOKYO IMPORT &   │
　　　　　　　　　　　　　　　　　　│ EXPORT CORPORATION │
　　　　　　　　　　　　　　　　　　└────────────────────┘
　　　　　　　　　　　TOKYO IMPORT & EXPORT CORPORATION
　　　　　　　　　　　　　　　　　　山　田

操作指南 ➡ 审核单据的注意事项

1. 汇票审核要点
(1)汇票金额不得超过信用证允许的金额,且大小写和货币名称必须一致。
(2)付款期限应符合信用证的规定。
(3)汇票的付款人应为开证行和信用证指定的付款行,不应以申请人为汇票的受票人。
(4)出票人印章或签字和名称与受益人的名称一致。
(5)包括信用证所要求的必要条款,如信用证号、开证行名称、对价条款。
(6)如果受款人为出票人指示性抬头,是否已由出票人背书。
(7)出票人、受款人、付款人都必须符合信用证的规定。
(8)汇票的出票日期应在信用证规定的有效期内。

2. 发票审核要点
(1)确保发票由信用证的受益人出具,在信用证支付方式下,发票的签发人必须是信用证的受益人。
(2)除非信用证另有规定,信用证的申请人应为发票的抬头人。
(3)货物的描述必须与信用证商品描述相符。
(4)信用证提及的发票显示的事项如唛头、数量/重量、价格、装运、包装、运费及其他相关的信息须与信用证一致,并与其他单据一致。
(5)发票的货币、金额必须与信用证的一致,发票的金额不得超过信用证的金额,如数量、金额有"大约"或类似字样的,可以允许增减10%。

续

(6)如不允许分批装运,发票必须包括信用证要求装运的全部货物。
(7)提交的正本和副本份数正确。
3. 海运提单的审核要点
(1)应提交全套或信用证规定份数的正本提单。
(2)必须是已装船的清洁提单,可以是预先印就"已装船"提单加注日期。
(3)贸易条件是 CIF 或 CFR 时,提单必须注明"运费预付"或"运费已付",贸易条件是 FOB 时,提单应该注明"运费代收"。
(4)提单注明信用证规定的装运港和卸货港。
(5)提单收货人符合信用证规定,如为指示提单,背书应符合信用证的规定。
(6)提单上的货物描述与发票上的描述不相抵触。
(7)提单正面注明承运人的名称,应由船公司签字。
(8)提单在要求的期限内交付。
(9)被通知人的名称和地址与信用证的规定一致。
4. 保险单的审核要点
(1)保险单据的名称应与信用证规定相符,除非信用证特别规定,保险凭证和暂保单不得代替保险单,但保险单可以代替保险声明书。
(2)保险单的被保险人名称应与信用证规定相符,如未规定,通常以出口商名义投保,然后再做成空白背书。
(3)保险单据由保险公司、保险商或代理人签发,且签发日期或保险责任的生效日期最迟应在已装船或已发运或接受监管之日。
(4)保险金额或货币必须符合信用证的规定。
(5)对保险货物的描述必须与发票上的货物描述相符。
(6)明确表示按信用证规定的险别投保。
(7)提交签发的正本保险单据。

工作任务二　　办理借单手续

上海进出口贸易公司在办理完承兑手续后,由于付款时间未到,但货物已到达上海吴淞港,为了能及时出售,上海进出口贸易公司填写提货担保申请书向中国银行上海分行借单提货,并与中国银行上海分行签订担保提货保函,向 KILIN TRANSPORT CORPORATION 船公司提货。

提货担保申请书

致：中国银行

信用证号：XUT17345　发票金额：USD 95 000.00　开证日期：2012 年 8 月 22 日

船名：　COSCO V.861　　　　　提单号：　EX060511

货名：　WRENCH

数量：　60 CARTONS

发票号码/唛头：TIEX060930

以上有关货物之记载以正本提单为准。

　　兹因上述货物的正本提单未到，我公司特请贵行向 KILIN TRANSPORT CORPORATION 船公司签发《担保提货保函》，以便我公司先行提货。为此，我公司已将上述货款全额存入在贵行的保证金专户，并保证如下：

　　1. 因按我公司要求提取贵行保函项下的货物而产生的任何性质的责任性损坏或损失，均由我公司负责赔偿，贵行无需为此承担任何责任。

　　2. 如因提取上述货物而引起对贵行的诉讼，我公司将随时提供足够的应诉费用，并保证无条件地承担由此而引起的一切责任和风险，赔偿贵行由此产生的一切直接和间接损失，前述责任、风险和费用包括但不限于赔偿责任、诉讼费用、律师费、进行诉讼的差旅费等。

　　3. 如果因此而使该船或属于该船东的其他船舶和财产遭到羁留或扣押，或是受到羁留和扣押威胁，我公司将负责获取保释或采取其他所需的安全措施使羁留或扣押不致发生，或把已被羁留或扣押的船只或财产保释出来。无论其羁留或扣押是否合法，由此产生的损失、损坏或费用均由我公司负责赔偿。

　　4. 在收到上述货物之单据时，无论其有无不符点，我公司放弃拒付的权利，贵行有权在规定时间内对外付款/承兑。

　　5. 一旦正本提单收到，我公司保证立即将其交给船公司以换回担保提货保函并交给贵行注销或由贵行直接交给船公司以换回担保提单保函注销。

签字：李莉

申请人（公章）：上海进出口公司

担保提货保函

编号：06109988

致：

信用证号：XUT17345　发票金额：USD 95 000.00　开证日期：2012 年 8 月 22 日

船名：COSCO V. 861　　　　　　提单号：EX060511

货名：WRENCH

数量：60 CARTONS

发票号码/唛头：TIEX060930

以上有关货物之记载以正本提单为准。

上述货物由 TOKYO IMPORT & EXPORT CORPORATION（托运人）交上述船舶运输。由于货物的正本提单未到而又急于提货，我行特请求贵公司在未见正本提单的情况下将该批货物交付给　上海进出口公司　并保证如下：

1. 因我行要求交付货物而产生任何性质的损坏或损失，均由我行承担，贵公司无须承担任何责任。

2. 如交付上述货物而引起对贵公司的诉讼，我方将随时提供足够的应诉费用并保证无条件承担由此而产生的一切费用，包括但不限于赔偿责任、诉讼费用、律师费、进行诉讼的差旅费等。

3. 如果因此而使该船或属于该船东的其他船舶和财产遭到羁留或扣押，或是受到羁留和扣押威胁，我行负责获取保释或采取其他所需的安全措施使羁留或扣押不致发生，或把已被羁留或扣押的船只或财产保释出来，并负责赔偿由此产生的损失、损坏或费用。

4. 我行一旦获得上述货物的正本提单，立即交与贵公司并换回本保函，我行责任便告终止，或本保函出具后期满一年自动失效。

5. 如果贵公司对保函下的责任人中的任何一方首先提起诉讼，不管其是否为参与方或直接责任人，我行无条件承担责任。

6. 本保函适用中华人民共和国法律并接受中国海事法院管辖。

签字：李莉　　　　　　　　　　　　　　　　签字：马密

提供单位盖章：　　　　　　　　　　　　　　担保方盖章：

（上海进出口公司 IMPORT & EXPORT CORPORATION SHANGHAI 印章）

（中国银行上海分行 担保专用章）

工作任务三　　办理入境货物报检手续

上海进出口公司办理好承兑借单后,根据我国出入境商品检验检疫有关法律法规的规定及时办理入境货物报检手续,填写入境货物报检单,并随附进口贸易合同、国外发票、提(运)单和装箱单等有关证单。由于手工工具扳手属于法定检验商品,须向出入境检验检疫局签发入境货物通关单。

操作指南　　入境货物报检的时间、地点及流程

1. 入境货物报检的时限

(1)输入微生物、人体组织、生物制品、血液及其制品或种畜、禽及其精液、胚胎、受精卵的应当在入境前 30 天报检;

(2)输入其他动物的,应在入境前 15 天报检;

(3)输入植物、种子、种苗及其他繁殖材料的,应在入境前 7 天报检;

(4)入境货物需对外索赔出证的,应在索赔有效期前不少于 20 天内向到货口岸或货物到达地的检验检疫机构报检。

2. 入境货物报检的地点

(1)审批、许可证等有关政府批文中规定检验检疫地点的,在规定的地点报检;

(2)大宗散装商品、易腐烂变质商品、废旧物品及在卸货时发现包装破损、数量短缺的商品,必须在卸货口岸检验检疫机构报检;

(3)需结合安装调试进行检验的成套设备、机电仪产品以及在口岸开件后难以恢复包装的商品,应在收货人所在地检验检疫机构报检并检验;

(4)其他入境货物,应在入境前或入境时向报关地检验检疫机构报检;

(5)入境的运输工具及人员应在入境前或入境时向入境口岸检验检疫机构申报。

3. 入境货物报检一般操作流程

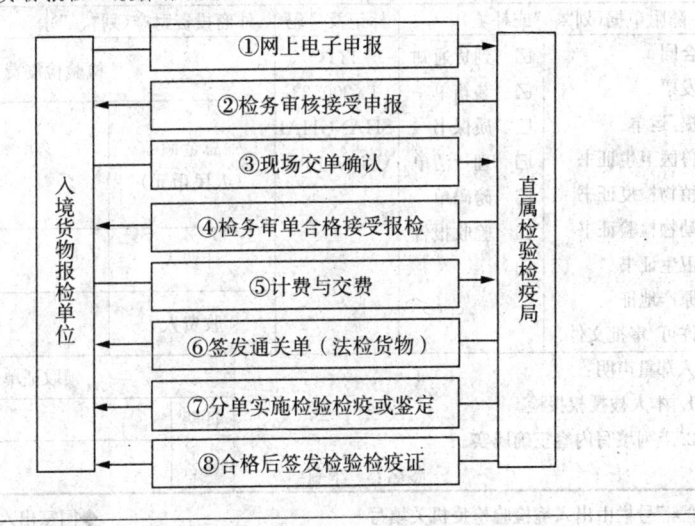

入境货物报检单位		直属检验检疫局
→	①网上电子申报	→
←	②检务审核接受申报	←
→	③现场交单确认	→
←	④检务审单合格接受报检	←
→	⑤计费与交费	→
←	⑥签发通关单(法检货物)	←
→	⑦分单实施检验检疫或鉴定	→
←	⑧合格后签发检验检疫证	←

李莉小姐填写入境货物报检单：

中华人民共和国出入境检验检疫
入境货物报检单

报检单位：（加盖公章） *编号：_____

报检单位登记号：1880298666 联系人：李莉 电话：56082266 报检日期：2012年10月4日

收货人	（中文）上海进出口公司	企业性质（划"√"）	☑合资 □合作 □外资
	（外文）SHANGHAI IMPORT & EXPORT CORPORATION		
发货人	（中文）东京进出口公司		
	（外文）TOKYO IMPORT & EXPORT CORPORATION		

货物名称（中/外文）	H.S.编码	产地	数/重量	货物总值	包装种类及数量
扳手 WRENCH	8204.1100	日本	6 000 SETS	95 000.00美元	60箱

运输工具名称及号码	COSCO V.861	合同号	TX200523
贸易方式	一般贸易	贸易国别（地区）	日本	提单/运单号	EX060511
到岸日期	2012.10.2	起运国家（地区）	日本	许可证/审批号	06-JZ5661168
卸毕日期	2012.10.2	起运口岸	东京	入境口岸	吴淞海关
索赔有效期至	2013.10.24	经停口岸		目的地	上海

集装箱规格、数量及号码

合同订立的特殊条款 以及其他要求		货物存放地点	上海市逸仙路5号
		用途	自营内销

随附单据（划"√"或补填）		标记及号码	*外商投资财产（划"√"）	□是 □否
☑ 合同	☑ 到货通知	TITC	*检验检疫费	
☑ 发票	☑ 装箱单	TX200523		
☑ 提/运单	□ 质保书	SHANGHAI	总金额	
□ 兽医卫生证书	□ 理货清单	C/NO.1-60	（人民币元）	
□ 植物检疫证书	□ 磅码单			
□ 动物检验证书	□ 验收报告		计费人	
□ 卫生证书	□			
□ 原产地证			收费人	
☑ 许可/审批文件				

报检人郑重声明： 1. 本人被授权报检。 2. 上列填写内容正确属实。 签名：李莉	领取证单
	日期
	签名

注：有"*"号栏由出入境检验检疫机关填写 ◆国家出入境检验检疫局制

248

操作指南　入境货物报检单的填制方法

1. 编号

由检验检疫机构报检受理人员填写。报检单编号前6位为检验检疫机构代码,第7位为报检类代码,第8、9位为年代码,第10至15位为流水号。

2. 报检单位

填写报检单位的全称,并加盖报检单位印章。

3. 报检单位登记号

填写报检单位在检验检疫机构备案或注册登记的代码。

4. 联系人

填写报检人员姓名。

5. 电话

填写报检人员的联系电话。

6. 报检日期

检验检疫机构实际受理报检的日期,由检验检疫机构受理报检人员填写。

7. 收货人(中/外文)

填写进口贸易合同中的买方,中英译文应一致。

8. 发货人(中/外文)

填写进口贸易合同中的卖方,中英译文应一致。

9. 货物名称(中/外文)

填写本批货物的品名,应与进口贸易合同和国外发票名称一致,如为废旧货物应注明。

10. H.S.编码

填写本批货物的商品编码,以当年海关公布的商品税则编码分类为准。商品编码为8位数或10位数编码。

11. 原产国(地区)

填写本批货物生产/加工的国家或地区。

12. 数/重量

填写本批货物的数/重量,应与进口贸易合同、国外发票上所列的货物数/重量一致,并应注明数/重量单位。

13. 货物总值

填写本批货物的总值及币种,应与进口贸易合同和国外发票上所列一致。

14. 包装种类及数量

填写本批货物实际运输包装的种类及数量,应注明包装的材质。

续

15. 运输工具名称及号码

填写装运本批货物的运输工具名称及号码。

16. 合同号

填写本批货物的进口贸易合同号,或订单、形式发票的号码。

17. 贸易方式

填写本批进口货物的贸易方式,如一般贸易、来料加工、进料加工、易货贸易、补偿贸易等。

18. 贸易国别(地区)

填写本批进口货物的贸易国家或地区名称。

19. 提单/运单号

填写本批进口货物的海运提单号或空运单号,有二程提单的应同时填写。

20. 到货日期

填写本批进口货物到达口岸的日期。

21. 起运国家(地区)

填写本批进口货物的起运国家或地区名称。

22. 许可证/审批号

需办理进境许可证或审批的进口货物应填写有关许可证号或审批号,不得留空。

23. 卸毕日期

填写本批进口货物在口岸卸毕的实际日期。

24. 起运口岸

填写装运本批进口货物起运口岸的名称。

25. 入境口岸

填写装运本批进口货物交通工具进境首次停靠的口岸名称。

26. 索赔有效期至

按进口贸易合同规定的日期填写,特别要注明截止日期。

27. 经停口岸

填写本批进口货物在到达目的地前中途曾经停靠的口岸名称。

28. 目的地

填写本批进口货物最后到达的交货地。

29. 集装箱规格、数量及号码

进口货物若以集装箱运输,应填写集装箱的规格、数量及号码。

30. 合同订立的特殊条款以及其他要求

填写在进口贸易合同中订立的有关质量、卫生等特殊条款,或报检单位对本批货物检验检疫的特别要求。

续

31. 货物存放地点
   填写本批进口货物存放的地点。
32. 用途
   填写本批进口货物的用途。用途根据实际情况选填种用或繁殖、食用、观赏或演艺、伴侣动物、实验、药用、饲用、其他。
33. 随附单据
   向检验检疫机构提供的实际单据名称前的"□"内打"√"。如没有,在"□"后补填其名称。
34. 标记及号码
   填写进口货物的标记及号码,应与进口贸易合同和国外发票等有关单据保持一致。若没有标记及号码,则填"N/M"。
35. 外商投资财产
   由检验检疫机构报检受理人员填写。
36. 报检人郑重声明
   由报检人员亲笔签名。
37. 检验检疫费
   由检验检疫机构计费人员填写。
38. 领取证单
   由报检人在领取证单时,填写实际领证日期并签名。

出入境检验检疫局签发入境货物通关单：

中华人民共和国出入境检验检疫
入境货物通关单

编号：T0608114

1. 收货人 上海进出口公司			5. 标记及唛码 TITC TX200523 SHANGHAI C/NO. 1-60
2. 发货人 TOKYO IMPORT & EXPORT CORPORATION			:::
3. 合同/提（运）单号 TX200523		4. 输出国家或地区 日本	:::
6. 运输工具名称及号码 COSCO V. 861		7. 目的地 上海	8. 集装箱规格及数量 - - - -
9. 货物名称及规格 扳手 WRENCH **********************	10. H.S. 编码 8204.1100	11. 申报总值 USD 95 000.00	12. 数/重量、包装数量及种类 6 000 SETS 60 CTNS
13. 证明 上述货物业已报验/申报，请海关予以放行。 （检验检疫专用章） 日期：2012年10月6日 签字：丁毅			
14. 备注			

◎ 工作任务四　　办理进口货物报关手续

上海进出口公司办理好报检手续后，李莉小姐根据外国发票、提单等有关内容填写进口货物报关单，在海关规定的时间内及时办理进口货物的报关。海关查验合格并征收进口关税后，予以放行，上海进出口公司方可提货。

体验活动四 自理进口贸易业务

李莉小姐填写进口货物报关单：

中华人民共和国海关进口货物报关单

预录入编号： 海关编号：

进口口岸 吴淞海关 2202	备案号		进口日期 2012.10.2	申报日期 2012.10.6
经营单位（0387124666） 上海进出口公司	运输方式 江海运输		运输工具名称 COSCO V.861	提运单号 EX060511
收货单位 0387124666	贸易方式 一般贸易		征免性质 一般征税	征税比例
许可证号 06-JZ5661168	起运国（地区） 日本		装货港 东京	境内目的地 上海
批准文号	成交方式 FOB	运费 502/1 100/3	保费 502/990/3	批准文号
合同协议号 TX200523	件数 60	包装种类 箱	毛重（千克） 175	净重（千克） 145
集装箱号	随附单据 B:T0608114		用途 自营内销	
标记唛码及备注	TITC TX200523 SHANGHAI C/NO. 1-60			

项号	商品编号	商品名称、规格型号	数量及单位	原产国（地区）	单价	总价	币制	征免
	8204.1100	WRENCH		日本			502	照章
01		HEX DEYS WRENCH	1 000 套		10.00	10 000.00		
02		DOUBLE RING OFFSET WRENCH	1 500 套		10.00	15 000.00		
03		COMBINATION WRENCH	2 000 套		20.00	40 000.00		
04		ADJUSTABLE WRENCH	1 500 套		20.00	30 000.00		

税费征收情况

	录入员 录入单位	兹声明以上申报无讹并承担法律责任	海关审单批注及放行日期（签章）	
报关员	3101045588 李莉	申报单位（签章） 上海进出口公司 报关专用章	审单	审价
			征税	统计
单位地址 上海市中山路 1321 号			查验	放行
邮编 200031 电话 56082266		填制日期 2012 年 10 月 6 日		

海关予以放行：

中华人民共和国海关进口货物报关单

预录入编号： 　　　　　　　　　　　　　海关编号：32444117252

进口口岸 吴淞海关 2202		备案号		进口日期 2012.10.2		申报日期 2012.10.6	
经营单位 (0387124666) 上海进出口公司		运输方式 江海运输		运输工具名称 COSCO V. 861		提运单号 EX060511	
收货单位 0387124666		贸易方式 一般贸易		征免性质 一般征税		征税比例	
许可证号 06-JZ5661168		起运国（地区） 日本		装货港 东京		境内目的地 上海	
批准文号		成交方式 FOB	运费 502/1 100/3		保费 502/990/3		杂费
合同协议号 TX200523		件数 60		包装种类 箱		毛重（千克） 175	净重（千克） 145
集装箱号		随附单据 B:T0608114			用途 自营内销		
标记唛码及备注	TITC TX200523 SHANGHAI C/NO. 1-60						

项号	商品编号	商品名称、规格型号	数量及单位	原产国（地区）	单价	总价	币制	征免
	8204.1100	WRENCH		日本			502	照章
01		HEX DEYS WRENCH	1 000 套		10.00	10 000.00		
02		DOUBLE RING OFFSET WRENCH	1 500 套		10.00	15 000.00		
03		COMBINATION WRENCH	2 000 套		20.00	40 000.00		
04		ADJUSTABLE WRENCH	1 500 套		20.00	30 000.00		

税费征收情况			
录入员　　　录入单位	兹声明以上申报无讹并承担法律责任	海关审单批注及放行日期（签章） 张玲　　2012.10.9	
报关员 3101045588 李 莉	申报单位（签章） 上海进出口公司 报关专用章	审单	审价
		征税	统计
单位地址　上海市中山路 1321 号			
邮编 200031　电话 56082266	填制日期　2012 年 10 月 6 日	查验 丸宁 放行 2012.10.9	

操作指南 ➡ **进口货物报关单的填制方法**

1. 进口口岸
按实际货物进口的口岸填写海关的名称及其海关"关区代码表"的代码。

2. 进口日期
填报进口货物所载的运输工具的进境日期,无实际进境的,则填申请办理货物进口手续的日期。

3. 申报日期
填制进口商或其代理人申请办理货物进口手续的日期,其不能早于进口日期。

4. 经营单位
应填写对外签订并执行进口货物贸易合同的中国境内企业的全称及其代码。

5. 提运单号
按进口货物提单或运单编号填写。

6. 收货单位
填入已知的进口货物在境内的最终消费单位的名称及其代码。

7. 征免性质
按海关对进口货物实施征、减、免税管理的性质类别和代码填报。一份报关单只允许填一种征免性质。

8. 征税比例
此项仅用于"进料非对口"贸易方式下的进口报关单,填报海关规定的实际应征税的比率,例如,5%填报5。

9. 许可证号
属于进口许可证范围的,必须在此栏目填报进口货物许可证的编号,不得为空。一份报关单只允许填一个许可证号,如有多个许可证号,必须分单申报。

10. 起运国(地区)
根据进口货物始发的国家(地区)的名称及其代码填写。

11. 装运港
填写进口货物在运抵我国关境前的最后一个境外装运港的名称及代码,无实际进出境的,填"中国境内0142"。

12. 境内目的地
填写进口货物在国内的消费地或最终运抵地的名称及代码。

13. 批准文号
本栏目应填入进口付汇核销单编号。

14. 运费

续

应注明该批货物的运费并注明币制代码,如为 CIF 或 CFR,则可不填。

15. 保费

填报该批货物的全部保险费和币制代码,如为 CIF,可不填。

16. 合同协议号

注明进口货物合同(协议)的全部字头和号码。

17. 用途

按进口货物的实际用途和用途代码进行填报,如"以产顶进 13"。

18. 原产国(地区)

根据进口货物的生产、开采或加工制造国家(地区)的名称及其代码填写。

上海 海关 进口关税 专用缴款书

收入系统:

海关系统　　　填交日期　2012 年 10 月 9 日　　　号码:269874123

收款单位	收入机关	中央金库			缴款单位(人)	名称	上海进出口公司
	科目	进口关税	预算级次	中央		账号	SZR80066686
	收款国库	中国银行上海分行				开户银行	中国银行上海分行

税号	货物名称	数量	单位	完税价格(¥)	税率(%)	税款金额(¥)
16258698	WRENCH	60	箱	7 676 000	1.0	76 000.00

金额人民币(大写)柒佰陆拾柒万陆仟圆整

申请单位编号	0387124666	报关单编号	32444117252	填制单位 (上海进出口公司 印章)	收款国库(银行) 中国银行上海分行 收款专用章
合同(批件)号	TX200523	运输工具(号)	COSCO V. 861		
缴款期限	2012.10.16	提/装货单号	XY05111		

备注　一般征税　照章征税　20121002 进
　　　USD 95 000.00
成交:FOB

制单人:350
复核人:

从填发缴款书次日起,限 7 日内(星期日和法定假日除外)缴纳,逾期按日征收税款总额千分之一的滞纳金。

上海 海关 代征增值税 专用缴款书

收入系统：

税务系统　填发日期　2012年10月9日　　　号码：269874123

收款单位	收入机关	中央金库			缴款单位（人）	名称	上海进出口公司
	科目	进口关税	预算级次	中央		账号	280066686
	收款国库	中国银行上海分行				开户银行	中国银行上海分行

税号	货物名称	数量	单位	完税价格（¥）	税率（%）	税款金额（¥）
16258698	WRENCH	60	箱	7 676 000	1.0	76 000.00

金额人民币（大写）柒佰陆拾柒万陆仟圆整

申请单位编号	0387124666	报关单编号	32444117252	填制单位	收款国库（银行）
合同（批件）号	TX200523	运输工具（号）	COSCO V. 861		中国银行上海分行 收款专用章
缴款期限	2012.10.16	提/装货单号	XY05111		

备注：一般征税　照章征税　20121002进
USD 95 000.00
成交：FOB

制单人：350
复核人：567

◆ 工作任务五　　办理进口付汇核销手续

上海进出口公司在汇票到期日办理好付汇手续后，填写贸易进口付汇核销单。银行审核无误后，将第一联交外汇管理局，第二联退还给上海进出口公司，由该公司的核销员向外汇管理局提供贸易进口付汇核销单、进口货物报关单付汇水单，并填写贸易进口付汇到货核销表，办理核销报审手续。

李莉小姐填写进口付汇核销单：

贸易进口付汇核销单(代申报单)

印单局代码：099210		核销单编号：3002698741	
单位代码：3145897564	单位名称：上海进出口公司		所在地外汇局名称：上海
付汇银行名称：中国银行上海分行	收款人国别：日本		交易编码：01156
收款人是否保税区：是□ 否☑		进口商品名称：扳手	
对外付汇币种：美元	对外付汇总额：USD 95 000.00		折美元总额：USD 95 000.00
其中：购汇金额 USD 95 000.00	现汇金额		
人民币账号：SZR80066686	外汇账号		

付汇性质

☑正常付汇
□不在名录　　　　□90天以上信用证　　　□90天以上托收　　　□异地付汇
□90天以上到货　　□转口贸易　　　　　　□境外工程使用物资　□真实性审查
备案表编号：6366

| 预计到货日期：2012年10月2日 | 进口批件号 | 合同/发票号：TX200523/TIEX060930 |

结算方式

信用证　90天以内☑　90天以上□　承兑日期 2012.10.6　付汇日期 2012.11.20　期限 60天

托收　　90天以内□　90天以上□　承兑日期　　　　　付汇日期　　　　　期限　天

汇款	预付货款□	货到付款(凭报关单付款)□	付汇日期	
	报关单号	报关日期	报关单币种	金额
	报关单号	报关日期	报关单币种	金额
	报关单号	报关日期	报关单币种	金额
	报关单号	报关日期	报关单币种	金额
	报关单号	报关日期	报关单币种	金额
	(若报关单填写不完,可另附纸。)			

其他□　　　　　　　　　　　　　　　　　　付汇日期

以下由付汇银行填写
申报号码：07010322
业务编号：9821546781

(付款银行签章)　　　　　中国银行上海分行 收款专用章
审核日期：2012年10月6日

进口单位(签章)：上海进出口公司　　　　　　　　　　2012年11月21日

李莉小姐填写进口付汇到货核销表：

贸易进口付汇到货核销表

进口单位名称：上海进出口公司　　　进口单位编号：3145897564　　核销单编号：3002698741

序号	核销单号	备案表号	付汇情况					报关到货情况				与付汇差额		凭报关单付汇	备注
			付汇币种金额	付汇日期	结算方式	付汇银行名称	应到货日期	报关单号	到货企业名称	报关币种金额	报关日期	退汇	其他		
1	300269 8741	6666	USD 95 000	11.21	信用证	中国银行上海分行	10.2	4441 17252	上海进出口公司	USD 95 000	10.6				

付汇合计笔数：1　　至本月累计笔数：2	付汇合计金额：USD 95 000　　至本月累计金额：USD 106 000	到货报关合计笔数：1　　至本月累计笔数：2	到货报关合计金额：USD 95 000　　至本月累计金额：USD 106 000	退汇合计金额：　　至本月累计金额：	凭报关单合计金额：　　至本月累计金额：

填表人：李莉　　　负责人：方力　　　填表日期：2012 年 11 月 22 日
本核销表内容无讹。（盖章）

（上海进出口公司 IMPORT & EXPORT CORPORATION SHANGHAI）

注：
1. 本表一式二联，第一联送外汇局，第二联由进口单位留存。
2. 本表合计和累计栏金额为折美元金额；
3. 本表由各外汇局印制，供进口单位使用。
4. 货款汇款项下的付汇在"凭报关单付汇"栏填"√"；
5. 累计栏为本年年初至本月的累计数；
6. 一次到货多次付汇的，在"付汇情况"栏填写实际付汇情况，在"报关到货情况"栏只填写一次；
7. 一次付汇多次到货的，参照第 6 点处理。

综合业务模拟操作

操作一

1. 操作资料

上海玩具进出口公司收到中国银行上海分行来自出口商 TOKYO IMPORT & EXPORT CORPORATION 的全套议付单据,进行审单,核准无误后付款赎单。然后办理进口货物的报检、报关手续。

审单与填写报检单、报关单的有关资料如下:

买　方:	上海玩具进出口公司(SHANGHAI TOY IMPORT & EXPORT CORPORATION) 地址:13 FENXIANG ROAD SHANGHAI, CHINA TEL:021-56082212 FAX:021-56082211
银行账号:	WT056742
卖　方:	TOKYO IMPORT & EXPORT CORPORATION 地址:82-324 OTOLI MACHI TOKYO, JAPAN TEL:028-548-742 FAX:028-548-743
货名规格:	电子手掌玩具(ELECTRON PALM BAUBLE)(货号为 R222S、R333H、R666W、R888A)
单　价:	FOB TOKYO R222S USD 50.00/SET, R333H USD 45.00/SET, R666W USD 35.00/SET, R888A USD 20.00/SET
支付方式:	不可撤销跟单即期信用证(IRREVOCABLE DOCUMENTARY CREDIT AT SIGHT)
数　量:	R222S 1 000 套(1 000 SETS)、R333H 1 000 套(1 000 SETS) R666W 1 000 套(1 000 SETS)、R888A 1 000 套(1 000 SETS)
包　装:	每50套装一个出口纸箱(PACKED IN 1 CARTON OF 50 SETS EACH)
装运期:	不迟于2012年10月31日前装运(LATEST DATE OF SHIPMENT: 20121031)
装运港:	日本东京(TOKYO, JAPAN)
目的地港:	中国上海(SHANGHAI, CHINA)
分批装运:	允许(ALLOWED)
转运:	不允许(NOT ALLOWED)
合同号:	TX06238
信用证号:	XUT17123
信用证有效期:	2012年11月20日

提交单据:(1)已签字的商业发票一式三份,并显示合同号(THREE COPIES OF SIGNED COMMERCIAL INVOICE INDICATING CONTRACT NUMBER OF TX06238);

(2)装箱单一式三份(THREE COPIES OF PACKING LIST);

(3)品质证书一式二份,由厂商签发(TWO COPIES OF CERTIFICATE OF QUALITY/QUANTITY ISSUED BY MANUFACTURE);

(4)在装船后12小时内用传真向买方发出装运通知,其中包含合同号、货名、数量、毛重、提单号和装运日期等(WITHIN 12 HOURS AFTER THE GOODS ARE COMPLETELY LOADED, THE SELLER SHALL FAX TO NOTIFY THE BUYER OF THE CONTRACT NUMBER, NAME OF COMMODITY, QUANTITY, GROSS WEIGHT, B/L NO. AND THE DATE OF DELIVERY)。

通知银行:FUJI BANK TOKYO BRANCH

报检单位登记号:30125478Q

H. S. 编码:9503.9000

提单号码:TES0610589Q

提单日期:2012.10.20

运　　费:USD 820.00

保险费:USD 1 020.00

海关注册号:3018712462

2.操作要求

(1)请你以上海玩具进出口公司业务员张成的身份,根据上述资料、合同和信用证的有关规定审核以下单据并找出不符点。

TOKYO IMPORT & EXPORT CORPORATION

82-324 OTOLI MACHI TOKYO, JAPAN

TEL:028-548-742 FAX:028-548-743

COMMERCIAL INVOICE

| SHANGHAI TOY IMPORT & EXPORT TRADE CORPORATION
13 FENXIANG ROAD SHANGHAI, CHINA
TEL:021-56082212 FAX:021-56082211 | INVOICE NO. TIEX070930
DATE: OCT. 12, 2012
PAYMENT TERMS:
L/C AT SIGHT |

MARKS: N/M

SHIPPED FROM	SHIPPED TO	VESSEL/VOYAGE NO.		
TOKYO	SHANGHAI	HONGDA V. 026		
DESCRIPTION		QUANTITY (SET)	PRICE PER SET (USD)	TOTAL AMOUNT (USD)
ELECTRON PALM BAUBLE			FOB TOKYO	
R222S		1 000	USD 50.00	USD 50 000.00
R333H		1 000	USD 45.00	USD 45 000.00
R666W		1 000	USD 35.00	USD 35 000.00
R888A		1 000	USD 20.00	USD 20 000.00
L/C NO.: XUT17123 P/C NO.: RT06900 PACKING: PACKED IN ONE CARTON OF 50 SETS EACH				USD 150 000.00

SAY U. S. DOLLARS ONE HUNDRED AND FIFTY THOUSAND ONLY.

山田

TOKYO IMPORT & EXPORT CORPORATION

体验活动四　自理进口贸易业务

TOKYO IMPORT & EXPORT CORPORATION

82-324 OTOLI MACHI TOKYO, JAPAN

TEL:028-548-742 FAX:028-548-743

PACKING LIST

SHANGHAI TOY IMPORT & EXPORT TRADE CORPORATION

13 FENXIANG ROAD SHANGHAI, CHINA

TEL:021-56082212 FAX:021-56082211

INVOICE NO.	TIEX070930
DATE:	OCT. 12, 2012
PAYMENT TERMS:	L/C AT SIGHT

MARKS: N/M

SHIPPED FROM	SHIPPED TO	VESSEL/VOYAGE NO.		
TOKYO	SHANGHAI	HONGDA V. 026		
PACKAGES	DESCRIPTION	QUANTITY (SET)	GROSS WEIGHT (KGS)	NET WEIGHT (KGS)
80	ELECTRON PALM BAUBLE	1 000	50	40
	R222S	1 000	50	40
	R333H	1 000	50	40
	R666W	1 000	50	40
	R888A			
	L/C NO. : XUT17345 PACKED IN ONE CARTON OF 50 SETS EACH	4 000	200	160

SAY TOTAL EIGHTY(80)CARTONS ONLY.

山田

TOKYO IMPORT & EXPORT CORPORATION

No. TIEX070930

For USD 100 000.00

BILL OF EXCHANGE   TOKYO, OCT. 21, 2012
                                        Date

At ____****____ sight of this SECOND BILL of EXCHANGE (first of the same tenor and date unpaid) pay to the order of   FUJI BANK TOKYO BRANCH   the sum of
SAY U. S. DOLLARS ONE HUNDRED AND FIFTY THOUSAND ONLY

Drawn under   BANK OF CHINA SHANGHAI BRANCH

L/C No.   XUT17123   Dated   SEP, 29. 2012

To. BANK OF CHINA SHANGHAI BRANCH
     100 ZHONGSHAN No. 1 ROAD SHANGHAI, CHINA

TOKYO IMPORT & EXPORT CORPORATION

山田

商业发票审核结果：

装箱单审核结果：

汇票审核结果：

(2) 请你以上海玩具进出口公司业务员张成的身份，根据上述资料、合同和信用证的有关内容填写入境货物报检单。

中华人民共和国出入境检验检疫
入境货物报检单

报检单位（加盖公章）：				*编号：
报检单位登记号：	联系人：	电话：	报检日期：	年 月 日

收货人	（中文）	企业性质（划"√"）		□合资 □合作 □外资
	（外文）			
发货人	（中文）			
	（外文）			

货物名称（中/外文）	H.S.编码	产地	数/重量	货物总值	包装种类及数量

运输工具名称及号码		合同号	
贸易方式		贸易国别（地区）	提单/运单号
到岸日期		起运国家（地区）	许可证/审批号
卸毕日期		起运口岸	入境口岸
索赔有效期至		经停口岸	目的地

集装箱规格、数量及号码			
合同订立的特殊条款以及其他要求		货物存放地点	
		用途	

随附单据（划"√"或补填）		标记及号码	*外商投资财产（划"√"）	□是 □否
□合同	□到货通知		*检验检疫费	
□发票	□装箱单			
□提/运单	□质保书		总金额	
□兽医卫生证书	□理货清单		（人民币元）	
□植物检疫证书	□磅码单			
□动物检验证书	□验收报告			
□卫生证书	□		计费人	
□原产地证				
□许可/审批文件			收费人	

报检人郑重声明：		领取证单	
1. 本人被授权报检。		日期	
2. 上列填写内容正确属实。			
签名：		签名	

注：有"*"号栏由出入境检验检疫机关填写　　　　◆国家出入境检验检疫局制

(3)请你以上海玩具进出口公司业务员张成的身份,根据上述资料、合同和信用证的有关内容填写进口货物报关单。

中华人民共和国海关进口货物报关单

预录入编号: 　　　　　　　　　　　　　　　　　　　海关编号:

进口口岸		备案号		进口日期		申报日期	
经营单位		运输方式		运输工具名称		提运单号	
收货单位		贸易方式		征免性质		征税比例	
许可证号		起运国(地区)		装货港		境内目的地	
批准文号		成交方式		运费		保费		批准文号	
合同协议号		件数		包装种类		毛重(千克)		净重(千克)	
集装箱号		随附单据				用途	
标记唛码及备注							

项号	商品编号	商品名称、规格型号	数量及单位	原产国(地区)	单价	总价	币制	征免

税费征收情况			
录入员　　录入单位	兹声明以上申报无讹并承担法律责任	海关审单批注及放行日期(签章)	
报关员	申报单位(签章)	审单	审价
单位地址		征税	统计
邮编　　　电话　　　填制日期		查验	放行

操作二

1. 操作资料

上海进出口贸易公司收到中国银行上海分行来自出口商 PITER IMPORT & EXPORT CORPORATION 的全套议付单据，进行审单，核准无误后付款赎单。然后办理进口货物的报检、报关手续。

审单与填写报检单、报关单的有关资料如下：

买　方：上海进出口贸易公司(SHANGHAI IMPORT & EXPORT TRADE CORPORATION)

21 ZHONGSHAN ROAD SHANGHAI, CHINA

TEL：021-56082266 FAX：021-56082265

银行账号：WT012342

卖　方：PITER IMPORT & EXPORT CORPORATION

地址：NO. 324 TOLI MACH HAMBURG, GERMANY

TEL：128-54842 FAX：128-54843

货名规格：彩色喷墨打印机(COLOR INKJET PRINTERS)

单　价：FOB HAMBURG RO123 USD 110.00/SET，RO122 USD 125.00/SET，RO145 USD 120.00/SET，RO168 USD 115.00/SET

支付方式：见票后 30 天付款不可撤销跟单信用证(IRREVOCABLE DOCUMENTARY CREDIT AT 30 DAYS AFTER SIGHT)

数　量：RO123 1 000 套(1 000 SETS)、RO122 1 000 套(1 000 SETS)、RO145 1000 套(1 000 SETS)、RO168 1 000 套(1 000 SETS)

包　装：每 50 套装一个出口纸箱(PACKED IN 1 CARTON OF 50 SETS EACH)

毛　重：每箱 10 KGS

净　重：每箱 8 KGS

体　积：每箱 0.8 CBM

装运期：不迟于 2012 年 11 月 8 日前装运(LATEST DATE OF SHIPMENT：20121108)

装运港：德国汉堡(HAMBURG, GERMANY)

目的地港：中国上海(SHANGHAI, CHINA)

分批装运：允许(ALLOWED)

转　运：允许(ALLOWED)

船　名：HOGA. V. 086

合同号：TX07238

信用证号：XUT17456

信用证有效期：2012 年 12 月 8 日

提交单据：(1)已签字的商业发票一式三份，并显示合同号(THREE COPIES OF

SIGNED COMMERCIAL INVOICE INDICATING CONTRACT NUMBER OF TX07238);
(2)装箱单一式三份(THREE COPIES OF PACKING LIST);
(3)品质证书一式二份,由厂商签发(TWO COPIES OF CERTIFICATE OF QUALITY/QUANTITY ISSUED BY MANUFACTURE);
(4)在装船后12小时内用传真向买方发出装运通知,其中包含合同号、货名、数量毛重、提单号和装运日期等(WITHIN 12 HOURS AFTER THE GOODS ARE COMPLETELY LOADED, THE SELLER SHALL FAX TO NOTIFY THE BUYER OF THE CONTRACT NUMBER, NAME OF COMMODITY, QUANTITY, GROSS WEIGHT, B/L NO. AND THE DATE OF DELIVERY).

报检单位登记号： 06965Q
H. S. 编码： 9503.1000
提单号码： TE06107E
提单日期： 2012.11.5
运　费： USD 1 510.00
保险费： USD 1 590.00
海关注册号： 3017887333

2. 操作要求

(1)请你以上海进出口贸易公司业务员方为的身份,根据上述资料、合同和信用证的有关规定审核以下单据并找出不符点。

体验活动四　自理进口贸易业务

PITER IMPORT & EXPORT CORPORATION
NO. 324 TOLI MACH HAMBURG, GERMANY
TEL:128-54842 FAX:128-54843

COMMERCIAL INVOICE

SHANGHAI IMPORT & EXPORT TRADE CORPORATION 1321 ZHONGSHAN ROAD SHANGHAI, CHINA TEL:021-56082266 FAX:021-56082265	INVOICE NO. TIEX071030
	DATE: SEP. 10, 2012
	PAYMENT TERMS: 30 DAYS AFTER SIGHT L/C

MARKS: N/M

SHIPPED FROM	SHIPPED TO	VESSEL/VOYAGE NO.
TOKYO	SHANGHAI	HOGAV. 186

DESCRIPTION	QUANTITY (SET)	PRICE PER SET (USD)	TOTAL AMOUNT (USD)
COLOR INKJET PRINTERS 　RO123 　RO122 　RO145 　RO168 L/C NO: XUT17456 P/C NO: RT06900 PACKING: PACKED IN ONE CARTON OF 50 SETS EACH	1 000 1 000 1 000 1 000	CIF HAMBURG USD 110.00 USD 125.00 USD 120.00 USD 115.00	USD 110 000.00 USD 125 000.00 USD 120 000.00 USD 115 000.00 USD 470 000.00

SAY U.S. DOLLARS FOUR HUNDRED AND SEVENYY THOUSAND ONLY.

PITER
PITER IMPORT & EXPORT CORPORATION

PITER IMPORT & EXPORT CORPORATION

NO.324 TOLI MACH HAMBURG, GERMANY

TEL:128-54842 FAX:128-54843

PACKING LIST

SHANGHAI IMPORT & EXPORT TRADE CORPORATION 1321 ZHONGSHAN ROAD SHANGHAI, CHINA TEL:021-56082266 FAX:021-56082265	INVOICE NO. TIEX071031
	DATE: SEP. 10, 2012
	PAYMENT TERMS:
	30 DAYS AFTER SIGHT L/C

MARKS: N/M

SHIPPED FROM	SHIPPED TO	VESSEL/VOYAGE NO.		
HAMBURG	SHANGHAI	HOGA V. 086		
PACKAGES	DESCRIPTION	QUANTITY (SET)	GROSS WEIGHT (KGS)	NET WEIGHT (KGS)
60	COLOR INKJET PRINTERS			
	RO123	1 000	200	160
	RO122	1 000	200	160
	RO145	1 000	200	160
	RO168	1 000	200	160
	L/C NO: XUT17456 PACKED IN ONE CARTON OF 50 SETS EACH	4 000	800	640

SAY TOTAL SIXTY(60)CARTONS ONLY.

PITER

PITER IMPORT & EXPORT CORPORATION

商业发票审核结果：

装箱单审核结果：

(2)请你以上海进出口贸易公司业务员方为的身份,根据上述资料、合同和信用证的有关内容填写入境货物报检单。

中华人民共和国出入境检验检疫
入境货物报检单

报检单位(加盖公章):　　　　　　　　　　　　　　　　　　*编号:＿＿＿＿

报检单位登记号:＿＿＿　联系人:＿＿＿　电话:＿＿＿　报检日期:　年　月　日

收货人	(中文)		企业性质(划"√")			□合资 □合作 □外资
	(外文)					
发货人	(中文)					
	(外文)					
货物名称(中/外文)	H.S. 编码	产地	数/重量	货物总值		包装种类及数量

运输工具名称及号码		合同号	
贸易方式	贸易国别(地区)	提单/运单号	
到岸日期	起运国家(地区)	许可证/审批号	
卸毕日期	起运口岸	入境口岸	
索赔有效期至	经停口岸	目的地	
集装箱规格、数量及号码			
合同订立的特殊条款以及其他要求		货物存放地点	
		用途	

随附单据(划"√"或补填)		标记及号码	*外商投资财产(划"√")	□是 否
□ 合同	□ 到货通知		*检验检疫费	
□ 发票	□ 装箱单			
□ 提/运单	□ 质保书		总金额	
□ 兽医卫生证书	□ 理货清单		(人民币元)	
□ 植物检疫证书	□ 磅码单			
□ 动物检验证书	□ 验收报告			
□ 卫生证书	□		计费人	
□ 原产地证				
□ 许可/审批文件			收费人	

报检人郑重声明:	领取证单	
1. 本人被授权报检。	日期	
2. 上列填写内容正确属实。		
签名:	签名:	

注:有"*"号栏由出入境检验检疫机关填写　　　　◆国家出入境检验检疫局制

(3)请你以上海进出口贸易公司业务员方为的身份,根据上述资料、合同和信用证的有关内容填写进口货物报关单。

中华人民共和国海关进口货物报关单

预录入编号：　　　　　　　　　　　　　　　　　　　　　海关编号：

进口口岸		备案号		进口日期		申报日期	
经营单位		运输方式		运输工具名称		提运单号	
收货单位		贸易方式		征免性质		征税比例	
许可证号		起运国(地区)		装货港		境内目的地	
批准文号		成交方式		运费		保费		批准文号	
合同协议号		件数		包装种类		毛重(千克)		净重(千克)	
集装箱号		随附单据				用途		
标记唛码及备注								

项号　商品编号　商品名称、规格型号　数量及单位　原产国(地区)　单价　总价　币制　征免

税费征收情况

录入员　　录入单位	兹声明以上申报无讹并承担法律责任	海关审单批注及放行日期(签章)	
报关员	申报单位(签章)	审单	审价
单位地址		征税	统计
邮编　　　电话　　　填制日期		查验	放行

体验活动五　代理进口贸易业务

工作情景

上海食品进出口公司是一家专业进出口贸易公司，主要代理冷冻食品、粮油和酒类等产品的进出口业务，深受欧洲、东南亚国家和地区客户的信赖。近日，受上海华亭有限公司的委托，从法国进口一批威士忌酒（Whisky）。为此，业务员马君先生上网查阅法国供应商情况，收集产品的质量、规格和购货价格等各种信息，对其进行综合分析后选择其中一家出口商 DENSE LIGHT SEMICONDUCTORS PTE LTD. 进行洽谈，最后达成一致意见，采用 CIF 价格条件、电汇（30%前 T/T，70%后 T/T）支付方式、航空运输，并签订了购货合同书。

购货合同书签订后，马君先生着手办理 30% 的汇款。法国 DENSE LIGHT SEMICONDUCTORS PTE LTD. 收到货款后，按时发货装运、制单，并将全套结汇单据直接寄给上海食品进出口公司。上海食品进出口公司马君先生对外国商业发票、装箱单、空运单等有关单据进行审核，审核无误后进行购汇申请，将 70% 余款电汇至法国客商。于是，马君先生根据购货合同、外国商业发票和装箱单等有关单据填制入境货物报检单和进口货物报关单，办理报检、报关手续，经出入境检验检疫局与海关查验放行后，提货拨交，并办理付汇核销。

代理进口业务流程如下图所示：

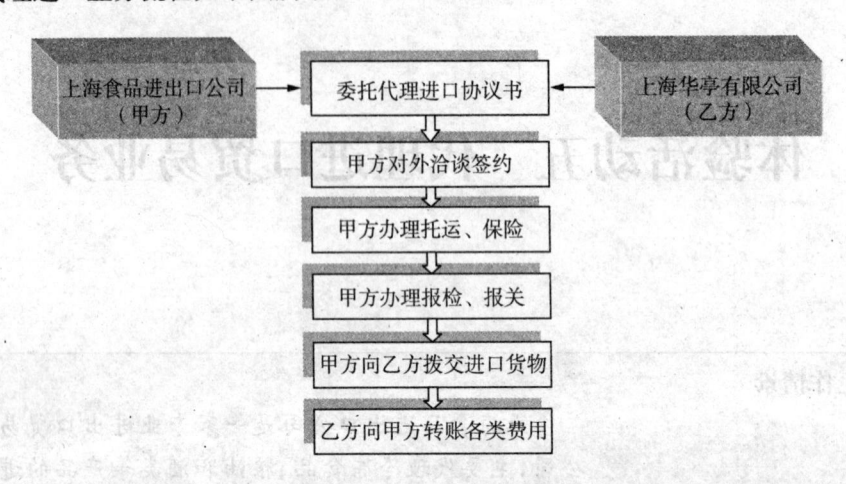

```
上海食品进出口公司 ──→ 委托代理进口协议书 ←── 上海华亭有限公司
    （甲方）                                        （乙方）
                            ↓
                    甲方对外洽谈签约
                            ↓
                    甲方办理托运、保险
                            ↓
                    甲方办理报检、报关
                            ↓
                    甲方向乙方拨交进口货物
                            ↓
                    乙方向甲方转账各类费用
```

实训一　进口交易磋商与合同签订

业务导入

近日，上海食品进出口公司受上海华亭有限公司的委托，从法国进口一批威士忌酒，品名规格为麦高伦18年(Macallen Highland Malt 18Yrs) 75cl 和皇家礼炮(Royal Salute) 70cl。为此，业务员马君先生上网查阅法国供应商情况，收集产品的质量、规格和购货价格等各种信息，并选择理想的出口商 DENSE LIGHT SEMICONDUCTORS PTE LTD. 进行洽谈。当双方就威士忌酒的规格、包装、价格、支付与运输方式等交易条件达成一致意见后，DENSE LIGHT SEMICONDUCTORS PTE LTD. 向上海食品进出口公司开出形式发票，作为办理进口许可证的材料，然后与其签订购货确认书。

合同商订的业务环节如下图所示：

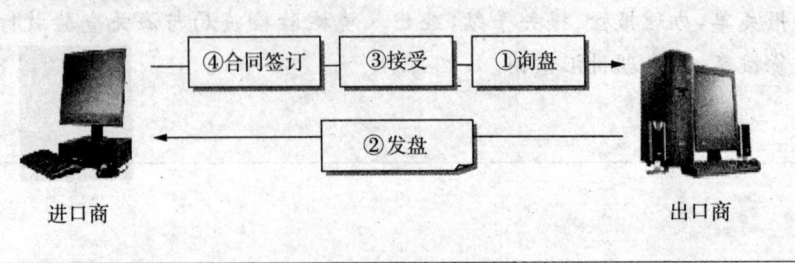

```
进口商 ←── ④合同签订 ── ③接受 ── ①询盘 ──→ 出口商
       ←───────────── ②发盘 ─────────────
```

工作任务一　　　　　　拟写询盘函

马君先生利用因特网和各种商务网站对法国威士忌酒市场的麦高伦18年和皇家礼炮进行调研，掌握市场的供求信息、价格动态。经过充分的分析后，确定 DENSE LIGHT SEMICONDUCTORS PTE LTD. 为出口商，向其进行询盘。

发件人：	MAJUN＜100 @ hotmail.com＞
发送：	2012-03-01
收件人：	DENSE＜119 @ hotmail.com＞
主题：	ENQUIRY

Dear Sir,

　　We are interested in your Whisky, especially Macallen Highland Malt 18Yrs 75cl, Royal Salute 70cl. We would be appreciated if you could quote us your best prices.

Macallen Highland Malt 18Yrs　　　　Royal Salute

Looking forward to hearing from you.

　　　　　　　　　　　　　　　　　　　　Yours truly,
　　　　　　　　　　　　　　SHANGHAI FOOD IMPORT & EXPORT CORPORATION
　　　　　　　　　　　　　　　　　　　　　Jun Ma
　　　　　　　　　　　　　　　　　　　MAR. 01, 2012

工作任务二　　　　　　拟写接受函

不久，上海食品进出口公司接到了出口商 DENSE LIGHT SEMI-CONDUCTORS PTE LTD. 的发盘，发盘中详细列明了各项交易条件。对此，上海食品进出口公司业务部门经慎重考虑，决定接受对方的发盘，并由马君先生拟写接受函。

收件人：	DENSE < 119 @ hotmail.com >
抄送：	
密件抄送：	
主题：	ACCEPTANCE

Dear Sir,

Thank you for your letter of MAR. 01, 2012.

We would like to inform you that we accept your proposal as follows:

GOODS OF DESCRIPTION	QUANTITY	UNIT PRICE
WHISKY		CIF SHANGHAI
MACALLEN HIGHLAND MALT18YRS 75cl	100 PCS	USD 55.00
ROYAL SALUTE 70cl	100 PCS	USD 55.00

Packing: Packed in 40 cartons of 5 pcs each
Shipment: not later than May 20, 2012 by air
Partial Shipments: Not Allowed
Transshipment: Allowed
Payment: by 30% T/T in advance, the others 70% T/T after shipment
Insurance: For 110 Percent Of The Invoice Value Covering All Risks And War Risk By The Buyer

We are glad that through our mutual effort finally we have reached the agreement.

Yours truly,
SHANGHAI FOOD IMPORT & EXPORT CORPORATION
Jun Ma
MAR. 10, 2012

◎ 工作任务三　　　申请签发自动进口许可证

由于麦高伦18年和皇家礼炮威士忌属于自动进出口许可证范围,因此上海食品进出口公司要求DENSE LIGHT SEMICONDUCTORS PTE LTD.出具形式发票。当上海食品进出口公司收到形式发票后,马君先生填写自动进出口许可证申请表,随附形式发票、主管部门有关批准进口文件等资料向上海市外经贸主管部门申请签发自动进口许可证。

体验活动五　代理进口贸易业务

DENSE LIGHT SEMICONDUCTORS PTE LTD. 出具形式发票：

DENSE LIGHT SEMICONDUCTORS PTE LTD.
6 CHANGJ NORTH STREET, PARIS

PROFORMA INVOICE
(WITHOUT ENGAGEMENT)

TEL: 65-64157986
FAX: 65-64157988

P/I NO.: INV. 04-00791
DATE: MAR. 13, 2012
P/C NO.: SOT0405127

TO:
SHANGHAI FOOD IMPORT & EXPORT CORPORATION

FROM　PARIS, FRANCE　　TO　SHANGHAI, CHINA
PARTIAL SHIPMENTS NOT ALLOWED. TRANSSHIPMENT ALLOWED

GOODS OF DESCRIPTION	QUANTITY	UNIT PRICE	TOTAL AMOUNT
WHISKY MACALLEN HIGHLAND MALT 18YRS 75cl ROYAL SALUTE 70cl	100PC 100PC	CFR PARIS USD 55.00 USD 55.00 TOTAL:	USD 5 500.00 USD 5 500.00 USD 11 000.00

TOTAL AMOUNT: SAY US DOLLARS ELEVEN THOUSAND ONLY
TERMS: BY 30% T/T IN ADVANCE, THE OTHERS 70% T/T AFTER SHIPMENT

Dense Light Semiconductors

This invoice is supplied to enable you to apply
for the necessary import licence to be valid up to ＿＿＿＿＿　PETER
AUTHORIZED SIGNATORY

上海食品进出口贸易公司填写自动进口许可证申请表：

中华人民共和国自动进口许可证申请表

1. 进口商： 代码：3147896523 上海食品进出口贸易公司		3. 自动进口许可证申请表号： 自动进口许可证号：		
2. 进口用户： 上海华亭有限公司		4. 申请自动进口许可证有效截止日期： 　　年　　月　　日		
5. 贸易方式： 　一般贸易		8. 贸易国（地区）： 　法国		
6. 外汇来源： 　购汇		9. 原产地国（地区）： 　法国		
7. 报关口岸： 　上海吴淞海关		10. 商品用途： 　自营内销		
11. 商品名称： 　威士忌	商品编码：8300000		设备状态：	
12. 规格、等级	13. 单位	14. 数量	15. 单价(USD)	16. 总值(USD)	17. 总值折美元
MACALLEN HIGHLAND MALT 18 YRS 75cl	100	瓶	55.00	5 500.00	5 500.00
ROYAL SALUTE 70cl	100	瓶	55.00	5 500.00	5 500.00
18. 总　　计	200	瓶		11 000.00	11 000.00
19. 备注： （上海食品进出口公司 FOOD IMPORT & EXPORT CORPORATION SHANGHAI 印章）		20. 签证机构审批意见：		

联　系　人：马君
联系电话：62781456
申请日期：2012年3月18日

◎ 工作任务四　　　　拟订购货合同书

　　上海食品进出口公司办理好自动进口许可证后，马君先生根据业务主管的指示拟订购货合同书一式两份，双方签章后，各留下一份作为履行合同的依据。

上海食品进出口公司
SHANGHAI FOOD IMPORT & EXPORT CORPORATION
328 SHANXI ROAD SHANGHAI, CHINA

购 货 合 同 书   P/C NO.: SOT0405127
PURCHASE CONTRACT   DATE: MAR. 22, 2012

买 方:
The Buyer: SHANGHAI FOOD IMPORT & EXPORT CORPORATION
328 SHANXI ROAD SHANGHAI, CHINA
TEL: 021-62781456 FAX: 021-62781454

卖 方:
The Sellers: DENSE LIGHT SEMICONDUCTORS PTE LTD.
6 CHANGJ NORTH STREET PARIS FRANCE
TEL: 65-64157986 FAX: 65-64157988

本合同由买卖双方订立,根据本合同规定的条款,买方同意购买,卖方同意出售下述商品:
This Contract is made by and between the Buyer and Seller, whereby the Buyer agrees to buy and the Seller agrees to sell the under-mentioned commodity according to the terms and conditions stipulated below.

1. 商品名称、规格、数量及单价:
COMMODITY, SPECIFICATIONS, QUANTITY AND UNIT PRICE:

商品名称及规格	数量	单 价	总 值
WHISKY MACALLEN HIGHLAND MALT 18 YRS 75cl	100 PCS	CIF SHANGHAI USD 1 100.00	USD 5 500.00
ROYAL SALUTE 70cl	100 PCS	USD 1 100.00	USD 5 500.00

2. 原产地国与制造商:
COUNTRY OF ORIGIN AND MANUFACTURER: FRANCE, Dense Light Semiconductors Pte Ltd.

3. 包装: 必须按照卖方标准中的适合海运、防湿、防潮、防震、防静电、耐粗暴搬运的方式包装,5件装1箱。
PACKING: To be packed in the Seller's standard export packing suitable for long distance ocean transport and well protected against dampness, moisture, shock, static and rough handling. Packed in 1 carton of 5 pcs each.

4. 唛头: S. F. C
SHIPPING MARK: SOT0405127
                 PARIS
                 C/NO. 1-40

5. 装运日期: 2012年5月20日前
DELIVERY: BEFORE MAY 20, 2008

6. 起运地: 巴黎机场
AIRPORT OF DEPARTURE: PARIS AIRPORT, FRANCE

7. 目的地：中国浦东机场
   AIRPORT OF DESTINATION：PUDONG AIRPORT，CHINA
8. 分批装运：不允许
   PARTIAL SHIPMENTS：NOT ALLOWED
9. 转运：允许
   TRANSSHIPMENT：ALLOWED
10. 付款条件：30％前 T/T、70％后 T/T
    TERMS OF PAYMENT：BY 30% T/T IN ADVANCE，THE OTHERS 70% T/T AFTER SHIPMENT
11. 保险：由卖方按发票全部金额加一成投保一切险和战争险
    Insurance：For 110 Percent Of The Invoice Value Covering All Risks By The Seller
12. 单据：卖方提供下列单据
    DOCUMENTS：The seller shall present the following documents to the paying bank．

    1)签字的商业发票 3 份，注明合同号。
      Three copies of Signed Commercial Invoice indicating contract number.
    2)装箱单 3 份。
      Three copies of Packing List.
    3)保险单正本 2 份
      Two Insurance Policy of Original.
    4)空运单正本 2 份
      Two Air Waybill of Original.
    5)卖方应在货物发运后 12 小时将合同编号、商品名称、数量、毛重、航次及日期电告买方。
      Within 12 hours after the goods are completely loaded, the Seller shall FAX to notify the Buyer of the contract number, name of commodity, quantity, gross weight, B/L No. and the date of delivery.

13. 检验和索赔：在本合同第 10 条规定的保证期限内，如发现货物的质量及/或规格与本合同规定不符或发现货物的缺陷包括内在缺陷或使用不良的原料(无论任何原因引起)，买方应申请商检局检验，并有权根据商检证向卖方索赔。卖方收到买方索赔通知后，如果在 30 天内不答复，应视为卖方同意买方提出的一切索赔。
    INSPECTION AND CLAIMS：Within the guarantee period stipulated in Clause 10 hereof should the quality/weight and/or the specifications of the goods be found not in line with the contracted stipulations, or should the goods prove defective for any reasons, including latent defect or the use of unsuitable materials, the Buyer shall arranges for an Inspection to be carried out by the Bureau and have the right to claim against the Sellers on the strength of the inspection certificate issued by the Bureau. Any and all claims shall be regarded as accepted if the Sellers fail to reply within 30 days after receipt of the Buyer's claim.

Buyer：   Seller：
SHANGHAI FOOD IMPORT & EXPORT CORPORATION   Dense Light Semiconductors Pte Ltd.
马君   PETER

体验活动五　代理进口贸易业务

综合业务模拟操作

操作一

1. 操作资料

近日,上海文化有限公司根据图书市场需求,从日本进口一批教学书籍(EDUCATIONAL BOOKS),委托上海图书进出口公司进口,双方签订了代理进口合同。上海图书进出口公司根据客户的要求直接向日本凡人株式会社(BOJINXYA LTD.,CO.)进行洽谈,双方达成一致意见后,签订购货合同书。双方具体磋商内容如下:

(1)2012 年 3 月 1 日上海图书进出口公司询盘:

"对贵公司出版的编号 SK0626215 教学书籍感兴趣,请报价 CIF SHANGHAI。"

(2)3 月 2 日上海图书进出口公司对日本凡人株式会社的发盘进行核定,表示接受全部发盘的条件。具体内容如下:

买　方：上海图书进出口公司(SHANGHAI BOOK IMPORT & EXPORT CORPORATION)
　　　　地址:288 NANXIANG ROAD SHANGHAI CHINA
　　　　TEL:021-65782312　　FAX:021-65782313
卖　方：BOJINXYA LTD.,CO.
　　　　地址:82 OTOLI MACHI TOKYO,JAPAN
　　　　TEL:028-548-742 FAX:028-548-743
货名规格:教学书籍(EDUCATIONAL BOOKS)Order No. SK0626215
单　价：CIP SHANGHAI USD 25.15
支付方式:提前电汇(BY T/T IN ADVANCE)
数　量：200 套(200 SETS)
包　装：每 20 套装一个出口纸箱(PACKED IN 1 CARTON OF 20 SETS EACH)
装运期：不迟于 2012 年 5 月 5 日前装运(LATEST DATE OF SHIPMENT:20120505)
起运地：日本东京机场(TOKYO AIRPORT,JAPAN)
目的地：中国浦东机场(PUDONG AIRPORT,CHINA)
分批装运:允许(ALLOWED)
转　运：不允许(NOT ALLOWED)
唛　头：由卖方制定(BY THE SELLER)
保　险：由卖方按发票金额的 110% 投保一切险(FOR 110 PERCENT OF THE INVOICE VALUE COVERING ALL RISKS BY THE SELLER)
合同号：TX200523
提交单据:1)已签字的商业发票一式三份,并显示合同号(THREE COPIES OF

SIGNED COMMERCIAL INVOICE INDICATING CONTRACT NUMBER）；

2)装箱单一式三份(THREE COPIES OF PACKING LIST)；

3)空运单正本二份(TWO AIR WAYBILL OF ORIGINAL)；

4)保险单正本二份(TWO INSURANCE POLICY OF ORIGINAL)；

5)在装船后 12 小时内用传真向买方发出装运通知,其包含合同号、货名、数量毛重、空运单号和装运日期等(WITHIN 12 HOURS AFTER THE GOODS ARE COMPLETELY LOADED, THE SELLER SHALL FAX TO NOTIFY THE BUYER OF THE CONTRACT NUMBER, NAME OF COMMODITY, QUANTITY, GROSS WEIGHT, AIR WAYBILL NO. AND THE DATE OF DELIVERY)。

2. 操作要求

(1)请你以上海图书进出口公司业务员张玉的身份,向日本凡人株式会社询盘,写一封询盘函。

询盘函：

(2)请你以上海图书进出口公司业务员张玉的身份,向日本凡人株式会社写一封接受函。

接受函：

(3)请你以上海图书进出口公司业务员张玉的身份,与日本凡人株式会社签订购货贸易合同书。

上海图书进出口公司
SHANGHAI BOOK IMPORT & EXPORT CORPORATION
288 NANXIANG ROAD SHANGHAI CHINA
PURCHASE CONTRACT

P/C NO.：_____

The Buyer：   DATE：_____
The Seller：

The Seller and the Buyer have confirmed this Contract with the terms and conditions stipulated below.

DESCRIPTIONS OF GOODS	QUANTITY	UNIT PRICE	AMOUNT

1. COUNTRY OF ORIGIN AND MANUFACTURER：
2. PACKING：
3. LATEST DATE OF SHIPMENT：
4. AIRPORT OF DEPARTURE：
5. AIRPORT OF DESTINATION：
6. PAYMENT：
7. PARTIAL SHIPMENTS：
8. TRANSSHIPMENT：
9. INSURANCE：
10. DOCUMENTS：THE SELLER SHALL PRESENT THE FOLLOWING DOCUMENTS TO THE PAYING BANK FOR NEGOTIATION：
    1) _____ COPIES OF SIGNED COMMERCIAL INVOICE INDICATING CONTRACT NUMBER.
    2) _____ COPIES OF PACKING LIST.
    3) ___ AIR WAYBILL OF ORIGINAL
    4) ___ INSURANCE POLICY OF ORIGINAL
    5) WITHIN_ HOURS AFTER THE GOODS ARE COMPLETELY LOADED, THE SELLER SHALL FAX TO NOTIFY THE BUYER OF THE CON-

TRACT NUMBER, NAME OF COMMODITY, QUANTITY, GROSS WEIGHT, AIR WAYBILL NO. AND THE DATE OF DELIVERY.

11. INSPECTION AND CLAIMS: IF THE QUALITY/WEIGHT AND/OR THE SPECIFICATIONS OF THE GOODS SHOULD BE FOUND NOT IN LINE WITH THE CONTRACTED STIPULATIONS, OR SHOULD THE GOODS PROVE DEFECTIVE FOR ANY REASONS, INCLUDING LATENT DEFECT OR THE USE OF UNSUITABLE MATERIALS, THE BUYER WOULD ARRANGE AN INSPECTION TO BE CARRIED OUT BY THE INSPECTION BUREAU AND HAVE THE RIGHT TO CLAIM AGAINST THE SELLERS ON THE STRENGTH OF THE INSPECTION CERTIFICATE ISSUED BY THE BUREAU. ALL CLAIMS SHALL BE REGARDED AS ACCEPTED IF THE SELLERS FAIL TO REPLY WITHIN 30 DAYS AFTER RECEIPT OF THE BUYER'S CLAIM.

Buyer: (上海图书进出口公司 SHANGHAI BOOK IMPORT & EXPORT CORPORATION)   Seller: BOJINXYA LTD., CO.

SHANGHAI BOOK IMPORT & EXPORT CORPORATION   BOJINXYA LTD., CO.

张玉   山田

操作二

1. 操作资料

近日,上海汽车进出口公司受上海浦东汽车制造公司的委托,从日本 AOYMA TRADING CORPORATION 进口汽车轮胎(TIRE),双方签订了代理进口合同。上海汽车进出口公司根据客户的要求直接向日本 AOYMA IMPORT & EXPORT CORPORATION 进行洽谈,双方达成一致意见后,签订购货合同书。双方具体磋商内容如下:

(1)2012年3月5日上海汽车进出口公司询盘:

"对贵公司的汽车轮胎,规格 TR681、TR682、TR683、TR684 感兴趣,请报价 FOB OSAKA。"

(2)3月8日上海汽车进出口公司对 AOYMA IMPORT & EXPORT CORPORATION 的发盘进行核定,表示接受全部发盘的条件。具体内容如下:

买方:	上海汽车进出口公司(SHANGHAI CAR IMPORT & EXPORT CORPORATION)
地址:	13 NANXIANG ROAD SHANGHAI CHINA
TEL:	021-56082212 FAX:021-56082211
卖方:	AOYMA IMPORT & EXPORT CORPORATION(代表为高田)
地址:	82-324 SKURA MACHI OSAKA, JAPAN
TEL:	028-688-744 FAX:028-688-743
货名规格:	汽车轮胎(TIRE)TR681、TR682、TR683、TR684
单价:	FOB OSAKA TR681 USD 10.00/PC、TR682 USD 11.00/PC、TR683 USD 8.00/PC
	TR684 USD 9.00/PC
支付方式:	BY 50% T/T IN ADVANCE,50% D/P AT SIGHT
数量:	每种规格各1 000只(1 000 PCS OF EACH)
包装:	每一只汽车轮胎装入一个复合无纺布(SPES)轮胎包装袋(PACKED IN A SPES TIRE BAG OF 1 PIECE EACH)
装运期:	不迟于2012年5月15日前装运(LATEST DATE OF SHIPMENT:20120515)
装运港:	日本大阪(OSAKA JAPAN)
目的地港:	中国上海(SHANGHAI, CHINA)
分批装运:	允许(ALLOWED)
转运:	不允许(NOT ALLOWED)
唛头:	由卖方制定(BY THE SELLER)
保险:	由买方按发票金额的110%投保一切险(FOR 110 PERCENT OF THE INVOICE VALUE COVERING ALL RISKS BY THE BUYER)

进口商代码:3245679218

合同号： RT061157W

提交单据：1)已签字的商业发票一式三份,并显示合同号(THREE COPIES OF SIGNED COMMERCIAL INVOICE INDICATING CONTRACT NUMBER);

2)装箱单一式三份(THREE COPIES OF PACKING LIST);

3)在装船后12小时内用传真向买方发出装运通知,其中包含合同号、货名、数量毛重、提单号和装运日期等(WITHIN 12 HOURS AFTER THE GOODS ARE COMPLETELY LOADED, THE SELLER SHALL FAX TO NOTIFY THE BUYER OF THE CONTRACT NUMBER, NAME OF COMMODITY, QUANTITY, GROSS WEIGHT, B/L NO. AND THE DATE OF DELIVERY).

2. 操作要求

(1)请你以上海汽车进出口公司业务员王伟的身份,向日本 AOYMA IMPORT & EXPORT CORPORATION 询盘,写一封询盘函。

询盘函：

(2)请你以上海汽车进出口公司业务员王伟的身份,向日本 AOYMA IMPORT & EXPORT CORPORATION 写一封接受函。

接受函：

(3) 请你以上海汽车进出口公司业务员王伟的身份，填写自动进口许可证申请表，向主管部门申请签发自动进口许可证。

中华人民共和国自动进口许可证申请表

1. 进口商： 代码：	3. 自动进口许可证申请表号： 自动进口许可证号：						
2. 进口用户：	4. 申请自动进口许可证有效截止日期： 年 月 日						
5. 贸易方式：	8. 贸易国(地区)：						
6. 外汇来源：	9. 原产地国(地区)：						
7. 报关口岸：	10. 商品用途						
11. 商品名称：	商品编码			设备状态：			
12. 规格、等级	13. 单位	14. 数量	15. 单价(USD)		16. 总值(USD)		17. 总值折美元
18. 总　计							
19. 备注： 联系人： 联系电话： 申请日期：	20. 签证机构审批意见：						

(4) 请你以上海汽车进出口公司业务员王伟的身份，向日本 AOYMA IMPORT & EXPORT CORPORATION 签订购货贸易合同书。

上海汽车进出口公司
SHANGHAI CAR IMPORT & EXPORT CORPORATION
13 NANXIANG ROAD SHANGHAI CHINA

PURCHASE CONTRACT

TEL: _____   P/C NO.: _____
FAX: _____   DATE: _____
TO:

The Seller and the Buyer have confirmed this Contract with the terms and conditions stipulated below.

DESCRIPTIONS OF GOODS	QUANTITY	UNIT PRICE	AMOUNT

1. PACKING:
2. LATEST DATE OF SHIPMENT:
3. PORT OF LOADING:
4. PORT OF DESTINATION:
5. PAYMENT:
6. PARTIAL SHIPMENTS:
7. TRANSSHIPMENT:
8. INSURANCE:
9. DOCUMENTS: THE SELLER SHALL PRESENT THE FOLLOWING DOCUMENTS TO THE PAYING BANK FOR NEGOTIATION:
   1) _____ COPIES OF SIGNED COMMERCIAL INVOICE INDICATING CONTRACT NUMBER.
   2) _____ COPIES OF PACKING LIST.
   3) WITHIN _____ HOURS AFTER THE GOODS ARE COMPLETELY LOADED, THE SELLER SHALL FAX TO NOTIFY THE BUYER OF THE CONTRACT NUMBER, NAME OF COMMODITY, QUANTITY, GROSS WEIGHT, B/L NO. AND THE DATE OF DELIVERY.
10. INSPECTION AND CLAIMS: IF THE QUALITY/WEIGHT AND/OR THE SPECIFICATIONS OF THE GOODS SHOULD BE FOUND NOT IN LINE WITH THE CONTRACTED STIPULATIONS, OR SHOULD THE GOODS PROVE DEFECTIVE FOR ANY REASONS, INCLUDING LATENT DEFECT OR THE USE OF UNSUITABLE MATERIALS, THE BUYER WOULD ARRANGE AN INSPECTION TO BE CARRIED OUT BY THE INSPECTION BUREAU AND HAVE THE RIGHT TO CLAIM AGAINST THE SELLERS ON THE STRENGTH OF THE INSPECTION CERTIFICATE ISSUED BY THE BUREAU. ALL CLAIMS SHALL BE REGARDED AS ACCEPTED IF THE SELLERS FAIL TO REPLY WITHIN 30 DAYS AFTER RECEIPT OF THE BUYER'S CLAIM.

Buyer: Seller:

实训二　进口贸易合同履行——汇款

业务导入

购货合同书签订后，马君先生填写购买外汇申请书，获准后填写汇款申请书，支付手续费办理30%货款的电汇。法国 DENSE LIGHT SEMI-CONDUCTORS PTE LTD. 收到货款后，按时发货装运、制单，并将全套结汇单据直接寄给上海食品进出口公司。上海食品进出口公司马君先生对外国商业发票、装箱单、空运单等有关单据进行审核，核准无误后进行70%货款的购汇申请，将余款电汇至法国客商。

购汇、电汇付款的业务环节如下图所示：

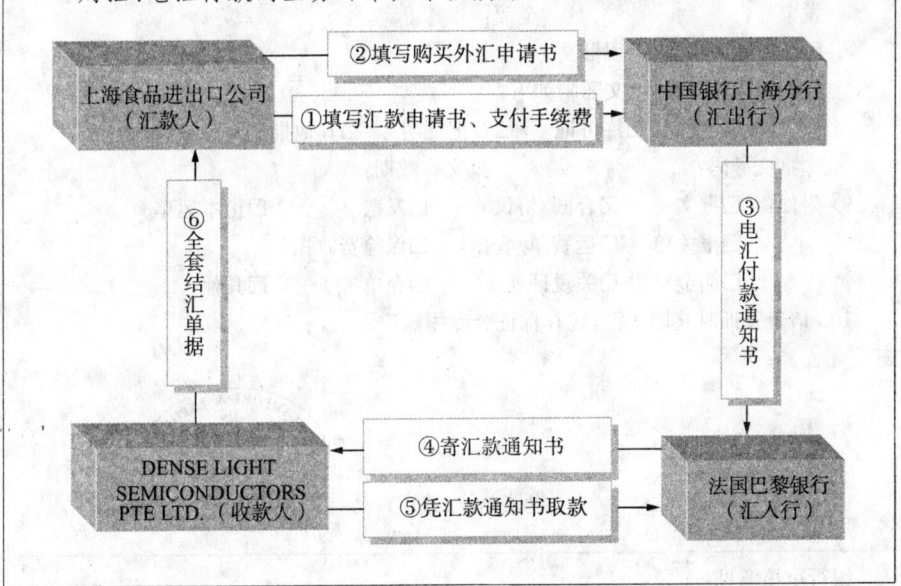

- 上海食品进出口公司（汇款人）
- ①填写汇款申请书、支付手续费
- ②填写购买外汇申请书
- 中国银行上海分行（汇出行）
- ③电汇付款通知书
- 法国巴黎银行（汇入行）
- ④寄汇款通知书
- ⑤凭汇款通知书取款
- DENSE LIGHT SEMICONDUCTORS PTE LTD.（收款人）
- ⑥全套结汇单据

工作任务一　办理电汇手续

近日，上海食品进出口公司收到了 DENSE LIGHT SEMICONDUCTORS PTE LTD. 回签的购货合同书后，马君先生持有关批文和证明材料向中国银行上海分行申请购买外汇，填写购汇申请书和电汇申请书。

马君先生填写购买外汇申请书：

中国银行上海市分行
购买外汇申请书

中国银行 __黄浦__ 分（支）行：

我公司为执行第 __SOT0405127__ 号合同项下对外支付，需向贵行购汇。现按外汇局有关规定向贵行提供下述内容及所附文件，请审核并按实际付汇日牌价办理售汇。所需人民币资金从我公司在贵行账户 SZR80066686 中支付。

1. 购汇金额： USD 3 300.00
2. 用　　途： ☑进口商品　□从附费用　□索退赔款　□其他
3. 支付方式： □信用证　□托收　☑汇款（□货到付款）　☑预付货款
4. 商品名称：WHISKY
5. 数量：200 瓶
6. 合同号：SOT0405127　　金额：USD 11 000.00
7. 发票号：　　　　　　　金额：
8. ☑一般进口商品，无须批文
   □控制进口商品，批文随附如下：
   　　□进口证明　□许可证　□登记证明　□其他批文
   　　批文号码：　　　　　批文有效期：
9. 附件： □批文　　☑合同/协议　□发票　　□正本运单
   　　　□报关单　□运费单/收据　□保险费收据
   　　　□佣金单　□关税证明　　□仓单　　□其他
10. 请于开证时立即售汇，转存保证金专用账户。

申请单位（盖章）：马君

银行审核意见：
上述内容与随附文件/凭证描述相符，拟按申请书要求办理售汇。

经办人：中迎　　复核人：张立　　核准人：李蓝

售汇日期：2012.3.24　　售汇专用章（黄浦）
（加盖售汇专用章）

马君先生填写汇款申请书：

中国银行上海市分行汇款申请书
BANK OF CHINA

外汇	汇款方式 Type of Remittance	电汇 T/T	✓	付款凭证(回单)	户名 Name of Account	上海食品进出口公司
		票汇 D/D		日期 2012年3月24日 Date	账号 Account No.	SZR80066686

请付 Pay	牌价 Rate	请付 Remit
25 080.00元	@7.60	USD 3 300.00

(汇款)大写金额 (Remit) Amount in word	叁仟叁佰美元整

收款人 Payee	DENSE LIGHT SEMICONDUCTORS PTE LTD.
住址 Address	6 CHANGJ NORTH STREET PARIS FRANCE
收款人所在地银行 Beneficiary's Bank	法国巴黎银行

汇款人 Remitter	上海食品进出口公司

附言 Remarks		中国银行上海分行 黄浦支行
		(付款单位银行盖章)

复核 张立　　经办 中迎

操作指南 ➡ **汇出汇款业务**

1. 汇出汇款业务处理程序
(1)客户向进出口银行提交汇出汇款申请书并加盖印鉴。
(2)银行根据汇出汇款申请书,在落实头寸后办理对外汇款手续。
(3)银行定期对汇出款项进行核对,及时催促汇入行办理解付。
2. 办理汇出汇款业务事项
(1)对于首次办理汇出汇款的企业,应提交经营进出口业务证明文件、企业营业执照、企业法人代码证复印件等进出口银行要求的资料,并在进出口银行预留印鉴。
(2)对于货到付款项下的汇出汇款,客户应提交有效的商业单据、正本进口货物报关单、贸易进口付汇核销单、进口付汇备案表等。
(3)电汇、信汇如需退汇,需由汇款人提出书面申请,并交验汇款回单,银行凭此向汇入行要求退汇,待接到汇入行同意退汇的答复并收妥汇款头寸后办理退汇手续;票汇如需退汇,需由汇款人提出书面申请,交回原汇票正本并背书,银行审核无误后,在汇票上加盖"注销"印戳后办理退汇手续。

◇ **工作任务二　　　　审核进口单证**

法国 DENSE LIGHT SEMICONDUCTORS PTE LTD. 收到30%的货款后,按时发货装运、制单,并将全套结汇单据直接寄给上海食品进出口公司。上海食品进出口公司马君先生对外国商业发票、装箱单、空运单和保险单等有关单据进行审核,核准无误后办理进口货物报检报关手续。

马君先生审核进口单据：

DENSE LIGHT SEMICONDUCTORS PTE LTD. 6 CHANGJ NORTH STREET PARIS FRANCE TEL：65-64157986 FAX：65-64157988	**Commercial Invoice** INVOICE NO. EXY070931 DATE：MAY 12，2012
SHANGHAI FOOD IMPORT & EXPORT CORPORATION 328 SHANXI ROAD SHANGHAI, CHINA TEL：021-62781456 FAX：021-62781454	PAYMENT TERMS：30% T/T IN ADVANCE，70% T/T AFTER SHIPMENT

MARKS： S. F. C
　　　　SOT0405127
　　　　　PARIS
　　　　　C/NO. 1-40

SHIPPED FROM	PARIS	SHIPPED TO	SHANGHAI
DESCRIPTION	QUANTITY	UNIT PRICE	TOTAL AMOUNT
WHISKY MACALLEN HIGHLAND MALT 18YRS 75cl ROYAL SALUTE 70cl	100 PCS 100 PCS	CIF SHANGHAI USD 55.00 USD 55.00	USD 5 500.00 USD 5 500.00 USD 11 000.00

SAY U. S. DOLLARS ELEVEN THOUSAND ONLY.

　　　　　　　　　　　　　　　　PETER
　　　　　DENSE LIGHT SEMICONDUCTORS PTE LTD.

DENSE LIGHT SEMICONDUCTORS PTE LTD. 6 CHANGJ NORTH STREET PARIS FRANCE TEL: 65-64157986 FAX: 65-64157988	**Packing list** INVOICE NO. EXY070931 DATE: MAY 12, 2012
SHANGHAI FOOD IMORT & EXPORT CORPORATION 328 SHANXI ROAD SHANGHAI, CHINA TEL:021-62781456 FAX:021-62781454	PAYMENT TERMS: 30% T/T IN ADVANCE, 70% T/T AFTER SHIPMENT

MARKS: S. F. C
           SOT0405127
               PARIS
             C/NO. 1-40

SHIPPED FROM	PARIS	SHIPPED TO	SHANGHAI	
PACKAGES	DESCRIPTION	QUANTITY	GROSS WEIGHT	NET WEIGHT
40	WHISKY MACALLEN HIGHLAND MALT 18YRS 75cl ROYAL SALUTE 70cl	100 PCS 100 PCS	8/160 KGS 8/160 KGS	7/140 KGS 7/140 KGS
	TOTAL	200 PCS	320 KGS	280 KGS

SAY TOTAL FORTY CARTONS ONLY.

                              PETER
               DENSE LIGHT SEMICONDUCTORS PTE LTD.

体验活动五 代理进口贸易业务

Shipper's Name and Address	Shipper's Account Number	Not negotiable
DENSE LIGHT SEMICONDUCTORS PTE LTD. 6 CHANGJ NORTH STREET PARIS FRANCE TEL: 65-64157986 FAX: 65-64157988	01458798-54	Air Waybill **PARIS ASIA AIRWAYS COMPANY,LTD.** Issued by 2411 TOHNKAWA HNKWA PARIS FRANCE
Consignee's Name and Address	Consignee's Account Number	Copies 1,2 and 3 this Air Waybill are originals and have the same validity
SHANGHAI FOOD IMPORT & EXPORT CORPORATION 328 SHANXI ROAD SHANGHAI, CHINA TEL: 021-62781456 FAX: 021-62781454	SZR80066686	It is agreed that goods described herein are accepted in apparent good order and condition (except as noted) for carriage SUBJECT TO THE CONDITIONS OF CONTRACT ON THE REVERSE HEREOF. ALL GOODS MAY BE CARRIED BY ANY OTHER MEANS INCLUDING ROAD OR ANY OTHER CARRIER UNLESS SPECIFIC CONTRARY INSTRUCTIONS ARE GIVEN HEREON BY THE SHIPPER, AND SHIPPER AGREES THAT THE SHIPPMENT MAY BE CARRIED VIA INTERMEDIATE STOPPING PLACES WHICH THE CARRIER DEEMS APPROPRIATE. THE SHIPPER'S ATTENTION IS DRAWN TO THE NOTICE CONCERNING CARRIER'S LIMITATION OF LIABILITY. Shipper may increase such limitation of liability by declaring a higher value for carriage and paying a supplemental charge if required.

Issuing Carrier's Agent Name and City	Accounting Information
Sinotrans Air Transportation De 989DONGFANG ROAD SHANGHAI P.R. OF CHINA	FREIGHT: PREPAID ☐ **MAP**

Agents IATA Code	Account No.	
08321550		D =20 (1.6 CBM)

Airport of Departure (Addr. Of First Carrier) and Requested Routing
PARIS AIRPORT

To	By First Carrier	Routing and Destination	To	By	To	By	Currency	Chgs Code	WT/VAL PPD / COLL	Other PPD / COLL	Declared Value for Carrier	Declared Value for Customs
							USD		xx /	xx /	N.V.D	N.C.V

Airport of Destination	Requested Flight/Date	Amount of Insurance	If shipper requests insurance in accordance with the conditions thereof indicate amount to be insures in figures in box marked "Amount of Insurance".
PUDONG SHANGHAI	JAA0614		

Handing Information

No. of Place RCP	Gross Weight	kg lb	Rate Class Commodity Item No.	Chargeable Weight	Rate / Charge	Total	Nature and Quantity of Goods (Incl. Dimensions or Volume)
40	320	K	Q	320	4.12	1 319.00	WHISKY 1.6 CBM

Prepaid	Weight Charge	Collect	Other Charges
	1 319.00		
	Valuation Charge		AWB FEE : 81.00
	Tax		
	Total other Charges Due Agent 81.00		Shipper certifies that particular's on the face hereof are correct and agrees THE CONDITIONS ON REVERSE HEREOF: OSAKA / AIR EXPORT 小山 一郎
	Total other Charges Due Carrier		Signature Shipper or his Agent
Total Prepaid 1 400.00		Total Collect	Carrier certifies that the goods described hereon are accepted for carriage subject to THE CONDITION OF CONTRACT ON THE REVERSE HEREOF. The goods then being in apparent good order and condition except as noted hereon. MAY 20,2012 PARIS,FRANCE PARIS ASIA AIRWAYS COMPANY,LTD
Currency Conversion Rate		CC Charges in Dest. Currency	Executed on (date) at (place) Signature of issuing Carrier
For Carriers Use only at Destination		Charges at Destination	Total Collect Charges 788-905 0945

THE PEOPLE'S INSURANCE COMPANY OF CHINA PARIS BRANCH
MARINE CARGO TRANSPORTATION INSURANCE POLICY

Invoice No. EXY070931　　　　　　　　　　　　　　　　　　　　Policy No. 06399101

Insured: DENSE LIGHT SEMICONDUCTORS PTE LTD.

This policy of Insurance witnesses that The People's Insurance Company of China Paris branch. (hereinafter called "The Company"), at the request of the Insured and consideration of the premium paid by the Insures, undertakes to insure the under-mentioned goods in transportation subject to the condition of this Policy as per the Clauses printed overleaf and other special clauses attached hereon.

Descriptions of Goods	Packing Unit Quantity	Amount Insured
WHISKY MACALLEN HIGHLAND MALT 18YRS ROYAL SALUTE	40 CARTONS	USD12 100.00

Condition: FOR 110% OF THE INVOICE VALUE COVERING ALL RISKS AS PER PICC

Marks of Goods: AS PER INVOICE NO. EXY070931

Total Amount Insured: SAY U.S. DOLLARS TWELVE THOUSAND ONE HUNDRED ONLY

Premium As arranged Per conveyance S.S DONG FEN V. 841 Slg. On or abt MAY 20, 2012

From　PARIS　　　　　To　SHANGHAI

In the event of loss or damage which may result in a claim under this Policy, immediate notice must be given to the Company's Agent as mentioned hereunder. Claims, if any, one of the Original Policy which has been issued in TWO Original(s) together with the relevant documents shall be surrendered to the Company, If one of the Original Policy has been accomplished, the others to be void.

THE PEOPLE'S INSURANCE COMPANY OF CHINA, SHANGHAI BRANCH

98 ZHONGSHAN ROAD SHANGHAI CHINA

TEL: O21-52436571

Claim Payable at　SHANGHAI

Date　MAY 14, 2012

The People's Insurance Company of China Paris Branch

THE PEOPLE'S INSURANCE COMPANY OF CHINA PARIS BRANCH

General Manager　凡依玲

综合业务模拟操作

操作一

1. 操作资料

近日,上海图书进出口公司与日本凡人株式会社(BOJINXYA LTD.,CO.)签订了购货合同书。为此,上海图书进出口公司根据合同的规定办理电汇付款。具体资料如下:

买　方：　上海图书进出口公司(SHANGHAI BOOK IMPORT & EXPORT CORPORATION)
　　　　　地址：288 NANXIANG ROAD SHANGHAI CHINA
　　　　　TEL：021-65782312　FAX：021-65782313

卖　方：　BOJINXYA LTD.,CO.
　　　　　地址：82 OTOLI MACHI TOKYO,JAPAN
　　　　　TEL：028-548-742 FAX：028-548-743

货名规格：　教学书籍(EDUCATIONAL BOOKS)Order No. SK0626215
单　价：　CIP SHANGHAI USD 25.15
支付方式：　提前电汇(BY T/T IN ADVANCE)
数　量：　200套(200 SETS)
包　装：　每20套装入一个出口纸箱(PACKED IN 1 CARTON OF 20 SETS EACH)
装运期：　不迟于2012年5月5日前装运(LATEST DATE OF SHIPMENT：20120505)
装运港：　日本东京机场(TOKYO AIRPORT,JAPAN)
目的地港：　中国浦东机场(PUDONG AIRPORT CHINA)
分批装运：　允许(ALLOWED)
合同号：　TX200523
购汇银行：　中国银行浦东分行
银行账号：　SZR80066686
用　途：　进口商品
附　件：　合同一份
汇　率：　1∶65
汇入银行：　日本东京银行

2. 操作要求

(1)请你以上海图书进出口公司业务员张玉的身份,根据上述资料填写购买外汇申请书。

中国银行上海市分行
购买外汇申请书

中国银行_____分（支）行：

　　我公司为执行第_____号合同项下对外支付，需向贵行购汇。现按外汇局有关规定向贵行提供下述内容及所附文件，请审核并按实际付汇日牌价办理售汇。所需人民币资金从我公司在贵行账户_____中支付。

1. 购汇金额：
2. 用　　途：□进口商品　　□从附费用　　□索退赔款　　□其他
3. 支付方式：□信用证　　　□托收　　　□汇款（□货到付款　　□预付货款）
4. 商品名称：
5. 数量：
6. 合同号：　　　　　　金额：
7. 发票号：　　　　　　金额：
8. □一般进口商品，无须批文
　　□控制进口商品，批文随附如下：
　　　　□进口证明　　□许可证　　□登记证明　　□其他批文
　　批文号码：　　　　　　批文有效期：
9. 附件：□批文　　　□合同/协议　　□发票　　□正本运单
　　　　 □报关单　　□运费单/收据　□保险费收据
　　　　 □佣金单　　□关税证明　　　□仓单　　□其他
10. 请于开证时立即售汇，转存保证金专用账户。

　　　　　　　　　　　　　　　　　　　　　　　申请单位（盖章）：

银行审核意见：

　　上述内容与随附文件/凭证描述相符，拟按申请书要求办理售汇。

　　经办人：　　　　复核人：　　　　核准人：

　　售汇日期：

　　（加盖售汇专用章）

(2)请你以上海图书进出口公司业务员张玉的身份，根据上述资料填写汇款申请书。

中国银行上海市分行汇款申请书
BANK OF CHINA

外汇	汇款方式 Type of Remittance	电汇 T/T		付款凭证(回单)		户 名 Name of Account	
		票汇 D/D		日期　年　月　日 Date		账 号 Account No.	

请 付 Pay		牌价 Rate	请 付 Remit

(汇款)大写金额 (Remit) Amount in word	

收款人 Payee	
住 址 Address	
收款人所在地银行 Beneficiary's Bank	

汇款人

Remitter

附言

Remarks

(付款单位银行盖章)

复核　　　　　　　　经办

操作二

(1)请你以上海汽车进出口公司业务员王伟的身份,根据上述资料填写购买外汇申请书。

中国银行上海市分行

购买外汇申请书

中国银行_____分(支)行:

  我公司为执行第_____号合同项下对外支付,需向贵行购汇。现按外汇局有关规定向贵行提供下述内容及所附文件,请审核并按实际付汇日牌价办理售汇。所需人民币资金从我公司在贵行账户_____中支付。

1. 购汇金额:
2. 用 途: □进口商品 □从附费用 □索退赔款 □其他
3. 支付方式: □信用证 □托收 □汇款(□货到付款 □预付货款)
4. 商品名称:
5. 数量:
6. 合同号: 金额:
7. 发票号: 金额:
8. □一般进口商品,无须批文
  □控制进口商品,批文随附如下:
    □进口证明 □许可证 □登记证明 □其他批文
    批文号码: 批文有效期:
9. 附件:□批文 □合同/协议 □发票   □正本运单
    □报关单 □运费单/收据 □保险费收据
    □佣金单 □关税证明 □仓单   □其他
10. 请于开证时立即售汇,转存保证金专用账户。

申请单位(盖章):

银行审核意见:
  上述内容与随附文件/凭证描述相符,拟按申请书要求办理售汇。
  经办人: 复核人: 核准人:
  售汇日期:
  (加盖售汇专用章)

(2) 请你以上海汽车进出口公司业务员王伟的身份，根据上述资料填写汇款申请书。

中国银行上海市分行汇款申请书
BANK OF CHINA

外汇	汇款方式 Type of Remittance	电汇 T/T	付款凭证（回单）	户　名 Name of Account	
		票汇 D/D	日期　　年　月　日 Date	账　号 Account No.	

请 付 Pay	牌 价 Rate	请 付 Remit

（汇　款）大 写 金 额
(Remit) Amount in word

收款人 Payee	
住　址 Address	
收款人所在地银行 Beneficiary's Bank	

汇 款 人
Remitter

附　言
Remarks

（付款单位银行盖章）

复　核　　　　　　经　办

实训三　进口贸易合同履行——入境货物报检、报关、汇款及核销手续

业务导入

上海食品进出口公司马君先生在对外国商业发票、装箱单、空运单和保险单等有关单据进行审核后，办理报检与报关手续。然后，进行购汇申请，填写购买外汇申请书，获准后将70％余款电汇至法国客商，并办理付汇核销手续。

报检、报关、汇款及付汇核销的业务环节如下图所示：

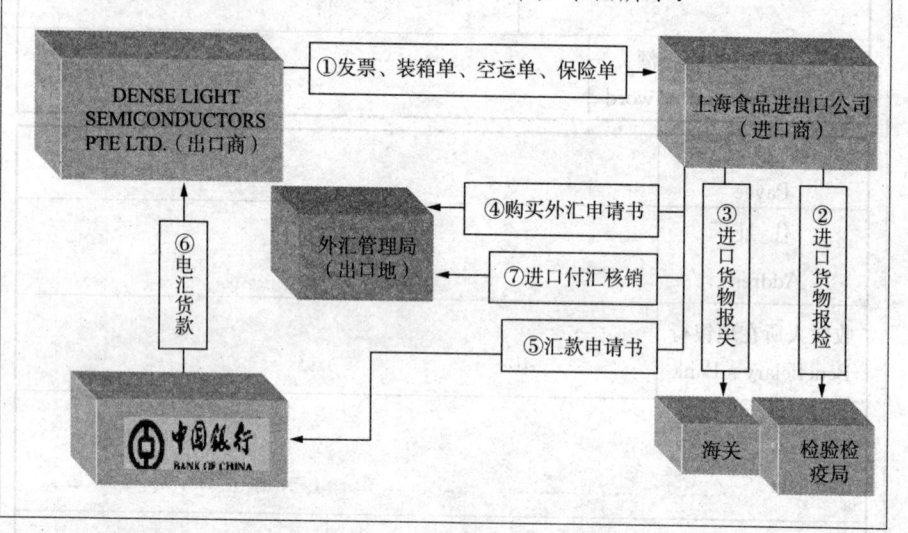

```
DENSE LIGHT SEMICONDUCTORS PTE LTD.（出口商）
   │①发票、装箱单、空运单、保险单→ 上海食品进出口公司（进口商）
   │                                    │③进口货物报关
   │                                    │②进口货物报检
   │          外汇管理局（出口地）
   │          ④购买外汇申请书
   │          ⑦进口付汇核销
   │⑥电汇货款
   │          ⑤汇款申请书
   中国银行 BANK OF CHINA ← 海关 检验检疫局
```

◇ 工作任务一　办理入境货物报检手续

上海食品进出口公司马君先生在对外国商业发票、装箱单、空运单和保险单等有关单据进行审核后，及时办理报检手续。为此，马君先生根据国外商业发票、装箱单、空运单和自动进口许可证的有关内容填写报检单。

马君先生填写入境货物报检单：

中华人民共和国出入境检验检疫
入境货物报检单

报检单位(加盖公章)：

报检单位登记号： 联系人：马君 电话：62781456 报检日期：2012年5月22日

*编号：7712152478

收货人	（中文）上海食品进出口公司	企业性质（划"√"）	□合资 □合作 □外资
	（外文）SHANGHAI FOOD IMPORT & EXPORT CORPORATION		
发货人	（中文）		
	（外文）DENSE LIGHT SEMICONDUCTORS PTE LTD.		

货物名称(中/外文)	H.S.编码	原产国	数/重量	货物总值	包装种类及数量
WHISKY MACALLEN HIGHLAND MALT 18YRS 75cl ROYAL SALUTE 70cl	830000	法国	200PCS	11 000.00美元	40箱

运输工具名称及号码			合同号	SOT0405127
贸易方式	一般贸易	贸易国别（地区）法国	提单/运单号	TU108286
到货日期	2012.5.21	起运国家（地区）法国	许可证/审批号	312098734
卸货日期	2012.5.21	起运口岸 巴黎	入境口岸	吴淞海关
索赔有效期至	2013.5.21	经停口岸	目的地	上海

集装箱规格、数量及号码			
合同订立的特殊条款 以及其他要求		货物存放地点	上海市逸仙路100号
		用 途	自营内销

随附单据（划"√"或补填）		标记及号码	*外商投资财产（划"√"）	□是 □否
☑ 合同	□ 到货通知		*检验检疫费	
☑ 发票	☑ 装箱单	S.F.C SOT0405127 PARIS C/NO. 1-40	总金额 （人民币元）	
☑ 提/运单	□ 质保书			
□ 兽医卫生证书	□ 理货清单			
□ 植物检疫证书	□ 磅码单		计费人	
□ 动物检验证书	□ 验收报告			
□ 卫生证书	□			
□ 原产地证			收费人	
☑ 许可/审批文件				

报检人郑重声明： 1. 本人被授权报检。 2. 上列填写内容正确属实。 签名：马君	领取证单
	日期
	签名

注：有"*"号栏由出入境检验检疫机关填写 ◆国家出入境检验检疫局制

出入境检验检疫局签发入境货物通关单：

中华人民共和国出入境检验检疫
入境货物通关单

编号：ST0805114

1. 收货人 上海食品进出口公司			5. 标记及唛码 S.F.C OT0405127 PARIS C/NO. 1-40
2. 发货人 DENSE LIGHT SEMICONDUCTORS PTE LTD.			
3. 合同/提(运)单号 TU108286	4. 输出国家或地区 法国		
6. 运输工具名称及号码	7. 目的地 上海		8. 集装箱规格及数量
9. 货物名称及规格 WHISKY MACALLEN HIGHLAND MALT 18YRS 75cl ROYAL SALUTE 70cl ********************************	10. H.S.编码 830000	11. 申报总值 USD 11 000.00	12. 数/重量、包装数量及种类 200 PCS 40 CTNS
13. 证明 上述货物业已报验/申报，请海关予以放行。 签字：丁毅			（检验检疫专用章） 日期：2012年5月24日
14. 备注			

◇ **工作任务二　　办理进口货物报关手续**

上海食品进出口公司马君先生办理好报检后，根据海关的有关规定办理进口货物报关手续，根据国外商业发票、装箱单、空运单和自动进口许可证的有关内容填写报关单。海关对该票货物查验合格后，征收进口关税，并在报关单上盖放行章。

体验活动五　代理进口贸易业务

马君先生填写进口货物报关单：

中华人民共和国海关进口货物报关单

预录入编号：　　　　　　　　　　　　　　　　　　　　海关编号：

进口口岸 吴淞海关 2202	备案号	进口日期 2012.05.21	申报日期 2012.05.23
经营单位 (0387124666) 上海食品进出口公司	运输方式 航空运输	运输工具名称	提运单号 TUO105286
收货单位 上海食品进出口公司	贸易方式 一般贸易	征免性质 一般征税	征税比例
许可证号 312098734	起运国（地区） 法国	装货港 巴黎	境内目的地 上海
批准文号	成交方式 CIP	运费	保费	批准文号
合同协议号 SOT0405127	件数 40	包装种类 箱	毛重（千克） 320	净重（千克） 280
集装箱号	随附单据 B: T0805114		用途	

标记唛码及备注　S.F.C
　　　　　　　　 OT0405127
　　　　　　　　 PARIS
　　　　　　　　 C/NO. 1-40

项号	商品编号	商品名称、规格型号	数量及单位	原产国（地区）	单价	总价	币制征免
	830000	威士忌		法国			502 照章
01		MACALLEN HIGHLAND MALT 18YRS 75cl	100 PCS		55.00	5 500.00	
02		ROYAL SALUTE 70cl	100 PCS		55.00	5 500.00	

税费征收情况

录入员　　录入单位	兹声明以上申报无讹并承担法律责任	海关审单批注及放行日期（签章）	
报关员　31078965218 马 君	申报单位（签章） 上海食品进出口公司 报关专用章	审单	审价
单位地址　上海市山西路 328 号		征税	统计
邮编 653214　电话 62781456	填制日期　2012 年 5 月 23 号	查验	放行

305

马君先生填写进口货物报关单：

中华人民共和国海关进口货物报关单

预录入编号：　　　　　　　　　　　　　　　　　　　　　　　　　　　　海关编号：

进口口岸 吴淞海关 2202	备案号		进口日期 2012.05.21	申报日期 2012.05.23
经营单位（0387124666） 上海食品进出口公司	运输方式 航空运输	运输工具名称		提运单号 TUO105286
收货单位 上海食品进出口公司	贸易方式 一般贸易		征免性质 一般征税	征税比例
许可证号 312098734	起运国（地区） 法国		装货港 巴黎	境内目的地 上海
批准文号	成交方式 CIP	运费	保费	批准文号
合同协议号 SOT0405127	件数 40	包装种类 箱	毛重（千克） 320	净重（千克） 280
集装箱号	随附单据 B: T0805114		用途	

标记唛码及备注　S. F. C
　　　　　　　　0T0405127
　　　　　　　　　PARIS
　　　　　　　　C/NO. 1-40

项号	商品编号	商品名称、规格型号	数量及单位	原产国（地区）	单价	总价	币制征免
	830000	威士忌		法国			502 照章
01		MACALLEN HIGHLAND MALT 18YRS 75cl	100PCS		55.00	5 500.00	
02		ROYAL SALUTE 70cl	100PCS		55.00	5 500.00	

税费征收情况

录入员　录入单位	兹声明以上申报无讹并承担法律责任	海关审单批注及放行日期（签章） 张玲　2012.05.24
报关员 31078965218 马君	申报单位（签章） 上海食品进出口公司 报关专用章 单位地址 上海市山西路 328 号	审单　　　　　审价
		征税　　　　　统计
邮编 653214　电话 62781456　填制日期 2012 年 5 月 23 号		查验　　　　　放行 张民　2012.05.24

上海食品进出口公司缴纳关税。

上海 海关 进口关税 专用缴款书

收入系统：

海关系统　　填发日期　2012年5月24日　　　　　　　号码：169874144

收款单位	收入机关	中央金库			缴款单位（人）	名称	上海食品进出口公司
	科目	进口关税	预算级次	中央		账号	SZR80066686
	收款国库	中国银行上海分行				开户银行	中国银行上海分行

税号	货物名称	数量	单位	完税价格（¥）	税率（%）	税款金额（¥）
1.6258698	威士忌	200	瓶	83 600	5	4 180

金额人民币（大写）捌万叁仟陆佰元整

申请单位编号	0387124666	报关单编号	8541172525	填制单位	收款国库（银行）
合同（批件）号	SOT0405127	运输工具（号）			BANK OF CHINA SHANGHAI BRANCH
缴款期限	2012.6.14	提/装货单号	TUO105286		
备注	一般征税　照章征税　10060932 进 USD 11 000.00 成交：CIP			制单人：220 复核人：	

从填发缴款书次日起，限七日内（星期日和法定假日除外）缴纳，逾期按日征收税款总额千分之一的滞纳金。

上海 海关 代收增值税 专用缴款书

收入系统：

税务系统　　填发日期　2012年5月24日　　　　　　　号码：269874123

收款单位	收入机关	中央金库			缴款单位（人）	名称	上海食品进出口公司
	科目	进口关税	预算级次	中央		账号	SZR80066686
	收款国库	中国银行上海分行				开户银行	中国银行上海分行

税号	货物名称	数量	单位	完税价格（¥）	税率（%）	税款金额（¥）
1.6258698	威士忌	200	瓶	83 600	5	4 180

金额人民币（大写）捌万叁仟陆佰元整

申请单位编号	0387124666	报关单编号	8541172525	填制单位	收款国库（银行）
合同（批件）号	SOT0405127	运输工具（号）			BANK OF CHINA SHANGHAI BRANCH
缴款期限	2012.6.14	提/装货单号	TUO105286		
备注	一般征税　照章征税　10060932 进 USD 11 000.00 成交：CIP			制单人：220 复核人：	

海关在报关单上加盖放行章。

中华人民共和国海关进口货物报关单

预录入编号：　　　　　　　　　　　　　　　　海关编号：8541172525

进口口岸 吴淞海关 2202	备案号	进口日期 2012.05.21	申报日期 2012.05.23
经营单位（0387124666） 上海食品进出口公司	运输方式 航空运输	运输工具名称	提运单号 TUO105286
收货单位 上海食品进出口公司	贸易方式 一般贸易	征免性质 一般征税	征税比例
许可证号 312098734	起运国（地区） 法国	装货港 巴黎	境内目的地 上海
批准文号	成交方式 CIP	运费	保费	批准文号
合同协议号 SOT0405127	件数 40	包装种类 箱	毛重（千克） 320	净重（千克） 280
集装箱号	随附单据 B: T0805114		用途	
标记唛码及备注　S.F.C OT0405127 PARIS C/NO.1-40			

项号	商品编号	商品名称、规格型号	数量及单位	原产国（地区）	单价	总价	币制征免
	830000	WHISKY		法国			502 照章
01		MACALLEN HIGHLAND MALT 18YRS 75cl	100PCS		55.00	5 500.00	
02		ROYAL SALUTE 70cl	100PCS		55.00	5 500.00	

税费征收情况

录入员	录入单位	兹声明以上申报无讹并承担法律责任	海关审单批注及放行日期（签章） 张玲 2012.05.24
报关员	31078965218 马君	申报单位（签章） 上海食品进出口公司 报关专用章	审单　　审价
单位地址	上海市山西路328号		征税　　统计
邮编 653214	电话 62781456	填制日期 2012年5月	查验　　放行 张民 2012.05.24

◇ 工作任务三　　　　办理电汇手续

　　上海食品进出口公司根据海关的有关规定办理进口货物的报关手续，经海关对该票货物查验放行后，马君先生凭提货单在指定地点提货。然后进行购汇申请，填写购买外汇申请书，获准后将70%余款电汇至法国客商，并办理付汇核销手续。

马君先生填写购买外汇申请书：

中国银行上海市分行
购买外汇申请书

中国银行___黄浦___分（支）行：

  我公司为执行第___SOT0405127___号合同项下对外支付，需向贵行购汇。现按外汇局有关规定向贵行提供下述内容及所附文件，请审核并按实际付汇日牌价办理售汇。所需人民币资金从我公司在贵行账户___SZR80066686___中支付。

1. 购汇金额：USD 7 700.00
2. 用　　途：☑进口商品　□从附费用　□索退赔款　□其他
3. 支付方式：□信用证　□托收　☑汇款（☑货到付款　□预付货款）
4. 商品名称：WHISKY
5. 数　　量：200 瓶
6. 合同号：SOT0405127　　　金额：USD 11 000.00
7. 发票号：EXY070931　　　　金额：USD 11 000.00
8. □一般进口商品，无须批文
  ☑控制进口商品，批文随附如下：
   □进口证明　☑许可证　□登记证明　□其他批文
   批文号码：312098731　　批文有效期：2012.9.20
9. 附件：□批文　☑合同/协议　☑发票　☑正本运单
   ☑报关单　□运费单/收据　☑保险费收据
   □佣金单　□关税证明　□仓单　□其他
10. 请于开证时立即售汇，转存保证金专用账户。

申请单位（盖章）：马君　（上海食品进出口公司 印章）

银行审核意见：
  上述内容与随附文件/凭证描述相符，拟按申请书要求办理售汇。
  经办人：中迎　　复核人：张立　　核准人：李蓝

售汇日期：2012.5.24　　｜售汇专用章｜
（加盖售汇专用章）　　 ｜（黄浦）　｜

马君先生填写汇款申请书：

中国银行上海市分行汇款申请书
BANK OF CHINA

外汇	汇款方式 Type of Remittance	电汇 T/T	✓	付款凭证（回单） 日期 2012 年 5 月 24 日 Date	户　名 Name of Account	上海食品进 出口公司
		票汇 D/D			账　号 Account No.	SZR80066686

请付 Pay	牌价 Rate	请付 Remit
58 520.00 元	@7.60	USD 7 700.00

（汇款）大写金额 (Remit) Amount in word	柒仟柒佰美元整

收款人 Payee	DENSE LIGHT SEMICONDUCTORS PTE LTD.
住　址 Address	6 CHANGJ NORTH STREET PARIS FRANCE
收款人所在地银行 Beneficiary's Bank	法国巴黎银行

汇款人　上海食品进出口公司 Remitter

附　言 Remarks	中国银行上海分行 黄浦支行 （付款单位银行盖章）

复　核　张立　　　经　办　中迎

工作任务四　　办理进口付汇核销手续

　　马君先生在办理付汇后，填写贸易进口付汇核销单。银行对其核准后，将第一联交外汇管理局，第二联退还给上海食品进出口公司。由该公司的核销员向外汇管理局提供贸易进口付汇核销单、进口货物报关单付汇水单，并填写贸易进口付汇到货核销表，办理核销报审手续。

体验活动五 代理进口贸易业务

马君先生填写贸易进口付汇核销单：

贸易进口付汇核销单（代申报单）

印单局代码：099210　　　　　　　　　　　　　　核销单编号：30126987788

单位代码：3145897564	单位名称：上海食品进出口公司	所在地外汇局名称：上海
付汇银行名称：中国银行上海分行	收款人国别：法国	交易编码：01156
收款人是否在保税区：是□ 否☑	进口商品名称：威士忌	
对外付汇币种：美元	对外付汇总额：USD 11 000.00	折美元总额：USD 11 000.00
其中：购汇金额 USD 11 000.00 人民币账号：SZR80066686	现汇金额 外汇账号	

付 汇 性 质		
☑正常付汇			
□不在名录	□90天以上信用证	□90天以上托收	□异地付汇
□90天以上到货	□转口贸易	□境外工程使用物资	□真实性审查
备案表编号：6666			

预计到货日期：2012年5月21日	进口批件号：312098734	合同/发票号：SOT0405127/ EXY070931

结 算 方 式					
信用证	90天以内□	90天以上□	承兑日期	付汇日期	期限　天
托 收	90天以内☑	90天以上□	承兑日期	付汇日期 2012.9.30	期限　天

汇款	预付货款□	货到付款（凭报关单付款）□		付汇日期
	报关单号	报关日期	报关单币种	金额
	报关单号	报关日期	报关单币种	金额
	报关单号	报关日期	报关单币种	金额
	报关单号	报关日期	报关单币种	金额
	报关单号	报关日期	报关单币种	金额
	（若报关单填写不完，可另附纸。）			

其他□		付汇日期

以下由付汇银行填写
申报号码：06010322
业务编码：98215467_

（上海食品进出口公司 盖章）　　　　　　（BANK OF CHINA SHANGHAI BRANCH 盖章）
　　　　　　　　　　　　　　　　　　　　（付款银行签章）
　　　　　　　　　　　　　　　　　　　　审核日期：2012.5.26

进口单位（签章）：上海食品进出口公司　　　　　　　　　　　　　2012年5月24日

马君先生填写贸易进口付汇到货核销表：

贸易进口付汇到货核销表

进口单位名称：上海食品进出口公司　　进口单位编号：3145897564

核销单编号：30126987788

<table>
<tr><th colspan="7">付汇情况</th><th colspan="6">报关到货情况</th><th rowspan="2">备注</th></tr>
<tr><th>序号</th><th>核销单号</th><th>备案表号</th><th>付汇币种金额</th><th>付汇日期</th><th>结算方式</th><th>付汇银行名称</th><th>应到货日期</th><th>报关单号</th><th>到货企业名称</th><th>报关币种金额</th><th>报关日期</th><th>与付汇差额
退汇 / 其他</th><th>凭报关单付汇</th></tr>
<tr><td>1</td><td>30126987788</td><td>5555</td><td>USD 11 000</td><td>9.30</td><td>电汇</td><td>中行</td><td>5.20</td><td>854117 2525</td><td>上海食品进出口公司</td><td>USD 11 000</td><td>5.23</td><td></td><td></td><td></td></tr>
<tr><td></td><td></td><td></td><td></td><td></td><td></td><td></td><td></td><td></td><td></td><td></td><td></td><td></td><td></td><td></td></tr>
<tr><td colspan="2">付汇合计笔数：
1
至本月累计笔数：</td><td colspan="2">付汇合计金额：
USD 11 000
至本月累计笔数：</td><td colspan="3">到货报关合计笔数：1
至本月累计笔数：</td><td colspan="3">到货报关合计金额：
USD 11 000
至本月累计金额：</td><td colspan="3">退汇合计金额：
至本月累计金额：</td><td colspan="2">凭报关单合计金额：
至本月累计金额：</td></tr>
</table>

填表人：马君　　负责人：方力　　填表日期：2012年5月27日

本核销表内容无讹。（盖章）

注：
1. 本表一式二联，第一联送外汇局，第二联由进口单位留存；
2. 本表合计和累计栏金额为折美元金额；
3. 本表由各外汇局印制，供进口单位使用；
4. 汇款项下的付汇在"凭报关单付汇"栏填"√"；
5. 累计栏为本年年初至本月的累计数；
6. 一次到货多次付汇的，在"付汇情况"栏填写实际付汇情况，在"报关到货情况"栏只填写一次；
7. 一次付汇多次到货的，参照第6点处理。

体验活动五　代理进口贸易业务

综合业务模拟操作

操作一

1. 操作资料

日本凡人株式会社(BOJINXYA LTD.，CO.)收到上海图书进出口公司的货款后,及时办理托运、保险等手续,并直接将商业发票、装箱单、空运单和保险单等全套单据寄送至上海图书进出口公司。上海图书进出口公司收到单据及时审单,确认无误后,办理进口货物的报检与报关手续。具体资料如下:

买　　方:　上海图书进出口公司(SHANGHAI BOOK IMPORT & EXPORT CORPORATION)
　　　　　　地址:288 NANXIANG ROAD SHANGHAI CHINA
　　　　　　TEL:021-65782312　FAX:021-65782313

卖　　方:　BOJINXYA LTD.，CO.
　　　　　　地址:82 OTOLI MACHI TOKYO, JAPAN
　　　　　　TEL:028-548-742　FAX:028-548-743

货名规格:　教学书籍(EDUCATIONAL BOOKS)Order No. SK0626215

H. S. 编码:　4901.9900

单　　价:　CIP SHANGHAI USD 25.15

支付方式:　提前电汇(BY T/T IN ADVANCE)

数　　量:　200套(200 SETS)

包　　装:　每20套装入一个出口纸箱(PACKED IN 1 CARTON OF 20 SETS EACH)

毛　　重:　每箱10千克

净　　重:　每箱8千克

装运期:　不迟于2013年5月5日前装运(LATEST DATE OF SHIPMENT:20130505)

起运地:　日本东京机场(TOKYO AIRPORT, JAPAN)

目的地:　中国浦东机场(PUDONG AIRPORT ,CHINA)

分批装运:　允许(ALLOWED)

航　　班:　USX0832-W

空运单号:　JR07842

合同号:　TX200523

购汇银行： 中国银行浦东分行
银行账号： SZR80066686
用途： 进口商品
附件： 合同一份
汇率： 1∶65
汇入银行： 日本东京银行
报检单编号： 1230508111
报检单位登记号：13684Q
海关编号： 3106547878
海关注册号： 0387124666
报关员： 张玉(3108976547)
印单局代码： 089210
核销单编号： 30126987123
单位代码： 3145897432
交易编码： 08153
人民币账号： SW80066435
备案表编号： 6235789

2.操作要求

(1)请你以上海图书进出口公司业务员张玉的身份,根据上述资料填写入境货物报检单。

中华人民共和国出入境检验检疫
入境货物报检单

报检单位(加盖公章):　　　　　　　　　　　　　　　　＊编号:＿＿＿＿＿＿

报检单位登记号:　　　联系人:　　电话:　　　　　　报检日期:　年　月　日

收货人	(中文)			企业性质(划"√")		□合资□合作□外资	
	(外文)						
发货人	(中文)						
	(外文)						
货物名称(中/外文)		H.S.编码	产地国	数/重量	货物总值	包装种类及数量	
运输工具名称及号码				合同号			
贸易方式		贸易国别(地区)		提单/运单号			
到岸日期		起运国家(地区)		许可证/审批号			
卸毕日期		起运口岸		入境口岸			
索赔有效期至		经停口岸		目的地			
集装箱规格、数量及号码							
合同订立的特殊条款以及其他要求				货物存放地点		上海市逸仙路100号	
				用途		自营内销	
随附单据(划"√"或补填)				标记及号码	＊外商投资财产(划"√")		□是□否
□ 合同		□ 到货通知			＊检验检疫费		
□ 发票		□ 装箱单					
□ 提/运单		□ 质保书			总金额		
□ 兽医卫生证书		□ 理货清单			(人民币元)		
□ 植物检疫证书		□ 磅码单					
□ 动物检验证书		□ 验收报告			计费人		
□ 卫生证书							
□ 原产地证					收费人		
□ 许可/审批文件							
报检人郑重声明:					领取证单		
1. 本人被授权报检。							
2. 上列填写内容正确属实。					日期		
签名:					签名		

注:有"＊"号栏由出入境检验检疫机关填写　　　　　◆国家出入境检验检疫局制

(2)请你以上海图书进出口公司业务员张玉的身份,根据上述资料填写入境货物报关单。

中华人民共和国海关进口货物报关单

预录入编号:　　　　　　　　　　　　　　　　　　海关编号:

进口口岸	备案号	进口日期	申报日期
经营单位	运输方式	运输工具名称	提运单号
收货单位	贸易方式	征免性质	征税比例
许可证号	起运国(地区)	装货港	境内目的地
批准文号	成交方式	运费　　保费	批准文号
合同协议号	件数	包装种类　毛重(千克)	净重(千克)
集装箱号	随附单据	用途	

标记唛码及备注

项号	商品编号	商品名称、规格型号	数量及单位	原产国(地区)	单价	总价	币制	征免

税费征收情况

录入员　　录入单位	兹声明以上申报无讹并承担法律责任	海关审单批注及放行日期(签章)	
报关员	申报单位(签章)	审单	审价
单位地址		征税	统计
邮编　　电话	填制日期	查验	放行

316

(3) 请你以上海图书进出口公司业务员张玉的身份，根据上述资料填写贸易进口付汇核销单。

贸易进口付汇核销单(代申报单)

印单局代码： 核销单编号：

单位代码：	单位名称：	所在地外汇局名称：
付汇银行名称:中国银行上海分行	收款人国别：	交易编码：
收款人是否在保税区：是□ 否□	进口商品名称：	
对外付汇币种：	对外付汇总额：	折美元总额：
其中：购汇金额	现汇金额	
人民币账号：	外汇账号	

付 汇 性 质
□正常付汇
□不在名录　　　　　□90天以上信用证　　□90天以上托收　　　　□异地付汇
□90天以上到货　　　□转口贸易　　　　　□境外工程使用物资　　□真实性审查
备案表编号：
预计到货日期：　　　　　　　进口批件号：　　　　　合同/发票号：

结 算 方 式					
信用证	90天以内□	90天以上□	承兑日期　付汇日期	期限	天
托　收	90天以内☑	90天以上□	承兑日期　付汇日期	期限	天

	预付货款□　　货到付款(凭报关单付款)□　　付汇日期			
汇款	报关单号	报关日期	报关单币种	金额
	报关单号	报关日期	报关单币种	金额
	报关单号	报关日期	报关单币种	金额
	报关单号	报关日期	报关单币种	金额
	报关单号	报关日期	报关单币种	金额
	(若报关单填写不完,可另附纸。)			

其他□	付汇日期

以下由付汇银行填写
申报号码：
业务编号：
(付款银行签章)
审核日期：

进口单位(签章)：　　　　　　　　　　　　　　　　　　　　　年　月　日

317

操作二

1. 操作资料

上海汽车进出口公司向日本 AOYMA TRADING CORPORATION 电汇50%的货款后,及时办理托运和保险手续,并通知 AOYMA TRADING CORPORATION 有关船名、航次、到达装运港日期等有关信息。当货物装运后,AOYMA TRADING CORPORATION 将商业发票、装箱单、提单等全套单据寄送至代收行中国银行上海分行托收。上海汽车进出口公司收到单据及时审单,确认无误后支付50%的托收款,并办理进口货物的报检、报关和付汇核销手续。具体资料如下:

买　　方：	上海汽车进出口公司(SHANGHAI CAR IMPORT & EXPORT CORPORATION)
	地址:13 NANXIANG ROAD SHANGHAI CHINA
	TEL:021-56082212 FAX:021-56082211
卖　　方：	AOYMA IMPORT & EXPORT CORPORATION(代表为高田)
	地址:82-324 SKURA MACHI OSAKA, JAPAN
	TEL:028-688-744 FAX:028-688-743
合同号：	RT061157W
货名规格：	汽车轮胎(CAR TIRE)TR681、TR682、TR683、TR684
单　　价：	FOB OSAKA TR681 USD 10.00/PC, TR682 USD 11.00/PC, TR683 USD 8.00/PC, TR684 USD 9.00/PC
支付方式：	BY 50% T/T IN ADVANCE, 50% D/P AT SIGHT
数　　量：	每种规格各1 000只(1 000 PCS OF EACH)
包　　装：	每一只汽车轮胎装入一个复合无纺布(SPES)轮胎包装袋(PACKED IN A SPES TIRE BAG OF 1 PIECE EACH)
毛　　重：	5KG/只
订舱委托书号:	WY083452
装运期：	不迟于2013年5月15日前装运(LATEST DATE OF SHIPMENT: 20130515)
装运港：	日本大阪(OSAKA JAPAN)
目的地港：	中国上海(SHANGHAI CHINA)
分批装运：	允许(ALLOWED)
转　　运：	不允许(NOT ALLOWED)
船　　名：	COSCO V. 167
运　　费：	USD 1 410.00
提单号：	COS345672
保　　险：	由买方按发票金额的110%投保一切险(FOR 110 PERCENT OF THE INVOICE VALUE COVERING ALL RISKS BY THE BUYER)

保险费： USD 1 480.00
报检单位登记号： 6612547
商品编码： 4011100010
自动进口许可证号：SH08976549
海关编号： 3017887452
海关注册号： 3018712462
入境货物通关单： SH08976532
印单局代码： 089876
核销单编号： 87626987123
单位代码： 31999982
交易编码： 08199
人民币账号： RT76066435-QV
备案表编号： 2335789

2. 操作要求

(1)请你以上海汽车进出口公司业务员王伟的身份,根据上述资料填写进口订舱委托书。

进口订舱委托书

编号： 日期：

货名（英文）			
重量		尺码	
合同号		包装	
装运港		交货期	
装货条款			
发货人名称、地址			
发货人电挂			
订妥船名		预抵港口	
备注		委托单位	

1. 危险品须注明性能,重大件注明每件重量及尺码。
2. 装货条款须详细注明。

(2)请你以上海汽车进出口公司业务员王伟的身份,根据上述资料与中国人民保险公司上海分公司签订进口货物运输预约保险合同。

中国人民保险公司
进口货物运输预约保险合同

合同号: 　　　　　　　　　　　　　　　　　　　　日期:

甲方:

乙方:

　　双方就进口货物的运输预约保险拟订以下条款,以资共同遵守:

　　一、保险范围

　　甲方从国外进口的全部货物,不论运输方式,凡贸易条款规定由买方办理保险的,都属于本合同范围之内。甲方应根据本合同规定,向乙方办理投保手续并支付保险费。

　　乙方对上述保险范围内的货物,负有自动承保的责任,在发生本合同规定范围内的损失时,均按本合同的规定,负责赔偿。

　　二、保险金额

　　保险金额以货物的到岸价(CIF)即货价加运费加保险费为准(运费可用实际运费,亦可由双方协定一个平均运费率计算)。

　　三、保险险别和费率

　　各种货物需要投保的险别由甲方选定并在投保单中填明。乙方根据不同的险别规定不同的费率。现暂定如下:

货物种类	运输方式	保险险别	保险费率

　　四、保险责任

　　各种险别的责任范围,按照所属乙方制定的"海洋货物运输保险条款"、"海洋运输货物战争险条款"、"海运进口货物国内转动期间保险责任扩展条款"、"航空运输一切险条款"和其他有关条款的规定为准。

　　五、投保手续

　　甲方一经掌握货物发运情况,即应向乙方寄送起运通知书,办理投保手续。通知书一式五份,由保险公司确认后,退回一份。如不办理投保,货物发生损失,乙方不予赔偿。

　　六、保险费

　　乙方按甲方寄送的起运通知书照前列相应的费率逐笔计收保费,甲方应及时付费。

　　七、索赔手续和期限

　　本合同所保货物发生保险责任范围内的损失时,乙方应按制定的"关于海运进口保险货物残损检验的赔款给付办法"和"进口货物施救整理费用支付办法"迅速处理。甲方应尽力采取防止货物扩大受损的措施,对已遭受损失的货物必须积极抢救,尽量减少货物的损失。向乙方办理索赔的有效期限,以保险货物卸离海港之日起满一年终止。如有特殊需要,可向乙方提出延长索赔期。

　　八、合同期限

　　　　本合同自　　　年　　月　　日起开始生效。

　　　　甲方:　　　　　　　　　　　　　　　　　　　　乙方:

(3)请你以上海汽车进出口公司业务员王伟的身份,根据上述资料填写入境货物报检单。

中华人民共和国出入境检验检疫
入境货物报检单

报检单位(加盖公章):					*编号:	
报检单位登记号:		联系人:	电话:	报检日期:	年 月 日	

发货人	(中文)		企业性质(划"√")		□合资 □合作 □外资	
	(外文)					
收货人	(中文)					
	(外文)					

货物名称(中/外文)	H.S.编码	产地	数/重量	货物总值	包装种类及数量

运输工具名称及号码		合同号	
贸易方式		提单/运单号	
到岸日期	起运国家(地区)	许可证/审批号	
卸毕日期	起运口岸	入境口岸	
索赔有效期至	经停口岸	目的地	
集装箱规格、数量及号码			
合同订立的特殊条款	货物存放地点		
以及其他要求	用 途		

随附单据(划"√"或补填)		标记及号码	*外商投资财产(划"√")	□是 □否
□ 合同	□ 到货通知		*检验检疫费	
□ 发票	□ 装箱单		总金额	
□ 提/运单	□ 质保书		(人民币元)	
□ 兽医卫生证书	□ 理货清单			
□ 植物检疫证书	□ 磅码单		计费人	
□ 动物检验证书	□ 验收报告			
□ 卫生证书	□		收费人	
□ 原产地证				
□ 许可/审批文件				

报检人郑重声明:	领取证单	
1. 本人被授权报检。		
2. 上列填写内容正确属实。	日期	
签名:_____	签名	

注:有"*"号栏由出入境检验检疫机关填写　　　　◆国家出入境检验检疫局制

(4)请你以上海汽车进出口公司业务员王伟的身份,根据上述资料填写进口货物报关单。

中华人民共和国海关进口货物报关单

预录入编号:　　　　　　　　　　　　　　　海关编号:

进口口岸	备案号	进口日期	申报日期
经营单位	运输方式	运输工具名称	提运单号
收货单位	贸易方式	征免性质	征税比例
许可证号	起运国(地区)	装货港	境内目的地
批准文号	成交方式	运费	保费	批准文号
合同协议号	件数	包装种类	毛重(千克)	净重(千克)
集装箱号	随附单据		用途	
标记唛码及备注				

项号	商品编号	商品名称、规格型号	数量及单位	原产国(地区)	单价	总价	币制	征免

税费征收情况

录入员	录入单位	兹声明以上申报无讹并承担法律责任	海关审单批注及放行日期(签章)	
报关员		申报单位(签章)	审单	审价
单位地址			征税	统计
邮编	电话	填制日期	查验	放行

(5)请你以上海汽车进出口公司业务员王伟的身份,根据上述资料填写贸易进口付汇核销单。

贸易进口付汇核销单(代申报单)

印单局代码:　　　　　　　　　　　　　　　　　　核销单编号:

单位代码:	单位名称:	所在地外汇局名称:
付汇银行名称:中国银行上海分行	收款人国别:	交易编码:
收款人是否在保税区:是□ 否□	进口商品名称:	
对外付汇币种:	对外付汇总额:	折美元总额:
其中:购汇金额	现汇金额	
人民币账号:	外汇账号	

<table>
<tr><td colspan="3" align="center">付 汇 性 质</td></tr>
<tr><td colspan="3">□正常付汇</td></tr>
<tr><td>□不在名录</td><td>□90天以上信用证　　□90天以上托收</td><td>□异地付汇</td></tr>
<tr><td>□90天以上到货</td><td>□转口贸易　　　　　□境外工程使用物资</td><td>□真实性审查</td></tr>
<tr><td colspan="3">备案表编号:</td></tr>
<tr><td>预计到货日期:</td><td>进口批件号:</td><td>合同/发票号:</td></tr>
<tr><td colspan="3" align="center">结 算 方 式</td></tr>
<tr><td>信用证　90天以内□</td><td>90天以上□　承兑日期　付汇日期</td><td>期限　天</td></tr>
<tr><td>托　收　90天以内□</td><td>90天以上□　承兑日期　付汇日期</td><td>期限　天</td></tr>
</table>

	预付货款□	货到付款(凭报关单付款)□	付汇日期	
汇款	报关单号	报关日期	报关单币种	金额
	报关单号	报关日期	报关单币种	金额
	报关单号	报关日期	报关单币种	金额
	报关单号	报关日期	报关单币种	金额
	报关单号	报关日期	报关单币种	金额
	(若报关单填写不完,可另附纸。)			
其他□		付汇日期		

以下由付汇银行填写
申报号码:
业务编号:

　　　　　　　　　　　　　　　　　　　　　　　(付款银行签章)
　　　　　　　　　　　　　　　　　　　　　审核日期:

进口单位(签章):　　　　　　　　　　　　　　　　　　年　月　日

附 录

附录1 常用出口货物报关单的填制代码

1. 地区性质代码表

地区性质代码	地区性质名称
1	经济特区
2	沿海开放城市
3	经济技术开发区
4	经济开放区
5	海南省
6	西藏自治区
7	广东省
8	福建省
9	北京市、新疆
A	保税工业区
B	新技术开发园区

2. 企业性质代码表

企业性质代码	企业性质名称
1	国有
2	合作
3	合资
4	独资
5	集体
6	私营
7	报关
8	其他

3. 国别(地区)代码表(略)

国别代码	中文国名(地区名)	英文国名(地区名)	优/普税率标记
100	亚洲	Asia	
101	阿富汗	Afghanistan	H
109	朝鲜	Korea, DPR	L
110	中国香港	Hong Kong	L
111	印度	India	L
112	印度尼西亚	Indonesia	L
114	伊拉克	Iraq	L
115	以色列	Israel	L
116	日本	Japan	L
121	澳门	Macao	L
122	马来西亚	Malaysia	L
128	巴勒斯坦	Palestine	H
129	菲律宾	Philippines	L
132	新加坡	Singapore	L

续表

国别代码	中文国名(地区名)	英文国名(地区名)	优/普税率标记
133	韩国	Korea Rep.	L
136	泰国	Thailand	L
138	阿联酋	United Arab Emirates	L
141	越南	Vietnam	L
142	中国	China	L
143	中国台湾	Taiwan prov.	L
200	**非洲**	Africa	
201	阿尔及利亚	Algeria	L
209	中非	Central African Rep.	U
236	尼日利亚	Nigeria	L
300	**欧洲**	Europe	
302	丹麦	Denmark	L
303	英国	United Kindom	L
304	德国	Germany	L
305	法国	France	L
306	爱尔兰	Ireland	L
307	意大利	Italy	L
309	荷兰	Netherlands	L
311	葡萄牙	Portugal	L
312	西班牙	Spain	L
326	挪威	Norway	L
330	瑞典	Sweden	L
331	瑞士	Switzerland	L
344	俄罗斯联邦	Russia	L
345	塔吉克斯坦	Tadzhikistan	L
400	**拉丁美洲**	Latin America	
402	阿根廷	Argentina	L
429	墨西哥	Mexico	L
500	**北美洲**	North America	
501	加拿大	Canada	L
502	美国	United States	L
600	**大洋州**	Oceania	
601	澳大利亚	Australia	L
609	新西兰	New Zealand	L

4. 国内地区代码表(略)

地区代码	地区名称	地区性质标记
11083	北京新技术产业开发区	B
11132	北京经济技术开发区	3
11909	北京其他	9
12043	天津新技术产业园区	B
12072	天津经济技术开发区	3
12074	天津港保税区	A
12909	天津其他	2

续表

地区代码	地区名称	地区性质标记
21022	大连经济技术开发区	3
21023	大连高新技术产业园区	B
21024	大连大窑湾保税区	A
21029	大连其他	2
23012	哈尔滨经济技术开发区	3
31019	黄浦	2
31029	南市	2
31039	卢湾	2
31043	上海漕河泾新兴技术开发区	B
31049	徐汇其他	2
31052	上海经济技术开发区	3
31059	长宁	2
31069	静安	2
31079	普陀	2
31089	闸北	2
31099	虹口	2
31109	杨浦	2
31112	上海闵行经济技术开发区	2
31119	闵行其他	2
31222	上海浦东新区	3
31224	上海外高桥保税区	A
31229	浦东其他	2
31909	上海其他	2
32013	南京浦口高新技术外向开发区	B
32019	南京其他	2
32023	无锡高新技术产业开发区	B
32029	无锡其他	

5. 货币代码表(略)

货币代码	货币符号	货币名称
110	HKD	港币
116	JPY	日本元
142	CNY	人民币
143	TWD	台币
300	EUR	欧元
303	GBP	英镑
304	DEM	德国马克
305	FRF	法国法郎
331	SF	瑞士法郎
501	GAD	加拿大元
502	USD	美元
601	AUD	澳大利亚元
609	NZD	新西兰元

6. 计量单位代码表(略)

计量单位代码	计量单位名称	计量单位代码	计量单位名称
001	台	020	片
002	座	021	组
003	辆	022	份
004	艘	023	幅
005	架	025	双
006	套	026	对
007	个	027	棵
008	只	028	株
009	头	030	米
010	张	032	平方米
012	支	033	立方米
013	枝	035	千克
014	根	036	克
015	条	037	盆
016	把	046	匹
017	块	047	公担
018	卷	067	英尺
019	副		

7. 成交方式代码表

成交方式代码	成交方式名称
1	CIF
2	CFR/CNF/C&F
3	FOB
4	C&I
5	市场价
6	垫仓

8. 监管证件名称代码表(略)

许可证或批文代码	许可证或批文名称
1	进口许可证
4	出口许可证
A	检验检疫入境货物通知单
B	检验检疫出境货物通知单
H	文物出口证书
N	机电产品进口证明

9. 结汇方式代码表

结汇方式代码	结汇方式名称
1	信汇
2	电汇
4	付款交单
5	承兑交单

续表

结汇方式代码	结汇方式名称
6	信用证
7	先出后结
8	先结后出
9	其他

10. 贸易方式(海关监管方式)代码表(略)

监管方式代码	监管方式简称	贸易方式全称
0110	一般贸易	一般贸易
0130	易货贸易	易货贸易
0214	来料加工	来料加工装配贸易进口料件及加工出口货物
0243	来料以产顶进	来料加工成品以产顶进
0245	来料料件内销	来料加工料件转内销
0255	来料深加工	来料深加工结转货物
0258	来料余料结转	来料加工余料结转
0265	来料料件复出	来料加工复运出境的原进口料件
0300	来料料件退换	来料加工料件退换
0345	来料成品减免	来料加工成品凭征免税证明转减免税
0420	加工贸易设备	加工贸易项下外商提供的进口设备
0446	加工设备内销	加工贸易免税进口设备转内销
0456	加工设备结转	加工贸易免税进口设备结转
0466	加工设备退运	加工贸易免税进口设备退运出境
0513	补偿贸易	补偿贸易
0615	进料对口	进料加工(对口合同)
0700	进料料件退换	进料加工料件退换
0715	进料非对口	进料加工(非对口合同)
1110	对台贸易	对台直接贸易

11. 用途代码表(略)

用途代码	用途名称
01	外贸自营内销
02	特区内销
03	其他内销
04	企业自用
05	加工返销
08	免费提供
10	货样、广告品

12. 运输方式代码表(略)

运输方式代码	运输方式名称
2	江海运输
3	铁路运输
4	汽车运输

续表

运输方式代码	运输方式名称
5	航空运输
6	邮运
9	其他

13. 关区代码表(略)

关区代码	关区名称	关区代码	关区名称
0100	北京关区	2200	上海海关
0101	机场货管	2201	浦江海关
0102	京监管处	2202	吴淞海关
0103	京关展览	2203	沪机场关
0111	京五里店	2208	宝山海关
0112	京邮办处	2209	龙吴海关
0113	京中关村	2210	浦东海关
0200	天津关区	2233	浦东机场
0201	天津海关	5100	广州海关
0202	新港海关	5101	广州新风
0203	津开发区	5102	新风罗冲
0204	东港海关	5103	清远海关

14. 征免性质代码表(略)

代码	征免性质简称	征免性质全称
101	一般征税	一般征税进出口货物
401	科教用品	大专院校及科研机构进口科教用品
503	进料加工	进料加工贸易进口料件及出口成品
506	边境小额	边境小额贸易进口货物
601	中外合资	中外合资经营企业进出口货物
602	中外合作	中外合作经营企业进出口货物
603	外资企业	外商独资企业进出口货物

15. 征减免税方式代码表(略)

征减免税方式代码	征减免税方式名称
1	照章征税
2	折半征税
3	全免
5	随征免性质
6	保证金
7	保证函
9	全额退税

附录2　各国主要航运公司及标识

标识	中文名称	英文名称	简　称	注册地
	中国外运股份有限公司	SINOTRANS Container Lines Co.，Ltd.	SINOTRANS	中国
	中海集装箱运输股份有限公司	China Shipping Container Lines Co.，Ltd.	CSCL	中国
	天海海运有限公司	Tinhai Marine Shipping Co.，Ltd.	TMSC	中国
	海丰国际航运集团有限公司	SITC Maritime（Group）Co.，Ltd	SITC	中国
	上海浦海航运有限公司	Shanghai Puhai Shipping Co.，Ltd.	PUHAI	中国
	万海航运有限公司	Wan Hai Lines Co.，Ltd.	WHL	中国台湾
	长荣海运股份有限公司	Evergreen Marine Co.，Ltd.	EVG	中国台湾
	正利航业股份有限公司	Cheng Lie Navigation Co.，Ltd.	CNC	中国台湾
	京汉海运有限公司	CO HEUNG Shipping Co.，Ltd.	CO-HEUNG	中国香港
	韩进海运有限公司	Hanjin Shipping Co.，Ltd.	HJS	韩国
	长锦商船船务有限公司	Sinokor Merchant Marine Co.，Ltd.	SKR	韩国
	现代商船有限公司	Hyundai Merchant Marine Co.，Ltd.	HMM	韩国
	高丽海运有限公司	Korea Marine Transport Co.，Ltd.	HMTC	韩国
	日本邮船有限公司	Nippon Yusen Kaisha Line Ltd.	NYK	日本
	川崎汽船有限公司	Kawasaki Kisen Kaisha Ltd.	KLINE	日本
	大阪商船三井船舶有限公司	Mitsui O.S.K. Lines，Ltd.	MOSK	日本

附 录

标 识	中文名称	英文名称	简 称	注册地
PIL	太平船务有限公司	Pacific International Lines Ltd.	PIL	新加坡
misc	马来西亚国际船运有限公司	Malaysia International Shipping Corporation	MISC	马来西亚
ANL	澳洲国家航运	Australian National Line	ANL	澳大利亚
	马士基海陆有限公司	Maersk Sealand Co., Ltd.	MSK	丹麦
W&W	华轮威尔森航运公司	Wallenius Wilhelmsen ASA	WALLENIUS	挪威
CMA CGM	达飞海运集团	CMA CGM Group	CMA	法国
	达贸国际轮船公司	Delmas S. A.	DMS	法国
	赫伯罗特航运公司	Hapag-Lloyd Container Line GmbH	HLC	德国
	地中海航运有限公司	Mediterranean Shipping Company S. A.	MSC	瑞士
ITALIA	意大利海运公司	Italia Marittima SpA.	ITS	意大利
APL	美国总统轮船股份有限公司	American President Lines Co., Ltd.	APL	美国
TMM	墨西哥航运有限公司	Grupo TMM	TMM	墨西哥
	智利国家航运公司	Compania Chilena de Navegacion Interoceanica S. A.	CCNI	智利

附录3 国际商务单证常用英语词组、语句和缩略词

Business Negotiation（交易磋商）

inquiry/enquiry 询盘
offer 发盘
firm offer 实盘
offer firm 发实盘
bid/bidding 递盘
bid firm 递实盘
to withdraw an offer 撤回报盘
to decline an offer 或 to turn down an offer 谢绝报盘
counter offer 还盘
cable reply 电复
indent 订单
book/booking 订货/订购
reply immediately 速复
usual practice 习惯做法
reference price 参考价
price indication 指示性价格
without engagement 不受约束
subject to reply… 限……复
subject to reply reaching here… 限……复到
time of validity 有效期限
valid till… 有效至……
purchase contract 购货合同
sales contract 销售合同
purchase confirmation 购货确认书
sales confirmation 销售确认书
originals of the contract 合同正本
copies of the contract 合同副本
to make a contract 签订合同
to sign a contract 签合同
to draw up a contract 拟订合同
to draft a contract 起草合同
to get a contract 收到合同
to countersign a contract 会签合同
subject to seller's confirmation 需经卖方确认
subject to our final confirmation 需经我方最后确认
May I have an idea of your prices? 可以了解一下你们的价格吗?
Please let us know your lowest possible prices for the relevant goods.
请告知你们有关商品的最低价。

If your prices are favorable, I can place the order right away.
如果你们的价格优惠,我们可以马上订货。
Your enquiry is too vague to enable us to reply you.
你们的询盘不明确,我们无法答复。
China National Silk Corporation received the inquiry sheet sent by a British company.
中国丝绸公司收到了英国一家公司的询价单。
We'd rather have you quote us FOB prices.　我们希望你们报 FOB 价。
Would you tell us your best prices C. I. F. Hamburg for the chairs?
请告诉你方椅子到汉堡到岸价的最低价格。
Will you please tell the quantity you require so as to enable us to sort out the offers?
为了便于我方报价,可以告诉我们你们所要的数量吗?
How long does it usually take you to make delivery?
你们通常要多久才能交货?
Could you make prompt delivery?　可以即期交货吗?
Could you tell me which kind of payment terms you'll choose?
能否告知你们将采用哪种付款方式?
Could you please send us a catalog of your rubber boots together with terms of payment?
你能给我们寄来一份胶靴的目录,连同告诉我们付款方式吗?
He inquired about the varieties, specifications and price, and so on and so forth.
他询问了品种、花色和价格等情况。
We have inquired of Manager Zhang about the varieties, quality and price of tea.
我们向张经理询问了茶叶的品种、质量、价格等问题。
Thank you for your inquiry.　谢谢你们的询价。
Do you always make out a contract for every deal?
每笔交易都需要订一份合同吗?
Are we anywhere near a contract yet?
我们可以签合同了吗?
We can repeat the contract on the same terms.
我们可以按同样条件再订一个合同。
My offer was based on reasonable profit, not on wild speculations.
我的报价以合理利润为依据,不是漫天要价。
I think the price we offered you last week is the best one.
相信我上周的报价是最好的。
The price you offered is above previous prices.
你方报价高于上次。
It was a higher price than we offered to other suppliers.
此价格比我们给其他供货人的出价要高。
We can't accept your offer unless the price is reduced by 5%.
除非你们减价 5%,否则我们无法接受报盘。
I'm afraid I don't find your price competitive at all.
我看你们的报价毫无任何竞争性。
Let me make you a special offer.　好吧,我给你一个特别优惠价。
We'll give you the preference of our offer.　我们将优先向你们报盘。

You'll see that our offer compares favorably with the quotations you can get elsewhere.
你会发现我们的报价比别处要便宜。
Our offers are for 3 days.　我们的报盘三天有效。
The offer holds good until 5 o'clock p. m. 22nd of June，1997，Beijing time.
报价有效期到1997年6月22日下午5点，北京时间。
All prices in the price lists are subject to our confirmation.
报价单中所有价格以我方确认为准。
This offer is subject to your reply reaching here before the end of this month.
该报盘以你方回复本月底前到达我地为有效。
subject to 以……为条件，以……为准
offer subject to our final confirmation 以我方最后确认为准的报盘
I'm afraid the offer is unacceptable.　恐怕你方的报价不能接受。
Please renew your offer for two days further.　请将报盘延期两天。
We regret we have to decline your offer.　很抱歉，我们不得不拒绝你方报盘。
The offer is withdrawn.　该报盘已经撤回。
Let's have you counter-offer.　请还个价。
I appreciate your counter-offer but find it too low.
谢谢您的还价，可我觉得太低了。
Your price is too high to interest buyers in counter-offer.
你的价格太高，买方没有兴趣还盘。
I'll respond to your counter-offer by reducing our price by three dollars.
我同意你们的还价，减价3元。

Transportation（运输）

move　运输
transport　运输
mode of transportation　运输方式
way of transportation　运输方式
to transport by sea　海运
to transport by railway　陆运
transport by container　集装箱运输
cargo by rail　铁路运输
cargo by road　公路运输
multimodal combined　多式联运
combined transportation　联运
through transport　直达运输
train-air-truck（TAT；TA）　"陆-空-陆"联运或"陆空联运"
transportation by sea，land，air and mail　海、陆、空、邮运输
regular shipping liner　班轮
direct vessel　直达船只
to do charter　租船
time charter　定期租船
time charter trip　航次期租
single voyage charter　单程租船

附 录

return voyage charter　回航次租船
voyage charter　定程租船
lighter　驳船
tanker　油轮
cargo space　货舱
shipping space　舱位
original B/L　正本提单
bill of lading (B/L)　提单
on board B/L　已装船提单
shipped B/L　已装船提单
received for shipment B/L　备运提单
direct B/L　直达提单
transshipment B/L　转船提单
through B/L　联运提单
clean B/L　清洁提单
unclean B/L 或 foul B/L　不清洁提单
straight B/L　记名提单
open B/L　不记名提单
bearer B/L　不记名提单
order B/L　指示提单
long form B/L　全式提单
short form B/L　简式提单
on deck B/L　舱面提单
stale B/L　过期提单
ante dated B/L　倒签提单
advanced B/L　预借提单
combined transport documents (CTD)　联合运输单据
transport document　运输单据
shipping documents　装船单据
freight at destination B/L　运费到付提单
freight prepaid B/L　运费预付提单
cargo receipt　陆运收据
airway bill　空运提单
carriage　运费
cargo freight　运费
freight　运费
transport charge　运输费
carriage expense　运费
transportation expense　运输费用
carload rate　整车运费
carriage free　免收运费
carriage paid　运费已付
carriage forward　运费待付

335

liner's freight tariff 班轮运价表
basic rate 基本运费率
heavy lift additional 超重附加费
over length additional 超长附加费
A. V. (Ad. Val) 从价运费
optional charges 选港费
wharfage 码头费
landing charges 卸货费
port dues 港口税
freight ton 运费吨
weight ton 重量吨
measurement ton 尺码吨
non-negotiable 未议付的
master 船长
shipper 托运人
consignor 发货人
consignee 收货人
port of shipment 装运港
optional port 选择港
port of discharge 卸货港
port of destination 目的港
immediate shipments 立即装运
prompt shipments 即期装运
to take delivery of goods 提货
transportation cost 运输成本
cargo mark (shipping mark) 货物装运标志
transportation company (corporation) 运输公司
carton/cartons (CTN/CTNS) 纸箱
piece/pieces (PCE/PCS) 只、个、支
dozen (DOZ/DZ) 一打
package (PKG) 包、捆、扎、件
weight (WT) 重量
gross weight (G. W.) 毛重
net weight (N. W.) 净重
each (EA) 每个、各
merchant vessel (M/V) 商船
steamship (S. S) 船运
metric ton (MT 或 M/T) 公吨
document (DOC) 文件、单据
packing list (P/L) 装箱单、明细表
express mail special (PC EMS) 特快专递
shipping marks (S/M) 装船标记
container yard (CY) 集装箱堆场

full container load（FCL） 整箱货
less than container load（LCL） 拼箱货
container freight station（CFS） 集装箱货运站
twenty-feet equivalent units（TEU） 20英尺换算单位
optional charges to be borne by the buyers 或 optional charges for buyers' account 选港费由买方负担
shipment during January 或 January shipment 一月份装船
shipment not later than Jan. 31st 或 shipment on or before Jan. 31st 一月底装船
shipment during Jan./Feb. 或 Jan./Feb. shipment 一/二月份装船
shipment during…in two lots 在……（时间）分两批装船
shipment during…in two equal lots 在……（时间）平均分两批装船
in three monthly shipments 分三个月装运
in three equal monthly shipments 分三个月，每月平均装运
shipments within 30 days after receipt of L/C 收到信用证后30天内装运
partial shipment allowed 允许分批装船
How do you usually move your machines? 你们出口机器习惯使用哪种运输方式？
Please dispatch the TV sets we ordered by sea. 请将我们订购的电视机采用海运方式。
Please have the goods transported by air. 请空运此批货。
We don't think it is proper to transport the goods by railway.
我们认为此货不适合用铁路运输。
Can you have them sent by railway? 能采用陆运方式吗？
Will you please tell us the earliest possible date you can make shipment?
你能告知我们最早船期吗？
Agreed to employ "combined transportation" to ship the goods.
双方决定联运货物。
Since there is no direct vessel, we have to arrange multimodal combined transport by rail and sea. 由于没有直达船只，我们只好安排海陆联运。
A part of the goods were damaged in transit. 一部分货物在运输途中受损。
Please quote your current tariffs. 请报你公司的最新运费表。
Freight for shipment from Shanghai to Hongkong is to be charged to your account.
从上海到香港的运费由贵方负担。
The bill of lading should be marked as "freight prepaid".
提单上应该注明"运费预付"字样。
This is one set of the shipping documents covering the consignment.
这是一套本批货的装运单据。
We'll send you two sets of the shipped, clean bill of lading.
我们将寄送两套已装运清洁提单。

Quality（品质）

good quality 好质量
fine quality 优质
better quality 较好质量
high quality 高质量
sound quality 完好的质量

best quality 最好的质量
superior quality 优等的质量
first-class 一等品
choice quality 或 selected quality 精选的质量
prime quality 或 tip-top quality 第一流的质量
first-class quality 或 first-rate quality 头等的质量
above the average quality 一般水平以上的质量
below the average quality 一般水平以下的质量
common quality 一般质量
standard quality 标准质量
average quality 平均质量
fair average quality (f. a. q.) 大路货
bad quality 劣质
low quality 低质量
inferior quality 次质量
poor quality 质量较差
We are responsible to replace the defective ones. 我们保换质量不合格的产品。
It's really something wrong with the quality of this consignment of bicycles.
这批自行车的质量确实有问题。
I regret this quality problem. 对质量问题我深表遗憾。
We hope that you'll pay more attention to the quality of your goods in the future.
希望贵方将来多注意产品的质量问题。
Upon arrival, we found the shipment of wool was of poor quality.
货到后，我们发现羊毛的质量较差。
The quality of the fertilizer is inferior to that stipulated in the contract.
化肥质量次于合同中规定的。
If you find the quality of our products unsatisfactory, we're prepared to accept return of the rejected material within a week.
如果贵方对产品质量不满意，我们将在一星期内接受退货。
This is a quality product. 这是一种高质量的产品。
Our price is a little bit higher, but the quality of our products is better.
虽然价格偏高，但我们的产品质量很好。
Your goods are superior in quality compared with those of other manufacturers.
和其他厂商相比，贵方产品质量上乘。
Our products are very good in quality, and the price is low. 我们的产品质高价低。

Price（价格）

trade term/price term 价格术语
price 单价
total value 总值
amount 金额
net price 净价
discount/allowance 折扣
discount (DCT) 打折

customs duty   关税
wholesale price   批发价
retail price   零售价
spot price   现货价格
forward price   期货价格
current price / prevailing price   时价
world market price   国际市场价格
You wish to have a discussion of the price terms of washers.
您是想谈谈洗衣机的价格条件吧。
I can give you a definite answer on the price terms.   我可以就价格条件答复你方。
All of the price terms are acceptable.   各种价格条件都是可以接受的。
CIF is the price term normally adopted by you，right?
CIF 是你们经常采用的价格条件,是吗?
Sometimes FOB and CFR are also employed.   有时也用 FOB 或 CIF 价。
Your price inacceptable /unacceptable.   你方价格可以接受/不可以接受。
Your price is reasonable /unreasonable.   你方价格合理/不合理。
The goods are /not competitively priced.   此货的定价有竞争力/无竞争力。
Price is turning high/low.   价格上涨/下跌。
Price is high/low.   价格高/低。
Price is up /down.   价格上涨/下跌。
Price is looking up.   价格看涨。
Price has risen perpendicularly.   价格直线上升。
Your price is on the high side.   你方价格偏高。
Price has advanced.   价格已上涨。
The goods are priced too high.   货物定价太高。
The Japanese yen is strengthening.   日元坚挺。
The U. S. Dollar is weakening.   美元疲软。
Your price is much higher than the price from U. K. France and Germany.
你方价格比英、法、德的都高。
DM210 is equivalent to 400 RMB.   210 德国马克折合人民币 400 元。
You said yesterday that the price was ＄60/mt，C. I. F. Brussels.
您昨天说价格定为每公吨 60 英镑 C. I. F. 布鲁塞尔。
Your price is quoted CFR Xingang at DM200 per washer，right?
你方报价是每台洗衣机 200 德国马克,CFR 新港价,对吗?
Since the prices of the raw materials have been raised，I'm afraid that we have to adjust the prices of our products accordingly.
由于原材料价格上涨,我们不得不对产品的价格做相应的调整。
Is it possible for you to raise (lift) the price by 5%?
你们能否把价格提高 5%?

Commission(佣金)

commission (com.)   佣金,手续费
price including commission   含佣价
return commission   回佣

two items of commission　两笔佣金
all commissions　所有佣金
to pay the commission　支付佣金
rate of commission or scale of commission　佣金率
commission agent　代理商
commission charges　佣金手续费
commission system　佣金制
commission agency　代理贸易
selling commission　代销佣金
buying commission　代购佣金
commissions earned　佣金收入
What about the commission?　佣金是多少？
We'll give you a 3% commission on every transaction.
每笔交易我们都付给百分之三的佣金。
We expect a 5% commission.　我们希望能得到百分之五的佣金。
We're usually paid with a 5% commission of the amount for every deal.
对每笔交易的成交量，我们通常付给5%的佣金。
The above price includes your commission of 2%.　上述价格包括百分之二的佣金在内。
The above price excludes your commission.　上述价格不包括佣金在内。
Our quotation is subject to a 4% commission.　我方报价包括百分之四的佣金在内。
You can get a higher commission rate if you order a bigger quantity.
如果你们订货量大，佣金率就会高。
Commission is allowed to agents only.　我们只对代理付佣金。
The commission has been increased to 5% in your favour.　贵方佣金已增至百分之五。
You can grant us an extra commission of 2% to cover the additional risk.
你们可以获得另外百分之二的佣金，以补偿所受的额外风险。
For every additional 10 pieces of pianos sold, we'll give you 0.2% more commission.
每笔交易若能多卖出10架钢琴，你们可以多得百分之零点二的佣金。
We can't agree to increase the rate of commission.　我们不能同意增加佣金率。
A higher commission means a higher price.　如果佣金提高了，价格也要提高。
A 4% commission is the maximum.　我们最多给百分之四的佣金。
Is it possible to increase the commission to 4%?　能不能把佣金提高到百分之四呢？
2% commission is not enough, is it?　百分之二的佣金是不是少了点？

Payment Terms(付款)

payment　支付，付款
to pay　付款，支付，偿还
the refusal of payment　拒付
deferred payment　延期付款
payment respite　延期付款
progressive payment　分期付款
payment by installment　分期付款
payment on terms　定期付款
payment at maturity　到期付款

payment in part 部分付款
payment in full 全部付讫
pay order 支付凭证
payment by banker 银行支付
payment order 付款通知
payment in advance 预付(货款)
cash with order (C. W. O) 随订单付现
cash on delivery (C. O. D) 交货付现
cash against documents (C. A. D) 凭单付现
pay on delivery (P. O. D) 货到付款
payment in kind 实物支付
the bank interest 银行利息
payment terms 支付条件
the mode of payment 付款方式
cash against payment 凭单付款
discount 贴现
draft 汇票
promissory note 本票
cheque 支票
clean bill 光票
documentary bill 跟单汇票
sight bill 即期汇票
time bill 远期汇票
usance bill 远期汇票
commercial bill 商业汇票
banker's bill 银行汇票
commercial acceptance bill 商业承兑汇票
bankers' acceptance bill 银行承兑汇票
performer invoice 形式发票
recipe invoice 收妥发票
certified invoice 证明发票
manufacturers' invoice 厂商发票
invoice(INV) 发票
certificate of origin (C. O) 一般原产地证
generalized system of preferences (G. S. P.) 普惠制
customs declaration (C/D) 报关单
import (IMP) 进口
export (EXP) 出口
document (DOC) 文件、单据
packing list (P/L) 装箱单、明细表
style (STL.) 式样、款式
sales contract (S/C) 销售确认书
amount (AMT) 数额

at sight　即期，见票即付
at…days (month) after sight　付款人见票后若干天(月)付款
at…days sight　付款人见票后若干天即付款
at…days after date　出票后若干天付款
at…days after B/L　提单签发后若干天付款
remittance　汇付
mail transfer (M/T)　信汇
demand draft (D/D)　票汇
telegraphic transfer (T/T)　电汇
collection　托收
clean bill for collection　光票托收
documentary bill for collection　跟单托收
collection advice　托收委托书
advice of clean bill for collection　光票托收委托书
collection bill purchased　托收出口押汇
trust receipt　信托收据
documents against payment (D/P)　付款交单
documents against payment at sight (D/P sight)　即期付款交单
documents against payment after sight (D/P sight)　远期付款交单
documents against acceptance (D/A)　承兑交单
letter of credit (L/C)　信用证
form of credit　信用证形式
terms of validity　信用证有效期
expiry date　有效期
Date of issue　开证日期
L/C amount　信用证金额
L/C number　信用证号码
to open by airmail　信开
to open by cable　电开
to open by brief cable　简电开证
to amend L/C　修改信用证
sight L/C　即期信用证
usance L/C　远期信用证
buyer's usance L/C　买方远期信用证
revocable L/C　可撤销的信用证
irrevocable L/C　不可撤销的信用证
confirmed L/C　保兑的信用证
unconfirmed L/C　不保兑的信用证
confirmed irrevocable L/C　保兑的不可撤销信用证
irrevocable unconfirmed L/C　不可撤销不保兑的信用证
transferable L/C　可转让信用证
untransferable L/C　不可转让信用证
revolving L/C　循环信用证

附 录

reciprocal L/C　对开信用证
back to back L/C　背对背信用证
banker's acceptance L/C　银行承兑信用证
trade acceptance L/C　商业承兑信用证
red clause L/C　红条款信用证
anticipatory L/C　预支信用证
credit payable by a trader　商业付款信用证
credit payable by a bank　银行付款信用证
usance credit payment at sight　假远期信用证
method of reimbursement　索汇方法
without recourse　不受追索
opening bank' name & signature　开证行名称及签字
beneficiary　受益人
guarantor　保证人
exporter's bank　出口方银行
importer's bank　进口方银行
seller's bank　卖方银行
buyer's bank　买方银行
paying bank　付款行,汇入行
remitting bank　汇出行
opening bank　开证行
issuing bank　开证行
advising bank　通知行
notifying bank　通知行
negotiating bank　议付行
drawee bank　付款行
confirming bank　保兑行
presenting bank　提示行
transmitting bank　转递行
accepting bank　承兑行

Additional Words and Phrases

pay bearer　付给某人
bearer　来人
payer　付款人
consignee　受托人
consignor　委托人
drawer　出票人
principal　委托人
drawee　付款人
acceptor　承兑人
trustee　被信托人
endorser　背书人
discount　贴现

343

endorsee 被背书人
endorse 背书
holder 持票人
endorsement 背书
payment against documents 凭单付款
payment against documents through collection 凭单托收付款
payment by acceptance 承兑付款
payment by bill 凭汇票付款
letter of guarantee（L/G） 保证书
bank guarantee 银行保函
payment guarantee 付款保证书
repayment guarantee 还款保证书
import guarantee 进口保证书
tender/bid guarantee 投标保证书
performance guarantee 履约保证书
documents of title to the goods 物权凭证
What's your reason for the refusal of payment? 你们拒付的理由是什么？
Collection is not paid. 托收款未得照付。
We'll not pay until shipping documents for the goods have reached us.
见不到货物装船单据，我们不付款。
Of course payment might be refused if anything goes wrong with the documents.
如果单据有问题，当然可以提出拒付。
What is the mode of payment you wish to employ? 您希望用什么方式付款？
This is the normal terms of payment in international business.
这是国际贸易中惯用的付款方式。
We can't accept any other terms of payment. 我们不能接受其他的付款条件。
Please protect our draft on presentation. 请见票即付。
The draft has not been collected. 汇票之款尚未收进。
We've drawn a clean draft on you for the value of this sample shipment.
我们已经开出光票向你方索取这批货的价款。
The draft has been handed to the bank on clean collection.
汇票已经交银行按光票托收。
We're sending our draft through Bank of China for documentary collection.
我们将汇票交中国银行按跟单托收。
We'll draw on you by our documentary draft at sight on collection basis.
我们将按托收方式向你方开出即期跟单汇票。
We'll agree to change the terms of payment from L/C at sight to D/P at sight.
我们同意将即期信用证付款方式改为即期付款交单。
We can do the business on 60 days D/P basis. 我们可以按60天付款交单的方式进行交易。
We agree to draw at 30 days D/P. 我们同意开立30天期的付款交单汇票。
We'll draw D/P against your purchase. 我们按付款交单方式收你方这批货款。
We can't agree to draw at 30 days D/A. 我们不同意开具30天期的承兑交单汇票。
I suppose D/P or D/A should be adopted as the mode of payment this time.

附 录

我建议这次用付款交单或承兑交单方式来付款。
It would help me greatly if you would accept D/A or D/P.
如果您能接受 D/P 或 D/A 付款,那可帮了我们大忙。
Could you make an exception and accept D/A or D/P?
您能否来个例外,接受 D/A 或 D/P 付款方式?
We insist on a letter of credit.　我们坚持用信用证方式付款。
We still intend to use letter of credit as the term of payment.
我们仍然想用信用证付款方式。
We always require L/C for our exports.　我们出口一向要求以信用证付款。
L/C at sight is normal for our exports to France.
我们向法国出口一般使用即期信用证付款。
We pay by L/C for our imports.　进口我们也采用信用证汇款。
Our terms of payment is confirmed and irrevocable letter of credit.
我们的付款条件是保兑的不可撤销的信用证。
What do you say to 50% by L/C and the balance by D/P?
百分之五十用信用证,其余的用付款交单,您看怎么样?
Please open letter of credit in good time.　请及时开出信用证。
We'll open the letter of credit at sight.　我们会按时开证。
I agree to use letter of credit at sight.　我同意用即期信用证付款。
Is the credit at sight or after sight?　信用证是即期的还是远期的?
Our letter of credit will be opened early March.　我们在 3 月初开出信用证。
We'll open the credit one month before shipment.　我们在装船前 1 个月开立信用证。
Please open the L/C 20 to 30 days before the date of delivery.
请在交货前 20 到 30 天开出信用证。
This letter of credit expires on 15th July.　这张信用证 7 月 15 日到期。
The validity of the L/C will be extended to 30th August.　信用证的有效期将延至 8 月 30 日。
The seller will request to amend the letter of credit.　卖方要修改信用证。
Please amend L/C No. 205 as follows.　请按下述意见修改第 205 号信用证。

Insure(保险)

insurer　保险人
underwriters　保险商
insurance company　保险公司
insurance underwriter　保险承保人
PICC (People's Insurance Company of China)　中国人民保险公司
insurance applicant　投保人
insurant/the insured　被保险人
insurance broker　保险经纪人
insure　保险、投保
insurance　保险、保险费
insurance against risk　保险
insurance expense　保险费
premium　保险费
insurance proceeds　保险金

insured amount　保险金额
premium rate　保险费率
additional premium　附加保险费
insurance rate　保险费率表
premium rebate　保险费回扣
insurance instruction　投保通知
insurance act　保险条例
insurance clause　保险条款
insurance treaty　保险合同
cover note　保险证明书
insurance claim　保险索赔
risk insured，risk covered　承保险项
to cover insurance　投保
to provide the insurance　为……提供保险
insurance coverage/risks covered　保险范围
insurance slip　投保单
insurance document　保险单据
certificate of insurance　保险凭证
insurance conditions　保险条件
risk　险别
ocean marine cargo insurance clauses　海洋运输货物保险条款
transportation insurance　运输保险
overland transportation insurance, land transit insurance　陆上运输保险
insurance against air risk, air transportation insurance　航空运输保险
parcel post insurance　邮包运输保险
ocean marine cargo insurance, marine insurance　海运货物保险
all risks　一切险
insurance free of (from) particular average (FPA)　平安险
risk of breakage　破碎险
risk of clashing　碰损险
risk of rust　生锈险
risk of hook damage　钩损险
risk of packing breakage　包装破裂险
risk of contingent import duty　进口关税险
insurance against war risk　战争险
air transportation cargo war risk　航空运输战争险
overland transportation insurance war risk　陆上运输战争险
insurance against strike, riot and civil commotion (SRCC)　罢工、暴动、民变险
insurance against extraneous risks, insurance against additional risks　附加险
risk of theft, pilferage and nondelivery (TRND)　盗窃提货不着险
risk of fresh and/of rain water damage　淡水雨淋险
risk of leakage　渗漏险
risk of shortage in weight/quantity　短量险

risk of sweating and/or heating　受潮受热险
risk of bad odour/change of flavour　恶味险、变味险
risk of mould　发霉险
on deck risk　舱面险
average　海损
ceding, retrocession(for reinsurance)　分保
I'm looking for insurance from your company.　我是到贵公司来投保的。
Please fill in the application form.　请填写一下投保单。
After loading the goods on board the hip, I go to the insurance company to have them insured.　装船后，我到保险公司去投保。
When should I go and have the tea insured?　我什么时候将这批茶叶投保？
The underwriters are responsible for the claim as far as it is within the scope of cover.　只要是在保险责任范围内，保险公司就应负责赔偿。
The loss in question was beyond the coverage granted by us.　损失不包括在我方承保的范围内。
The extent of insurance is stipulated in the basic policy form and in the various risk clause.　保险的范围写在基本保险单和各种险别的条款里。
What kind of insurance are you able to provide for my consignment?　贵公司能为我的这批货保哪些险呢？
These kinds of risks suit your consignment.　这些险别适合你要投保的货物。
Generally speaking, aviation insurance is much cheaper than marine insurance.　空运保险一般要比海运保险便宜。
What is the insurance premium?　保险费是多少？
The total premium is 800 U. S. dollars.　保险费总共是 800 美元。
The insurance rate for such kind of risk will vary according to the kind.　这类险别的保险费率将根据货物种类而定。
Can you give me an insurance rate?　您能给我一份保险率表吗？
Could you find out the premium rate for porcelain?　您能查一下瓷器的保险费率吗？
FPA stands for "Free from Particular Average".　FPA 代表平安险。
W. P. A. stands for "With Particular Average".　WPA 代表水渍险。
I'll have the goods covered against Free from Particular Average.　我将为货物投保平安险。
Free from Particular Average is good enough.　只保平安险就可以了。
The goods are to be insured F. P. A.　这批货需投保平安险。
What you've covered is Leakage.　你所投保的是渗漏险。
The coverage is W. P. A. plus risk of breakage.　投保的险别为水渍险加破碎险。
You'll cover SRCC risks, won't you?　你们要保罢工、暴动、民变险,是吗？